Into the Fight

Pickett's Charge at Gettysburg

by

John Michael Priest

 WHITE MANE BOOKS

Copyright © 1998 by John Michael Priest

This White Mane Books publication
was printed by
Beidel Printing House, Inc.
63 West Burd Street
Shippensburg, PA 17257-0152 USA

In respect for the scholarship contained herein, the acid-free paper used in this book meets the guidelines for permanence and durability of the Committee on Production Guidelines for Book Longevity of the Council on Library Resources.

For a complete list of available publications
please write
White Mane Books
Division of White Mane Publishing Company, Inc.
P.O. Box 152
Shippensburg, PA 17257-0152 USA

Library of Congress Cataloging-in-Publication Data

Priest, John M., 1949–
    Into the fight : Pickett's charge at Gettysburg / by John Michael
    Priest.
        p.   cm.
    Includes bibliographical references and index.
    ISBN 1-57249-138-8 (alk. paper)
    1. Gettysburg (Pa.). Battle of, 1863.   2. Pickett, George E.
(George Edward), 1825–1875.   I. Title.
E475.53.P93   1998
973.7'349--dc21   98-7695
                                                                   CIP

To our grandchildren,
Michael Hunter Priest
and
Miranda Elizabeth Secula

Contents

Illustrations

Maps

Acknowledgements

As in any work of this type, I received assistance from a variety of individuals who willingly shared information and resources with me. Special thanks to Earl B. McElfresh. The base maps in this work are adapted from The Gettysburg Maps, McElfresh Map Company, 1994 with the permission of the publisher. Gordon Grahe and David Kincherf sent me valuable information on the role of the 7th Tennessee during the battle and on the captured flags. Gary Kross shared his first edition copy of the Pennsylvania Supreme Court case over the placement of the 72nd Pennsylvania's monument. What a terrific goldmine of information. Morris M. Penny, co-author of *Law's Alabama Brigade*, provided me with a roster of the 5th Alabama Battalion. Robert Poirier sent me his notes about Major Edmund Rice of the 19th Massachusetts. Steven Stubbs unselfishly allowed me to use his unpublished manuscript on the history of the 11th Mississippi. Not many authors would have been so generous. I genuinely appreciate his kindness.

As always, I wish to express my gratitude to Ted Alexander and Paul Chiles at Antietam National Battlefield for allowing me to use the research library there. I also thank the library staff at Gettysburg National Battlefield for opening their research library to me. Dr. Richard Sommers and his staff in the Manuscripts Division and Michael Winey and Randy Hackenberg from the Photo Archives Division at the Unites States Army Military History Institute, Carlisle, Pennsylvania have been tremendously helpful in leading me to several great resources about the battle. The Saint Augustine Historical Society, The Eleanor S. Brockenbrough Library at the Museum of the Confederacy, the Virginia Historical Society, The Special Collections Departments at Duke University, the University of Virginia, and Yale University have graciously given me permission to use the material in their files.

I appreciate the time Mike Winey took to review this manuscript. I genuinely appreciate his comments and suggestions. Any mistakes that might be in the book are the responsibility of the author.

Writing takes a great deal of time and sacrifice. I could never have completed this project without the patience of my wife, Rhonda. She suggested I write this book.

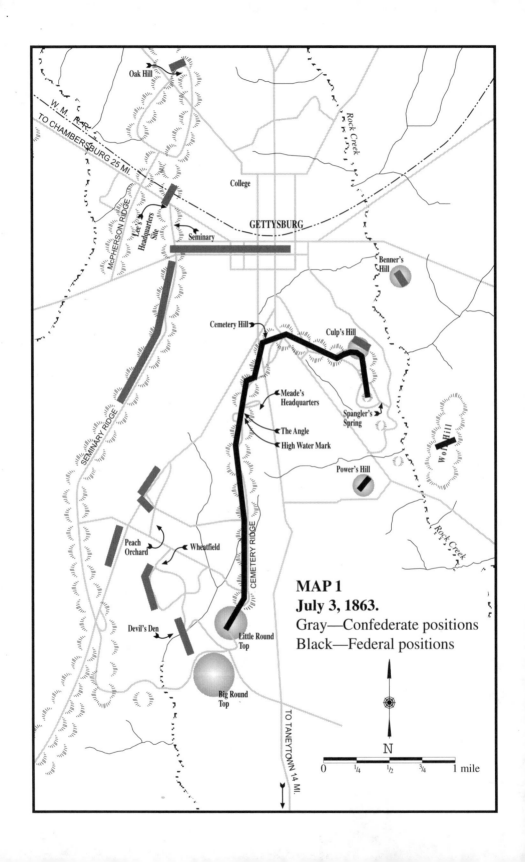

Oak Hill

W. M. R.R.
TO CHAMBERSBURG 25 MI.

Rock Creek

College

McPHERSON RIDGE

Lee's Headquarters Site

Seminary

GETTYSBURG

Benner's Hill

Cemetery Hill

Culp's Hill

SEMINARY RIDGE

Meade's Headquarters

The Angle

High Water Mark

Spangler's Spring

Wolf Hill

Power's Hill

Peach Orchard

Wheatfield

CEMETERY RIDGE

Rock Creek

Devil's Den

Little Round Top

Big Round Top

MAP 1
July 3, 1863.
Gray—Confederate positions
Black—Federal positions

TO TANEYTOWN 14 MI.

N

0   ¼   ½   ¾   1 mile

1 *Predawn through 1:00 p.m.*

July 3, 1863—Predawn Hours
The Southern End of the Confederate Lines

Captain Merritt Miller's Third Company of the Washington Artillery (three 12-pounder Napoleons) was roused with the rest of Major Benjamin F. Eshleman's Battalion at 2:00 a.m. In the darkness, artilleryman Napier Bartlett heard the human wreckage of the previous day's battle moaning loudly enough, he thought, to awaken the bloating corpses around the guns. He could not forget the ghastly dry rattles of the dying as they rasped out their last breaths. His lieutenant, Andrew Hero, Jr., felt just as uneasy. During the night, having had no blanket, he did what most veterans in his condition had done before; he snuggled up next to a sleeping man to share body warmth until daylight. He awoke briefly while it was still dark to tell the fellow how cold blooded he had become. When Hero arose in the morning, in the shadows, he took a closer look at the other soldier's still face only to discover that he had slept with a corpse.[1]

Colonel E. Porter Alexander, whom Lieutenant General James Longstreet had appointed Chief of Artillery for the Army of Northern Virginia's First Corps for the duration of the battle, was busily rearranging his forty-eight field pieces to support the impending infantry attack against Cemetery Ridge. He kept Major Mathias W. Henry's battalion of eighteen guns on the extreme right, south of the Peach Orchard along the Emmitsburg Road facing east toward Little Round Top.[2]

The artillery line which he intended to use to support the impending assault began at Trostle's lane with his battalion under the direct command of his good friend, Major Frank Huger. At that point, on the rise south of the lane, Captains Tyler C. Jordan's and William W. Parker's Virginia batteries held the right of the line, facing north. Captain Osmond B. Taylor's Virginia Artillery was in battery on the western side of the Emmitsburg Road, across from them, with his guns facing northeast. Parts of Colonel Henry C. Cabell's Battalion and what was left of Eshleman's Louisiana Battalion would occupy the line from the Sherfy house to the small knoll north of Spangler's lane on the southwestern and southern side of the Rogers house.[3]

Alexander expected Major James Dearing's eighteen field pieces to further supplement the corps' offensive ability between Eshleman's left flank and the first ridge east of Spangler's Woods, which would bring his total armament to eighty-five pieces.[4] Rather than risk wasting ammunition which he could not spare, Alexander specifically forbade his battalion commanders to engage in any artillery duels. They could, if necessary, send one or two rounds at the Yankees, if the situation necessitated it, but no more than that. With his guns exposed to the Federal rifled pieces on Little Round Top, he did not want to be enfiladed before the assault began.[5] To safeguard against an infantry attack, he sent Brigadier General Cadmus Wilcox's bloodied Alabama Brigade to Eshleman's and Cabell's support. Wilcox, with his left flank on the south side of Spangler's lane, put his regiments in the hollow 200 yards west of the road. As the men went prone, their officers passed among them, telling them they were going to remain there during the bombardment which would occur sometime later in the day.[6]

Nevertheless, just past first light, the Yankees dropped a few 20-pounder shells among Alexander's crews while they maneuvered their guns into formation. A pair of them screamed into Eshleman's Washington Artillery Battalion while the four batteries wheeled into front along the Emmitsburg Road north of the Sherfy house. One of them burst over the Fourth Company, Captain Joe Norcom's Napoleon section. It knocked the captain down, slightly wounding him and killing one of the drivers and two of the horses from the Third Company.[7] Lieutenant Henry A. Battles replaced him on the field.[8]

Federal Lines—Cemetery Hill
Stannard's Brigade, I Corps

Lieutenant George G. Benedict (A.D.C. to Stannard) and his orderly, under Brigadier General George J. Stannard's directive, had spent the entire evening and early hours of July 2–3, 1863, meandering from campfire to campfire along the back roads east of Cemetery Ridge, looking for the I Corps ammunition trains. In the pitch darkness they stumbled across several large Pennsylvania stone and brick barns, which were serving the Army of the Potomac as rear line hospitals. The lieutenant grimaced at the memory of one of those makeshift hospitals. The recollections of the unattended casualties which filled the surrounding yard and of a bloody pile of amputated arms and legs next to the door flashed through his mind. He could still see the disabled men lying all about, wrapped in their blankets, stoically waiting for their time upon the surgeons' tables. He later wrote, "It seemed to me as if every square yard of the ground, for many square

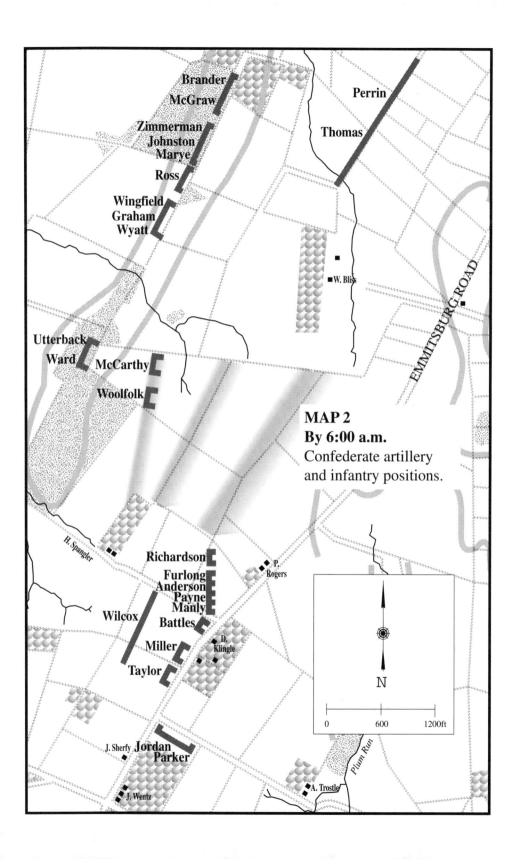

Brander
McGraw
Zimmerman
Johnston
Marye
Ross
Wingfield
Graham
Wyatt

Perrin

Thomas

■
■ W. Bliss

Utterback
Ward
McCarthy
Woolfolk

EMMITSBURG ROAD

MAP 2
By 6:00 a.m.
Confederate artillery
and infantry positions.

H. Spangler
Richardson
Furlong
Anderson
Payne
Manly
Wilcox
Battles
Miller
Taylor

■
■ P. Rogers

D, Klingle

N

| 0 | 600 | 1200ft |

J. Sherfy Jordan
Parker

J. Wentz

A. Trostle

Plum Run

miles, must have its blood stain." After being stopped repeatedly by wounded men asking for directions to their division hospitals, he finally realized that the bloodletting of the previous day had reached monstrous proportions.[9]

Unable to find the ammunition wagons, he glanced into the sky, noted that the moon was setting, and decided to forget about them altogether. Abandoning his orderly, who was meandering about somewhere in the night, he decided it was time to return to headquarters. The lieutenant quietly spurred his horse onto a road which he supposed led toward Rock Creek Church. A short time later, he passed under what appeared to be an arch. Two field pieces stood silently in the road in front of him pointing in the direction he was heading. While working his horse between them, Benedict was startled by someone standing up in the shadows next to one of the guns and asking where he was going. The lieutenant told him he was look-ing for Headquarters, Third Brigade, Third Division, I Corps. The artilleryman bluntly told him he was only going to find the Rebels if he kept his present bearing. Benedict quietly turned his horse about and rode under the arch of the cemetery gate house.[10]

Troop Dispositions—Army of the Potomac

In the dark, the exhausted lieutenant had meandered into Battery I, 1st Ohio Light Artillery, Captain Hubert Dilger's command, which belonged to Major Thomas Osborn's XI Corps artillery brigade. This day marked the brigade's second morning on Cemetery Hill, the most critical, yet the weak-est point of the Federal line. Captain Michael Wiedrich's bloodied Battery I, 1st New York (six Ordnance Rifles) still occupied the earthen lunettes on the northeast side of the Baltimore Pike, facing Benner's Hill and the Con-federate left flank. His position formed the northeastern side of the bend in what later became the "fish hook" of the Federal line.

To Wiedrich's left rear Dilger's Ohioans formed the westerly bend in the hook. With his right flank on the eastern side of the Baltimore Pike, he placed his guns along the crest of Cemetery Hill north of the gate house with their muzzles aimed toward Gettysburg and the railroad cut on the high ground northwest of the town.[11] Forty-four-year-old Captain Elijah Taft with his six 20-pounder Parrotts (5th New York Independent Battery) were deployed as they had been during the previous afternoon. Two sections were on the western side of the Baltimore Pike south of the gate house well below Wiedrich's right flank. Facing northeast, they would counter any fire from Benner's Hill. Captain Frederick M. Edgell's Battery A, 1st New Hampshire Artillery (four 3-inch rifles) were in a cornfield to his right front on the eastern side of the Baltimore Pike. Taft's remaining two rifled guns were in battery to the left rear of Dilger, facing west.[12]

The shank of the hook began at the intersection of the Emmitsburg Road and the Taneytown Road. The 55th Ohio on the right of Colonel Orland Smith's three regiments lay down with its colors at the intersection.

The right wing, taking cover in the Emmitsburg Road, faced northwest toward the town along about a 200-foot front. The left wing went prone behind the stone wall along the western side of the Taneytown Road. The 73rd Ohio with the 136th New York on its left occupied about another nine hundred feet of the line.[13]

A two hundred yard gap separated the left flank of the 136th New York from the right rear of Lieutenant Emerson L. Bicknell and his twenty men from the 1st Company of Massachusetts Sharpshooters on the western edge of Ziegler's Grove.[14] They and the 126th New York on their left were the right flank of a line which extended for about three fourths of a mile to the south. The New Yorkers lay on the eastern slope of the ridge, supporting Lieutenant George A. Woodruff's six Napoleons (Battery I, 1st U.S. Artillery), which had rolled into battery on the top of the ridge to the regiment's left front.[15] The remaining three regiments of Colonel Eliakim Sherrill's small brigade were on line to its left below the line of sight of the Confederate skirmishers in the fields to the west. Colonel Thomas A. Smyth's brigade continued the formation on the crest to the south until it contacted Captain William A. Arnold's six Ordnance Rifles (Battery A, 1st Rhode Island Artillery). His left flank ended where the stone wall turned west.

To Arnold's left, Battery A, 4th U.S. Artillery, Lieutenant Alonzo H. Cushing, commanding, added another six 3-inch rifles to the line. A copse of trees separated Cushing from Lieutenant T. Fred Brown's Battery B, 1st Rhode Island Artillery (four 12-pounder Napoleons). The 69th Pennsylvania held the wall immediately west of the trees in the area later known as "The Angle." They were the only infantry in front of the guns from Arnold's left to Brown's left. The 71st Pennsylvania was lying among Cushing's limbers on the eastern side of the ridge with their right flank to the left of Arnold's limbers. The 72nd Pennsylvania were prone to their left rear.[16] The rest of Brigadier General John Gibbon's division filled out the line to the south of the 69th Pennsylvania with assorted regiments from the I Corps on their left. Those infantry regiments were behind a low earthwork which they constructed as an extension of the wall in front of the Pennsylvanians.

Captain James Rorty's Battery B, 1st New York Artillery, consisting of four 10-pounder Parrotts was in battery about one hundred yards south of Brown. For the next mile there were no other artillery on line from his left to the northern base of Little Round Top. In that area, battered I, II, and III Corps troops and a division of the VI Corps held the woods east of Cemetery Ridge, but they were not going to do anything to precipitate an engagement. Daylight would find the Union position along Cemetery Ridge looking less than formidable to their Confederate opponents on Seminary Ridge to the west of them.[17]

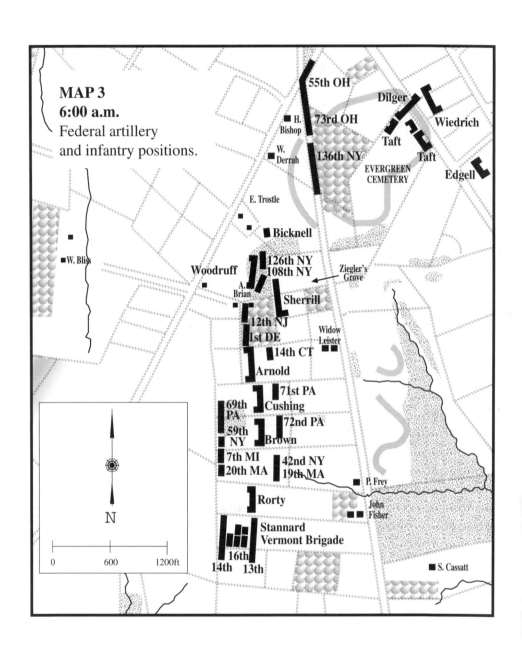

MAP 3
6:00 a.m.
Federal artillery and infantry positions.

55th OH

Dilger

Wiedrich

H. Bishop

73rd OH

Taft

W. Derrah

136th NY

Taft

EVERGREEN CEMETERY

Edgell

E. Trostle

W. Bliss

Bicknell

Woodruff

126th NY

108th NY

Ziegler's Grove

A. Brian

Sherrill

12th NJ

1st DE

Widow Leister

14th CT

Arnold

71st PA

69th PA

Cushing

59th NY

72nd PA

7th MI

Brown

20th MA

42nd NY

19th MA

P. Frey

Rorty

John Fisher

Stannard
Vermont Brigade

16th

14th   13th

S. Cassatt

N

0   600   1200ft

Chambersburg Pike—South Side of Marsh Creek

Major General George E. Pickett's Confederate division awoke at 3:00 a.m.[18] The men stirred the coals of their old coffee fires and prepared what Second Lieutenant W. Nathaniel Wood (Company A, 19th Virginia) called their "frugal" breakfasts. His men's joking and laughter dispelled any latent sense of doom.[19] Captain Robert McCulloch (Company B, 18th Virginia), whose regiment also belonged to Brigadier General Richard B. Garnett's brigade, awakened with the memory of the previous night's star bedecked sky still sparking in his mind. With the exception of occasional picket shots from the direction of the Lutheran Seminary, he had spent a very restful night.[20]

Farther along the line, in Brigadier General James L. Kemper's brigade, the very perceptive First Lieutenant John E. Dooley (Company C, 1st Virginia) arose with an unsettling dread of the forthcoming day. The contemptuous jeers and laughter of the women of Chambersburg echoed in his ears as did the piteous sobs of a girl who had peered into one of the regimental ambulances while it moved out along the Chambersburg Pike. When she saw the ill Second Lieutenant Aldophus Blair, Jr. (Company D) among the sick, she blurted something about her brother having been killed at Second Manassas. Her intense grief reminded Dooley of the hundreds of mourning Southern families back in Virginia. He wrote in his journal, "Sorrow makes the whole world kin." The march from Chambersburg had been unusually quiet—a foreboding omen. He went to sleep that night more worried for his safety than he had ever been before. An intangible, gut churning fear lingered over him throughout the night punctuated by the recurring visions of horribly mutilated corpses and horrific suffering which intensified as the hours passed. With each conscious thought of what lay ahead the images of gore became more diverse and more vivid. This morning's darkness merely heightened his concern.[21]

Captain James Risque Hutter (Company H, 11th Virginia, Kemper's brigade) awakened that morning believing what his long-time friend, Colonel Armistead L. Long, Lee's personal secretary, had told him. Long reassured Hutter that, in his personal opinion, Pickett's men were going to follow up the rest of the Army of Northern Virginia—nothing more.[22] The rumor traveled fast among the regiments and by daylight it had progressed to the rear of the division to Brigadier General Lewis Armistead's brigade, where Junior Second Lieutenant John H. Lewis (Company G, 9th Virginia) readily accepted it as the absolute truth. He sincerely hoped the division would be used only in pursuit of the Federals.[23]

It took the men less than an hour and a half to eat their breakfasts. Shortly before daylight, Pickett's fifteen regiments were in column and moving out toward the front.[24] Brigadier General James L. Kemper's brigade (1st, 3rd, 7th, 11th, and 24th Virginia) led the division, followed by Brigadier General Richard B. Garnett's five regiments (8th, 18th, 19th, 28th, and 56th Virginia). Brigadier General Lewis A. Armistead's brigade (9th, 14th, 38th, 53rd, and 57th Virginia) brought up the rear.[25]

After going a very short distance east along the Chambersburg Pike, the column turned south along the Knoxlyn Road, which Private Robert B.

Colonel Armistead L. Long

Lee's personal secretary, he honestly believed that Pickett's Division would not be actively engaged on July 3, 1863.

Miller, *Photographic History*

Damron (Company D, 56th Virginia) described as a farm lane.[26] General Robert E. Lee, on horseback, watched Kemper's men swing past. Lieutenant Dooley (1st Virginia) studied the general's anxious expression. His utter silence reflected his uncertainty—odd behavior for a man who seldom betrayed any feelings in his face.[27]

Three-fourths of a mile south of the Chambersburg Pike, Pickett's brigades forked east onto Hereter's Mill Road.[28] The two wood-lots which paralleled both sides of Herr Ridge not only masked the column's approach from the Federals on Cemetery Hill but sheltered them from the intense sunlight which blanketed the battlefield.[29] Captain McCulloch (18th Virginia) thought the morning was glorious, a completely different perspective than that of Lieutenant Wood (19th Virginia), who savored the relative coolness of their tree-lined route.[30]

The Federal Skirmishers
The Eastern Side of the Emmitsburg Road

One battalion of the 16th Vermont, under Colonel Wheelock G. Veazey (General Officer of the Day) lay in the creek bottom of Plum Run, anchoring the skirmish line south of the Codori Farm.[31] Private O. P. Blaisdell (Company H) nestled low to the ground at the southwestern corner of Trostle's Woods, a bit too close to the barn to his liking and to its ghastly collection of wounded and dying men.[32]

At 4:00 a.m., Captain William Watts Parker's Virginia Battery from its position along Trostle's lane opened fire into the predawn shadows at Companies B, F, D, and E from the 19th Maine, under Captain William H. Fogler (Company D) when they walked into the hollow east of Codori's barn. Some of the New Englanders crawled into the Emmitsburg Road with their right near the barn while the rest of them refused the line to the southeast. Shots echoed across the fields between them and the Confederates. Having not been fed since the previous morning, the Yankees ignored the pot shots to listen to their stomachs growl and churn while they waited out the morning.[33]

To the west, along the Emmitsburg Road, Second Lieutenant Frank E. Moran (Company H, 73rd New York), who had been wounded in the ankle and the left eye, and other prisoners from the fighting of July 2, awakened from a brief slumber in the basement of the Rogers house to the sounds of sporadic rifle fire. The Rebels had brought them there, forlorn and dejected, from the Sherfy house shortly after midnight. As the bullets zipped across the road around them, the Yankee prisoners knew that the Army of the Potomac was on the field to stay. There was not going to be another Chancellorsville.[34]

Smyth's Brigade, II Corps

Farther to the north, a desultory skirmish began at daylight (4:27 a.m.) along the II Corps' picket line. Confederate sharpshooters, having reoccupied the Bliss barn during the night, were sniping at any Federals who gave them a clear target.[35] Three minutes later, Captain Edward S. McCarthy's Virginia section of two 12-pounder Napoleons, having rolled into battery on the crest of the third ridge east of Spangler's Woods opened fire.[36] The gunners caught Companies B and D from the 14th Connecticut off guard while they were moving forward (west) from the reserve picket posts. As the Yankees stood up to climb over the post and rail fence along the Emmitsburg Road a shell smashed into the western side of the fence and sent a rail spinning madly through Company B. Every man but Private Augustus Guild instinctively dodged out of its path. The rail caught him in the small of his back, just at the waist, and sent him sprawling onto the road bed. His comrades left him for dead and crawled through the wheat field toward the next fence row to the west.[37] McCarthy's men fired twenty rounds before losing Private Dewees Ogden to small arms fire. By then, orders arrived to retire to the first ridge east of Spangler's Woods.[38]

The forty New Englanders spread out at intervals of two to three fence posts between each of them and went prone. They loaded their rifles while on their backs then rolled over and propped them on the bottom rails to fire. With the tall wheat hiding them from each other and from the Rebels, they occasionally called out to reassure themselves that they had not taken any casualties. In Company B, Private Hiram Fox, to the left of Sergeant Elnathan B. Tyler, hollered that Corporal Samuel G. Huxam had not responded to his call. The sergeant told him to crawl over to see if the corporal was still all right. Fox quickly scurried back. Huxam was dead—shot through the head. Tyler surmised that the dead man, having tired of firing prone, had foolishly kneeled to get a clean shot when a Rebel dropped him.[39]

Southern End of Cemetery Ridge
McGilvery's Brigade

With the sounds of the artillery fire from the Bliss farm rumbling south across the fields, Lieutenant Colonel Freeman McGilvery began deploying his small brigade. Captain James Thompson's Batteries C and F, Pennsylvania Light Artillery (five 3-inch rifles) rolled onto the crest of Cemetery Ridge to the left of Stannard's Vermonters.[40] Within a few minutes, Captain Patrick Hart, riding ahead of his four 12-pounder Napoleons (15th New York Battery), reined in beside Thompson and asked where he wanted his battery deployed. Thompson ordered him to leave enough room between them for Phillips' Battery E, 5th Massachusetts Artillery.[41] Very shortly thereafter, Captain Charles A. Phillips and his six 3-inch rifles filled the gap.[42] Their presence increased the number of Federal guns along Cemetery Ridge to fifty-one. Not too long after, First Lieutenant Edwin Dow (Battery F, 6th Maine Artillery) sent his four 12-pounders into line about one hundred yards to Hart's left. McGilvery immediately ordered the gunners to entrench.[43] As the artillerymen scooped up the ground with the tools from their caissons, Major General Winfield Scott Hancock rode into the woods behind them and ordered what was left of the Irish Brigade into the space between Hart and Dow. The 116th Pennsylvania, on the right of the brigade, fell in to Hart's left. The battered veterans pulled rocks from the ground, scoured up fence rails, and scraped up dirt with their tin plates—anything to provide them some type of cover.[44] Before too long they had constructed an irregular two-foot-high berm from Weikert's lane to Phillips' right flank—a distance of about 1,160 feet.[45]

Lieutenant Colonel
Freeman McGilvery

His strategic deployment of the Federal artillery on the southern end of Cemetery Ridge contributed greatly to the failure of Longstreet's charge.

MOLLUS, USAMHI

Henry's Battalion

The movement along McGilvery's line attracted E. Porter Alexander's attention. He dispatched a courier south along the Emmitsburg Road to Major Mathias Henry's Battalion, which was on Warfield Ridge, about one and one-half miles below Trostle's Lane. The one-armed Major John C. Haskell, Henry's superior, received the message to reinforce the line to Parker's right. His gunners, who had been banging away at Little Round Top for about half an hour, ceased fire and prepared to move out. Leaving Reilly's North Carolina and Bachman's South Carolina Batteries with Henry (the junior officer of the two), Haskell took Captains Alexander C. Latham's North Carolina and Hugh R. Garden's South Carolina Batteries north at a gallop. Alexander personally posted them when they arrived at the northern end of the Peach Orchard. The nine guns rolled into battery to Parker's right, facing northeast and east, parallel with the ridge on the eastern side of the orchard.[46]

Hays' Division along the Emmitsburg Road

The increased firing along the 14th Connecticut's skirmish line prompted Brigadier General Alexander Hays to feed more bodies into the fields west of the Emmitsburg Road. The job fell to Companies F

Colonel E. Porter Alexander

Saddled with the responsibility of actually ordering when the charge was to begin, he carefully documented his every move on July 3, 1863.

Miller, *Photographic History*

and G of the 111th New York.[47] Captain Benjamin W. Thompson and his Company F had not been fed in over a day; they did not want to go out. Suppressing his gnawing stomach with pipe tobacco and a tin of water, Thompson thought it a mean business to expect his men to fight on empty stomachs. He and his only lieutenant, John B. Drake, grudgingly pushed their forty-eight enlisted men toward the right of the New Englanders. He hated this particular type of work, because he considered it to be nothing short of deliberate murder.

His marksmen bellied up to the first fence west of the Emmitsburg Road and set to work in earnest. It did not take long for the Confederates to reinforce their own position. Thompson and Drake walked upright from man to man, directing their fire and setting examples of personal courage which they believed their commissioned ranks demanded of them. By not lying down, they made conspicuous targets.

Three Confederate sharpshooters quickly got their range on the captain. The third shot convinced him to be more careful. When the next rifle ball zipped close by, he flopped onto his back and played dead. A minute later, he rolled over to the closest man on his flank then stood up until he got sniped at again. Once more he dropped apparently lifeless, then rolled aside. The three Rebels, however, gave him no respite. When he realized that they were wise to him, he took a rifle from one of his men and picked off one of them. (It was the first and only time he discharged a weapon during the war.)[48]

Cemetery Ridge—East of the Codori Farm

By then the weary Lieutenant George G. Benedict (A.D.C. to Stannard) had returned to his own headquarters along the southern end of the II Corps line on Cemetery Ridge. The Confederate artillery made him uneasy.[49] Captain William W. Parker's Virginia Battery slammed a shell into the ground close to Benedict's feet the moment he dismounted. Within sixty seconds another one snapped the leg on an orderly's horse not ten feet away. A third ripped the hoof off yet another horse. Figuring that the Confederate gunners were sighting in on their mounts, Stannard and his officers sent them below the eastern crest of the ridge.[50] As the shooting continued, the Federal artillery returned fire.[51]

The half of the 16th Vermont which had not gone forward as skirmishers remained prone in column of divisions (two company front) behind the wooded knoll to its front.[52] An incoming round exploded one of Rorty's caissons to the right rear of the brigade and killed several men in the 14th Vermont. For a moment Lieutenant Benedict believed the entire battery had gone up. Stannard decided to redeploy his line. The 14th Vermont advanced over the crest of the hill and took cover along a scattered line of bushes and trees along its western base within 100 feet of the brigade skirmish line.[53]

The 13th Vermont went into line to its right rear on the slightly wooded crest of the ridge to the right of the 16th Vermont. There were no other Federal troops to the brigade's front. Benedict warned the general that it might be exceedingly bad on morale to have the men deploy among the corpses of both armies which were scattered all over the ground to the west, and suggested they be covered with blankets. Stannard agreed and immediately assigned the task to Benedict and an orderly.[54]

Severe small arms fire broke out to the right rear of the Federal line in the direction of Culp's Hill.[55] To Stannard's immediate right, the remnants of the 80th New York and the 151st Pennsylvania, having been badly mauled during the first day of battle, were more interested in getting fed than in worrying about the security of their surroundings. The few men who were present rifled their haversacks for any edibles. They had not eaten in twenty-four hours. A corporal in the 80th New York, who happened upon an entire piece of hard cracker, shared it with his captain, John D. S. Cook (Company I).[56]

Lieutenant Benedict glanced at his watch. It was a little before 6:00 a.m. The volleying to the northeast sounded to him like one unrelenting crashing noise which neither receded nor advanced. There seemed to be no modulation in the volume, indicative of a severe standup fight with neither side giving ground. The billowing smoke from the small arms fire ascending above the tree tops told him all he needed to know.[57]

Seminary Ridge between McMillan's Woods and Spangler's Woods

Before daylight, Brigadier General James Johnston Pettigrew had placed his badly mauled division along the western slope of Seminary Ridge (south of the Lutheran Seminary). Colonel John M. Brockenbrough's four Virginia regiments (55th, 47th, 40th, and 22nd Virginia Battalion) occupied about 360 feet of line directly across from the Long Lane where it ended on the northern side of the Bliss farm.[58] Brigadier General Joseph Davis' brigade (55th North Carolina, 2nd, 42nd, and 11th Mississippi), numbering about 1,143 officers and men, fell in to Brockenbrough's immediate right.[59] Colonel James K. Marshall (52nd North Carolina), who had assumed brigade command when Pettigrew replaced the wounded Major General Henry Heth on July 1, placed his 1,205-man brigade (26th, 11th, 47th, and 52nd North Carolina) next in line to the south.[60] Colonel Birkett D. Fry (13th Alabama) anchored the extreme right of the division with Brigadier General James J. Archer's 900-man brigade (5th Alabama Battalion, 7th and 14th Tennessee, 13th Alabama, 1st Tennessee).[61] During the early morning, Brigadier General James H. Lane positioned the 1,076 men (28th, 37th, 7th, 18th, and 33rd North Carolina) of his own brigade and Colonel William Lee J. Lowrance's 840-man North Carolina brigade (38th, 13th, 34th, 22nd, and 16th North Carolina) in line to the right rear of Fry's brigade. At that point, Major General Isaac Trimble assumed command of the very small division, and Lane returned to his own brigade.[62]

A very piqued Lieutenant General James Longstreet met with Lee while Pickett was en route from the Chambersburg Pike. Lee had waited until a short time before to personally reinforce what he had told Longstreet by messenger during the previous evening. Pickett's division would make an early morning assault. About an hour and one-half past daylight with no Pickett on the field Lee had yet to identify the objective of the attack.[63] Having decided that Longstreet's First Corps would attack the Federals' left center, Lee sat on a log beside his "Old Warhorse" behind the ridge and informed him that Major Generals Lafayette McLaws' and John B. Hood's divisions with Pickett's support were to sweep over the ground of the previous day's battle and smash through the Union lines.[64]

That would not do, Longstreet protested. His men had failed to maintain their position on Cemetery Ridge the day before when they were fresh and at near full strength. The Yankees had entrenched, he said. His men had heard them digging throughout the night. The Federal line extended for a mile along his right. If he moved those two divisions to the north to support the assault, the Yankees would have him flanked and in the event of a defeat, they would smash through the right and cut the army off from the Potomac River. He asserted that he needed 30,000 men to carry off Lee's plan. He *had*, however, about 13,000 left; they would have to cross one mile of open ground under constant artillery fire with the last 1,000 yards under long range small arms fire. Conditions had changed since the Napoleonic Wars, he argued. Surely, Lee knew that the ranges of field batteries and small arms had increased with the advent of new technology.[65]

Lee would not listen, having made his decision, and wanted Longstreet to consent to it. At this point Colonel Armistead L. Long (Lee's military secretary) impertinently interjected that the Confederate artillery would suppress the Federal guns on Little Round Top with counterbattery fire.[66] Lee added that the distance was not more than 1,400 yards. Nevertheless, Hood's and McLaws' battered divisions could stay in reserve. Lee, having already anticipated Longstreet's objection, decided to use some of Lieutenant General Ambrose P. Hill's Corps in conjunction with Pickett's division. How many men would be involved? Longstreet asked. Lee replied, 15,000. Longstreet emphatically protested that "the fifteen thousand men who could make successful assault over that field had never been arrayed for battle." Lee impatiently cut him off by saying that he was tired of talking. When the cannonading from Ewell's position north of Culp's Hill reverberated across the fields to Seminary Ridge it became evident to Longstreet that the commanding general had already made up his mind to carry off his grand assault whether he agreed to it or not. [67]

Stannard's Brigade, I Corps

Lieutenant Albert Clark (Company G, 13th Vermont) approached Colonel Francis V. Randall with the suggestion that volunteers tear down a rail fence across their front and construct breastworks to the left front of the much smaller 151st Pennsylvania. Sergeant George H. Scott and at least twenty other men from the lieutenant's company responded to the call. They completed the work in remarkably short order amid the cheers of their own men. Low works were more protection than none at all.[68]

The Emmitsburg Road—
Immediately West of Ziegler's Grove

Shortly before 6:00 a.m. Captain David Lewis (Company G), commanding both Companies G and K on the 8th Ohio's advanced picket line 400 feet west of the Emmitsburg Road, reported increased Confederate activity in the low ground along his front.[69] Lieutenant Colonel Franklin Sawyer told his adjutant, First Lieutenant John W. DePuy, to alert the men. He walked into the regiment, which was sleeping in the dirt track of the

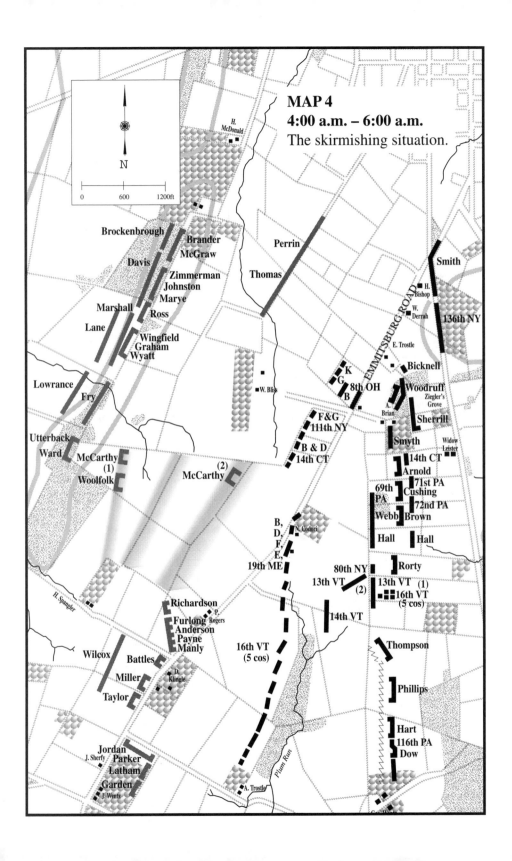

MAP 4
4:00 a.m. – 6:00 a.m.
The skirmishing situation.

N

0   600   1200ft

H. McDonald

Brockenbrough
Brander
McGraw
Davis
Zimmerman
Johnston
Marye
Marshall
Ross
Lane
Wingfield
Graham
Wyatt
Lowrance
Fry
Utterback
Ward
McCarthy
(1)
Woolfolk
McCarthy
(2)

Perrin
Thomas

W. Bliss

Smith

H. Bishop
W. Derrah
E. Trostle

EMMITSBURG ROAD

136th NY

K
G
B   8th OH

Bicknell
Woodruff
Ziegler's Grove
A. Brian
Sherrill

F&G
111th NY
B & D
14th CT

Smyth
Widow Leister
14th CT
Arnold
71st PA
Cushing
69th PA
72nd PA
Webb   Brown
Hall   Hall

B,
D,
F,
E,
19th ME

N. Codori

80th NY
13th VT
(2)

Rorty

13th VT   (1)
16th VT
(5 cos)

H. Spangler

Richardson
P.
Furlong   Rogers
Anderson
Payne
Manly
Wilcox
Battles
Miller
Taylor

D. Klingle

14th VT

16th VT
(5 cos)

Thompson

Phillips

Hart
116th PA
Dow

Jordan
J. Sherfy   Parker
Latham
Garden
J. Wentz

A. Trostle

Plum Run

road, and awakened Sergeant Thomas F. Galwey. He told him to take Company B to the picket line.[70]

Galwey organized his men behind the deep road bank. A volley burst along the low ground beyond the pickets. Sawyer gave the command to move out. A few steps beyond the road, a bullet punched a hole in the colonel's hat, knocking him senseless in the wake of the attack.[71] The Westerners charged across the 400-foot interval to the post and rail fence which paralleled the road. They quickly threw themselves behind the piled up fence rails. Nestling among the corpses of their dead skirmishers from the fighting on July 2, the Ohioans returned fire. As soon as Company B occupied his section of the line, Captain Wilbur Pierce retired his Company K at a run for the Emmitsburg Road.[72]

Cemetery Ridge
Smyth's Brigade, II Corps

The incoming Confederate small arms rounds which passed over their intended targets along the Emmitsburg Road plopped harmlessly among the sleeping soldiers of the 1st Delaware without disturbing them to any great extent.[73] At 7:00 a.m., after enduring about two and one-half hours of harassment Brigadier General Alexander Hays, their division commander, decided to clean out the Bliss farm yard as he had done the day before. He personally ordered First Lieutenant John L. Brady (Company E, 1st Delaware) to drive the Rebels out of the barn and to hold it "at all hazards."

The lieutenant gathered up twenty-seven men from his regiment and three or four volunteers from the 12th New Jersey. Slipping to the right, with the stone wall covering their flank, they halted just north of the Brian barn, near the eastern end of the farm lane which fed directly into the Emmitsburg Road. Stripping themselves of all of their superfluous equipment, except their belts, cap boxes, cartridge boxes, and weapons, they raced toward the road. Striking it, they jigged left, then right into Bliss' long farm lane.[74] They dragged Captain William Kenney (Company B), acting major of the 8th Ohio, and Companies G and H with them. On the way to the rise west of the road, Company B, 8th Ohio joined in the movement. "...as far as I know," Sergeant Thomas Galwey later wrote, "without any orders, we charged straight ahead."[75]

The Confederates in the barn let them cover all but the last fifty feet of the track when they opened fire from slits in the upper story. On the Federal left, all but six of the Yankees went down in the blast. The raiders, hurriedly dragging their wounded with them, limped back toward their lines, leaving Corporal John B. Sheets and Private William J. Dorsey (both Company D) dead upon the field.[76] The three companies of the 8th Ohio managed to push the Confederates back onto the ridge west of the Bliss farm house.[77] Captain James W. Wyatt's Virginia Battery (three 3-inch rifled pieces) and Captain Joseph Graham's 1st North Carolina Artillery (two 12 pounder Napoleons) responded quickly to the threat.[78] Several rounds of canister and the appearance of Confederate reinforcements not 200 yards to the west abruptly stopped the three companies. Halting, they reformed, and, firing as they went, they inched their way back to the fence rails west of the road. They took cover behind the destroyed fence and settled down to steady skirmishing.[79] Their foray cost them eleven wounded and two dead, one of whom was Sergeant John G. Peters.[80]

One hundred skirmishers under Captain Sebastian D. Holmes (Company D, 111th New York) and a couple of companies from the 125th New York rushed to the relief of Companies F and G, 111th New York, south of the Bliss farm lane.[81] Simultaneously, Companies C, F, H, and K from the 126th New York with Companies A and C of the 108th New York (Sherrill's brigade), on the far right of the line, supported the 8th Ohio's withdrawal by deploying in extended order west of the Taneytown Road.[82] They were going to dislodge Confederate skirmishers who had infiltrated the northern end of the Emmitsburg Road beyond the Ohioans' right flank.

The two regiments charged the Rebels. A round dropped the orderly sergeant of Company A, 108th New York. First Lieutenant Dwight H. Ostrander immediately replaced him with the skinny Corporal William H. Raymond.[83] Coming on line with the 8th Ohio, they ran into a prone Confederate brigade. The Confederates met them with a withering fire. The 126th New York went to the ground in a futile effort to protect themselves. In short order, the Rebels killed Captains Charles M. Wheeler (Company K) and Orin J. Herendeen (Company H). Captain Isaac Shimer (Company F), while lying between two of his men, raised his head to see where the fire was coming from when a bullet slammed into his forehead. He died without making a sound. Four of his men hurriedly rolled him onto their muskets and carried him off the field as soon as the Confederates loosed the next volley at them.[84] Captain Winfield Scott (Company C) lost his only lieutenant, Sidney E. Brown, and over one-third of his company in one of the bitterest "scrapes" he had ever experienced. He retired to the Emmitsburg Road with bullet holes in his hat, his pants and his coat.[85] The two companies from the 108th remained on the forward line despite the loss of three killed and four wounded.[86]

As the four companies from the 126th New York pulled back, Colonel Eliakim Sherrill dispatched the picket reserves to the eastern side of the Emmitsburg Road on the brigade's right front. Company A, 126th New York, under Captain Morris Brown and Captain Samuel C. Armstrong (Company D) quickly occupied the Emanuel Trostle house and yard.[87]

Cushing's Battery, North of the Copse of Trees
The Confederate sharpshooters also pelted Battery A, 4th U.S. Artillery with several annoying rounds. As soon as Lieutenant Alonzo Cushing

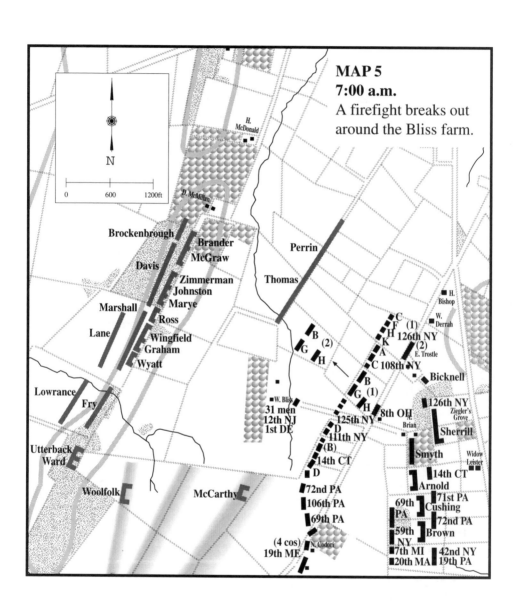

MAP 5
7:00 a.m.
A firefight breaks out
around the Bliss farm.

N

0   600   1200ft

H. McDonald

D. McMillan

Brockenbrough

Brander

McGraw

Davis

Zimmerman

Johnston

Marye

Marshall

Ross

Lane

Wingfield

Graham

Wyatt

Lowrance

Fry

Utterback

Ward

Woolfolk

McCarthy

Perrin

Thomas

H. Bishop

W. Derrah

C
F   (1)
H   126th NY
K
A   (2)
       E. Trostle
C 108th NY

Bicknell

126th NY
Ziegler's Grove

Sherrill

Smyth

Widow Leister

14th CT

Arnold

71st PA
Cushing
72nd PA

Brown

42nd NY
19th PA

B
G   (2)

H

W. Bliss

31 men
12th NJ
1st DE

B
G   (1)
H

8th OH
Brian

125th NY

D
111th NY
(B)

14th CT

D

72nd PA
106th PA
69th PA

(4 cos)
19th ME

N. Codori

69th
PA

59th
NY

7th MI
20th MA

ordered his six guns to load, then open fire upon the barn, Brigadier General Henry Hunt (Chief of Artillery, Army of the Potomac) rode into the rear of the battery.[88] Dismounting below the line of sight of the Rebel sharpshooters, on the eastern side of the crest, twelve feet behind Limber Number Three, he called Cushing and First Sergeant Frederick Fuger over to give them directions to the reserve ammunition train. The two artillerists stood close to the general while he produced a piece of paper and began penciling in the location of the ammunition train on a rough map. The Number Seven men for guns One, Two, and Three had just opened the lids on the ammunition chests to execute Cushing's command when a Confederate shell whirled in on top of Number Two Limber.[89]

An horrendous blast shattered the ammunition chest. The earth trembled and rolled; the concussion threw men to the ground and sent Cushing, Hunt, and Fuger running for cover with a burst of sulfurous smoke and bright flames skyrocketing into the air high above the ridge. The intense heat flashed laterally to both flanks, detonating the ammunition in Limbers One and Three and hurling the wheel driver of Arnold's Number Six gun, Private Thomas M. Aldrich, to the ground. [90]

The lead and swing horses reared. Breaking free from lead driver Patrick Lannegan and horse holder Private John Healy, they tried to bolt to the rear but got tangled in their harnesses. The two enlisted men threw themselves on the horses' heads, grabbed their halters and pulled them back into line.[91] Aldrich picked himself up in time to see the entire team from Cushing's Number One limber racing pell-mell for the Rebel lines. Leaping over a low spot in the western side of the Angle, they careened toward a downed section of the fence along the Emmitsburg Road and kept on running until he lost sight of them.[92] The stunned Pennsylvanians along the wall quickly recovered and grabbed the teams from Numbers Two and Three before they could escape. The tails of the wheel horses were still smoldering when they brought them back to the battery.[93]

By the time the smoke had cleared, Hunt was nowhere to be seen. Cushing and Fuger returned to the limbers to check the damage and to count their casualties. To Fuger's surprise the Number Seven men had miraculously escaped injury. In the distance, they could see the North Carolinian and Virginian artillerymen jumping up and down. Seconds later the annoying "yips" of the Rebel Yell rippled across the fields into the Yankee lines.[94] Cushing ordered the caissons, which were stationed not more than fifty feet behind the limbers, forward. He was not going to let the Rebels off so easily.[95]

Spangler's Farm Lane

The severity of the action around the Bliss farm posed a potential threat to Alexander's guns in the vicinity of the Rogers house. Major General Richard H. Anderson, whose division had spread out along the southern end of Seminary Ridge, ordered Colonel David Lang to the artillery's support. Skirmishers sprayed out to the front of the brigade; loping to the crest of the hill west of the Rogers house, they went to ground behind the guns. Lang's Floridians passed through Spangler's orchard. Crossing the fence in front of them, they lied down on the hillside on the north side of the farm lane, to Wilcox's immediate left.[96]

Cemetery Ridge
Smyth's Brigade, II Corps

It did not take long for Company A, 108th New York to expend its ammunition and the spare cartridges gathered from its casualties. Corporal William Raymond reported the problem to Lieutenant Ostrander who ordered him to take a detail to the rear for more. The corporal hesitated, unwilling to arbitrarily command men to risk their lives. To escape the responsibility, he asked the lieutenant to call for volunteers. "I don't care how it is done, as long as you obtain the ammunition," Ostrander snapped at him. When no one responded to the corporal's plea for volunteers, Raymond raced across the bullet-swept ground to Ziegler's Grove.

Lieutenant Colonel Francis E. Pierce (108th New York) commandeered a thousand-round box and advised the corporal, "Raymond, you have taken your share of risk; let someone else take this down to the skirmish line." The corporal refused, arguing that he as much as anyone else had the right to run the gauntlet. With the fatalistic "good-byes" of some officers and men fading behind him, he hoisted the crate upon his shoulder and ran toward the skirmishers. Reaching the company, he dragged the crate from man to man. Seven bullets tugged through his uniform without hitting meat or bone. Raymond, who had been teased for being too tall and skinny to cast a shadow came through the action without a scratch.[97]

Lieutenant Alonzo Cushing, Company A, 4th U.S. Artillery

Cushing (standing in the center) serviced his artillery with tremendous heroism until a Confederate bullet snuffed out his life.

MOLLUS, USAMHI

Just before Cushing sent his first round roaring toward Seminary Ridge, General Hays ordered Smyth to silence the skirmishers in the Bliss barn. The colonel, in turn, commanded Major John Hill (12th New Jersey) to execute the order. Hill passed the responsibility to Companies A, C, D, F, and K under

Captain Richard S. Thompson (Company K). Within half of an hour, the detachment picked up First Lieutenant John L. Brady (Company E) and the men from the 1st Delaware who were not on the picket line for their second attempt at the house.[98]

Cushing's Battery, North of the Copse of Trees

From 8:00 a.m. until 8:30 a.m. Alonzo Cushing's guns and Lieutenant George A. Woodruff's Battery I, 1st U.S. Artillery (in Ziegler's Grove) hurled shells at Wyatt's battery on Seminary Ridge.[99] Cushing's men worked their pieces methodically as if they were at drill.[100] With his six guns returning fire as soon as possible, they caught Captain Henry H. Carlton's section of 10-pounder Parrotts while they attempted to join McCarthy's section of Napoleons on the first ridge east of Spangler's Woods. A shell screamed into the hollow between the woods and the western side of the ridge just as the Troup Artillery executed a right wheel on the grassy slope. The round tore away the entire left buttock of a lead horse, literally painting the grass in bright red. Alexander, having never seen so much blood fly, rode toward the right of his line, leaving Carlton to fume over his spoiled drill book maneuver.[101] Shortly, a Rebel limber chest burst into flames and the Yankees leaped to their feet and cheered.[102] Before long, Cushing spied several mounted officers grouped together under a cluster of trees on the opposite ridge. The lieutenant, who was standing between Number Three and Four guns, turned to Acting Gunnery Sergeant Edward Drummond and yelled, "Sergeant, train your gun on that group." The first shot whirled over the Confederates. Thirty seconds later, the next one burst above their heads, unhorsing one of them and scattering the rest.[103]

That shell fell among Sir Arthur Fremantle (Coldstream Guards) and Lee's and Longstreet's staff officers who were patrolling the lines on a reconnaissance. It cut down the horse from under Colonel James B. Walton, who temporarily commanded Longstreet's artillery reserve. Satisfied that his good friend was not dead, the Englishman spurred on toward safer ground, closer to Pickett's division which had just arrived upon the field.[104]

Once again the "manly huzzah" reverberated among the Federals at the Angle.[105] The persistent firing irritated Captain John G. Hazard, Cushing's brigade commander. Trotting up to the lieutenant, he loudly reprimanded him, "Young man, are you aware that every round you fire costs the government two dollars and sixty-seven cents?" The battery fell silent very shortly after the captain rode away.[106]

The small arms fire spread south, along the fields west of the Codori farm as Brigadier General Alexander Webb dispatched 125 men under Captain James C. Lynch (Company B, 106th Pennsylvania) forward from the brigade line near the copse of trees. The captain's party consisted of a small contingent from Companies A and B of his own regiment, a detachment from two companies of the 72nd Pennsylvania, and some men from the 69th Pennsylvania.[107] The general instructed him to "hold on as long as he could."[108] The skirmishers advanced about ninety feet west of the road between the men from the 19th Maine and the 14th Connecticut and went prone.[109] The 69th held the left with the 106th and the 72nd on the center and the right, respectively. Second Lieutenant Robert Stewart's men from Company A of the 72nd Pennsylvania threw up a low breastwork of fence rails and prepared for a confrontation.[110]

Thompson's Raiders[111]

At the same time Captain Richard S. Thompson (Company K, 12th New Jersey) and his 200 men slipped north along the stone wall on the western slope of Cemetery Ridge to the corner of the Brian barn. Darting into the lane, they cut west to the Emmitsburg Road then moved south a very short distance to the point where the Bliss lane entered the road.[112] The Federals dashed into the chest-high wheat field west of the road. Using the rising ground in front of them as cover, they quickly formed in column of companies with Company F, 12th New Jersey in the front, followed respectively by Companies A, C, and K.[113] At the command, the raiders, with their weapons at trail arms, charged the farm buildings at the double-quick. Artillery and small arms fire slammed into them the moment they crested the rise.[114] Private William P. Haines (Company F) saw First Lieutenant John J. Trimble reel under the impact of a slight wound. At what seemed like the same instant three enlisted men went down. Private W. Henry Stratton bolted to the front and hurled himself to the ground to the right of the column. Private George W. Adams turned to the rear of Company F and fell away from the column's path. Private Will H. Johnson cut to the left and crumbled in the wheat along the fence row which paralleled the Yankees' line of advance. Their comrades left the four where they dropped without checking upon the condition of their wounds.[115]

1st Minnesota

On the far left of the corps line, while the firing died away along the Emmitsburg Road, Private Lafayette W. Snow (Company B) informed Sergeant Patrick H. Taylor (Company E) that he had seen his brother's corpse lying on the ground to the left rear of the regimental line. Taylor without saying much of anything, got up with two of his friends and wandered away from the regiment. Finding Isaac's body, they set to work to give him a proper burial.[116]

Seminary Ridge, North of Spangler's Woods
Fry's Brigade

Second Lieutenant John H. Moore (Company B, 7th Tennessee) stared in disbelief as Lieutenant Furgerson S. Harris (Company H, 7th Tennessee), commanding Major General Henry Heth's division sharpshooters, shooed some old men, women and children from the Bliss farm house for the Confederate lines while his skirmishers fell back toward the barn.[117] Their sudden retreat flushed the rest of their men out into the open. None of them stopped running until they reached a row of low, thick bushes west and north of the barn.

Captain Thompson hurried his raiders to the barn. The men charged under the overhang on the east side and burst into the lower level stable.[118] Sergeant James White (Company F) skittered to a basement window on the western side of the barn while his comrades crawled up through the stalls onto the main floor.[119] Hoping to shoot one of the Rebels, who were running through the orchard, in the back, he poked his rifle through the window when he heard, "Don't shoot, I'll give up." White shouted at the Confederate, who had flattened his back against the outside wall, to come in through the window, which he did without any hesitation.[120] In short order, the Yankees captured a Confederate major and several enlisted men.[121] On the main floor, a bullet smashed both of Corporal Abel K. Shute's knees as he tried running across the open doorway on the west side of the barn.[122] He lay exposed in the open screaming for someone from Company F to help him. Sergeant White, having turned his prisoner over to Sergeant Henry M. Avis, pulled the mortally wounded corporal to cover.[123] Sergeant Frank Riley hoisted himself up on a joist in the barn and walked the beam to a lattice in the north end of the wall. From his perch he could see a Confederate officer trying to urge his men back into action against the barn. His comrades loaded and passed their rifles up to him in assembly line fashion so he could take pot shots at the Rebels.[124]

From the main floor, the Yankees watched a great many Confederates disappear behind the bush row along the far edge of the wheat field northeast of the barn and suspected the Rebels might be flanking them. Captain Thompson sent a captain with a reconnaissance party into the open to feel out the position. The Rebels got to them first. A nasty firefight erupted. The scouting party took several hits, including their officer, and limped back to report the obvious—"the bushes are full of them."

In the meantime, the Confederates, having rolled a battery into the wheat west of the orchard, slammed four solid shot into the barn's long side. Stone shards, masked in a cloud of pulverized mortar, ricocheted around the inside of the building, startling the men and coating them with limestone dust. The situation had gotten too hot for them to stay. Thompson gave the order to clear out. "Come down! come down quickly! They are trying to capture us!" Riley heeded his friends' warning. While lowering himself from the rafters, he shot a quick glance out through the lattice and saw what appeared to be an entire brigade closing in on the barn from the north.[125]

At the signal, the 12th New Jersey, their wounded and prisoners in tow, took off at the double-quick toward the brush with the Confederate gunners firing at their flank. Without warning, they halted, fronted, and riddled the shrubbery with buck and ball. Woodruff's Regular battery (I, 1st U.S.), on the right front of the Federal line along Cemetery Ridge, immediately slammed the position with canister. The Rebels broke and ran while the Yankees headed in the opposite direction back to their own lines.[126]

As the panting Yankees neared the top of the ridge where they first came under fire, Private Haines ran out to check on Company F's casualties. Upon discovering that George Adams was dead, Haines left him where he lay and went to Henry Stratton's side. He could stand with Haines' assistance but could not walk. Haines called to his men and at least three came over and carried Stratton, Captain Azariah Stratton's older brother, off the field. (He died on the way to the hospital.) Several others hauled Will Johnson away. (He was dead before the day ended.)[127]

The Confederates, however, had not dispersed as much as Thompson had hoped they would. By the time the Federals had gotten to the east side of the Emmitsburg Road, the Confederate skirmishers were regrouping and moving back toward their forward position in and around the Bliss buildings.[128] Snipers reoccupied the barn and peppered Captain William A. Arnold's artillerymen (A, 1st Rhode Island) on the crest of Cemetery Ridge south of Hays' line.[129]

9:00 a.m.—Seminary Ridge

While Thompson's raiders were struggling to gain control of the Bliss farm, Brigadier General William N. Pendleton, Chief of Artillery for the Army of Northern Virginia, inspected Alexander's work. Riding alongside Alexander, the general complimented the colonel upon his deployment. As they discussed the matter further, the general mentioned that Colonel R. Lindsay Walker, commanding A. P. Hill's artillery reserve, had eight 12-pounder howitzers which he could not use against Cemetery Ridge because of the extreme range. Would the colonel have any use for them? Alexander, without telling the general how he intended to use the guns, did not hesitate to accept them, saying that he had the "very place for them." Pendleton, Alexander and his courier, Private Arthur C. Catlett (Bedford Artillery) rode back to Seminary Ridge to the southern end of Hill's line. One gun came from Ward's Mississippi Battery; he took two each from Graham's North Carolina and Brooke's Virginia Batteries. Wyatt's Virginia Battery loaned him one more howitzer and Grandy's Virginia Light Artillery supplied him with the last two guns.[130] Placing Major Charles Richardson from Lieutenant Colonel John J. Garnett's Battalion in command of the detachment, Alexander directed the guns to the thinly wooded hollow on the western side of Seminary Ridge near Pitzer's house where Pitzer's Run flowed east into the swale opposite the Bliss farm. Alexander gave the major explicit instructions to wait there until he sent for him. At the same time he cautioned Private Catlett to remember exactly where the guns were.

Keeping his intentions to himself, Alexander headed toward the left of his line. Had Richardson or the cautious Pendleton known that the mountain howitzers were going to be used exclusively to provide close support to Pickett's division by advancing immediately behind the infantry, neither one of the officers might have been so willing to relinquish them to Alexander's command. The colonel joined Lee, Longstreet and their staffs in the vicinity of the northeast corner of Spangler's Woods. They gave him more specific advice about the placement of Pickett's division and their intended line of march. Equipped with that information, he began to readjust his line to concentrate his fire upon the Federal guns along Cemetery Ridge from the copse of trees to Ziegler's Grove. While they were conversing, Major James Dearing's Battalion

**Brigadier General
William N. Pendleton**

Colonel E. Porter Alexander wisely concealed his intended use of the Army of Northern Virginia's howitzers from the very cautious Pendleton.

Miller, *Photographic History*

(Pickett's division) arrived. Alexander ordered him into position immediately south of the fence which paralleled the northern edge of Spangler's Woods.[131]

Pickett's Division

In the heat of the day, Pickett's sweating infantrymen, for the most part, did not pay attention to the time. First Lieutenant George W. Finley (Company K, 56th Virginia) of Garnett's brigade mistakenly believed that it was around 8:00 a.m. (It was probably closer to 10:00 a.m.)[132] While the batteries along the northern end of Seminary and Cemetery Ridges banged away at each other and the 12th New Jersey conducted its futile charge against the Bliss farm, Pickett's brigades deployed for what would later be recorded as one of the most spectacular charges in history. His infantry began moving before Dearing brought his guns up.[133]

About the same time, Brigadier General Cadmus Wilcox, his field glasses in his hand, returned to his brigade in the low ground south of the Rogers house.[134] Having spent some time on the crest of the hill along the Emmitsburg Road studying the Federal lines, he had decided to change the brigade's position. The Alabamians got to their feet and reformed their lines, which prompted Lang to do the same with his Floridians. Edging their

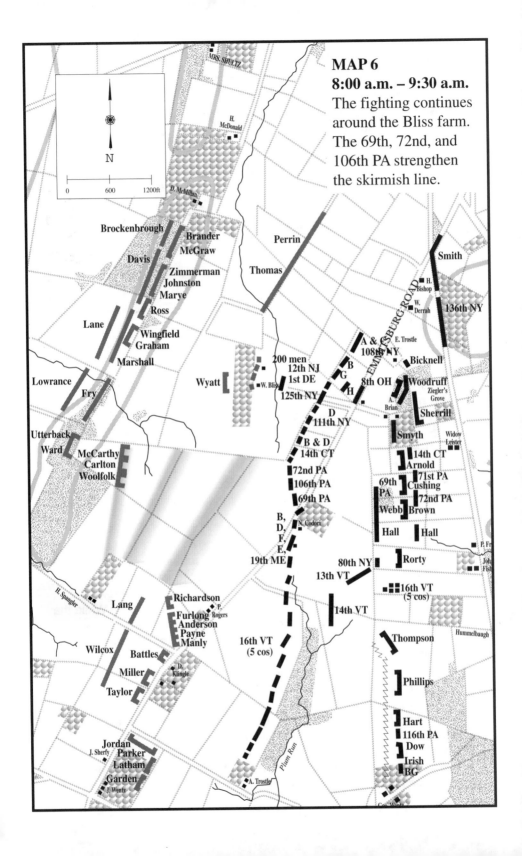

MAP 6
8:00 a.m. – 9:30 a.m.
The fighting continues
around the Bliss farm.
The 69th, 72nd, and
106th PA strengthen
the skirmish line.

way toward the top of the ridge, Wilcox's men went prone in the tall grass about forty yards behind Eshleman's artillery. Captain George Clark (Company B, 11th Alabama) watched the men around him shake their heads in grim resignation to their fates. A rumor traveled through the ranks that their brigadier, "Old Billy Fixin," having not lost enough men on July 2, intended to sacrifice the rest of them before the present day ended.[135] To the north side of Spangler's lane, Lang's brigade moved to within twenty feet of some of the guns. Almost immediately a good many of the veterans unsheathed their bayonets and began scraping out a small trench, while others scrounged up fence rails and loose stones. According to First Lieutenant Raymond J. Reid (Adjutant, 2nd Florida) they had constructed quite a "formidable breastwork" in a very short amount of time.[136]

Adjutant Raymond J. Reid, 2nd Florida

First Lieutenant Reid left behind an informative account of the Florida Brigade's role in the action of July 3, 1863.

Florida State Archives

Kemper's Brigade

With those two brigades out of his way, Kemper marched his regiments into the low ground west of the Spangler farm. Company D of the 1st Virginia and Company D from the 11th Virginia, respectively, sprayed forward as skirmishers to the open ground in front of Lang's and Wilcox's men.[137] Behind them, on the south side of the farm lane, the 24th Virginia (442 effectives) filed into the hollow south of Spangler's orchard and halted. The 11th Virginia (405 effectives) went into line on its left. As the brigade emerged from the cover of Spangler's Woods into the brilliant sunlight, Captain John Holmes Smith (Company G, 11th Virginia) fixed his eyes upon his soldiers. While directing them into the regimental line he noticed how short their legs seemed in comparison to the extremely long shadows which stretched out behind them. The absurd impression that his men were shorter than he had ever remembered them lingered with him throughout the morning.[138] The 1st Virginia (218 effectives), the 7th Virginia (359 effectives), and the 3rd Virginia (351 effectives), respectively continued the line to the north side of Spangler's lane.[139]

A feeling of relief swept over First Lieutenant John E. Dooley (Company C, 1st Virginia) as his regiment stood to arms in Spangler's little apple orchard. He preferred being in the torrid sunlight to waiting in the cooler woods where the burial details were interring the scattered remains of the previous days' fatalities. (Very few of the bodies were intact. After passing a decapitated body he discovered its fragmented skull lying not too far away in bloodied puddles.) The report of an artillery piece drew his attention to the red brick Sherfy house on the ridge bordering the Emmitsburg Road. (He estimated the distance between his men and the house was about one fourth of a mile.) As he stood there watching the battery near the house fire to the north, a green apple fight erupted among his twenty-seven-man company. His "boys," while remaining in place, stooped down, snatched up the crab apples at their feet, and chucked them at each other. For several minutes he participated in his first small unit action at Gettysburg.[140]

Garnett's Brigade

Along the western face of Spangler's Woods, Garnett's brigade stood to arms, waiting to advance. Company G from the 18th Virginia and Company H from the 8th Virginia sprinted forward from the line. Cutting through the swale east of Spangler's Woods, they rushed up to the top of the forward ridge and threw themselves down onto grass among McCarthy's and Carlton's field pieces.[141]

The 56th Virginia (430 effectives) held the left of the line. The 28th Virginia (376 effectives), lying in the field, was the next regiment to the right, followed respectively by the 19th (426 effectives), 18th (371 effectives), and 8th Virginia regiments (242 effectives).[142] Private Robert D. Damron (Company D, 56th Virginia) stared through the thin belt of woods to his front at the four guns on the first ridge east of the woods.[143]

Fry's Brigade

Fry's Tennesseeans and Alabamians, having spent the entire morning lying below the western crest of Seminary Ridge, had no genuine idea of what lay before them. The suspense having become overpowering, Orderly Sergeant Junius "June" Kimble (Company A, 14th Tennessee) ventured over the ridge, fifty yards beyond his regiment to study the Federal lines. What he saw, at first, did not seem daunting. The two worm fences—one west of the Bliss farm, the other near the Emmitsburg Road—did not seem formidable. Sunlight danced off the burnished tubes of the Yankees' 12-pounders. Scanning the Federal position from Ziegler's Grove to Little Round Top, he could not help but taste the fear of having to face them. "June Kimble," he blew through his teeth, "are you going to do your duty today?" After a moment's pause he replied out loud, "I'll do it, so help me God." An unexplainable calm settled over him—a genuine peace of spirit. When he returned to the regiment, Lieutenant Pembrook S. Waters (Company A) asked, "How does it look, June?" "Boys," the sergeant coolly answered, "if we have to go, it will be hot for us, and we will have to do our best."[144]

Second Lieutenant John H. Moore (Company B, 7th Tennessee), who was lying with his men along the western crest of Seminary Ridge, did not feel encouraged by the menacing sight of the Federal batteries massed along Cemetery Ridge. General Lee in the company of Lieutenant Generals A. P. Hill and James Longstreet rode along the brigade's front. Every now and then they would glance at the prone Tennesseeans and Alabamians but, for the most part, they kept their field glasses focused upon the Federal line. The three officers trooped the ridge no less than three times. Their apparent indecisiveness showed. Moore took their pacing as an ominous portent of the hazardous duty which lay ahead.[145]

He watched them ride behind the line. About sixty paces to the right rear of the division, they dismounted and sat upon a fallen tree trunk. Private Robert D. Damron (Company D, 56th Virginia) recognized Lee, Longstreet and Major Walter H. Taylor, Lee's assistant adjutant general. A cordon of sentries immediately surrounded the officers, facing away from them. It must have been a war council, Damron surmised. Colonel Birkett D. Fry, who was mounted behind his brigade, noticed them poring over a map and earnestly discussing something.[146]

Moore and Fry warily watched the generals remount. Lee rode north alone, behind his regiments. Staff officers and couriers scattered in every direction like a covey of frightened birds. Then the generals rode the front of Fry's brigade again. It occurred to Moore that Lee and his officers were vacillating about their next move. Their nervous pacing of the line made him feel very uneasy.[147] A veteran's intuition told Private Wiley Woods (Company F, 1st Tennessee), the color bearer, they were going to be thrown into a very desperate situation. Since the regiment had no official color guard he told Sergeant Stant Denson (Company A), who stood nearby, to keep an eye upon him. If he went down during the advance Stant was to pick up the flag.[148] He did not expect to live out the assault.

Marshall's Brigade

Captains Thomas J. Cureton (Company B) and Samuel P. Wagg (Company A) left the 26th North Carolina and strolled to the top of the ridge. In the distance, across the wide, slightly undulating fields, they studied the Federal position. No cover "...not even a hill to protect a charging line from the artillery," Cureton recalled. "The ridge we occupied was splendid for defense." He dreaded leaving its protection.[149]

Fry's Brigade

A few minutes later, Brigadier General J. Johnston Pettigrew rode up to Fry to tell him that the infantry would advance after the shelling stopped. The colonel distinctly remembered the general's admonition, "They will of course return the fire with all the guns they have; we must shelter the men as best we can, and make them lie down." With that, Pettigrew ordered Fry to see Pickett immediately to get an understanding of which brigade would be the brigade of direction.

Fry found Pickett in an excellent frame of mind—almost exuberant. Old comrades from the Mexican War, the two politely greeted each other. This charge would be just like the good old days when they stormed Chapultapec together, the general reminded Fry. Pickett reassured his friend that their men would drive the Yankees away after the Confederate guns had completely demoralized them. Garnett joined them. After a short discussion, he agreed that Fry's brigade would be the brigade of direction.[150]

While Fry returned to his regiments, Pickett turned his particular attention to his close friend, Richard Garnett. When Garnett asked for specific instructions, Lieutenant Colonel Norborne Berkeley (8th Virginia) overheard Pickett tell him, "Dick, old fellow, I have no orders to give you, but I advise you to get across those fields as quick as you can, for in my opinion you are going to catch hell!" Garnett, who had been kicked by a mule the night before, had been advised by his surgeon not to participate in the charge. Despite the order from Lee that all officers were to go in dismounted, he requested to ride his gelding. Pickett assented. Dick Garnett, in an old blue overcoat, would be aboard Red Eye, which at $1400 was the second most expensive thoroughbred in Longstreet's Corps.[151] Pickett relayed his instructions to his brigade commanders.

Dearing's Battalion rolled into the hollow along the eastern side of the woods and swung into battery on the right of Lieutenant James Woolfolk's guns, which stood in front of the northeast corner of the woods. At that Garnett gave the command for his brigade to advance to their support. From the center of the brigade, Second Lieutenant W. Nathaniel Wood (Company A, 19th Virginia) walked away from his regiment to the crest of the hill just beyond the woods as Dearing galloped by him heading south. "That hill must fall," he heard the young major scream at his approaching guns. With the words still echoing in his ears, Wood walked back to his men, all the while watching the most artillery he had ever seen roll into position on or below the crest behind him.[152]

Orders traveled along the 56th Virginia to furl its colors and for the men to stoop low as they marched into the open field between them the guns to their front.[153] The limbers and caissons from Carlton's and McCarthy's sections disrupted the left wing of the 56th Virginia. Lieutenant George W. Finley (Company K), whose company was the second from the left of the line, broke his men to the rear while the rest of the regiment went prone along the base of the ridge with the limbers and caissons behind their line. They had no respite from the suffocating humidity and the severe heat. He watched his men welter in their own sweat and waited for someone to tell them what was going on.[154] Major Edmund Berkeley (8th Virginia) kneeled down in the open field north of Spangler's orchard and began scraping up earth to bury the deck of cards which he, his younger brother, Lieutenant Colonel Norborne Berkeley (8th Virginia), Colonel Eppa Hunton (8th Virginia), and Richard Garnett had used at Fredericksburg.[155]

Kemper's Brigade

Garnett's advance crowded Kemper's line at Spangler's orchard, forcing his regiments to move to the hillside immediately east of the orchard. The men in the 1st Virginia dropped their green apples and picked up their weapons. Advancing with the brigade, they crossed the open ground between the orchard and the base of the hill, and tore down the fence along their front before lying down on the slope along the line formerly occupied by Lang's Floridians. On the right, the 11th and the 24th Virginia fell in along Wilcox's old position. First Lieutenant John Dooley (Company C, 1st Virginia) warily noted that it "looks like work." He was right. Shortly thereafter, the field and staff told their men that every Confederate field piece was going to open fire. The cannonading would last an hour after which they were to charge and sweep everything before them. To the anxious Dooley, the time passed very, very slowly.[156]

The word quickly spread through the regiments that they were to make an advance. On the far left, among the ranks of the 3rd Virginia, the men were exceedingly quiet. "Still and thoughtful as Quakers at a love feast," Colonel Joseph C. Mayo, Jr. later recalled. Strolling over to the 7th Virginia, to his right, he found Colonel Waller Tazwell Patton standing on the hillside in front of his regiment and expressed his concern about his soldiers' morale. "This news has brought about an awful seriousness with our fellows, Taz."

Tazwell Patton, a no-nonsense individual, replied, "Yes, and well they may be serious if they really know what is in store for them. I have been up where Dearing is and looked across at the Yankees." The somberness in his voice said it all. Realizing that he had disturbed his friend, Patton attempted to lighten things up a little by telling a story about Dearing.

Dearing had ridden out on the skirmish line, well beyond his guns, when Lee sent a courier to him. The young officer thought Lee wanted him to report on what he had seen.

Major James Dearing

The gallant major trooped his artillery line, flag in hand, to inspire his men and the infantry on the slope behind him to do their all on that fateful day.

Miller, *Photographic History*

Instead, he received a reprimand. "Major Dearing," the note from the commanding general read, "I do not approve of young officers needlessly exposing themselves; your place is with your batteries."[157]

Armistead's Brigade

Armistead's brigade ran southeasterly on the western side of a ridge which extended from the northeastern end of Spangler's Woods into the open ground west of the Spangler House. Four of his regiments (38th, 57th, 53rd, and 9th Virginia) lay in the woods, about 200 yards southwest of Garnett's brigade with the 14th Virginia in the field on the right of the line. Altogether they occupied about a 1,750-foot front.[158]

Private Erasmus Williams (Company H, 14th Virginia) took out his case knife and unsheathed his bayonet; he began scooping up earth and tossing it in a pile at the head of his "ditch." Second Lieutenant Philip P. Guerrant, who was leaning against a sapling behind him, laughed at his efforts. "Why, Williams," he teased, "you are a coward." "You may call me what you please," the private snapped, "but when the time comes I will show up all right, and when the artillery begins, the hole I am digging will be a good place for me to be in." He kept digging, heedless of his lieutenant's guying.[159]

Alexander's Artillery

By 10:00 a.m., Alexander had his battalions arranged from Spangler's Woods to the Peach Orchard. Captain Henry H. Carlton with a section of 10-pounder Parrotts and the 12-pounder Napoleon section from McCarthy's guns (Colonel H. C. Cabell's Battalion) occupied the far left with their right near the northeast corner of Spangler's Woods. (Carlton kept his two 12-pounder howitzers below the crest of the ridge behind his rifles because the Federal lines were beyond their range.)[160] Lieutenant James Woolfolk's two Napoleons and two 20-pounder Parrotts were in battery to the right, with his right flank near the northeast corner of the woods.[161] Dearing's Battalion (eighteen guns) was to his right, the guns' positions conforming to the contour of the ridge which ran southeasterly toward the northwest corner of Spangler's orchard. Captain Joseph O. Blount's battery held the left of the battalion with Captains Miles C. Macon's, William H. Caskie's, and Robert M. Stribling's guns to his right. The entire battalion faced northeast toward the copse of trees. Eshleman's Battalion continued the line to the right front on the hilltop in front of Lang's brigade with two 12-pounder Napoleons under Captain John B. Richardson. The rest of Cabell's Battalion—less Captain Basil C. Manly's two light howitzers—filled the gap between Richardson's section and Lieutenant Henry A. Battles' section of Napoleons (Eshleman's Battalion) with his remaining eight guns. Battles' guns were in the high ground along the Emmitsburg Road immediately south of Spangler's lane. Captain Merritt B. Miller's four guns completed

Eshleman's line with Captain Osmond B. Taylor's battery from Huger's Battalion to his right. (The major kept Lieutenant George E. Apps' two 12-pounder howitzers in reserve.)[162] At that point, the artillery line crossed the road at about a ninety degree angle. Captains William W. Parker's and Tyler C. Jordan's Virginia batteries continued the line along Trostle's lane, about 200 feet north of the Peach Orchard. Latham's and Garden's nine pieces, facing east at right angles to the orchard, covered Alexander's flank.[163] With sixty-four longer range pieces in the line and his twelve 12-pounder and 24-pounder howitzers in reserve Alexander hoped to suppress the Federal batteries along Cemetery Ridge and provide close fire support for the advancing infantry.[164] His fifty-five guns became the southern end of an artillery line which stretched intermittently for two

Captain Frank Huger

He assumed command of Colonel E. P. Alexander's artillery battalion throughout the day on July 3, 1863. He is shown with a colonel's rank.

Miller, *Photographic History*

and one-half miles to the north to Oak Hill and east another two and three-eighths miles to Benner's Hill on the far left of the Confederate line.[165]

The 8th Ohio, West of the Emmitsburg Road

The Ohioans had been under what Sergeant Thomas Galwey called "murderous" fire since 8:00 a.m. and were not going to attempt another charge across the killing ground between the Confederates in the Long Lane and the Bliss farm. The Rebels in their butternut uniforms were extremely hard to detect. Only the telltale puffs of smoke following each shot betrayed a hint of any sharpshooter's location in the wheat field. The Westerners resorted to a "scientific" method of eliminating the Rebels with what they morbidly referred to as "Turning a Jack." Working in gangs of four or five, all of whom had loaded rifles, they would wait for a Rebel to fire. The second the Yankees saw the smoke rise above the wheat, they would all volley at its point of origin.

Nevertheless, the Confederates fearlessly exploited every advantage. By 9:30 a.m. it had become extremely hazardous for a skirmisher on either side to risk standing up. A couple of Rebel sharpshooters had picked off careless soldiers throughout the morning, much to the chagrin of the Westerners. Without warning, the Ohioans heard, "Don't fire, Yanks!" Instinctively, many men in Company B got up to see what was going on in the wheat. A Rebel, his rifle slung across his back, popped out from behind the large shade tree which stood in the center of the field about thirty yards west of the Yankees. Several of them raised their rifles to their shoulders to cut him down, but their comrades stopped them. They wanted to see what the skirmisher was going to do. The Rebel held a canteen in his hand. Walking halfway into the field between him and the Yankees, he kneeled down to give water to a wounded Ohioan. One of Company B cried out, "Bully for you! Johnny!" A cheer rose above the field as the entire company got to its feet. The Confederates along the skirmish line quit shooting and also stood up to see what was going on. When he ran out of water, the Confederate walked back to his tree, from which he yelled, "Down, Yanks, we're going to fire." The skirmishers on both sides went to ground and began sniping again.[166] Company B of the 8th Ohio weltered in the intense heat and humidity. The men coped with it as best they could.

Sergeant Galwey (Company B), struck with an hunger pang, scraped his fingers along the inside of his haversack, trying to retrieve the few crumbs of hard crackers which remained. All along the line, he spotted exhausted skirmishers, lying motionless like dead men in the trampled wheat—asleep. Shortly thereafter, Lieutenant Colonel Franklin Sawyer retired all but Company H back to the deep road cut north of the Brian farm lane.[167]

Cemetery Ridge
Harrow's Brigade, II Corps

Major General George G. Meade (Army of the Potomac, commanding) shuffled troops north along Cemetery Ridge to reinforce his weak center. Brigadier General William Harrow's brigade, which had been badly mauled the day before, passed behind Stannard's men as it deployed north to support the II Corps artillery near the copse of trees. Lieutenant William Lochren (1st Minnesota) whose stalwart regiment had lost eighty-two percent of its effective strength in a forlorn hope less than twenty-four hours before, noticed how clean Stannard's men were and how large their regiments were compared to those of his brigade. (The 1st Minnesota, including Company F which had just returned from skirmish duty at Little Round Top, mustered about one hundred forty officers and men. Company C, with its estimated ten officers and men, still remained at division headquarters. Captain Wilson B. Farrell, having gained headquarters' attention by dressing his men in the regulation frock coats and the ostrich-plumed Jeff Davis hat, was considered a "favorite" at the divisional level.)[168] Harrow's battle-wearied veterans began fortifying their line with fence rails and field stones. For added security they reinforced their knee-high breastworks with dirt-filled knapsacks. Unlike the Vermonters, who were too nervous to relax, many of the westerners nestled down behind their "works" and napped.[169]

Hays' Division, II Corps

The 12th New Jersey and the 1st Delaware returned to their brigade only to be asked "Why didn't you burn the barn?" The mere insinuation that the men had not done their duty irked Private William Haines (Company F, 12th New Jersey) for over thirty years. He later wrote, "I am positive that none of our company had orders to burn it, or it would have been done..."

Brigadier General Alexander Hays ordered the 14th Connecticut (Smyth's brigade) to silence the noisome Rebels for good. Major Theodore Ellis decided to detach the right wing of his regiment from the line southeast of the Brian barn.[170] At around 10:00 a.m., he sent Lieutenant Frederick P. Doten, the regimental adjutant, to Captain Samuel A. Moore with orders to pull his Company F, with Companies G, I, and A (fifty to sixty men) from the one hundred fifty-nine-man regiment. Moore immediately deployed them to finish the job once and for all.[171] First Lieutenant Frederick S. Seymour (Company I) asked Colonel Smyth, "If in the event of capturing the house and barn, the rebs make it so hot we can't hold them, shall we fire them?" The colonel hesitated a moment then gave permission to torch the farm.[172] Slipping north along the stone wall past Hays' headquarters at the Brian house, the raiders followed the same route used by Thompson. Once they reached the lane, Moore ordered each man to charge the barn on his own. The New Englanders, with Moore in the lead, ran helter-skelter across the 600 yards of wheat under a scattering fire from the sharpshooters in the barn and the skirmishers from Thomas' and McGowan's brigade which had them flanked on the right from the "Long Lane."[173] Private Thomas J. Brainard (Company F) sprang ahead of his company, shouting, "Come on you cowards!" when a round struck him through his lowered shoulder and lodged in his chest.[174] He screamed. Captain John C. Broatch (Company A) looked up to see the impact of the round lift the private off his feet and drop him to the ground. He was writhing in terrible pain and crying out, "My God! my God! I'm hit. O' how it hurts me!" as Sergeant Major William B. Hincks ran by him.[175] Second Lieutenant Samuel H. Seward (Company I) went down with a bullet in his stomach. Frederick S. Seymour, the company's remaining lieutenant, caught a round through the leg and fell without telling anyone to fire the buildings.

Most of the Confederates in the barn scattered before the Yankees reached them. Moore, the first of the raiders to reach the lower level door, darted inside and captured a few of the slower running sharpshooters. His men, piling in after him, soon found themselves coming under fire from the farm house which was about 150 feet to the northeast, and from the orchard west of the barn.[176]

Seeing that Moore's raiders were pinned down, Hays sent Major Ellis with Companies C, E, H, and K to their relief.[177] Leaving the color guard with the flag behind they made a wild dash from the road through the wheat field toward the house. The sight of Ellis' unexpected rush sent the Rebels inside the house scattering for safer ground. Firing as they ran, they wounded Private John Fox (Company A) in the thigh and killed Sergeant George W. Baldwin (Company I). Sergeant J. Samuel Scranton (Company G) very calmly returned fire, amazing First Lieutenant Henry P. Goddard with his unflinching steadiness as he deliberately picked off a Rebel in the doorway of the house.[178] Once the major, however, discovered that the house offered nominal protection, he retired most of his men to the barn.[179]

Unfortunately the west side of the barn (the long side facing the Confederates) had no apertures in it. Blind to the Confederates' movement, the Yankees found themselves in a very precarious situation.[180] Without warning, an artillery round burst through the north gable, wounding a few more men and killing Private Moses G. Clement (Company G). A piece of debris slammed Commissary Sergeant Julius W. Knowlton so hard in the back that he swore it nearly broke his spine. One of the enlisted men handed a piece of the projectile to Ellis. It was a cast iron "grape shot" and not the smaller canister ball which the Federals used. The major concluded that it probably was a Confederate round.[181] With no place to go, Ellis' men returned fire from any open spots which they could find. The Confederates peppered the barn. A bullet cracked through one of its windows and prostrated Corporal Thomas W. Gardner (Company H), leaving him with a nasty groove across the top of his head.[182]

Osborn's Position—Cemetery Hill

While Hays' men charged the Bliss farm, Lieutenant General Richard S. Ewell's assault against Culp's Hill abruptly stopped. Major Thomas W. Osborn glanced at his watch. It was 10:00 a.m. Shortly thereafter aides from army headquarters trotted onto the hill and informed the major that Confederate infantry had been seen massing in heavy numbers on the left of the Federal line. General Hunt, who had dropped by several times since daylight, added that he expected the Confederates to bring as many guns as possible to bear upon Cemetery Hill to silence Osborn's batteries on the high ground before rolling up the left of the line. He authorized Osborn to get all of the field pieces and ammunition he needed from the Artillery Reserve and to deploy them as he saw fit.[183]

With the field relatively quiet, the major decided to act upon the general's suggestions. He closed Dilger's battery to the right, contracting the intervals between the guns from the regulation fourteen yards to fourteen feet.[184] He immediately called up four batteries from the Artillery Reserve which were located in the low ground between the Baltimore Pike and the Taneytown Road in the vicinity of Meade's Headquarters.[185] Leaving a gap large enough

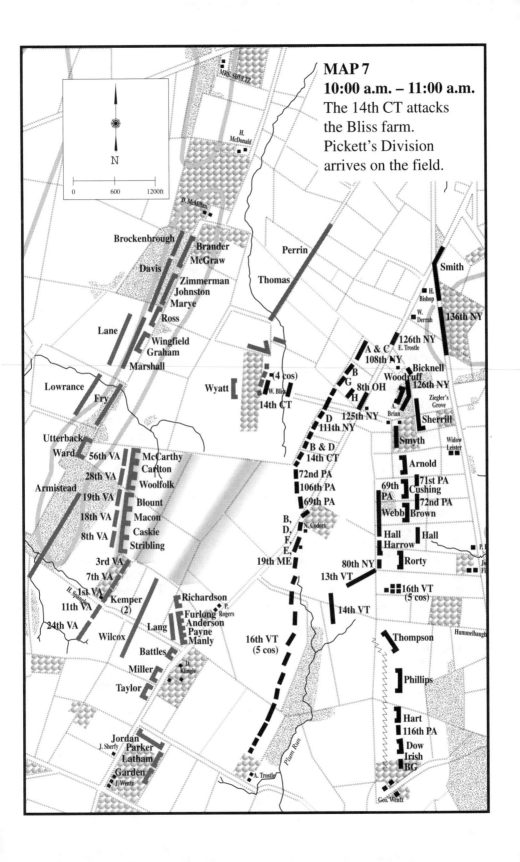

MAP 7
10:00 a.m. – 11:00 a.m.
The 14th CT attacks
the Bliss farm.
Pickett's Division
arrives on the field.

N

0   600   1200ft

MRS. SHULTZ

H. McDonald

D. McMillan

Brockenbrough

Brander
McGraw

Perrin

Smith

Davis

Thomas

H. Bishop

Zimmerman
Johnston
Marye

W. Derrah

136th NY

Ross

Lane

Wingfield
Graham

126th NY
E. Trostle

A & C
108th NY

Marshall

Wyatt

(4 cos)
W. Bliss

14th CT

B
G
H

8th OH

Woodruff

Bicknell
126th NY

Ziegler's
Grove

Lowrance

Fry

D
111th NY

125th NY

Brian

Sherrill

Utterback

Ward

56th VA

McCarthy
Carlton

B & D
14th CT

Smyth

Widow
Leister

Armistead

28th VA

19th VA

Woolfolk

72nd PA
106th PA

Arnold

71st PA
Cushing

18th VA

Blount

Macon

69th PA

69th
PA

72nd PA

8th VA

Caskie

Stribling

B,
D,
F,
E,

N. Codori

Webb

Brown

Hall

Hall

3rd VA

7th VA

19th ME

Harrow

80th NY

Rorty

H. Spangler 1st VA

11th VA

24th VA

Kemper
(2)

Richardson

P. Rogers

13th VT

16th VT
(5 cos)

Wilcox

Lang

Furlong
Anderson
Payne
Manly

14th VT

Hummelbaugh

Battles

Miller

Taylor

D. Klingle

16th VT
(5 cos)

Thompson

Phillips

Jordan
J. Sherfy

Parker
Latham

Hart
116th PA

Garden

J. Wentz

Plum Run

Dow
Irish
BG

A. Trostle

Geo. Wentz

to place another battery if required, Second Lieutenant Philip D. Mason (Battery H, 1st U.S. Artillery) placed his six Napoleons on the crest behind the center of the 136th New York.[186] Captain Wallace Hill's Battery C, 1st West Virginia Artillery (four 10-pounder Parrotts) then Second Lieutenant George W. Norton's six 3-inch rifles (Battery H, 1st Ohio Artillery) finished the formation to the left.[187] With his total complement of thirty-four guns, Osborn brought the aggregate number of Yankee field pieces from Cemetery Hill to the Weikert farm to eighty-three.

The Southern End of Cemetery Ridge

Sometime in the forenoon, Captain Andrew Cowan, commanding the 1st New York Independent Battery, having been detached to the I Corps from the VI Corps, arrived at the intersection of the Granite School House Road and the Taneytown Road looking for Major General John Newton. The battery halted before entering the intersection while the captain rode west toward the I Corps Headquarters flag which fluttered along the eastern face of a large grove about 500 yards to the west.

Major General Abner Doubleday introduced himself to Cowan as soon as he entered the woods with the explanation that he commanded the I Corps in Newton's absence. Newton was riding the line, the general explained and he really could not use the captain's guns at the time. Sensing Cowan's disappointment, Doubleday began walking west. "Come with me," he said, "and I will show you the situation." Passing to the western edge of the woods, they turned north, all the while keeping within the tree line.

In the open, to the left, the captain saw Union infantry hunkering down behind an extensive, formidable rifle pit. On the ridge beyond, past the Emmitsburg Road, he noticed Confederates walking about and the glint of sunlight reflecting off a bronze battery flashed in his eyes. Doubleday, motioning toward the Rebel guns, added that he could not deploy the New Yorkers without drawing the fire of all of the Confederate artillery along the Emmitsburg Road. The general did not want to needlessly lose men in a senseless skirmish. "Park your battery in some convenient place. Let your men get their breakfasts, send me word where you are, and when I can use you, I will send for you." Cowan turned away and quietly returned to his guns. They went into park about 100 yards east of the works.[188]

The 8th Ohio in the Emmitsburg Road

At 11:00 a.m., Colonel Charles Wood, Jr. (136th New York) sent a battalion into the open ground between Ziegler's Grove and the Emmitsburg Road to relieve the two companies of the 108th New York which were on the skirmish line.[189] At that time A. P. Hill's artillery from Seminary Ridge to Oak Hill opened fire upon the northern end of the Federal line. The ground rolled and thundered under the furious barrage.[190] It caught the 136th New York by surprise as it moved out from the Taneytown Road.

Sergeant Thomas Galwey (Company B, 8th Ohio) watched the New Yorkers go to ground under the protection of the road cut. The Ohioans

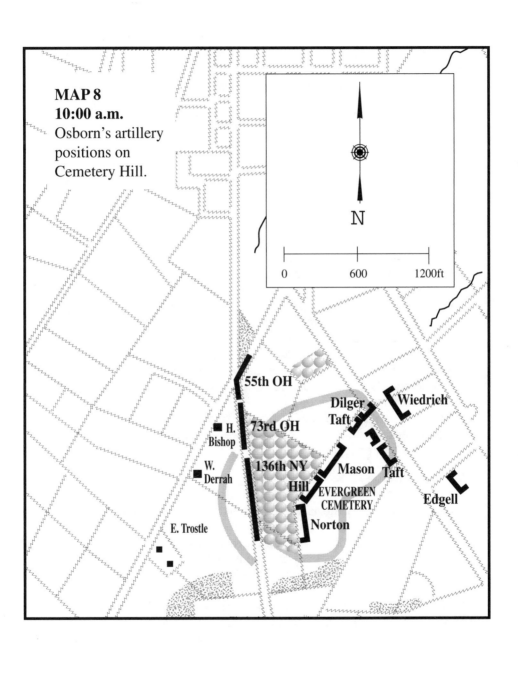

MAP 8
10:00 a.m.
Osborn's artillery
positions on
Cemetery Hill.

N

0   600   1200ft

55th OH

Wiedrich

Dilger
Taft

H.
Bishop

73rd OH

Mason   Taft

W.
Derrah

136th NY
Hill

EVERGREEN
CEMETERY

Edgell

E. Trostle

Norton

stood up, jeering at them and cursing them to face the fire like men. A handful of the more stout-hearted got up and stepped into the wheat. The rest of the New Yorkers reluctantly followed them out with their heads bowed and shoulders bent as if they were walking into a rain. Their officers lagged behind them.[191] Corporal Thaddeus S. Potter (Company H, 8th Ohio), glancing toward the road from the skirmish line, saw one of them take cover behind a tree near the road bank.[192] Several of his fellow officers hit the ground, afraid to go any farther. The irate Ohioans in the road showered them with curses and stones, forcing them to go out with their men.[193] Captain Wells W. Miller (Company H), hearing the ruckus, unsheathed his sword, and herded the fellow into the open amid the derisive laughter of his own men.[194]

The Taneytown Road

Back on the ridge, the rest of the 136th New York lay down between the stone walls along the Taneytown Road, trying to avoid the brutal sunlight. All morning long, sharpshooters in the houses on the southern end of town had peppered their position, making it impossible to put up shelter halves to shade themselves. Private George P. Metcalf (Company D) roasted in the intense heat and wondered when he would get fed next. The regiment had not eaten anything since July 1 when they slaughtered an ox which someone had driven into their bivouac.[195] The heat overpowered Corporal William Q. Huggins (Company F). Privates Milon O. Robinson and Marsena Stout picked up their unconscious corporal and carried him behind the lines. On the way back they plopped down under a tree to escape the heat when a case shot exploded over them. One of the balls ripped clear through Stout's chest. He was dead before the round exited his body and slapped into the ground behind him.[196]

Seminary Ridge

The unexpected artillery duel which suddenly flared up around the Bliss farm caught Colonel E. Porter Alexander in the Emmitsburg Road on the far right of his line. He had just finished getting the names of two Mississippi lieutenants who were trying to awaken their drunken surgeon when the battery near the Bliss barn opened fire into the farm yard. Furious that Hill's gunners were wasting much needed ammunition, and fearing that the contagion of combat would spread along his line, he immediately galloped to his battery officers within the immediate vicinity with orders not to shoot back. The command spread among his officers and the young colonel calmed down, mistakenly satisfied that none of his pieces had taken part in the skirmish.[197]

Cemetery Ridge—The Brian Farm

Meanwhile, Alexander Hays was growing restless. He sent a runner to Colonel Thomas Smyth with explicit instructions to "...have the men in the barn take that damned white house and hold it at all hazards." Smyth faced his staff who were standing nearby and said, "Gentlemen, you hear; who will take the order?" Captain J. Parke Postles, the brigade's acting assistant inspector general, was sitting on a rock close by. Sick with chronic diarrhea, with the reins of his horse looped over one arm, he buried his face in his hands in a vain attempt to rest. When it seemed like no one was going to volunteer, the feeble captain raised his head and said, "I will take it, sir." "Well, Postles," Smyth replied bluntly, "you need no instructions from me."

Mounting up, the captain walked his horse down the Brian farm lane, retracing the same trail which the raiders had used all morning. Once into the field west of the Emmitsburg Road, he spurred his horse into a gentle run. The Confederates sent rounds zipping about him and his horse. Postles, who expected to die at any moment, reassured himself that the Rebs could not hit a moving target. Reaching the barn, he dug his spurs into the horse and pulled back on the reins, making the animal dance on its hind legs. He hated injuring his horse. The poor creature was bleeding in the flanks from his spurs and from the mouth from the curb bit. He plunged and pitched, making both himself and Postles terrible targets. Major Ellis stepped out under the overhang and saluted. "Tell the officer in command here, to take that house with one company of sharpshooters, and hold it at all hazards," Postles screamed. The Connecticut officer saluted and the captain spurred away. Three hundred yards from the buildings, he reined his horse to a halt and pulling his cap from his head, he defiantly waved it at the Confederates, who responded with a vigorous Rebel Yell and stopped shooting at him.[198]

Major Theodore Ellis, 14th Connecticut

The intrepid Ellis fought his small regiment valiantly against the Confederates lodged in the Bliss farm buildings.

MOLLUS, USAMHI

In the mean time, Hays, who had been watching the action from the position of the 111th New York on the high ground in Brian's orchard, realized that as long as the buildings remained intact the Confederates would continue to harass his line. He turned to Colonel Clinton D. MacDougall (111th New York) and said that he needed a volunteer to carry an order to the Bliss barn. MacDougall turned to his regiment and repeated the request in a loud voice. Sergeant Charles A. Hitchcock (Company G), who was sitting nearby chewing on a hard cracker, looked around to see if anybody would step forward. MacDougall yelled again for volunteers. When no one responded, the sergeant stood up and told the general he would run the message.

Hays wanted him to instruct the officer in charge to fire the barn. The sergeant asked for some matches and cartridge paper, then took off across the open ground at a dead run. He reached the barn within seconds of Postles' departure, delivered the order with the paper and matches to Captain Moore, and left.[199] Moore and his men set the loose hay on fire while Ellis supervised the house's razing.[200] Private James A. Stroazzi and several others from Company A ignited a mattress in the house. Dragging their dead and wounded with them, and several of the farm's chickens, the New Englanders beat a hurried retreat to the Emmitsburg Road. By the time they reached it, the buildings were fully engulfed.[201] At the first sight of the flames lapping through the barn roof, the skirmishers from the 8th Ohio burst into a lusty cheer.[202]

The skirmishers from the 125th New York on the ridge north of the farm lane laid down a cover fire for the New Englanders. The fracas cost the 14th Connecticut two officers and fifteen enlisted men killed or wounded and three men missing—a heavy price for such a small regiment.[203] The survivors halted in a hollow east of the Emmitsburg Road. The wheezing Sergeant Hitchcock reported back to Hays with "General, I have executed your order." "I see you have, Sergeant," Hays replied, looking in the direction of the farm, "but the men are not assembled where I want them, go down there, Sergeant, and halt them at that place, and you had better stay there too." At that, Hitchcock trotted down to the Emmitsburg Road with orders to move the 14th Connecticut back to the Brian house.[204]

While the 14th Connecticut regrouped in the roadbed, the New Yorkers to the left of Company H, 8th Ohio kept shooting at the Confederates around the Bliss barn. Word was passed to Captain Wells W. Miller (Company H) to get them to cease fire. He, in turn, ordered Sergeant George M. Hitchcock to execute the order but the New Yorkers would not listen to him. Hitchcock pointed to the dead and wounded between the lines, hopelessly trying to impress upon them the need to stop drawing fire. To the sergeant's consternation, they would not listen to him. "Nein! Nein!" one of them yelled at him. "Sehet die Toten, und Verwundeten. Wir wollen schiessen!" [No! No! You saw the dead and those who were wounded. We want to shoot!"] Hitchcock returned to his captain, and the Germans continued to fire.[205]

As the noon hour approached, Lieutenant Colonel Franklin Sawyer (8th Ohio) replaced Company H with Company B. The men munched their rations, lay about, basting in the scorching heat of the summer sun, and wrote letters home. Some discussed the last two days of fighting—acting as if the battle were over.[206] Captain Winfield Scott (Company C, 126th New York) likened it to the peaceful quiet of a Sunday.[207] The eight companies of the 14th Connecticut marched up to the stone wall on the ridge north of Arnold's battery only to find the 1st Delaware in their former position. Major Ellis ordered the men to lie down behind Arnold's guns, about thirty-three yards to the east.[208]

Confederate Artillery Position—Seminary Ridge

The Confederate skirmishers, Captain Edward S. McCarthy's two Napoleons, and a section from Wyatt's artillery moved in closer to the Bliss farm to keep the Federals at bay. For another ten minutes a severe artillery duel raged between the farm and the batteries on Cemetery Ridge.[209] Cushing's battery across the fields from the Confederates further depleted its limited supply of shells.

Farther to the south, Captain James Rorty's Battery B, 1st New York Light Artillery, joined in the fray. While firing over the heads of Colonel Norman Hall's prone brigade, which was only fifteen feet away, a shell prematurely burst over the 20th Massachusetts. Men screamed as the searing metal shards struck them down. A fragment from the same projectile slapped into Second Lieutenant Henry Ropes (Company K) who was sitting against a tree, reading Dickens. "I am killed," he groaned as he fell over and died.[210] The field became terribly silent.

Cemetery Ridge—Gibbon's Headquarters

Brigadier General John Gibbon (II Corps commanding) and his staff officers walked their horses down to the peach orchard on the Taneytown Road, below the line of sight of the Confederate artillerymen. John, Gibbon's black servant, had their meal waiting for them. The aroma of freshly stewed "old and tough rooster," boiled potatoes, toast, bread, butter, tea, and coffee greeted them as they stepped up, according to rank, to get their portions. Gibbon invited Major General Winfield Scott Hancock (III Corps commanding) who just happened to be nearby to join in their repast. Lieutenant Frank A. Haskell, of Gibbon's staff, who had not eaten in about twenty-four hours, and whose only contribution to the officers' mess was a partially eaten cucumber pickle, eagerly joined the queue in front of the steaming pots.

The generals commandeered the officers' mess chest for their table and the only two camp stools in the headquarters. After they sat down, their subordinates lowered themselves onto the grass, balancing their plates upon their crossed legs.[211]

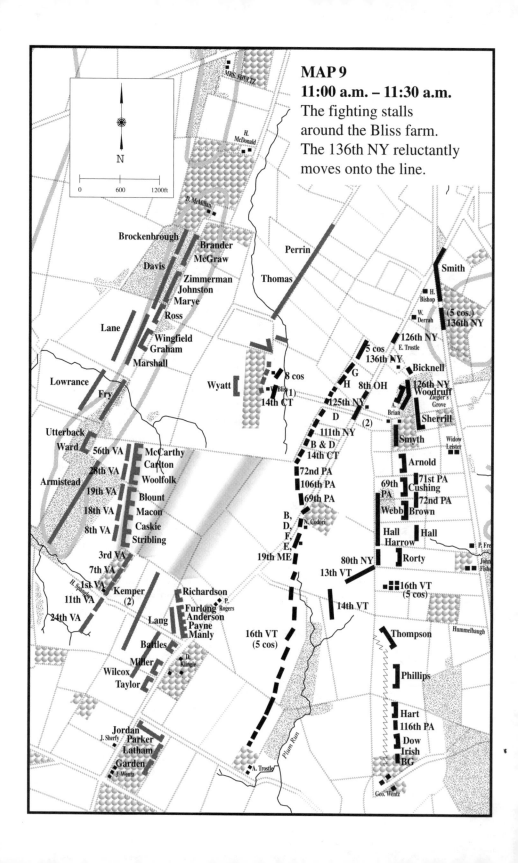

MAP 9
11:00 a.m. – 11:30 a.m.
The fighting stalls
around the Bliss farm.
The 136th NY reluctantly
moves onto the line.

MRS. SHULTZ

H. McDonald

N

0   600   1200ft

D. McMillan

Brockenbrough

Brander
McGraw

Perrin

Smith

Davis

Zimmerman
Johnston
Marye

Thomas

H. Bishop

W. Derrah

(5 cos.)
136th NY

Ross

Lane

Wingfield
Graham

126th NY

5 cos
136th NY

E. Trostle

Bicknell

Marshall

8 cos

Wyatt

Bliss (1)

G

Woodruff

126th NY

Ziegler's
Grove

Lowrance

Fry

14th CT

H

8th OH

A. Brian

Sherrill

Utterback

Ward

56th VA

McCarthy
Carlton

125th NY

D

(2)

Smyth

Widow
Leister

28th VA

Woolfolk

111th NY

Arnold

Armistead

19th VA

18th VA

Blount

Macon

B & D

14th CT

72nd PA

69th
PA

71st PA
Cushing

72nd PA

P. Fre

8th VA

Caskie

Stribling

106th PA

69th PA

Webb

Brown

John
Fishe

3rd VA

7th VA

B,
D,
F,
E,

N. Codori

Hall
Harrow

Hall

1st VA

H. S. plangh.

Kemper
(2)

19th ME

80th NY

Rorty

P. Fre

11th VA

24th VA

Richardson

13th VT

16th VT
(5 cos)

Furlong
Lang   Anderson
Payne
Manly

P.
Rogers

14th VT

Battles

16th VT
(5 cos)

Thompson

Hummelbaugh

Miller

Wilcox

Taylor

D.
Klingle

Phillips

Jordan
Parker

J. Sherfy

Latham

Garden

J. Wentz

Hart

116th PA

Dow
Irish
BG

A. Trostle

Plum Run

Geo. Wentz

While his aides gorged themselves, Gibbon walked a few hundred feet south along the road to the Leister House and invited Major General George Meade to share in their mess. Meade objected at first, saying he had to remain at Army Headquarters to review the reports which were constantly coming in. Gibbon showed him that his own headquarters were very close by and, after adding that it would only take a few minutes to eat and that he needed to keep up his strength, Meade consented.[212]

Frank Haskell's servant, George, scrounged up an empty hard cracker box for the commanding general while the lieutenant joined the other junior officers on the grass. Before too long, Major General John Newton, who had been given command of the I Corps over its rightful commander, Major General Abner Doubleday, and Major General Alfred Pleasonton, who commanded the Army of the Potomac's Cavalry Corps, with their aides meandered into the continually increasing luncheon circle. George "found" a couple of blankets for the corps commanders to sit on while their A.D.C.s plopped down among their peers. The entire affair reminded Haskell of "the scene of a smoking Turk."[213]

The observant aide probably never realized how accurately his comparison had described the internal politics behind the Army of the Potomac's command structure. On July 1, Hancock (who commanded the II Corps when the battle began), by Meade's direct order had assumed field command over his senior, the Radical Republican and abolitionist, Major General Oliver O. Howard of the XI Corps. On July 2, following the serious wounding of the III Corps' Major General Daniel Sickles, Hancock was given control of that corps over its abolitionist second in command, Major General David Birney. Brigadier General John Gibbon took over the II Corps. On July 2, Major General John Newton, commanding the Third Division, VI Corps, relieved Major General Abner Doubleday of the command of the I Corps. The fact that most of the officers of his choosing were Democrats and professional soldiers with whom he felt a genuine kinship no doubt influenced Meade's decisions. Following a heated repartee between Meade and the thoroughly miffed Birney during the evening conference on July 2, Gibbon told Meade that he felt awkward when referred to as a corps commander. Meade replied politely, "That is all right, I wanted you here." According to the loyal Gibbon, when Secretary of War Edwin Stanton reassured Meade that he had the complete backing of the War Department, "Meade took the responsibility of placing officers of his own choosing in places where he wanted them."[214]

Cushing's Battery

Shortly before noon Lieutenant Alonzo Cushing (A, 4th U.S.) ordered his men to stand down and get lunch. Cushing, Lieutenant Samuel Canby, and Lieutenant Joseph Milne, whom the men strongly disliked, retired to the rock outcroppings below the east side of the ridge to build coffee fires.

Private Christopher Smith (Battery A) watched them lay flat stones across their natural fire pit upon which to cook their rations. For a while it seemed like the battle had stopped.[215]

Near Spangler's Lane
Kemper's Brigade

While the Yankees slept or ate their way through the noon hour, the Confederates prepared to launch their offensive. The boiling heat drove Captain J. Risque Hutter (Company H, 11th Virginia) from his position behind the right wing of his regiment to the shade of a nearby apple tree. Being the only sizable shelter of any sort near the line it attracted a disproportionate number of officers. Chaplain John C. Granbery (11th Virginia) and Generals Longstreet and Pickett, with several staff officers, had plopped themselves down under its shade.

Presently, General Lee rode up to the group. Hutter only caught snatches of the conversation. He distinctly heard Longstreet protest, "...his command would do what any body of men on earth dared to do, but no troops could dislodge the enemy from their strong position." At that point Pickett interjected that he thought his men could drive the Yankees from the front. Hearing confirmation of what he wanted to believe, Lee told Longstreet, "Ask the men if they can dislodge them."

Turning to Hutter, Longstreet ordered him to take a couple of companies to the crest of the hill along the Emmitsburg Road to survey the position. Hutter with Captain Thomas Horton (Company B) solemnly followed their men to the top of the rise. They watched their men's reactions when they heard what was intended for them. With typical fatalism, the veterans turned to each other and shook hands as if they were embarking on distant journeys. Hutter heard one of them say, "Boys, many a one of us will bite the dust here to-day, but we will say to General Lee if he wants them driven out we will do it."[216]

Armistead's Brigade

By the time Colonel James G. Hodges (14th Virginia) approached Captain Richard Logan, Jr. (Company H) with the admonition that a "...cannonade is going to commence presently and a signal gun will begin it," Private Erasmus Williams had completed a respectable hole into which to throw himself. Flattening himself on his stomach, he snuggled against the freshly turned dirt despite Lieutenant Guerrant's jests. "I am going to stand right up here," the easygoing officer bragged, "and witness the whole proceeding."[217]

Northeast Corner of Spangler's Woods

Around noon Colonel Alexander, with one of Pickett's four division couriers, positioned himself in the northeast angle of Spangler's Woods to better observe the fire of his artillery. Brigadier General Ambrose R. Wright, one of A. P. Hill's brigade commanders joined him there as did Major John C. Haskell. It was Alexander's understanding that when the infantry was ready to advance, Longstreet would send the order to a section of the Washington Artillery (Eshleman's Battalion) to fire the two signal shots which placed the responsibility for the attack upon Longstreet. Shortly after noon, however, a courier delivered a very disturbing note to Alexander. The colonel read it with some trepidation.

> Colonel, If the Arty fire does not have the effect to drive off the enemy or greatly demoralize him so as to make our effort pretty certain, I wd prefer that you wd not advise Gen. Pickett to make the charge. I shall rely a great deal on your good judgment to determine the matter, & shall expect you to let Gen. Pickett know when the moment offers.

Alexander, who did not want that responsibility forced upon him, showed the note to the one-armed Haskell before he scribbled a defensive response to Longstreet. He would only be able to judge the effect of his artillery fire upon the Yankees' guns and not upon their infantry which were well hidden below the ridge. The smoke of the guns would further obscure his vision. Did the general have an alternative? If so, Alexander had to know because he had barely enough ammunition to carry off the present plan. If the assault failed he would not have enough ammunition left for a second assault. Regardless of the outcome of the attack, the human cost would be terrible.

A few minutes passed at which point Alexander received another message from Longstreet.

> Colonel. The intention is to advance the Infy, if the Arty. has the desired effect of driving the enemy's off, or having other effect such as to warrant us in making the attack. When that moment arrives advise Gen. P. & of course advance such Arty. as you can in aiding the attack.

After reading that communiqué, Wright turned to Alexander and said, "He has put the responsibility back upon you." "General," Alexander replied, "tell me exactly what *you* think of this attack." "Well, Alexander," Wright said matter-of-factly, "it is mostly a question of supports. It is not as hard to get there as it looks. I was there yesterday with my brigade. The real difficulty is to stay there after you get there—for the whole infernal Yankee army is up there in a bunch."

The colonel realized that the decision to attack had to be made before he opened fire with his guns. Once they cut loose, his visibility would be reduced to nothing. The timing for the attack was placed upon him, a mere colonel, and no one else. Resigned to his fate, he rode back into Spangler's Woods to consult with Pickett. Pickett, not realizing why the colonel was asking him about his morale, seemed buoyant and confident of success. Dejected, Alexander rode back to Carlton's section and wrote the following response to Longstreet:

General. When our fire is doing its best I shall give Pickett the signal to charge.

He sent his orderly, Catlett, to find Richardson's eight howitzers and bring them forward. He then began calculating how long his barrage would last. Twenty minutes, fifteen minutes, at the least, would be all that he would allow before sending Pickett's men across the open fields. Catlett returned with bad news. Richardson was not in the place where Alexander had left him. The colonel sent Catlett back with explicit orders to bring the guns forward.[218]

Lowrance's Brigade

His personal reconnaissance of the division completed, Captain Robert A. Bright returned to Spangler's Woods where he found Pickett conversing with an officer whom he did not know. Turning to Bright, the general said, "This is Colonel Gordon, who [was] once opposed to me in the San Juan affair, but now [is] on our side."

Ignoring the captain, Lieutenant Colonel George T. Gordon (34th North Carolina) continued his conversation with Pickett, "Pickett, my men are not going up to-day." "But, Gordon, they must go up; you must make them go up." Gordon, in his distinct English accent, pressed the issue. "You know, Pickett, I go as far with you as any other man, if only for old acquaintance sake, but my men have until lately been down at the seashore, only under the fire of heavy guns from ships, but for the last day or two they have lost heavily under infantry fire and are very sore, and they will not go up to-day."[219]

Near the Leister House
Gibbon's Headquarters

While the generals and their aides enjoyed their lunches, General Newton taunted Gibbon by referring to him as "this young North Carolinian" and by noting how his promotion to corps command had pushed him beyond his position. Gibbon reminded Newton that, in the light of his own recent field promotion, he did not have the credentials to make such comments.

Meade switched the topic. He expected the Rebels to attack his left wing again that evening but Hancock felt it would be directed toward the II Corps on the center of the line. When and if the Confederates did strike the center, Meade interjected, Hancock would assume control of the II Corps and Gibbon would revert to division command.[220] The commanding general turned to Gibbon. "General Gibbon," he said, "see that all your provost guards are sent to the front after the artillery ceases firing." Without waiting, Gibbon called over First Lieutenant William Harmon (Company C, 1st Minnesota), who was in charge of the provost guard. "Do you hear that, Harmon?" the general asked. "Yes." "Well, see that your company is there."[221] With that detail out of the way, Meade, Newton, and Pleasonton rode off toward their respective commands. Gibbon's officers dozed off to nap on the grass. Their horses, which were tied to nearby trees, munched oats from their nose bags. Gibbon and Hancock stood nearby.[222] The relative quiet which settled over the battlefield conveyed a false sense of security. It was too hot to fight.

Brian Farm along the Emmitsburg Road

Meanwhile Captain Sebastian D. Holmes and his skirmishers from the 111th New York were assembling behind the Brian tenant house when Major Hugo Hildebrand and his extremely small regiment, the 39th New York, approached the men from Ziegler's Grove. The major curtly ordered the captain to move away from the house because he wanted to post his men there. Holmes bluntly refused to comply until all of his men had come in from the picket line. The irate Hildebrand went for his side arm but the much quicker Holmes "got the drop" on him. The major wheeled his horse about and galloped to the eastern slope of Cemetery Ridge. Finding the 111th New York behind the orchard, the major reported the incident to Colonel Clinton MacDougall. When the captain brought in his detail, he was ordered to see MacDougall. After he explained what had happened, the colonel asked him why he did not shoot the irritating foreigner. Holmes said he would have had Hildebrand unholstered his pistol.[223]

Stannard's Brigade

Corporal Wesley C. Sturtevant (Company E, 14th Vermont) hunted up his cousin, Ralph O. Sturtevant of the 13th Vermont. With the firm belief that he would never see his home again, he asked his cousin to tell his family good-bye for him. He asked to be buried in his home town of Weybridge. He had just awakened from a death premonition and had resolved himself to his fate after having entrusted his soul to God. Turning his letters over to Ralph, he told him to give them to his mother and father. Ralph, who did not believe in dreams, tried to ease Wesley's concerns but failed. "Good-by," Wesley said with an eerie certainty as he returned to the 14th Vermont.[224]

Lee's plan to break the Union center and to exploit Meade's flanks between Little Round Top and Cemetery Hill, based upon the tactical deployment of his guns and infantry, initially appeared logical and achievable. His lines overextended the observable Federal positions on Cemetery Ridge. His guns from Benner's Hill to Oak Hill to Seminary Ridge had the Federals bracketed between convergent fire. Ewell's attack temporarily kept the Federals preoccupied at Culp's Hill. From his position on Seminary Ridge, Lee could readily assume he had fire superiority over the Federal guns north and south of the copse of trees. No one, however, on the general's staff or from Longstreet's Corps had, at this point in time, informed Wilcox or Lang of their anticipated roles in the forthcoming charge.

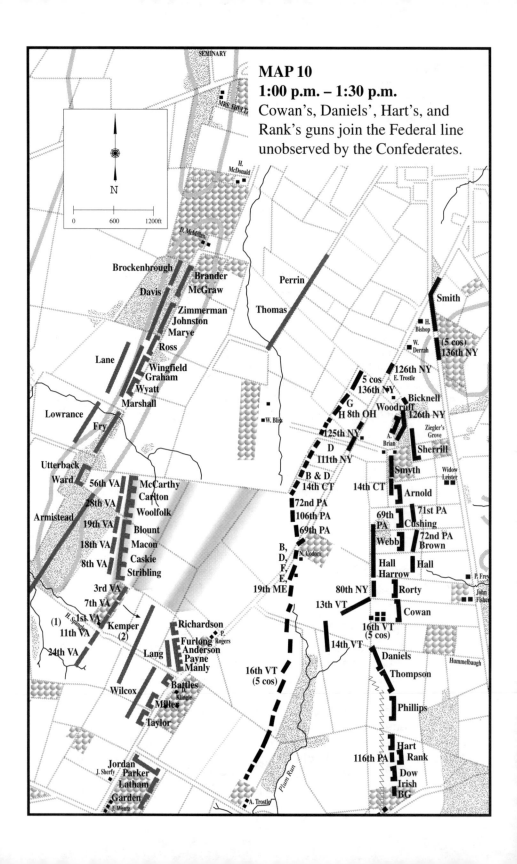

MAP 10
1:00 p.m. – 1:30 p.m.
Cowan's, Daniels', Hart's, and
Rank's guns join the Federal line
unobserved by the Confederates.

SEMINARY

MRS. SHULTZ

H. McDonald

N

0   600   1200ft

D. McMillan

Brockenbrough
Brander
Davis   McGraw
Zimmerman
Johnston
Marye
Ross
Lane
Wingfield
Graham
Wyatt
Marshall
Lowrance
Fry

Perrin

Thomas

Smith

H. Bishop
W. Derrah

(5 cos)
136th NY

5 cos
136th NY

E. Trostle

126th NY

G
H 8th OH

Woodruff
Bicknell
126th NY

Ziegler's
Grove

W. Bliss

125th NY

D
111th NY

A. Brian

Sherrill

Smyth

Widow
Leister

Utterback
Ward   56th VA
28th VA
19th VA
18th VA
8th VA

McCarthy
Carlton
Woolfolk
Blount
Macon
Caskie
Stribling

B & D
14th CT

72nd PA
106th PA
69th PA

14th CT

Arnold

69th
PA

71st PA
Cushing
72nd PA
Brown

Armistead

B,
D,
F,
E,

N. Codori

Webb
Hall
Harrow

Hall

P. Frey

Rorty

John
Fisher

3rd VA
7th VA
1st VA
11th VA
24th VA

(1) H. Spangler
(2)
Kemper

Richardson
P.
Furlong Rogers
Anderson
Payne
Manly

19th ME

80th NY
13th VT

Cowan

16th VT
(5 cos)

14th VT

Daniels

Hummelbaugh

Lang

Wilcox

Battles
D.
Klingle
Miller
Taylor

16th VT
(5 cos)

Thompson

Phillips

Jordan
J. Sherfy   Parker
Latham
Garden
J. Wentz

Hart
Rank

116th PA

Dow
Irish
BG

A. Trostle

Plum Run

2

1:00 p.m. through 2:00 p.m.

Seminary Ridge

Colonel Alexander placed himself behind a tree near the northeast corner of Spangler's Woods, from which he had a clear view of the Federal line at the Angle. Realizing that his guns had enough ammunition for about one hour of sustained long-range fire and the fact that he had to conserve ammunition to back up the charge, he decided to shell the Federals for no more than twenty minutes rather than risk exhausting his supply during the height of the attack.[1]

Very shortly before 1:00 p.m. a courier rode up to Colonel James B. Walton, who was with Miller's Washington Artillery near the Peach Orchard, and delivered the following message:

> Colonel:—Let the batteries open; order great care and precision in firing. If the batteries at the peach-orchard cannot be used against the point we intend attacking, let them open on the rocky hill.
>
> Most respectfully,
> J. Longstreet
> Lieut.Gen. Commanding.
> To Col. Walton, *Chief of Artillery*

Walton relayed the order to the battalion commander, Major Benjamin F. Eshleman, who passed the command to the right section (Third Company, Washington Artillery) under Lieutenant C. H. C. Brown.[2]

Oak Hill

Before Brown could relay the order to his section chief, Sergeant W. T. Hardie, the Alabamians commanding the Whitworth section on Oak Hill, a few miles to the north, opened fire with one gun. The puff of smoke, seen distinctly from Cemetery Hill, caught Major Osborn's attention. He automatically marked the time. It was 1:00 p.m. by his watch. In less than a minute the round traversed the two and one-fourth miles and shrilly whistled within a few feet above the major's head.³ "At ten minutes to one precisely, by my watch," Sergeant Thomas Galwey (Company B, 8th Ohio) wrote, "after a lull in the cannonade, a heavy gun was heard from the enemy's line."⁴ Lieutenant Frank A. Haskell (Gibbon's staff), who was contemplating taking a nap, glanced at his watch while shaking off a yawn. "It was five minutes before one o'clock," he remembered. Returning his watch to his pocket, he stretched out on the ground to doze off when the distinct "sharp sound" of a lone gun snapped him awake.⁵ Lieutenant William R. Driver, acting assistant adjutant general for Harrow's brigade, swore the first shot came from a gun near the Lutheran Seminary.⁶ Glancing at his watch, Colonel Adin B. Underwood (33rd Massachusetts), whose regiment was in line on the eastern base of Stevens' Knoll, recorded the time at 12:50 p.m.⁷ Both he and Captain Winfield Scott (Company C, 126th New York) watched a Whitworth shell from Oak Hill whistle over their heads toward Little Round Top.⁸ At the Angle, farther to the south, Private Anthony McDermott (Company I, 69th Pennsylvania) heard the same round scream above him.⁹

Emmitsburg Road
Brown's Section
Third Company, Washington Artillery

The Number Four man on Sergeant P. O. Fazende's gun pulled the lanyard. Nothing happened. The friction primer failed. The Number Three man hastily replaced it. Number Four attached the lanyard. The crew cleared the piece. The lanyard was pulled. The primer ignited and the gun fired.¹⁰ On Alexander's watch it was exactly 1:00 p.m.¹¹ To the right, Sergeant W. T. Hardie's Napoleon roared sending a shell hurtling toward the Federal lines.¹²

At the report of Fazende's gun soldiers instinctively glanced at their watches and noted the time. Captain Richard S. Thompson (12th New Jersey) said that the first round came in from the south. Striking the ground behind Hays' division, it lay on the surface unexploded.¹³ From the highest point on Little Round Top, Brigadier General Henry Hunt (Chief of Artillery, Army of the Potomac) turned his attention toward the Peach Orchard. He had just finished personally directing all of his battery commanders to withhold their fire for fifteen to twenty minutes into the expected cannonade when that solitary blast reverberated across the low ground to the northwest. He immediately wheeled his horse about and disappeared down the slope, heading north toward army headquarters.¹⁴

The prone soldiers of the 19th Massachusetts, who were on the eastern side of the ridge in Colonel Norman J. Hall's second line, jerked their faces toward the noise. A solid shot skipped over the crest from the southwest like a gigantic rubber ball. Passing by the officers who were enjoying a lunch on a spread blanket behind the regiment's rifle stacks, it instantly brought them to their feet. Seconds later another round hissed in, striking Lieutenant Sherman Robinson (Company A) as he wiped food from his mouth with his handkerchief. It hit him just below the left shoulder. Ripping his body to pieces, it left him in a gory puddle on the ground. A third ball quickly followed, scattering gun stacks behind the regiment.[15]

Shortly thereafter 144 Confederate field pieces from the Peach Orchard to Seminary Ridge to Oak Hill to Benner's Hill opened fire in succession as the reports of the guns to the south rolled into their batteries. The air over the Federal lines exploded with a fury which the men had never before experienced.[16] The suddenness of the cannonade took many of the Federals unaware.

Sherrill's Brigade

The Whitworths on Oak Hill screamed in on top of the 111th New York which had sheltered itself along the stone wall on the northern side of the open field east of the Brian orchard. Captain Benjamin W. Thompson (Company F), having spent the noon hour grousing to Colonel Clinton MacDougall about the shameful lack of rations, in a moment of unabashed terror, dove to cover along the base of the wall. The colonel shouted at his quaking line officer, "Captain, it won't do for us to lay here. We must get our place in line." Scrambling along the regiment as fast as they could, they shoved their men into some semblance of a line. But it unraveled faster than they could organize it as the soldiers clawed their way up the hill in squads to escape the plunging fire.[17]

While the New Yorkers hugged the ground, Hays sent Second Lieutenant David S. Shields (Company F, 63rd Pennsylvania) down the slope to Meade's Headquarters with a message. The captain, in delivering it, passed by a dismounted officer who was sitting against the stone wall on his right with his horse's reins in his hand. From the looks of his uniform, he appeared to be an infantry field officer. Upon his return, despite the terrible rain of shells, Shields ferreted out the officer. He found him in the same spot, still cowering against the wall. It angered him to no end to learn that he was Lieutenant Colonel Levi Crandall of the 125th New York. As the division A.D.C. Shields had to do something. He asked Crandall what he was doing there. Sick, came the reply. The boyish captain ordered the colonel to return to his regiment, adding that it was safer on the far side of the ridge than where he was. Crandall would not budge. He insisted he was too ill to go into combat. The disgusted A.D.C. left the frightened colonel alongside the wall and hurried toward Brian's orchard on the top of the hill.[18] Rather than have his men slaughtered before the infantry assault which would follow, Hays ordered Shields to send the 111th New York forward over the crest to the stone wall on the gentle western slope of the ridge.[19]

In passing through the orchard on the ridge, Thompson saw a direct hit on a coffee fire pulverize the three men who had gathered around it. At the same time, General Hays spied a handful of men bolt for the backside of the Brian house. He sent the captain after them then hurried south to speed the 125th New York and the 39th New York regiments into line.[20]

Smyth's Brigade

Amid the cries of "Down! Down!", the infantrymen frantically scurried to their places in the ranks and hit the dirt. The sky above them was filled with projectiles. Captain Richard Thompson (12th New Jersey) said there was "an avalanche of bursting shells." The regiment furled its colors to keep them from getting shredded. The smoke from the exploding projectiles, coupled with the heat nearly suffocated the prone infantry. Their lungs screamed for oxygen. The sulfuric taste of burned powder soured their mouths. Their eyes watered. It was the worst bombardment they had ever experienced.[21] The men hugged the ground while the left flank of the 111th New York bellied down on the sloping rocks behind the regiment's right wing.[22]

Part of Company F (12th New Jersey) took cover behind the hog pen adjacent to the Brian barn, believing that the muck would absorb incoming shot and minimize ricochets. Private William P. Haines, having never been so scared in his life, could not lie still. He rolled onto his back to watch the effects of the Confederate fire. The Brian barn and tenant house took several direct hits. [23]

A cannon ball snapped an entire board off the back wall of the barn as Captain Benjamin W. Thompson (Company F) herded his men from the 111th New York south toward the stone wall west of the house. Whirling through the air, the clapboard slapped the captain square across the face. The blow snapped his head back. His feet shot out from under him. Amid his men's laughter, he landed flat upon his back. Painfully regaining his feet, he staggered toward the regimental line, his head throbbing and ringing.[24] That same round, simultaneously, struck Gustavus Ritter, the cross-eyed corporal of Company D in the legs. The impact ripped both of them away below the knees. First Lieutenant Samuel B. Intyre (Company A) saw Ritter's comrades drag him on his back toward the northeast corner of the barn. They left him lying there with his hands hooked together under his bleeding stumps and there he bled to death—his arms still elevating his mangled legs.[25]

Benjamin Thompson threw himself down along the stone wall, wedging himself half between, half on top of two enlisted men. He ducked his throbbing head behind a boulder which jutted like an inverted keystone between the stones which were lodged against it. A deeply religious man, who detested any type of vulgarity or profanity, he could only describe his surroundings as a literal Hell.[26]

Solid shots brought down tree branches on the ridge behind the regiment. Others hammered into the opposite side of the stone wall, shaking its foundation. The earth pitched and trembled as one of Arnold's caissons, to the left rear, went up in a column of billowing flame and smoke.[27] Wounded men, rather than risk crossing the exposed higher ground where a good many of the shells were striking, stayed in the ranks and risked bleeding to death.[28] The 14th Connecticut, without orders, rushed into line at the feet of the 1st Delaware and hit the dirt.[29] Throughout it all, Hays refused to dismount. Trooping from one end of the stone wall to the other, he urged the men to scrounge around for discarded muskets. Within short order, Lieutenant David Shields' (A.D.C. to Hays) noted, most of the men had two to four muskets apiece besides their own weapons.[30]

Gibbon's Headquarters

In an instant every dozing officer rolled onto their hands and knees with a start, their eyes straining toward the batteries along the crest of Cemetery Ridge. A sulfuric cloud climbed into the humid sky, followed simultaneously with a head-jarring concussion. Before anyone could get to their feet the air was filled with more explosions. Shell fragments slapped into the ground around them.

Gibbon's two servants immediately deserted him. The officers' mounts neighed in terror and many of them broke free from their masters' hands or from the trees to which they had been casually tied. Gibbon started toward the top of the hill at a run, his sword in hand. He kept his eyes skyward, watching for the shot which he believed would kill him. The sky rained projectiles. The 12-pounders' solid shot arched gracefully overhead in high trajectories before thudding to the ground in the vicinity of the Taneytown Road. The rifled shells screamed through the air creating noticeable trails of hot air in their wakes. Some of the spent rounds tumbled end over end like misshapen minie balls. Those which burrowed into the ground without bursting showered the men nearby with dirt and shattered rocks. The shells which exploded, Gibbon clearly recalled, hurled "fragments about in a most disagreeably promiscuous manner."[31]

Lieutenant Frank Haskell, Gibbon's aide, called for his horse but when no one responded, he ran over to the tree where an orderly had tied him. The animal was still munching his oats, oblivious to the hell which reigned around him. Haskell slipped the bridle over the horse's head and was adjusting it when he saw a shell go off in front of the headquarters' mess wagon. One of the horses dropped in a bloody heap and dragged its mate down to the ground against a tree. In a panic, the driver let go of the reins and was thrown into a tangled pile along with the wagon. Simultaneously, an explosive round butchered two pack mules, spraying them and the contents of their ammunition crates all around.[32]

Within seconds Lieutenant Colonel Charles H. Morgan (Inspector General and Chief of Staff, II Corps) counted sixteen dead or dying horses among the generals' staffs and escorts. A panicked officer, upon seeing his mount severely disabled by a shell fragment, clattered into the Leister house to get his pistol. Firing wildly as he dashed outside, he immediately put two rounds into Captain James S. Hall's perfectly sound horse. Hall, the II Corps Signal Officer, disarmed the man before he could drop any more innocent bystanders.[33]

In all of the confusion, Hancock's Judge Advocate, Captain Henry H. Bingham, not only lost track of the general but he also discovered that someone else had taken his mount. He spent several minutes trying to procure another from one of the general's startled orderlies. He lost no time in racing north along the Taneytown Road toward the corps' right flank.[34] Captain George Meade, the commanding general's son and aide, whose horse died during the opening shots of the cannonade, could not find his orderly, who had run off with his spare mount.[35]

Gibbon's personal orderly, Private John Shehan (Battery B, 4th U.S. Artillery), swung into the saddle at the same time that Haskell leaped onto the back of his mount. Snatching the reins to the general's horse, he had barely put the spurs to his mount when a hot fragment tore open his chest. Dead—he released his grip on Gibbon's horse and toppled to the ground, leaving both animals to gallop away in a panic.

Upon seeing this, Haskell spurred toward Gibbon, intercepting him halfway between his headquarters and the crest of the ridge. By then another orderly, having snagged the general's mount, delivered it to him. Gibbon rode with Haskell toward the rock outcropping in the sharp hollow behind Cushing's battery and dismounted. The general intended to inspect the disposition of his division from there.[36] He did not like what he saw as he peered over the top of the hill. Most of the few infantrymen in the immediate area were lying down below the crest of the ridge or behind the stone wall near Arnold's battery. Satisfied that they were doing the best they could under the circumstances, he hunkered down with Haskell to wait it out.[37]

McGilvery's Batteries

Winfield Scott Hancock, unable to restrain himself, decided the Union artillery was not responding quickly enough to the Confederate guns. With his orderly, Corporal Uriah Parmelee (Company I, 6th New York Cavalry) right behind him, he spurred along the II Corps line. Finding Captain John Hazard, who commanded the corps artillery, he commanded him to open fire immediately upon the Confederates. Hazard respectfully told the general that he had been ordered to wait fifteen to twenty minutes before replying to the Rebels. He begged to let Hunt's directive stand. The impetuous general refused. All of Hazard's batteries were to commence firing at once. Nevertheless, Hazard waited until the prearranged time had lapsed before complying with Hancock's directive.

**Major General
Winfield Scott Hancock**

The commander of the II Corps, he suffered a particularly nasty groin wound just as Wilcox's and Lang's brigades struck the 14th Vermont during the last phase of Longstreet's charge.

Miller, *Photographic History*

Hancock raced toward McGilvery's three batteries, which also had not commenced firing. Riding into Hart's Battery, he emphatically told the captain to reply to the incoming fire. The determined Irishman refused to comply. Colonel Freeman McGilvery, who was standing there with Colonel Patrick Kelly (commanding the Irish Brigade) and Brigadier General Joshua "Paddy" Owens, immediately intervened. He calmly informed the general that he had been instructed to wait and that the time to fire had not arrived yet. Where did he get those directives? Hancock demanded. From the Chief of Artillery, the colonel replied. The Chief of Artillery, Hancock shot back, did not have any concept of the intensity of the bombardment when he issued that command. McGilvery countered by saying that Hunt had accurately anticipated such an artillery barrage and that his orders were specifically designed to meet the present circumstances.

"My troops cannot stand this cannonade," Hancock shouted back, "and will not stand if it is not replied to." He commanded McGilvery to deliver fire at once, but the colonel adamantly refused to do so pursuant to Hunt's instructions.[38] Hancock, whose estimation of his own military judgment verged on infallibility, rode north into Captain Charles P. Phillips' battery. He furiously threatened the captain with force unless he obeyed. Phillips, frustrated by the dense smoke which obscured his vision, hated hurling rounds at the Rebels but did so nonetheless until McGilvery ordered him to stop.[39]

Granite School House Road—Taneytown Road

Captain Andrew Cowan (1st New York Independent Battery, VI Corps) having just returned from a private reconnaissance which took him almost to the copse of trees, decided he needed a brief rest in the grove east of the intersection. Turning his horse over to Bugler Lewis C. Talman, he flopped down on his overcoat to take a nap rest, when the Confederates opened fire. The first round sailed overhead, followed immediately by a deluge of others. Bursting in the tree tops, well above his artillerymen, they showered leaves and branches down upon them. A considerable number of the New Yorkers scattered before Cowan realized what had happened.

Leaping to his feet, he threw his overcoat on top of the closest caisson and yelled for Talman to bring up his horse. The moment Cowan reached for the reins, a shell splinter killed the bugler's mount. "Stand to horse!" the captain commanded. "Cannoneers, to your posts!" His veterans turned about and assembled around their pieces. At the command, the battery wheeled to the west into column in the Granite School House Road, with the lead team at the intersection with the Taneytown Road.[40]

Cemetery Hill

The Confederates had such a precise range on the hill that their shots literally missed the mounted officers by inches. Osborn immediately ordered his junior officers to dismount. Fragments from blasted limbers and caissons pelted the gunners and the horses behind them. Personal pride alone kept Osborn on horseback. He led by example. Captain Craig Wadsworth, son of Brigadier General James Wadsworth (I Corps) and an aide de camp to Meade, rode up to Osborn, bringing some instructions from army headquarters. With his mount alongside Osborn so that they could face each other, the young officer began delivering his instructions when a 10-pounder percussion shell shattered directly beneath them. Neither horse nor officer flinched. Osborn, however, never forgave himself for inadvertently pulling his stare away from Wadsworth to see where the projectile landed.

The major did not tolerate cowardice, real or inferred on the part of anyone, in particular himself. Battery H, 1st Ohio had not taken a serious beating of any sort to mention. A Rebel sharpshooter sent Sergeant Ritchie, a member of Lieutenant William A. Ewing's left section, to the ground with a bullet in the abdomen, and a shell fragment badly bruised Private John E. Wilcox (Norton's section) on the foot.[41] It angered Osborn to no end when, several minutes into the artillery barrage, an orderly informed him that Norton's Ohioans were pitching their ammunition into the clump of trees behind them. The major galloped to the battery and furiously swore at Norton for attempting to quit the field. Turning his back upon the frightened artillerists, he rode back toward the center of his line.[42] Norton paid no mind to the major. He merely hunted up Captain James F. Huntington, his brigade commander, and reported that he would have to leave because he had expended his ammunition.[43]

Huntington headed toward the Artillery Reserve south of the cemetery to get a replacement battery. As he swung onto the saddle a shell landed in the ground to his right front and went off. Clods of dirt pelted his side and leg as he felt for the stirrup with his right foot. It took but a second for him to realize that one fragment had cut the stirrup away from his saddle and another had broken the leg of his orderly's horse.[44]

As Osborn approached Mason's Regular battery a shell ripped the arm away from an enlisted man at the shoulder. The fellow, who had served as Osborn's orderly for a short while, screamed a word of recognition as he fell to the ground. The major, being the professional he was, would not allow himself to show any grief as the fellow bled to death in front of him. "Look, Major, see the cowards," one of the nearby artillerymen shouted. Osborn fumed at the sight of Norton's battery, its men mounted on the ammunition chests, careening down the Baltimore Pike for the alleged safety of the hollow.[45]

Alexander at Spangler's Woods

Ten to fifteen minutes into the bombardment, which Alexander compared to a terrific volcanic eruption, the Federal II Corps gunners returned fire. He thought it madness to order any infantry across the open fields between the two armies. Nevertheless, he decided to extend his barrage beyond the original fifteen minutes, fearing that he would not be able to silence the Federals sufficiently enough to order the charge.[46] At the same time, his courier, Catlett, returned with the disturbing news that the eight howitzers which Alexander had placed in reserve were not to be found. He had looked everywhere but they were gone.[47]

Southern Cemetery Ridge near the Taneytown Road

Racing his horse northeast from Little Round Top, Hunt headed for the southern side of the Granite School House Road, intending to send his Reserve Artillery and the ammunition trains to the front. To his dismay, he found couriers standing where he had last seen the guns. He left word behind to hurry the batteries forward when the cannonading ceased, then spurred west into the Taneytown Road, where the remains of several destroyed caissons provided him with the explanation behind the Artillery Reserve's and the supply train's rapid retreat to the east.[48] He rode west into the I Corps headquarters in the woods north of George Weikert's house.

Lieutenant Colonel Edward R. Warner (1st New York Artillery), following in the general's wake, stopped long enough in the crossroads to order Cowan's battery to the southern end of the II Corps' line. While rushing forward toward Newton's headquarters, the captain detached his caissons to remain in the pasture along the eastern side of the woods. With Warner in the lead, the battery cleared the far side of the wood lot, then turned north under his direction. As they trotted forward under a very dangerous fire, one of Cowan's men, with a grin, jokingly suggested, "Captain, if you have no objection, I'll lose a day." Private Otis C. Billings, however, whom Cowan knew to be very courageous, did not jest. His face drained of its color, he matter-of-factly said, "Captain, I am very sick today; please, let me go back to the caissons." Cowan, his nerves taut from the fearful shelling, shot back, "No, Billings, this is no time to be sick." His six rifles rumbled into battery to Rorty's left, firing, in succession, as they unlimbered to the left oblique.[49]

A little over 100 yards to the south Captain Jabez Daniels (9th Michigan Battery) wheeled his six 3-inch rifles into position on the right of McGilvery's line. At the same time a section of ordnance rifles from Battery H, 3rd Section, Pennsylvania Heavy Artillery, under Captain William Rank, pulled into the works on Hart's left.[50]

Stannard's Brigade

Lieutenant George G. Benedict (A.D.C. to Stannard) tuned his ears to the particular sounds of the various projectiles. The standard rifled shells whizzed and burst with popping noises. The hexagonal Whitworth bolts rang like metal striking against metal. Case shot rattled against the rails and pelted the men's backs. Cannon balls bounded along like gigantic marbles, gouging chunks of earth out of the fields on both sides of the brigade line.[51] He took out his watch. In sixty seconds he counted six black spots rippling through the air above his head.[52] Stannard's untried soldiers hugged the ground, their heads toward the Confederates, their faces in the dirt. Every now and then a round hit a man, but the pressure was too great to evacuate any of the casualties. A great many of the shells dropped among the 14th Vermont, claiming, in all, about sixty casualties who had to lie in their own gore. Stannard and his officers stayed on their feet, continually walking the regimental lines, waiting for the barrage to cease.[53]

On his right, the veterans of the 151st Pennsylvania and the 80th New York spread themselves flat behind the pile of rails which served as their only breastworks. Solid shot repeatedly knocked the rails about, usually injuring someone in the process. Shell splinters also found their marks with uncomfortable frequency. Captain John D. S. Cook (Company I, 80th New York) squirmed about, taking in everything around him. It occurred to him that if he even entertained the thought of deserting, he would not survive the gauntlet of incoming rounds long enough to get over the ridge behind him. There was no safe place to hide. A round ball "swished" over him. He watched it strike the ground not too far to his left rear and ricochet over the head of the soldier who was lying there. The air current hurled the man's forage cap twenty feet into the air and bounced him nearly end over end with a peculiar "flopping" sound. His comrades guffawed at him for overreacting to the close call. When he did not respond to them, Cook and a couple of the enlisted men crawled to his side to revive him. He was dead—no marks at all upon his body—but dead nonetheless. The captain had never seen anything like it in his life.[54] General Hunt, who witnessed everything from behind the ridge, believed that a rifled bolt killed the fellow.[55]

A very short distance to the north, the battered 1st Minnesota took the shelling in stride. The tremendous racket, the men later recalled, far surpassed the noise made by the artillery at either Antietam or at Fredericksburg.[56] The Confederates, by concentrating their fire upon the Federal artillery behind the prone infantry, tended to overshoot Harrow's brigade. The shells seemed to destroy caissons every few minutes. The blasts, while covering most of the Minnesotans with dirt, injured relatively few men. Despite the intensity of the assault and the horrendous noise, some of the exhausted westerners slept through it all.[57]

Lieutenant George G. Benedict (A.D.C. to Stannard) believed the Confederates fired twice as fast as their own gunners. A solid shot smashed into a caisson belonging to a battery to the left of Stannard's brigade, exploding one of the ammunition chests. Smoke rolled into the air while the six-horse team panicked and clattered to the rear, dragging what was left of the caisson with them.[58]

Meade's Headquarters

The firing having grown too intense, Meade moved his headquarters into the barn across the road. When word arrived that Slocum had a signal man at his headquarters along the Baltimore Pike, the general decided to move to that location.[59] As his father headed northeast from the barn toward Stevens Knoll, young Meade and Lieutenant Charles W. Woolsey (General Seth Williams' A.D.C.) took off after him on foot.[60]

Northeast Corner of the Angle

Arnold's battery, to the left rear of the 14th Connecticut, blasted away over the heads of its own infantry. Sergeant Major William B. Hincks lay three paces behind the regiment's left wing, his right arm draped protectively over Sergeant Eddy Hart (Company G). Each discharge of the gun behind him blanketed him in a white, sulfuric tasting cloud and stung him with gravel picked up by the muzzle blast. The smoke blocked out every ray of sunlight. The suffocating midday heat, coupled with the fiery reports of the guns, bathed him in his own sweat. He studied the huge drops of sweat fall from his face into the dust beneath and create a salty mud puddle under him.

Through it all Hincks distinctly heard the gunnery sergeant, then his replacement, hoarsely belt out the commands to aim, load, and fire the gun nearest to him as if on a holiday drill. The battery was so shot up that drivers replaced the artillerymen at the pieces.[61] Second Lieutenant John B. Geddis (126th New York) and several volunteers from his Company D stepped forward to also assist at one of the guns.[62] Once or twice, Hincks glanced behind him only to see confused clusters of men shifting about in the smoke to evade the shells. At one point, a shot plucked a rail from the rider on top of the stone wall and sent it sailing through the air like a jack straw.[63]

Sherrill's Brigade

While the infantrymen cringed in the dirt, the artillerymen went about their business with monotonous regularity. Captain Winfield Scott (Company C, 126th New York), whose regiment was on the eastern side of the knoll to the right of Lieutenant Woodruff's Battery I, 1st U.S. Artillery, admired their pluck and their no nonsense discipline. "Number one, fire! Number two, fire!" he heard the section chiefs repeatedly holler. The artillerymen, defiant of the rain of shot, fragments, and case shot which filled the air and slammed into the ground around them, continued to work their pieces. The captain noticed how the Number Five and the Number Six men at the limber chests continually ran their ammunition forward. It seemed as if the artillery crews were being cut down by the score. Every time a limber chest or a caisson went up men and horses were smashed into pieces too small to count. Scott saw men vaporized by direct hits.[64]

Scott's chief desire at that moment was to be about five feet under the ground. The New Yorker flattened himself out, trying to mold himself into the earth. As the barrage continued, it became evident that the regiment was in a relatively safe place. Most of the shells, as elsewhere along the line, fell behind the ridge among the headquarters orderlies and the field hospitals or right along the crest among the guns.[65]

The 108th New York, behind and among Woodruff's guns, took a terrible drubbing. Large branches thudded down upon their heads. At the shriek of an incoming round passing close by, Corporal Chauncey L. Harris (Company F) snapped his head up in time to see it shatter a caisson and wound several men. At the same time a pile of shells with attached powder bags, which the artillerymen had stacked too close to the guns and the New Yorkers, went up in an horrendous explosion. A great many of the infantrymen leaped to their feet to run, but Second Lieutenant Dayton T. Card (Company H), with his drawn sword, and Hays' mounted A.D.C., Lieutenant David Shields, herded them back into the ranks. They reluctantly complied.[66]

Second Lieutenant Theron Parsons (Company D) gaped in horror as a fragment ripped Card's chest apart and carried away part of his face. Before he had time to react, a round slew First Lieutenant Carle V. Amiet (Company I). Corporal William Fairchild (Company D) died very shortly thereafter in the same spot and Second Lieutenant John L. Graham (Company K) fell, seriously wounded.[67]

Corporal Harris swore that the regiment had never before lain under such a destructive barrage. A substantial oak tree, measuring three feet in diameter, which stood about five feet from him, took five direct hits from solid shots, one of which bored clear through the trunk. A shell also burst above his feet, killing Sergeant Maurice Welch and Private John Fitzner (both from Company F).[68]

Smith's Brigade—Taneytown Road

The XI Corps' regiments lying on the higher ground east of Ziegler's Grove took a terrible beating from two directions. The Confederate shells which overshot the troops to the west burst over their heads while their own guns in the cemetery behind them sent projectiles hurtling over them toward the Confederates. The 136th New York hugged the ground between the stone walls which bordered the Taneytown Road while their own batteries in the cemetery—less than seventy-eight feet away—fired over them. The sounds all blended together in a deadly crescendo. The sheer volume of the counterbattery fire numbed nineteen-year-old Private George P. Metcalf (Company D) who could not mentally separate the sound of one shell from the next. The wooden sabots from the 1st West Virginia's 10-pounder Parrotts slammed into the New Yorkers' backs, badly bruising a number of them.

Colonel Thomas Smyth

Despite his nick on the nose during the cannonade, Smyth remained with his men until the artillery ceased fire.

Miller, *Photographic History*

Unable to respond to the fire from either side, Metcalf and his section leader, Corporal Aaron Walker, who lay to his left, rolled over onto their backs. Propping themselves against the wall with their heads below the top row of stones, they were watching their own shells scream overhead when one of them prematurely burst over them. Walker grabbed his left arm, struck by a hot fragment. Metcalf reacted immediately. Pulling away Walker's field blouse at the point of entry, he fingered the wound to determine how serious it was. After fishing through the jacket and Walker's blouse, he pried out a piece of jagged iron about the size of a copper penny. Walker did not stay around. Crawling on his hands and knees, he headed down the road to a field hospital.[69]

Toward the center of the line the color guard sheathed the flag and got as low to the ground as they could. A shot crashed into the wall, snapped the flag staff in half, killed two men outright and wounded three others. The survivors uncased their colors to assess the damage and found thirteen holes in the flag.[70] With Walker gone, Metcalf (Company D) intensely studied the incoming Confederate rounds. Every thirty seconds a black speck would momentarily hover high above him before plummeting to the ground where it invariably bounced and whirled away from the line. Someone told Metcalf the Rebs were throwing railroad iron at them.[71]

Cemetery Hill

The moment Osborn responded to the artillery along Seminary Ridge, his gunners came under an enfilade from Captain Charles I. Raine's section of 20-pounders on Benner's Hill. A single round, whirling in low to the ground from the right, gutted three pairs of horses which were harnessed to three parallel limbers. Then a caisson or two exploded in flame and smoke, wounding more men and horses. The major, who dismounted, ordered Hill's six rifled guns from the line into the open space between Taft's and Edgell's rifles on the eastern side of the hill.[72] A 20-pounder bolt screamed in on Dilger's Ohio Battery from the right. Knocking down Private McLaughlin when it struck him on the side, it slammed against Second Lieutenant Z. Clark Scripture's left hip. The lieutenant went down in a heap while the round continued onward. It ripped the left hand away from Private Alonzo Silsby at the wrist before burrowing itself into the ground nearby. The dazed Scripture, upon regaining his senses, checked himself for his injuries. His new revolver, shattered beyond repair, still dangling in the mangled holster from his belt, had saved his life. Badly bruised, and suffering from shock, he earned a well-deserved convalescent furlough.[73]

A few minutes later, General Meade and a staff officer galloped up to Osborn. Could the major hold the place? the general asked hurriedly. Osborn said he could. The result of the battle depended upon keeping the hill, Meade added, to which the major calmly replied that he believed the Rebels felt the same way. "Can you stay here? Are your men thoroughly in hand?" Meade anxiously shot back. Osborn firmly reassured the commanding general that his officers and enlisted men were in good condition and that they would not abandon the hill. At that, the general abruptly wheeled his horse about and rode away.[74] He had not gone very far when he met his son and Lieutenant Charles W. Woolsey trudging up from the Leister house. When his son informed him he had lost his horse, the general curtly told him to take one of the orderlies' mounts, then rode south, leaving his namesake behind.[75]

Smyth's Brigade—Hays' Division

The 111th New York regiment on the right of the brigade showed signs of a panic.[76] The regiment was taking quite a pounding. An explosion on the other side of the stone wall in front of Captain Benjamin W. Thompson (Company F) drove the rock behind which he lay against his skull. The impact flipped him unconscious onto his back as if his feet were hinged to the ground. From all appearances, he seemed dead. Gravel-sized pieces of rock peppered his already bruised face. Colonel Clinton MacDougall, who could not leave his position behind the center of the regiment, watched

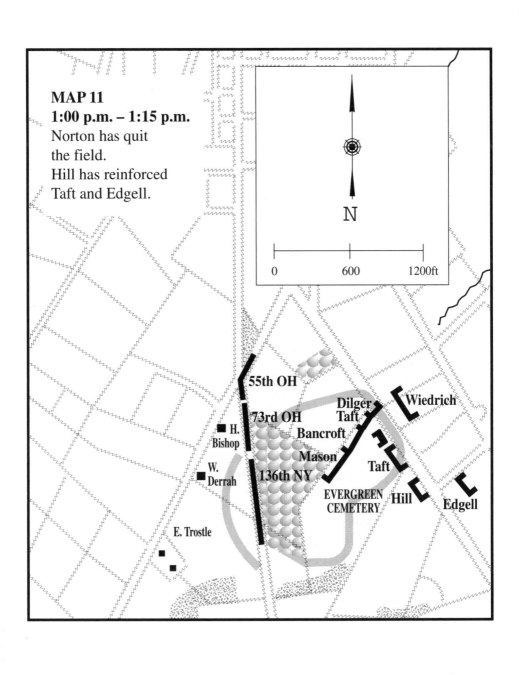

MAP 11
1:00 p.m. – 1:15 p.m.
Norton has quit
the field.
Hill has reinforced
Taft and Edgell.

N

0   600   1200ft

55th OH

73rd OH

H. Bishop

W. Derrah

Dilger
Taft

Wiedrich

Bancroft

Mason

Taft

136th NY

EVERGREEN
CEMETERY

Hill

Edgell

E. Trostle

his "dead" captain rise unsteadily to his feet and stagger over to him. Oblivious to everything around him, the stalwart Thompson wiped the blood from his face and told the colonel the obvious—he was wounded. MacDougall told him to leave the line, which he did.[77]

Nearby, on the right of Company F, a fragment killed First Lieutenant John B. Drake within fifteen feet of Captain Sebastian D. Holmes (Company D). The fighting had gotten too hot and too close for Holmes. He moved into the doorway in the south wall of the Brian barn to sit out the cannonade.[78] Near the northeast corner of the barn, one of the enlisted men from Company A stood up for reasons known only to himself when a solid shot struck him square in the face. His lifeless body collapsed across Sergeant Thomas Geer, who was lying to his right, splattering the startled sergeant with blood and brains.[79]

Colonel Thomas Smyth, commanding the brigade, rushed toward the 111th New York to restore order when a shell fragment cut his nose. Rather than leave the field, he walked into Ziegler's Grove to sit out the barrage along a fence row with two officers from the 108th New York—Second Lieutenant Theron E. Parsons (Company D) and Lieutenant Charles Schaeffer. Within seconds, another ball sent the fence rail behind their heads sailing through the woods. Striking Schaeffer across the back, it glanced harmlessly off Parsons' hip. Smyth suddenly decided to escort Schaeffer to a field hospital.

They had barely left the fence when Brigadier General Hays rode up to Parsons and told him to place Lieutenant Colonel Franklin Pierce (108th New York) in charge of the brigade. The lieutenant rushed toward his horse and was about to grab the reins when an unexploded shell gutted it. Abandoning his "useless" animal, he darted across the ridge to deliver the order.[80] Within a few minutes, Captain Henry H. Bingham reined in alongside of Hays looking for Hancock. The aide had barely asked if Hays had seen Hancock on the right of the line when a spent bullet glanced off the captain's skull. The impact would have unhorsed him if Hays had not kept him from falling. Blood trickled from Bingham's scalp. Hays bound the wound with his own handkerchief and told him to get it properly dressed at a hospital. The captain pulled away, heading east toward the Taneytown Road.[81]

The Rock Outcropping behind Cushing's Guns

The bulk of the Confederate fire smashed into the area immediately around the copse of trees. Dense, sulfuric clouds engulfed the entire area. Artillerymen rapidly flittered through the choking veil, their feet and legs alone being visible to the men lying down behind the crest.[82] General Gibbon, Lieutenant Frank Haskell, Captain Francis Wessels (Company K, 106th Pennsylvania), and several orderlies remained huddled below the brow very intent upon sitting out the bombardment. Close by, a solid shot bounced over the top of the rise. Striking the knapsack on the back of a soldier who was carrying canteens toward the front, it ripped it completely from its straps and scattered its contents all over the ground behind him. Non-plused, the fellow halted, felt his back for the missing knapsack and ambled nonchalantly on his way, ignoring the chaos around him.

His courage steeled Haskell. The lieutenant noticed an enlisted man crouching in a fetal position behind a rock about the size of a gallon bucket. He upbraided the fellow, "Do not lie there like a toad. Why not go to your regiment like a man?" The terrified soldier, his face paled from fright, slowly turned his head and fixed his blank eyes upon the lieutenant. Then he turned his face back, his nose toward the ground. Within moments a cannon ball smashed the rock into gravel, yet the man remained unmoved, and unscathed. Several orderlies not thirty feet away fared worse. A shell landed in the bushes where they had taken cover and killed two of them and one of the horses they were holding.[83]

Cushing's Battery

One of Cushing's men standing by his open ammunition chest caught Gibbon's attention.[84] Suddenly one of the caissons behind the officers exploded followed almost instantly by another. The earth rolled and heaved. Flaming splinters and shards of iron pelted the ground around them.[85] The artilleryman hobbled away, the flesh of his one leg dangling in bloody ribbons from what was left of the bone.[86]

Private Christopher Smith recalled hearing one shot come in from the left. A second screamed in from the right. The third, a solid shot, came in directly from the west. Glancing off the ground in front of the officers who were cooking their lunch in a stone pit behind the guns, it slammed into their makeshift cooking pit and sent their cooking stones flying all over the place. The Regulars sprang to their pieces immediately. For fifteen agonizing minutes they withstood a hellish barrage which completely obscured their position in a suffocating cloud of smoke. Cushing finally gave the order to load.

As the command traveled along the battery to open fire, a cannon ball crashed into Number Three, dismounting a wheel. The gun crashed down on its axle. Sergeant Thomas Whetston panicked and started to bolt to the rear. Cushing, his pistol drawn, stopped him cold. "Sergeant Whetston," he screamed, "come back to your post. The first man who leaves his post again I'll blow his brains out!" The sergeant regained his senses. Within minutes, his men had taken the spare wheel from the caisson and had put the piece back in service.[87]

Brown's Battery

Battery B, 1st Rhode Island Light Artillery had four 12-pounder Napoleons in line on the ridge, immediately south of the copse of trees. The artillerymen and the drivers lay on the ground behind the guns, waiting for Stable Sergeant Robert A. Niles to bring up their rations.[88] First Lieutenant

William S. Perrin, having assumed command when First Lieutenant T. Fred Brown was wounded the day before, personally directed the left section. Second Lieutenant Charles A. Brown had the right section.[89]

Glancing down toward the Taneytown Road, Lance Corporal John H. Rhodes, one of the battery's lead drivers, saw the "fearless" Niles galloping toward the guns leading four mules.[90] As soon as the Confederates opened fire, Perrin's men sprang to their guns. Niles turned about and headed to the rear with the only meal the men would have had within the last twenty-four hours. Perrin placed his pieces in a "V" formation. Sergeant Anthony B. Horton and Corporal Samuel J. Goldsmith held the extreme right with gun Number Three. Gun Number Four, under Sergeant Albert Straight and Corporal James M. Dye, stood to the left front with Sergeant Alanson A. Williams' and Corporal John F. Hanson's Number Two piece to its left. Sergeant Richard H. Gallup and Corporal Pardon S. Walker went into position with the Number One Napoleon on the left rear.[91] For ten to fifteen agonizing minutes, they waited, until ordered to return fire.

"They [the shells] came so thick and fast there was no dodging," Sergeant Albert Straight (Gun Number Four) later informed his brother. The sergeant's piece took a direct shell burst on the axle. Nevertheless, the artillerymen continued to service the piece. Sergeant Straight never forgot the horrifying moments which followed. Private William Jones, Number One on the gun, stepped up to the piece, sponged the bore and, inverting the staff, tapped the muzzle twice with the rammer before placing himself between the wheel and the muzzle, his face toward the Confederates. At the same time Number Two, Private Alfred Gardner, who stood across from him, reached around the left wheel of the gun and took the shell from Number Five. Gardner turned to the left and was about to insert the fixed round into the bore when a fourth shell barreled in on top of them.

Striking the left side of the muzzle it exploded. Blood sprayed all over the place. A fragment violently threw Gardner down in a ghastly heap, with his lifeless left arm and shoulder barely attached to his body. Jones' head, struck from the lower left, shattered into pieces. As his body thudded to the ground, the sponge staff flew from his right hand and landed about three yards away from his body. At the same time, Number Three, who tended the vent, staggered away from the gun, severely wounded.

Corporal James M. Dye, the gunner, turned to the left only to find his Number Four man, the fellow in charge of the lanyard, lying on the ground. He pulled on the man, trying to get him to his feet but he did not budge. Dye ordered him to tend the vent. The man would not respond. He remained motionless on the ground—too frightened or too exhausted to obey.

While Dye wrapped a rock in a piece of his torn shirt and laid it over the vent to seal it, Straight rushed to Gardner's side. Send his Bible to his wife, Gardner told his tentmate. Tell her he died happy. The sergeant left his friend lying in his own blood. Grabbing the sponge staff, he yelled for another round. In the background, Gardner shouted, in his delirium, "Glory to God! I am happy! Hallelujah!" Dye shoved a fixed shot into the muzzle. The ball did not slip down the bore. The corporal supported it with both hands while Straight pounded it repeatedly with the rammer.

Lieutenant Brown, seeing they had difficulty with the charge, bawled at a nearby artilleryman to get an ax from the limber. As the fellow stepped up to pound the ball down the bore, a third shell exploded against the cheek. A spoke shattered. The gun reared up on one wheel then slammed back down on the damaged wheel. The frantic gunners tried to pry the ball out of the muzzle but it was stuck fast. Gun Number Four was no longer in Federal service.[92]

Rorty's Battery

To Brown's left, Captain James Rorty's Battery B, 1st New York Light, took a devastating beating. Almost as soon as the Confederates opened, Rorty lost five horses and the drivers of his right caisson. They were writhing among the infantrymen supporting their line. His third gun took a direct hit and was dismounted. The Rebels also knocked out one of his right guns. Very shortly thereafter, a caisson exploded, followed immediately with a hit on his left piece. The Confederates slaughtered the gunners. He did not have enough bodies to man his remaining Parrott.[93]

The Confederate Position on Seminary Ridge
Kemper's Brigade

The artillery barrage caught Kemper's men lying down on the slope west of the Rogers house. Colonel Joseph Mayo, Jr. (3rd Virginia) initially intended to inspire his men with a foolish act of bravado. At the sound of the first signal gun he walked to the front center of his regiment and plopped down on the hillside on a blanket in front of the colors. He remained but a short time before the oppressive heat drove him back to an apple tree to the right rear of his regiment. Crowding in between Lieutenant Colonel Alexander Callcote of his regiment, and Colonel Tazwell Patton of the 7th Virginia, he tried to share what little shade there was with them and a handful of file closers.

Fifteen to twenty minutes into the Confederate bombardment, the Federals replied. The first two shots passed harmlessly overhead. The third projectile burst directly over the top of the tree, showering the men underneath with bark, splinters, and branches. The fourth shell exploded to the right over the 7th Virginia. Colonel Patton ran toward the shrieks emanating from that part of the line and quickly returned with an assessment of the casualties—two killed and three wounded. The words had barely left his mouth when a solid shot plowed through Company F in the middle of the 3rd Virginia. It killed Second Lieutenant Patrick H. Arthur and a private outright, while mortally wounding acting Orderly Sergeant Elisha

Murray and Third Lieutenant John C. Arthur. It also smashed First Lieutenant Azra P. Gomer's left thigh and wounded three more enlisted men before bounding away.[94]

The Federal rounds which overshot the guns fell among the prone
Virginians with terrifying effect. First Lieutenant John Dooley (Company C,
1st Virginia) got as low to the ground as he could. All around him it seemed
that men were getting killed or wounded. Nearby a man raised his head
only to get struck in the face and to become horribly disfigured. Another
fellow flopped spread-eagled on his stomach, his arms and legs involun-
tarily quivering in death.

Every now and then Dooley looked behind him to watch Major James
Dearing prancing about on horseback behind his guns, all the while defiantly waving a division flag at the Yankees.[95] Frightened to the point of
exhaustion, Dooley mentally recorded the sounds of each incoming round.
"...they schreech, sing, scream, whistle, roar, whirr, buzz, bang, and whizz,"
he later wrote.[96]

The artillery fire randomly killed and maimed. Toward the right of the
brigade line, Captain James R. Hutter (Company H, 11th Virginia) lay on
the ground next to a close friend, their faces in the grass. Hearing his
friend mumble to him, Hutter asked him what he had just said. Seconds,
which seemed like minutes, lapsed without a response. The colonel turned
his head toward his friend and, to his horror, found him dead. Hutter never
heard the shot that killed him.[97] Not everyone attempted to take cover.
The selfless Methodist Episcopalian Bishop John C. Granbery (Chaplain,
11th Virginia), his faith secure in Christ, abandoned the nominal safety of
the apple tree, and scurried from place to place to pray with and for the
wounded and the dying.[98] Company E lost more men than Company G,
which was in line to its immediate left. Before the bombardment, Captain
John H. Smith (Company G) tallied twenty-nine men present for duty. The
artillery killed and wounded no less than ten men—among them Privates
Thomas and William Jennings, brothers who died from the same shell.[99]

Sergeant Major David E. Johnston (7th Virginia), under the shade of
a lone apple tree, lay in his assigned post behind the last private in the rear
rank on the left flank of the 7th Virginia. Colonel Joseph Mayo, Jr. (3rd
Virginia) was to his immediate left. Colonel W. "Taz" Patton stood at Mayo's
feet.[100] A solitary shell exploded over Company E, killing Privates John D.
Canaday, Alec Legg, and Willis and Joseph Welsh.[101] The carnage momentarily overwhelmed the young sergeant major. The dense smoke obscured the sun. Heads, arms, and legs occasionally bounded across the
grass or dangled momentarily in the air before falling sharply to the ground.
The earth heaved and rolled. A solid shot slammed into the ground under
Private Albert Dodson (Company G). The impact, which killed him instantly,
lifted his body a full three feet off the ground.[102]

To the skirmishers on the ridge along the Emmitsburg Road, it seemed like the Yankees had their range from the very beginning. Solid shot and shells tore up the earth in front of Company D, 11th Virginia, First Lieutenant John T. James recollected. While lying with their faces in the thick, stifling grass, several of his men succumbed to sunstroke.[103]

Garnett's Brigade

The 19th Virginia, in the center of the brigade line, miraculously escaped most of the plunging fire, Second Lieutenant W. Nathaniel Wood (Company A) recalled. With the exception of a round or two from Little Round Top way off to the regiment's right flank, few of the Federal projectiles found their mark. Those that did, hit with horrible effect. Wood distinctly remembered a solid shot which came skipping in from the right behind the regiment. "Look out!" someone screamed. Without thinking, Lieutenant Colonel John T. Ellis, who was lying in a small wash in the hillside, raised his head to see what he had to avoid. The ball hit him full in the face. Friends quickly dragged him to Spangler's Woods and left him to die alone in the shade.[104]

Armistead's Brigade

Within minutes Private Erasmus Williams (Company H, 14th Virginia), in his personal trench, found himself blanketed with dirt. At the screech of another incoming round he pushed his head deeper into the ground. Blood spattered his back and his sleeves. Without looking, he knew that the shell had mangled the defiant Lieutenant Guerrant. Almost immediately another one thudded onto the earth next to him. Without thinking, he reached over, pulled the burning fuse from it, then flattened himself out in his hole.[105]

North of Spangler's Woods
Davis' Brigade

The 11th Mississippi joined the left of its brigade in McMillan's Woods (on the western side of the ridge several hundred yards south of the farm house) shortly before the shelling began.[106] The regiment, which took hits with the first Federal fire, hugged the ground. A shell struck in front of Company F on the right of the line. At the sound of the impact, Lieutenant William H. Peel (Company C) immediately rolled onto his back in time to see something he hoped never to witness again. The projectile, in ricocheting, penetrated Second Lieutenant Daniel Featherston's chest and exploded. The blast threw the 200-pound officer ten feet into the air while hurling him another twenty feet to the rear as if he were a twig. Private Andrew J. Baker (Company A) vividly recalled seeing the lieutenant's skull being "split wide open."[107]

A shell exploded over the University Greys (Company A), horribly mangling Sergeant Jeremiah S. Gage, the only enlisted man in the company who had not lain down. A piece of shrapnel ripped away most of his left arm between the elbow and the shoulder. Another nearly cut him in half. Passing left to right across his body, it tore away most of his bladder, a great deal of his intestines, and over a third of his pelvis. His friends wrapped him in a blanket to keep him in tact, placed him on a stretcher, and hurried him to Surgeon Joseph Holt, who had established a field hospital in the north-south leg of McMillan's sunken lane. Seeing Doctor William Shields, the dying soldier called out, "Doctor, they have got Jere Gage at last. I thought I would get through safely, but they got me." "I hope not, Jere. I hope not." Gage told his men to set him down gently and asked the doctors to look at the wound.

Holt initially thought the sergeant had only lost his arm. When he tried to encourage Gage, the boy replied, "Why, Doctor, that is nothing; here is where I really hurt." Gage pulled his blanket aside to expose his abdomen. The doctor quickly noticed the acute absence of any hemorrhaging and mentally noted that the indescribable mangling had twisted the soldier's guts up too much to bleed. Surgeon LeGrand Wilson (42nd Mississippi) examined the wound more closely—stomach torn away, spleen and one rib missing. "Doctor, how long do I have to live?" Gage asked Doctor Holt. "A very few hours." "Doctor," the dying man gasped, "I am in great agony; let me die easy, dear Doctor; I would do the same for you." The surgeon assured him he would "die easy." Holt called Jim Rowell, his knapsack bearer, to give him his two-ounce bottle of black drop (concentrated opium). The doctor quickly poured a tablespoon into a cup of water and was handing it to Gage when he stopped. "Have you no message to leave?" The young soldier snapped out something about his mother. He had to write her. Using the hospital knapsack as a table and with the doctor supporting him, Gage scrawled his last message in pencil to his mother.

He told her that he was probably dying and that he was dying like a man. She needed to handle his loss. He was dying for his country and he regretted that Mississippi was not free and that he could no longer be of any use to his sisters. She would not be able to bring his body home. He could not write more. Tell his sisters the contents of his note, he admonished her. Send his dying words to Miss Mary. He signed the note and, after pressing the clean side to his wound, added the superfluous postscript, "This letter is stained with my blood." Handing the paper to the surgeon, he reminded him of his promise to "die easy." The doctor handed him the cup. Offering the opiate as a final personal toast to victory and his friends, he drained it. The attendants laid him on his back and covered him from head to foot with a blanket. (Four hours later, he died.)[108]

Fry's Brigade

The ground quaked and bounced with each concussion, producing after shocks, the likes of which Sergeant June Kimble (Company A, 14th

Tennessee) had never seen before. "...loose grass, leaves, and twigs arose from six to eight inches above the ground, hovered and quivered as birds about to drop," he vividly recollected years later.[109] A shell fragment ripped into Colonel Birkett D. Fry's right shoulder. Despite the intense pain, he refused to give up the command of the brigade. He was not going to let his regiments go in without him.[110] A solid shot, traveling at a very slow speed, and losing altitude fast, dropped with a tremendous thud in front of the 7th Tennessee within inches of Sutler Jim Bradley's head.[111]

East of McMillan's Woods
Cutt's Battalion

Private Felix R. Galloway's 10-pounder Parrott (Battery A), in the orchard on the left of the battalion, fired about forty rounds before the Federals responded. To his amazement Cemetery Ridge went up in a blaze, he recalled. He bowed his

Colonel Birkett D. Fry

Disregarding his shoulder wound, the stoic Fry led Archer's brigade into the charge until prostrated near the Angle.
Miller, *Photographic History*

head to meet the inevitable. Seconds later the air around him filled with projectiles. Tree branches rained down upon them. Leaves showered them, covering the ground around their feet with a green blanket. Dazed though he was by the incessant concussions, he gripped his sponge staff tighter and stayed at his post as the Number One man on the piece.

The Yankees never got the section's exact range. Their rounds either burst well above them or struck the steep ridge immediately in front of the guns. The rounds which ricocheted off the ridge usually bounded over the gunners' heads. Every now and then Galloway felt the hot breath of an exploded shell kissing the back of his neck. After about forty-five minutes of constant firing, the tube had become quite heated. With each round the piece bounced higher in the recoil.

Every time he sponged the bore, he eyed the breech to see a reassuring spurt of water shoot out of the vent. By the ninetieth round he was black with powder which clung to his sweating body. He continually kept his eyes on the Number Two man who loaded the rounds. Without enough men to handle the gun, he had no Number Three man to tend the vent. His nervousness showed. Each time he rammed a fixed charge down the bore,

Galloway expected to have his arms and hands sent across the field by a premature discharge. At one point, the Number Two man yelled at him, "Say, where is your God and your mother's prayer?" "I am only wet with powder," Galloway shot back. "Not a bone is broken." With that he did not say another word. Only Captain L. E. Spivey continued to shout above the blasts, "Stand by your guns! Load! Fire!" Through it all, Galloway insisted that he only feared shrapnel because it would strike down a man before he ever heard the shell explode.[112]

Kemper's Brigade

Colonel Tazwell Patton (7th Virginia), who had lain down on the right of Sergeant Major Johnston, yelled over him at Colonel Joseph Mayo (3rd Virginia) to look up on the ridge behind them. Dearing was still on horseback, riding from gun to gun and conspicuously waving his large flag. He said that they should move their men closer to the guns around the Rogers house but Mayo said it was out of the question. They had no orders to advance. Besides, he added, the Federal fire was slackening. Without warning, the Confederates renewed their barrage and the Yankees responded in kind.[113]

Sergeant Major David Johnston (7th Virginia) never heard the proverbial shot which hit him. The intense heat forced him to raise his head to get a mouthful of fresh air. Senior Second Lieutenant James W. Brown (Company G), to his right, admonished him. "You had better put your head down or you may get it knocked off." "A man had about as well die that way as to suffocate for want of air," Johnston gasped. At that a shell screamed in from the left through Company D of the 3rd Virginia.[114] It sheared off two men's heads at their ears before bursting over the sergeant major, and splattered Mayo's left shoulder with a ghastly paste of earth, blood, and brains.[115] A piece of shrapnel wounded First Lieutenant John R. Stewart (Adjutant, 3rd Virginia), who was on Mayo's left, through the buttocks.[116] Johnston, Lieutenant Brown, and one other man were also hit.

The concussion threw Johnston onto his back, away from the line. For a brief time, he lay there unconscious. Gasping for breath, he awakened to discover that he was paralyzed on the left side. (At the time he had no way of knowing that the blast had broken all of his ribs on that side and had contused his lung.) Colonel Patton sprang over to him, asking him if he was severely wounded. Johnston asked for water. Sergeant Harry Snidow (Company D) and another enlisted man spread a blanket under the apple tree then carefully sat the semiconscious sergeant major upon it with his back against the trunk.[117]

Cemetery Ridge
Cushing's Battery

From where he stood Private Christopher Smith could occasionally see through the smoke and catch glimpses of the green rye across the Emmitsburg Road.[118] The Rebels severely pounded the battery. Early in the action, Cushing posted himself behind the prone Company I on the right of the 69th Pennsylvania. Standing in that position, he could see below the muzzle blasts of his guns on the crest of the hill. From there he screamed at his individual gunners to raise or lower the elevations of their pieces as needed.[119] Blinded as they were by the smoke, the artillerymen dutifully adjusted the elevations but did not train the guns on any specific targets before firing.[120] In a very short amount of time Confederate solid shots knocked the wheels off four of Cushing's rifles. His men hurriedly replaced them.[121]

Rorty's Battery

By 1:30 p.m., the Confederates had terribly reduced the crews of Battery B, 1st New York Light. Only three men and Captain James Rorty remained of the original 65 effectives.[122] To the left front, behind their hastily constructed earthwork, the enlisted men of the 13th Vermont thought the artillerymen were frozen beside their guns. Lieutenant Stephen Brown (Company K), armed with a camp hatchet, arbitrarily removed himself from camp arrest and ran up to them to ask what their problem was. Within short order, he reported back to Captain George G. Blake, his company commander, with a request for volunteers. Smith Decker, James Hagen, Daniel Manahan, Henry B. Meigs and several others followed the lieutenant back to the guns with the cheers of their comrades echoing off their backs.[123]

Throwing his sword and tunic aside, Rorty snatched up the rammer and assumed the position of the Number One man. When the bore proved too hot to take the round, he shouted for water to cool the tube. Second Lieutenant Moses Shackley (Company B, 19th Massachusetts) leaped forward, snatched the gun's water bucket and calmly walked down the east side of the ridge to the spring behind the Leister house. A cannon ball thudded into the earth between his feet without disturbing him. With the air around him filled with swirling dust and dirt, and shell fragments, he rushed back to Rorty. While passing by his prone company, he yelled, "The water is cold enough, boys, but it's devilish hot around the spring."[124]

Leaving the water with the artillerymen, he resumed his place in line next to the color guard. Rorty asked Colonel Arthur F. Devereaux for volunteers to man his one-gun battery.[125] The colonel ordered six volunteers forward. For several seconds, the men looked at each other, trying to see who would go first. "I'm one, boys," Private Samuel G. Snellen (Company G) exclaimed, who, having been struck by a case ball, painfully rose to his full height. "Who's the next?" Captain Andrew Mahoney (Company E) and Sergeant "Billy" McGinnis (Company K) followed. Sergeants Cornelius Linehan and Matthias Bixby (both from Company F) joined them. Lieutenant Shackley nudged Color Sergeant Benjamin H. Jellison. "Come, Jellison," he said, "let's go and help. We might as well get killed there as here."

By the time they reached the guns, Rorty had died. Lieutenant Stephen Brown (Company K, 13th Vermont) screamed at Devereaux, "For God's sake, Colonel, let me have twelve men to work my gun." Without waiting for orders, twenty more volunteers sprang forward. They replaced the wheels on one of the Parrotts and put the gun back into action.[126] Shackley, despite Devereaux's admonition that he did not have to join the volunteers, strutted back and forth between the two pieces, encouraging the men to keep at their posts.[127] The colonel ordered Jellison back into the ranks. He took his place but left his flag with another member of the colorguard.[128]

Emmitsburg Road

Farther to the north, the 8th Ohio dozed off between the steep banks of the Emmitsburg Road, seemingly oblivious to the terrible artillery fire which pelted their position. A spent shell fragment slapped against Sergeant Thomas F. Galwey's foot, jarring him awake. Sitting upright to rub his bruised foot, he glanced east across the road and saw Private Charley Gallagher lying severely wounded beneath a small tree. He had dropped off to sleep about the same time as Galwey and never knew what struck him down. The young sergeant was laughing about his "wound" when a second piece of shell struck him on the thigh and unceremoniously bowled him into the dirt. Picking himself up, he returned to his place against the western side of the road. As he hunkered down behind the road bank, he heard the company's perpetual pessimist, Private Joseph Lloyd, say that the next hit would be the fatal one.[129]

At least Galwey still had his senses about him. Some other wounded men, like the severely jarred Captain Benjamin W. Thompson (Company F) of the 111th New York had no concept of their surroundings. After leaving the regiment at Brian's stone wall along the western side of Cemetery Ridge, the captain meandered into the apple orchard on the ridge. His company clerk found him there, sitting beneath an apple tree, completely unaware of the shot which furrowed and gouged the earth around him. The corporal pulled the captain to his feet and walked him down the eastern side of the hill to the log barn behind Meade's headquarters at the Leister farm.

In so doing, they stepped from the proverbial pan into the fire. The place shook and rolled with the concussions of the Confederate overshoots. In all of the confusion, Thompson regained his senses. All around them lay dead horses. The artillery caissons in the hollow were being decimated. The longer they stayed there, the thirstier they became. When the fire slacked off, Thompson took his clerk's canteen and limped southeast, across the Taneytown Road to the creek on the opposite side. Kneeling down, he washed the blood from his head before picking the gravel from his face. When he realized that he was not as severely injured as he had thought, he decided to return to the regiment.[130]

Spangler's Woods

Colonel E. Porter Alexander glanced at his watch. It was 1:25 p.m., five minutes longer than he had desired for the cannonade to last. Unable to bring himself to order the deaths of hundreds of men, he had deliberately waited. Since the cannonading began, Pickett had pestered him twice with messengers, both of whom asked, "Is it time to charge yet?"[131] From his position behind Woolfolk's battery he realized that he could not postpone it any longer, despite the fact that the Federals were still laying out a good fire.

He anxiously scribbled a note to Pickett:

If you are coming at all you must come at once, or I cannot give you proper support, but the enemy's fire has not slackened at all. At least 18 guns are still firing from the cemetery itself.

Handing the note to a courier, he turned his large glass upon the copse of trees and anxiously waited for Pickett to respond.[132]

Pickett and Longstreet

The courier found Pickett with Longstreet in Spangler's Woods. He handed the paper to the division commander, who after reading it, passed it on to Longstreet who said nothing. "General, shall I advance?" Pickett asked. Knowing too well what awaited his men, Longstreet could not bring himself to reply out loud. He merely nodded his head in mute assent. The foppish Pickett threw himself onto his horse's back and galloped away to dispatch his aides to prepare the division to advance. He split them up. The general's brother, Major Charles Pickett, Captains Edward R. Baird and Robert A. Bright, and Lieutenant W. Stuart Symington departed with instructions to each of the brigade commanders and to Dearing.[133] Longstreet and a staff officer also mounted.[134]

Colonel E. Porter Alexander

Meanwhile, Alexander became increasingly impatient with what seemed like inordinate delay upon Pickett's part. Five minutes after he sent the first note, the Federal artillery fire perceptibly slackened near the copse of trees. Training his glasses upon the ridge, he noticed what appeared to be about three Federal batteries limbering up and leaving the field. He waited another five minutes to see if the Federals were reinforcing the position. Detecting no activity, he wrote another note to Pickett.

For God's sake come quick. The 18 guns have gone. Come quick or my ammunition will not let me support you properly.

His courier, Catlett, hurried away with the message. The time seemed to drag on interminably, with Alexander becoming more excitable and impatient for the infantry to arrive. Very shortly after Catlett left he dispatched an officer and a sergeant from Woolfolk's battery with verbal instructions for

Pickett to hurry up. With his glasses, he surveyed the area around the copse of trees, which he had mistakenly been informed, was at the cemetery.[135]

Cemetery Hill

About the same time that Alexander sent his first note to Pickett, General Hunt joined Major Osborn and General Howard on the high ground near the top of Cemetery Hill. He reiterated what both officers already knew—that the Rebels were massing to the southwest and were intent upon charging once the guns fell silent on Cemetery Hill. Osborn spoke up. Did Meade really want the Confederates to make a charge? "General Meade had expressed a hope that the enemy would attack, and he had no fear of the result." "If this is so, why not let them out while we are all in good condition?" the major suggested. If he ceased fire immediately the Rebels would have to conclude that the guns had been driven from the cemetery. Why not find Meade and get permission to cease fire? the major concluded.

Could Osborn control his men once they ceased fire? Hunt asked. The ever confident Osborn reassured him that he need not fear their steadfastness. Howard interjected that by following the suggestion they would find out exactly what the Confederates intended to do and in very short order. After sharing a few comments with Howard, Hunt took it upon himself to execute the order and then to consult Meade should he come upon him. He would personally order the guns along the stone wall to stop firing while the major tended to the guns on the hill.[136]

Unknown to Hunt, Osborn, or Howard, Meade had already decided to lure the Confederates into an assault by silencing his own batteries. He gave the message to one of his aides, Captain Charles E. Cadwallader, who he erroneously assumed would faithfully brave the deluge of shells pounding the Taneytown Road and deliver the order to Hancock. The captain, however, along with Chief Quartermaster of the Army of the Potomac, Brigadier General Rufus Ingalls, got as far as the stone wall near the Guinn house when they decided to take shelter from the incoming artillery rounds. Cadwallader caught sight of a young officer with a freshly bandaged head heading north from the hospital south of the Leister house. The captain hailed over the mounted officer and asked him if he belonged to Hancock's staff. Henry Bingham said he did. "Here is an order from General Meade for him, which I wish you would deliver," Cadwallader yelled as he handed Bingham a folded slip of paper. Bingham opened the three-inch by five-inch sheet and scanned the directives which were scribbled in pencil. Addressed to either Hancock or Hunt, it cautioned them to conserve their ammunition and not to fire it so quickly. The captain, who hoped to deliver the note to either general, sped away toward Ziegler's Grove.[137]

Meanwhile, Hunt departed for Cemetery Ridge and Osborn tended to his batteries. Calling for Second Lieutenant Eugene A. Bancroft to bring up his four 12-pounders (Battery G, 4th U.S. Artillery), Osborn crossed the road into Wiedrich's battery. After commanding the men to lie down beside their guns, he trooped his line. An estimated ten minutes elapsed between Hunt's departure and the time when Mason's guns fell silent.[138] By then, Bancroft's guns had filled the open space between Taft's section of 20-pounder Parrotts and Mason's six 12-pounders.[139]

The Federal Position at and South of the Copse of Trees

Arnold's Battery A, and Brown's Battery B of the 1st Rhode Island Light Artillery, having been shot up beyond useful service, limbered up to leave the field.[140] At the same time, Captain Bingham, having been unable to find Hunt or Hancock, took it upon himself to order the II Corps batteries along Cemetery Ridge to cease fire. Beginning with Woodruff's Battery, he spurred along the ridge toward the south.[141]

The counterbattery fire also stopped as suddenly as it had begun. The smoke quickly dissipated along the line. Sergeant Major William B. Hincks (14th Connecticut) stared at the welcome sunlight. Arnold's drivers brought up the teams for the two serviceable guns they had left. When the pieces withdrew, the aching infantrymen from the 14th Connecticut stood up to stretch the cramps out of their arms and legs. They began telling each other that the battle was over. Major Theodore Ellis overheard them. "No," he said abruptly within the sergeant major's hearing, "they mean to charge with all their infantry." The command to "Fall in Fourteenth," echoed along the line. Ellis marched the regiment up to the stone wall, along Arnold's former front.[142] Their 100 men deployed in a single rank to wait out the assault.[143]

On the ridge, northeast of the copse of trees, with solid shot and Whitworth bolts screaming overhead, Brigadier General Alexander Webb stepped over to Colonel R. Penn Smith, whose regiment, the 71st Pennsylvania, occupied the crest from the west-north angle of the stone wall, and commanded Captain Charles H. Banes, his assistant adjutant general, to bring up batteries from the reserve artillery.[144]

Captain William A. Arnold, Company A, 1st Rhode Island Artillery

Having expended all of their ammunition during the cannonade, he ordered the guns from the field long before Longstreet's Confederates reached the stone wall north of the Angle.

MOLLUS, USAMHI

Cowan's Battery

Bingham, whom Captain Andrew Cowan (1st New York Independent Battery) did not know, galloped along the line, ahead of Banes, from the right, shouting, "Cease firing. Hold your fire for the infantry." The captain, unable to see through the smoke, initially prepared to unload several more rounds upon the Confederates when Banes reined up to him. "Report to General Webb on the right," he said. Cowan hesitated. As a VI Corps battery attached to the I Corps, he was not under the authority of anyone in the II Corps. Looking to the north, he saw an officer, whom he later discovered to be Webb, anxiously waving his hat at him. By the time Cowan turned to his men, most of whom had stripped to their shirts, and commanded, "Limber to the right," Bingham had intercepted Hunt and delivered Meade's order. Yipping and cheering, Cowan's veterans, implements in hand, leaped upon the limbers.[145] Battery B, 1st New York Light Artillery, its crews decimated, and its officers down, had almost exhausted its ammunition supply.[146] It too fell silent.

Stepping out into the open with Lieutenant Frank Haskell, General Gibbon, whose division held the left of the II Corps line, decided to inspire his men by his personal example. Believing he would be safer if he moved closer to the front, he headed directly toward Cushing's battery. Without warning three of the battery's limbers exploded, sending voluminous columns of smoke and fragments billowing into the sky. In the distance the Confederates' cheering echoed across the fields. Passing by the left of the guns north of the copse of trees, Gibbon stepped up to the rear rank of the prone 69th Pennsylvania. Motioning the men aside, he and Haskell went over the wall and took cover behind a high clump of brush to observe the Confederate line. All the while projectiles screamed overhead. Rolling clouds of sulfuric smoke marked the Confederate artillery positions. Through it all, he could see no infantry movement. Within a few minutes one of Hancock's aides, Major William G. Mitchell, approached the general and asked what Gibbon thought the cannonade meant only to be given an ambiguous answer. It was either the prelude to an assault or a retreat, Gibbon said. Mitchell left.[147] Several more minutes elapsed.

When he noticed the Confederate guns were still firing high, Gibbon decided to inspect the southern end of his line. Folding his arms, he paced the front of the division with complete indifference. It was a terrible and foolhardy gamble Captain John D. S. Cook (Company I, 80th New York) thought for a man of Gibbon's character to risk his life in such a manner. The captain, while understanding the general's purpose and observing the positive effect it had upon the troops, wondered what would happen to their morale if Gibbon were killed.[148] Sergeant Henry Taylor (Company E, 1st Minnesota) thought otherwise. The presence of his commanding general between him and the Confederates told him the general knew how to stare peril in the face. "See there, see General Gibbons [*sic*]," a number of them called out.[149]

While Gibbon and Haskell inspired their men, Webb directed Smith to move the 71st Pennsylvania forward to the front section of the stone wall with his left flank anchored on a sapling about five paces (twelve and one-half feet) to the right of the 69th Pennsylvania. While moving the line by companies from the left, by the right oblique into line, the colonel soon discovered that he did not have enough room to deploy the entire command. The two right companies, being cut off by the north wall of the Angle, filed by the right into line in Arnold's former position thereby contracting the 14th Connecticut's front.

Smith immediately trotted over to those two companies and ordered the officers and men to gather up all of the loaded and capped weapons which they had captured the day before. He then hurried down to Lieutenant Colonel C. Kochersperger who was at the front wall and ordered him not to fire until the Confederates crossed the Emmitsburg Road. At that time the men were to load and fire as rapidly as possible then fall back as soon as the Rebs got too close for the line to reload. In retiring from the front, the lieutenant colonel's eight companies were to watch out for the right wing, which would open with an enfilade as soon as they cleared the line of fire.[150]

Armistead's Brigade

Brigadier General Cadmus Wilcox rode up to Armistead, and saluting, asked him what he thought would follow the unusually heavy cannonade. Armistead supposed the division would charge and carry the Yankees' works. The fields had already been heavily fought over, Wilcox argued. The Yankees would have strengthened the stone wall. There would be great slaughter in the attempt to dislodge them. As Wilcox spurred his horse toward his own brigade, a shell ricocheted off a small hickory. Barely missing Armistead, it seriously wounded a private in the 53rd Virginia. The men instinctively huddled together. "Lie still, boys," Armistead said loud enough for them to hear, "there is no safe place here." Pacing up and down the front of the 53rd Virginia in the center of his line, the general tried to encourage them. "Men," he began, his voice booming over the sound of the guns, "remember what you are

Brigadier General
Lewis A. Armistead

Courageous to the end, he led his brigade right into the Federal lines at the Angle.

Miller, Photographic History

fighting for. Remember your homes, your firesides, your wives, mothers, sisters and your sweethearts."[151]

Presently, one of Pickett's A.D.C.s rode into the brigade and the order rippled through the regiments to pile up knapsacks, blankets, and excess equipment by companies.[152] The 53rd Virginia loaded and fixed bayonets. "I had participated in a number of engagements," Captain Benjamin L. Farinholt (Company E) wrote, "but this was the greatest and most imposing sight I ever witnessed." Armistead called to the regiment, "Attention, Battalion!"[153] The officers cautioned the men to reserve their fire until close to the enemy.[154]

Spangler's Woods
Colonel E. Porter Alexander

Coming out of the line near the right flank of Kemper's brigade, Longstreet and his aide calmly wheeled their horses north and trooped the line. Captain John H. Smith (Company G, 11th Virginia) distinctly remembered that Longstreet looked to neither side as he continued to the left of the line and disappeared from his view.[155] Placing themselves along the crest, behind the guns, the two rode the ridge, seemingly defying the occasional potshots from the Federal skirmishers to the east. A shell or two buried themselves in the ground near the general's horse, but he seemed oblivious to the danger. "Go to the rear," some of the men shouted. "You'll get your old fool head knocked off," others called out. "We'll fight without you leading us." Longstreet ignored them also. Continuing on, he disappeared into the northeast corner of the woods to the right of Company K, 56th Virginia.[156]

Alexander anxiously checked his watch again. It was 1:45 p.m.[157] Longstreet reined in by his side. Private Robert D. Damron (Company D, 56th Virginia) saw him stop behind one of the guns and observe the Federal lines through his glasses.[158] Alexander hurriedly told the general that the Yankees had withdrawn their guns and that the charge would get a favorable start. He also told him that the howitzers he had procured were no longer available and that his own artillery support might not be all that he had wanted to provide.[159] Alexander merely confirmed what Longstreet already knew.

"Go and halt Pickett right where he is, and replenish your ammunition," Longstreet ordered without taking the glasses from his eyes. "General," Alexander replied, "we can't do that. We nearly emptied the trains last night. Even if we had it, it would take an hour or two, and meanwhile the enemy would recover from the pressure he is now under. Our only chance is to follow it up now—to strike while the iron is hot." He only had about fifteen minutes more of ammunition left. "I don't want to make this attack," the general continued deliberately with emphatic pauses between each sentence. "I believe it will fail. I do not see how it can succeed. I would not make it even now, but that General Lee has ordered and expects

**Lieutenant General
James Longstreet**

Commander of Lee's First Corps, he reluctantly committed his men and A. P. Hill's men to a charge which he believed would never succeed.

Miller, *Photographic History*

it."[160] With that, Alexander turned to Haskell and ordered him to take all of the guns he could from the right of the line to support the charge and to help it in any way he could.[161] Alexander sensed that Longstreet wanted him to stop the charge but the colonel said nothing. He did not want the responsibility for causing a needless delay or for halting an attack which Lee had personally ordered.[162]

Garnett's Brigade

Longstreet had barely passed the front of the 56th Virginia when Pickett came racing out of the woods yelling something which Lieutenant George W. Finley (Company K, 56th Virginia) could not hear. As the regiment got to its feet it became apparent that he had ordered the brigade to "Attention."[163] One company from each regiment sprinted forward as skirmishers. Company H, 8th Virginia had explicit orders to tear down the fences crossing the brigade's line of march.[164] The regimental officers paced their line instructing their men to keep at the "common time," not to break ranks, and not to cheer. They could carry their arms "at will" but they were to continually close on the center as casualties were incurred.[165] (On the far left of the regiment, Company D received orders to carry their weapons at "trail arms" and to advance at the "quick step.")[166] Farther to the right, the 18th Virginia was already prepared to advance, Captain Charles F. Linthicum (Garnett's A.A.G.) having already instructed them that they would march when the guns ceased fire.[167]

Dearing's guns had fallen silent by the time the order to charge reached the 8th Virginia on the right of Garnett's line. The caissons wheeled through the regiment, temporarily disrupting its formation. "For God's sake wait till I get some ammunition," Dearing called to Colonel Eppa Hunton, "and I will drive every Yankee from the heights." Hunton, who was mounted because a Second Manassas injury kept him from walking, remembered how Dearing earlier had assured him that his artillery would go in with the brigade as it always had done. He also knew that it was too late. The charge was starting without the guns.[168] The artillery duel killed five men, leaving 200 effectives in the regimental line.

Kemper's Brigade

Pickett trotted up to the rear center of the 3rd Virginia; he shouted at them to rise up and to "Remember Old Virginia." The regiment got to its feet and closed ranks to the left. The many gaps in the ranks marked by the bodies of the dead, the wounded, and the sunstruck tore at Colonel Joseph C. Mayo's heart. His regiment appeared decimated. Close by lay the bloodied corpse of Color Sergeant Joshua Murden (Company B), the brand new regimental colors clasped in his hands.[169]

In the meantime, Captain Robert Bright had reached the 1st Virginia in the center of the brigade. General Kemper got up at the captain's approach, his face veiled by a handkerchief which he had tucked under his hat to protect him from flying stone chips. Pulling the veil away, he greeted Bright who instructed him, "You and your staff and field officers to go in dismounted; dress on Garnett and take the red barn for your objective point." "Bob, turn us loose, and we will take them," someone shouted from close by. Bright glanced toward the rear of the line, recognized his former schoolmate, Sergeant Major Robert McCandish Jones and made no response. He did not have the time. While instructing Kemper to have his officers go in dismounted, Colonel Lewis Williams hobbled over to him. "Captain Bright, I wish to ride my mare up." "Colonel Williams, you cannot do it," Bright insisted. "Have you not just heard me give the order to your general to go up on foot?" "But you will let me ride," Williams replied, "I am sick to-day, and besides that, remember Williamsburg."

The not so subtle retort reminded the captain that Williams had been wounded while defending the captain's hometown—a battle which he had missed. His honor stung, Bright relented. "Mount your mare, and I will make an excuse for you," he said before he rode back toward Spangler's Woods.[170] Kemper also disobeyed the directive.

The brigade line stood up. First Lieutenant John Dooley (Company C, 1st Virginia) noticed that quite a few of the men remained on the ground. They lay in their places dead, sick, wounded, or paralyzed by fear. A number of the men collapsed as they got to their feet, victims of the terrible heat. Dooley found himself thinking, "Oh, if I could just come out of this charge safely, how thankful I would be."[171] He was going into the charge bent upon returning alive. The intense heat also prostrated a considerable number of men in Company G, 11th Virginia. Captain James R. Hutter (Company H) tried to urge one of the unconscious men to his feet. "Captain Hutter," Captain John H. Smith (Company G) admonished him, "when he says he is sick, he is sick."[172] Hutter let go of the man and assumed his place behind the regiment.

By 2:00 p.m., Alexander's guns had effectively silenced all of the Federal artillery along Cemetery Ridge which he could see. Many of his rounds had hit their intended targets—the Federal artillery and their infantry supports behind the guns. At the same time the Union artillery fire and the sun had reduced Longstreet's assault columns by over two hundred effectives. The testimony of Colonel Gordon, Colonel Fry, Lieutenant Dooley, and others intimated that the North Carolinians and the Virginians did not relish going into the fight and that many of them did not expect to survive it. Confederate morale was not as high as it should have been.

3   2:00 p.m. through 2:45 p.m.

The Charge Begins
Pettigrew's Division

The cease fire relieved Colonel Birkett D. Fry, who commanded the brigade on the right of Pettigrew's division. The cannonade had cost him a number of officers and enlisted men. He preferred the movement of the impending charge to being slaughtered like cattle in a pen.[1] Orderly Sergeant June Kimble (Company A, 14th Tennessee) took a prolonged deep breath in anticipation of what would follow next.[2] Pettigrew signaled Fry to get his regiments moving. At the colonel's command, the men stood up, aligned themselves, and prepared to march.[3]

Meanwhile Pettigrew rode north to Colonel James K. Marshall, commanding the center brigade in his division, whom he found mounted in front of his line. His face bright with

**Brigadier General
J. Johnston Pettigrew**

He survived the charge with a serious wound only to get killed at Falling Waters during Lee's retreat into Virginia.
Miller, *Photographic History*

the prospect of battle, he shouted, "Now, Colonel, for the honor of the good old North State, forward." The colonel yelled the command and the regimental officers picked it up, sending it from the center of the brigade to both flanks.[4] On the far left of the line, Pettigrew passed the word to Brigadier General Joseph R. Davis to get his men to their feet.[5]

At the command "Forward!" Fry's brigade stepped off. Kimble heard no drums, only the rhythmic stamp and swish of veteran soldiers advancing in cadence. While the 14th Tennessee cleared the woods along the crest and moved past Poague's Battalion, the sergeant trotted ten feet ahead of his company. Turning his back upon the Federals, he faced the line and studied it from right to left. The magnificent spectacle of the regiments emerging into the open ground with the breathtaking precision of the Prussian Guards left an indelible impression upon him which he could never find the words to adequately describe.[6] Once the regiments cleared the tree line, Second Lieutenant John H. Moore (Company B, 7th Tennessee) knew there was no turning back. A Rebel Yell—a shrill "Yi! Yi!"—erupted from the far right of the line and traveled to the left. Unlike on previous occasions it did not spur the men into a rush. They marched steadily forward as if on parade.[7] The North Carolinians stepped off to the north, trying to keep the unwieldy formation aligned.

Davis' Brigade

At the clarion command "Attention!" the North Carolinians and Mississippians got to their feet. Lieutenant William H. Peel (Company C, 11th Mississippi) noticed how gray the men's faces seemed, confirming what they need not be told—a tremendous task lay before them. "Forward!" traveled along the brigade from south to north. The soldiers stepped off with a stoic determination.[8]

Brockenbrough's Brigade

Pursuant to orders, the brigade split. Colonel John M. Brockenbrough took the 40th Virginia and the 22nd Virginia Battalion forward on the left of Davis' brigade, leaving Colonel Robert M. Mayo of the 47th Virginia in charge of his own small regiment and the 55th Virginia. Brockenbrough gave explicit instructions to Colonel William S. Christian (55th Virginia) that his regiment and the 47th Virginia were to advance only at Mayo's command. As the distance increased between the two wings of the brigade, Christian became more uneasy. Unable to find Mayo anywhere, he consulted with Lieutenant Colonel John W. Lyell, commanding the 47th, as to what they should do. After asking around for Mayo, Lyell suggested that he had died during the artillery duel. At that, Christian assumed command of the wing and decided to march forward.[9] The delay staggered the Confederate advance and reduced the first line's frontage by around 250 feet.

Colonel E. Porter Alexander

Shortly before 2:00 p.m. Alexander looked behind him and to his relief saw Pickett's division moving up the rise behind his guns. Brigadier General Richard Garnett, with whom Alexander had traveled across the Plains with Armistead before the war, rode "Red Eye" in front of his brigade. Garnett and Longstreet exchanged salutes. Alexander mounted up

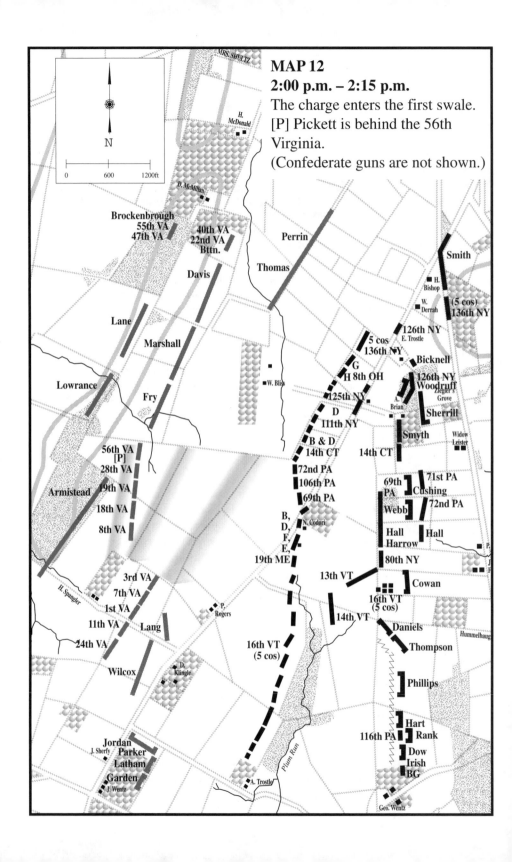

MAP 12
2:00 p.m. – 2:15 p.m.
The charge enters the first swale.
[P] Pickett is behind the 56th
Virginia.
(Confederate guns are not shown.)

N

0   600   1200ft

to escort Garnett a few yards beyond the guns, which had ceased fire. When Alexander turned back to attend to his pieces, Garnett wheeled south, toward his right flank.[10]

Pickett's Division

While Pettigrew's men crested Seminary Ridge to the north, Garnett's brigade marched into the swale east of Alexander's guns. On the left of the brigade, the 56th Virginia quickstepped with their weapons at trail arms over the ridge before closing to the right. Glancing over his shoulder, Private Robert D. Damron (Company D) fixed his eyes upon Pickett and Private Thomas R. Friend (Company C, 9th Virginia), the division color bearer and courier who were riding to the rear of the regiment. The headquarters flag rippled grandly in the breeze.[11]

Pickett, noticing that the division was generally drifting south, dressing on its own center, sent Friend with orders to correct the line of march. The courier found Garnett behind the 8th Virginia and ordered him to close to the left on Pettigrew.[12] Friend galloped away. Private George W. Hummer (Company H), Colonel Eppa Hunton's mounted orderly, turned to him and said, "Colonel Hunton, I don't think that order has been carried to General Kemper. Had not I better inform him of it?" The colonel agreed and Hummer took off on a southeasterly course toward the middle of Kemper's brigade.[13]

The 56th Virginia, correcting the alignment, extended the brigade line to the hedgerow which separated them from Fry's men, who had caught up with Garnett's left, and dragged the rest of the brigade with it.[14] By following the fence which separated Pickett's and Pettigrew's divisions, the line of march shifted from the southeast to the east. This pulled Pickett's brigades north and shortened his original front. Private James R. McPherson (Company C, 28th Virginia) gazed across the open fields toward Cemetery Ridge, and later recalled with the understatement of a man committed to the acceptance of his own mortality that he could "see" what he and his men were about to encounter.[15] First Lieutenant George W. Finley (Company K, 56th Virginia) looked up, as the brigade started into the first swale. Some Yankee skirmishers west of the Emmitsburg Road popped from cover and bolted for their own lines like flushed rabbits. At that moment, the steel glint of polished rifle barrels behind the low stone wall in the distance caught his attention.[16]

Spangler's Woods
Armistead's Brigade

Marching his brigade to the hill, Armistead briefly halted the line behind the guns on the first ridge. Walking over to Color Sergeant Leander C. Blackburn (Company E, 53rd Virginia) with Colonel Rawley Martin by his side, he asked him, "Sergeant, I want you and your men to plant your colors on those works. Do you think you can do it?" "Yes, sir," Blackburn honestly replied, "if God is willing." Armistead fished a flask of brandy from the satchel at his side and offered it to the sergeant. Blackburn took a small pull from it and handed it back.[17] With a voice that could be clearly heard above the din in the fields beyond, the general bellowed, "Right shoulder, shift arms. Forward, march." The commands traveled from the center to the brigade's flanks, and the men marched out at the quick step.[18] A military band on the right flank struck up a brisk tune, and the artillerymen, standing by their guns, waved their hats and cheered the brigade forward.[19]

While the center of Garnett's line topped the second ridge west of the Emmitsburg Road, Second Lieutenant W. Nathaniel Wood (Company A, 19th Virginia) looked behind him to see Armistead hurrying his regiments forward. They pressed on without wavering. "What a line of battle!" Wood mentally exclaimed. "How they keep together!" Turning about to tend to his section of the regimental line, the lieutenant cautioned his men. For a few moments, he mistakenly reassured himself that the Federal line had indeed collapsed. Then he noticed Cowan's and Fitzhugh's New Yorkers rolling into battery on the ridge south of the copse of trees.[20]

Cemetery Ridge
Sherrill's Brigade

The Rebels' skirmishers appeared first. Captain Winfield Scott (Company C, 126th New York) estimated them to be about two feet apart. A second and equally large skirmish line came out of the woods along Seminary Ridge about one hundred ten yards behind the first. Presently, a line of battle on brigade front stepped into the open at about the same distance from the second line. The Confederates carried their weapons at the right shoulder, bayonets fixed. The sun glistened and danced brilliantly off the burnished steel. "The whole line of battle looked like a stream or river of silver moving towards us," Scott recollected. The brigade officers and their orderlies followed the main line. The regimental flags flapped in the air. Presently a second brigade emerged into view. They all looked resplendent. Martial music from their regimental bands drifted across the fields.[21] The drum beats and the footsteps of the regiments reverberated off the hard ground in a mesmerizing cadence. "It was magnificent," Major Theodore Ellis (14th Connecticut) later wrote.[22] The men of the 14th Connecticut counted three brigade lines and a partial one behind them.[23] "Thank God!" an enlisted man in the 12th New Jersey shouted. "There comes the infantry!" Captain Richard S. Thompson (Company K, 12th New Jersey) agreed with him. It was far better to die fighting than to lie helpless under artillery fire.[24] Orders went throughout the brigade to hold its fire until the Rebels reached the Emmitsburg Road. In the prone 14th Connecticut one man insisted that if they listened carefully enough they could occasionally hear a Confederate officer shout, "Steady men, steady."[25] Lieutenant John L. Brady, commanding the depleted 1st Delaware, quickly surveyed his single line of men and wondered how they would ever hold against the

Confederates marching against them. At that moment, General Hays, whom the lieutenant adored, dismounted behind him. The general's silent, stoic presence calmed his fears.[26]

Company C, 1st Minnesota
The moment the shelling abated, Captain Wilson B. Farrell, the nominal commander of Company C, ordered First Lieutenant William Harmon to form the company and then stunned his subordinate by telling him he was going to take actual command. Farrell rarely assumed physical control in the field. As they started up the hill from Meade's Headquarters, an exploding shell mortally wounded Farrell.[27]

Federal Skirmishers
The skirmishers of the 8th Ohio saw the Confederates' bayonets glint against the tree line. "Boys," Captain Wells W. Miller (Company H) cautioned his men, "they are going to make a charge. See that your guns are in order."[28] He had no intention of buckling under their advance. At the same time, Colonel Clinton MacDougall detached First Lieutenant John I. Brinkerhoff and Company I of the 111th New York to the skirmish line on the right of the 8th Ohio. While the bulk of his line went to the front, Brinkerhoff and the picket reserve took cover in the Emmitsburg Road. Looking west, he fastened his eyes upon a solitary beech tree near the road. A 3-inch shell had bored a perfectly symmetrical hole through its trunk without snapping the trunk off.[29]

Seminary Ridge
Garnett's Brigade
When the brigade reached the second ridge, Rittenhouse's Parrotts on Little Round Top ripped into them. Rather than tear down the worm fence across their path, the 56th Virginia scrambled over it, then halted to reform.[30] A shell roared into the regiment. Exploding over Company D, it killed Third Lieutenant William E. Jones and Second Corporal James W. Spencer while wounding Privates James H. and William J. Banton and William J. Bishop.[31]

The Confederates pressed on through the terrible barrage which the guns on Little Round Top and Cemetery Hill laid into them. Another shell slammed into the company on Company K's right, catching it squarely on the flank as it shifted left to close a gap in the line. The lieutenant swore that a single explosion knocked out no less than thirty-five men. The regiment became engulfed in a walking wall of iron and flame. Projectiles burst everywhere—between the file closers and the rear rank, in front of the line—following the course of the line as it advanced. Colonel William D. Stuart never reached the second hollow. A shell fragment brought him down among the young corn shoots on the top of the second ridge, mortally wounded.[32]

The 28th Virginia developed a bulge in its line when Captain Michael P. Spessard (Company C), commanding the right wing, picked up the pace. Colonel Robert C. Allen ordered him to slow down, stay aligned with the colors and keep pace with the left wing.[33] Farther to the right, in the center of the brigade, Second Lieutenant W. Nathaniel Wood (Company A, 19th Virginia) audibly reassured himself, "That hill must fall." "Steady, boys." "Don't fire." "Close up." He found himself admonishing his men, though, in the pandemonium, it did not seem to him that he was actually talking. "Never mind the skirmish line," he warned as the Yankees along the Emmitsburg Road raced for Cemetery Ridge.[34] Well he should have warned his men. With each incoming round soldiers dropped from the ranks. Some were hit. Some went down, feigning injury. As the line went forward, the slightly wounded and the disheartened got up and walked to the rear.

1st Minnesota
Despite the gaps cut through their lines by the Yankee artillery, the Confederates closed up as if on parade and continued to march forward without hardly breaking step. The westerners admired their courage as only fellow soldiers could. The Confederates absorbed the fire like the professionals they were.[35] "No one who saw them could help admiring the steadiness with which they came on, like the shadow of a cloud seen from a distance as it sweeps across a sunny field," Captain John D. S. Cook (Company I, 80th New York) recollected.[36]

Trimble's Division
Farther to the north, Brigadier General Isaac R. Trimble, having personally admonished Lane's and Lowrance's brigades to withhold their fire until the Yankee line broke, assured them he would go with them to the limits of the advance. Hoping to avoid walking into the rounds which passed through or over Pettigrew's men, he held his men back until about one hundred fifty yards separated the two divisions. His men stepped out with the same precision as those to his front. "...with the deliberation and accuracy of men on drill," he later recalled.[37] Lowrance held the right of the line. Lane had the left. Trimble, being centered on them to the front, rode ahead of them to direct their lines of march.[38]

The Federal Position
Cemetery Hill and Cemetery Ridge
Alexander ordered the charge to commence believing his gunners had silenced every gun along the entire Union line when in reality he had permanently silenced only eight guns (Brown's and Rorty's) and had forced them to quit the field. Cushing's and Woodruff's had expended everything but their canister. Arnold withdrew because the battery had no ammunition left. Dow's four Napoleons on the left of McGilvery's line and the fifteen pieces on the right of his position as well as the eight field pieces from the

Cavalry Corps Artillery Reserve had ceased fire. Osborn's thirty-eight silent field pieces on Cemetery Hill added to the ominous quiet. Within a quarter of an hour the Confederates believed they had eliminated no less than one hundred five guns, when, in reality, they had only disabled fourteen and forced another twenty, on Cemetery Hill, to direct their fire toward Benner's Hill.

While the Confederates formed for their charge, the Federals brought more guns into the line. Captain Frederick Edgell's four Ordnance Rifles (Battery A, 1st New Hampshire Artillery) moved from the Baltimore Pike into Norton's former position.[39] At the same time, no less than five more batteries were swinging into battery along the Federal line. Lieutenant Gulian V. Weir's Regulars (Battery C, 5th U.S.) attempted to wheel into line southeast of Rorty's former position, but General Newton stopped the guns before they broke over the top of Cemetery Ridge. The general did not want 12-pounders on the line and sent them back to the reserve.[40] (Weir, who suffered from a severely ulcerated throat, refused to go to the hospital before the action opened.)[41] Lieutenant Augustus Parsons' Battery A, 1st New Jersey (six 10-pounders), having been ordered on the field by Hunt in person, did not check in with Newton. The battery unlimbered on the ridge northeast of Thompson's Pennsylvanians. Battery K, 1st New York, Captain Robert H. Fitzhugh commanding, with its six 3-inch rifles, followed farther to the right, northeast of the 9th Michigan.[42] Sterling's 2nd Connecticut Battery, consisting of four 10-pounder James guns, filled the space between the 3rd Pennsylvania Heavy Artillery and Dow's Mainers. Going into battery behind the 116th Pennsylvania, the four James guns were unlimbered and prepared to fire.[43] Captain Nelson Ames' Battery G, 1st New York Light Artillery (six 12-pounders) finished the line on the left to the Weikert house. With Cowan's guns redeploying to Cushing's left, not counting Rittenhouse, who had two of six 10-pounder Parrotts on Little Round Top which could bear down on any troops coming off Seminary Ridge, there were ninety-eight guns along Cemetery Ridge waiting to open upon the two divisions which were marching toward them.[44]

Cushing's Battery

Two incoming rounds sailed over Cushing's gunners into the caissons and limbers behind the ridge. One gutted a horse before exploding inside the one next to it. The other burst under one of the drivers, Private Arsenal H. Griffin, who with his horse, went down in a ghastly heap of entrails and pulverized flesh. Looking behind him, Private Christopher Smith saw Griffin futilely trying to repack his intestines into his torn abdomen. Deliberately putting the muzzle of his service revolver to his temple, he moaned, "Good-bye, boys," and blew his brains out. [45]

Cushing, who was bleeding from a bullet wound which carried away his right shoulder strap, no longer had enough men to handle his guns. He

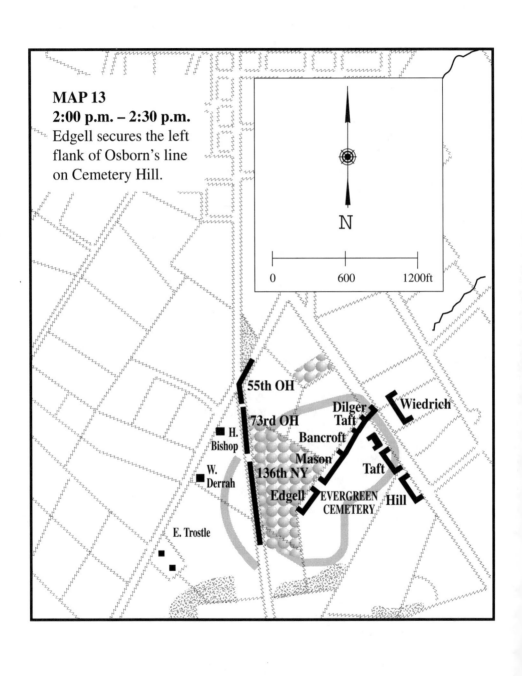

MAP 13
2:00 p.m. – 2:30 p.m.
Edgell secures the left
flank of Osborn's line
on Cemetery Hill.

N

0   600   1200ft

55th OH

Wiedrich

Dilger
Taft

73rd OH

Bancroft

H.
Bishop

Mason
136th NY

Taft

W.
Derrah

Edgell

EVERGREEN
CEMETERY

Hill

E. Trostle

ran over behind the ridge to the right front of the 72nd Pennsylvania, which was lying behind his caissons, to get some volunteers.[46] Major Samuel Roberts (72nd Pennsylvania) saw Cushing approach Webb, who was standing close by, and distinctly heard the lieutenant explain, "Webb, see, pretty much all of my men are disabled. If I had some men I could still work my guns."[47] Cushing then asked if he could move his guns forward toward the wall. Webb assented. Cushing went back to the north side of the copse of trees and gave the command to move the pieces.[48] As he stepped between the trails of Numbers Three and Four guns, a minie ball ripped through his scrotum, carrying away his testicles. Clamping his left hand over his bleeding crotch, he screamed for First Sergeant Frederick Fuger to stand by his side to relay orders. The sergeant, noticing how much pain his

Brigadier General Alexander Webb

He won the Medal of Honor at Gettysburg for his defense of the Angle and the copse of trees.

MOLLUS, USAMHI

lieutenant was in, told him to go to the rear. "No," Cushing grimaced, "I stay right here and fight it out or die in the attempt."[49]

Cowan's Battery

Webb personally directed Cowan's guns into Brown's former position. The general kept pointing west. Cowan looked up in time to see Garnett's skirmishers springing forward from the crest closest to Seminary Ridge and then understood why he had been ordered to cease fire.

Counting the report of each piece as it was brought to bear, he heard only five shots. His lead gun was nowhere in sight, having gotten detached in the confusion of the maneuver. Automatically assuming it had gone too far north, Cowan spurred his horse around the eastern side of the copse of trees to look for it. He found the stray gun, under Corporal Peter Mulally on the north side of the trees, within six yards of Cushing's Number Six rifle, unable to open fire.[50] Turning to Cushing, who was nearby, he blurted an apology for crowding the lieutenant's battery and noticed that Cushing had been wounded in the right shoulder and that he was bleeding from both legs. Turning around, Cushing rasped out, "By hand to the front." The two officers exchanged amenities, then returned to their guns. Cushing, in rolling his four serviceable ordnance rifles to within forty yards of the stone wall, closed the intervals between the pieces to nine yards.[51]

Stannard's Brigade

General Stannard glanced through the settling smoke. "There they come," he shouted. Lieutenant George Benedict, his A.D.C., noted how every man within his immediate range of sight snatched up his weapon. His heart palpitated at the scene unfolding before him.[52] The officers of the 13th Vermont trooped the line from company to company. "Steady, boys. Hold your position," they warned, "don't fire until the word is given, keep cool, lie low till [the] order is given to fire, make ready, take good aim, fire low."[53]

Sherrill's Brigade

General Hays, whose division held Ziegler's Grove, came alive. He cried out, "Now boys, look out; you will see some fun."[54] With that he moved his second line to the top of the ridge. The 126th New York with the 108th New York on its left marched out together. Behind the two regiments Lieutenant Colonel Francis E. Pierce (108th New York) locked arms with Captain Winfield Scott (Company C, 126th New York), his former classmate from the University of Rochester. "Well, Scott," Pierce said with deliberate understatement, "we have sat beside each other in the classroom many a day; but this is a new experience. This isn't much like digging out Greek roots."[55]

While those two regiments moved forward, Hays trotted back to the 125th New York and ordered the regiment to its feet. Flanking the New Yorkers south about 620 yards, he threw them into line below the brow of Cemetery Ridge on the eastern side of Brian's orchard. Without giving them a chance to take cover behind the dilapidated stone wall along their front, Hays pushed them over the top of the hill and down the western slope of the ridge to a position behind the 12th New Jersey and the 1st Delaware.[56]

Alexander's Artillery Support

Having left Garnett as the brigade descended into the swale between the first and the second ridges, Alexander returned to his artillery line. Despite the incoming Federal artillery rounds, most of which were directed toward the infantry, he rode from gun to gun. Starting with McCarthy's section of Napoleons on the far left of his line, he instructed each gunner to check his ammunition supply. Any gun with fifteen or more long range projectiles was to limber and follow the infantry toward the Emmitsburg Road. The others were to wait until the infantry advanced far enough to the front to fire over their heads and engage in counterbattery fire with the Federals.[57]

Sporadically along the line, drivers mounted up and brought their limbers to the guns. McCarthy's two Napoleons, followed to the right by

Lieutenant Columbus W. Motes' two howitzers and two 10-pounder Parrotts, rolled east into the hollow beyond the first ridge.[58] Continuing toward the Peach Orchard, Alexander ordered Battles' section of the 4th Company Washington Artillery and Brown's section of the 1st Company Washington Artillery with Moody's four 24-pounder howitzers to Dearing to support Pickett's flank.[59] While Alexander struggled to support the charge, the attack was getting away from him.

Pettigrew's Advance

The Federal rifled pieces opened fire as soon as the Confederates descended into the swale west of Bliss' orchard, gouging bloody holes in Fry's and Marshall's brigades. The Alabamians and Tennesseeans closed ranks as if on parade and kept on going.[60] At this point their bands quit the field. (They were needed to evacuate the casualties.)[61] Knocking down the first fence by hand or with their bayonets, they quickly moved into the low ground.[62] Private Wiley Woods (Company F, 1st Tennessee), carrying the regimental colors, looked around him. He never heard Stant Denson, who had been by his side, go down. Woods shouted at Private Thom Denson (Company C), who stood nearby, to take the colors if the Yankees dropped him. Denson agreed.[63]

Farther to the north, Lieutenant William Peel (Company C, 11th Mississippi) watched in awe as the overshots from the guns on Cemetery Hill splintered the tree line behind them. As the Federals adjusted their range, fragments thudded into the line.[64]

Cemetery Ridge
Hays' Division

Captain Winfield Scott (Company C, 126th New York) thought for a brief amount of time that the Confederates were not going to hit his sector of the line. One quarter of a mile across the field, however, they left half wheeled, moving northeast. The captain could see from the length of the lines that their left flank would hit the right flank, where his brigade was waiting, head on. He watched them so transfixed by the grandeur of their precision that he paid no attention to the Confederate shells bursting around him. Solomon's Song 6:10 suddenly popped into his head. "Fair as the moon, bright as the sun, and terrible as an army with banners," he muttered to himself, as if to subconsciously affirm the truth of the Scriptures.[65]

Pettigrew's Division

The Confederates did not plan the left half wheel which Captain Scott observed. Pettigrew's flank, in closing to the right, herded his two northern brigades into Fry's men.[66] The crowding, coupled with several accurate hits from Osborn's artillery on Cemetery Hill, rattled Marshall's line as they came out of the swale west of Bliss' orchard. Men streamed from the ranks in squads. Marshall valiantly tried to turn them back until a shell knocked him from his horse. With a large number of his men passing around them, an aide shoved the wounded colonel back into the saddle and, at Marshall's insistence, turned the mount toward the front.

The commotion caught Pickett's attention. After dispatching two of his aides, Captain Edward R. Baird and First Lieutenant W. Stuart Symington, to the north to stem the Carolinians' rout, he sent Captain Bright to the rear with orders to find Longstreet and to tell him the division could take the works but would have to have reinforcements to hold them.[67]

Symington and Baird failed to curb the stampede. Symington snatched at the 47th North Carolina's colors but succeeded only in tearing it from its staff. Like two boulders in a fast-moving stream, the two aides remained immobile and useless. Discouraged, they rode back to where they had last seen Garnett's brigade, only to discover that Pickett had galloped south toward Kemper's left flank as it advanced toward the crest of the hill immediately west of the Rogers house.[68]

Nothing could stop the refugees from Marshall's brigade. The panic spread to the left to Davis' regiments. Lieutenant William Peel of the 11th Mississippi, amid the terrifying scream of incoming shells and the numbing bursts, heard something he had never believed possible among the stalwarts of the Army of Northern Virginia. "Steady, boys." "Slow," a number of officers cautioned. "Don't break yourselves down by running."[69] A considerable number of men—mostly from the terribly decimated 2nd and 42nd Mississippi regiments—joined the rout.[70] Pettigrew immediately ordered Lieutenant William B. Shepard, his aide, into their ranks to stop them. He also failed to turn the retreating soldiers back.[71] They skirted around the leveled bayonets of the 7th North Carolina as it came down from the tree line on the right flank of Lane's brigade and escaped to the safety of the western slope of Seminary Ridge.[72] The front line on the northern end of the field shrank approximately 600 feet before it reached the eastern side of Bliss' orchard.

Kemper's Brigade

Having been informed by Private George W. Hummer (Company H, 8th Virginia) to dress to the left, Kemper could see Garnett's line, in the second hollow, guiding farther to the north as it followed the easterly running fence line on that flank. Had Garnett marched southeast there would have been about 352 feet separating the two brigades when he came abreast of Kemper. However, with the Federal guns continually reducing his front, the gulf between the two commands widened immensely long before they aligned with one another.[73]

Leaving their dead, wounded and disabled on the ground, Kemper's Virginians closed ranks to the north for about two hundred feet. At that point the regiments flanked about another three hundred feet to the north, then fronted, which put the 11th Virginia squarely in front of the Rogers house.[74] Color Bearer William M. Lawson, Sergeants Patrick Woods and Theodore R. Martin, Corporal John Q. Figg and Private William Mitchell automatically marched four paces to the front center of the 1st Virginia with the regimental flag. By the time the brigade stepped off at the common time toward the top of the hill, it had lost about 500 feet of the line to the sun and incoming artillery fire.[75] Longstreet's total command, which had begun the charge on about a 5,700-foot front, had been reduced to around 4,400 feet. The justifiably feint-hearted accounted for a large number of the "casualties."

From the top of the ridge, Adjutant James B. Johnson (5th Florida) rolled onto his side and saw the Virginians coming toward him. One of the Virginians collapsed on top of Johnson. The startled adjutant briefly caught a glimpse of the man's face and asked him if he was wounded. "No, sir," the frightened soldier blurted, "but I can't go forward. I know I am disgracing my family, but I can't go." The lieutenant punched him with his sword hilt and told him to roll off him and head to the rear. The unnerved Virginian asked where it was. Johnson pointed it out to him. Unbuckling his cartridge box, the soldier took off at a run for Seminary Ridge.[76]

Major Kirkwood Otey (11th Virginia) sent Adjutant H. Valentine Harris to Captain James R. Hutter (Company H) with orders to move his wing around the house. Hutter shot back that the maneuver should be done by regiment because the obstacle was too big. Nonetheless, he commanded "by right of company to the front." When he realized that his last company would not clear the house, he ordered the left company to move by the left flank to the front.[77]

The shifting of his line to the left bunched up the brigade's advance, forcing the 3rd Virginia, on the left of Kemper's line, once it cleared the front of the batteries, to march north.[78] The Rogers House nearly destroyed Kemper's formation. McGilvery's Artillery along Cemetery Ridge and Rittenhouse's pieces at Little Round Top devastated the ranks of the 11th Virginia. Within seconds after passing around the house, Adjutant Harris informed Captain Hutter that Major Otey was wounded. Hutter, who was desperately trying to reform the right wing of the regiment, told Harris to give Captain Andrew J. Jones (Company I) the right wing. Jones was wounded, Harris informed him. Hutter then yelled for Captain David G. Houston, Jr. (Company D), but he also had been mortally wounded. What about the captain's brother, Captain Andrew M. Houston (Company K)? Presumed dead, Harris responded. The situation seemed beyond redemption. With no captains remaining with his right wing and with the 24th Virginia closing up on his right flank, Hutter quickly found himself losing control of his regiment.

Federal Skirmishers

Many of the Federal skirmishers, south of the Ohioans and west of the Emmitsburg Road were not as game for a fight.[79] The men from the

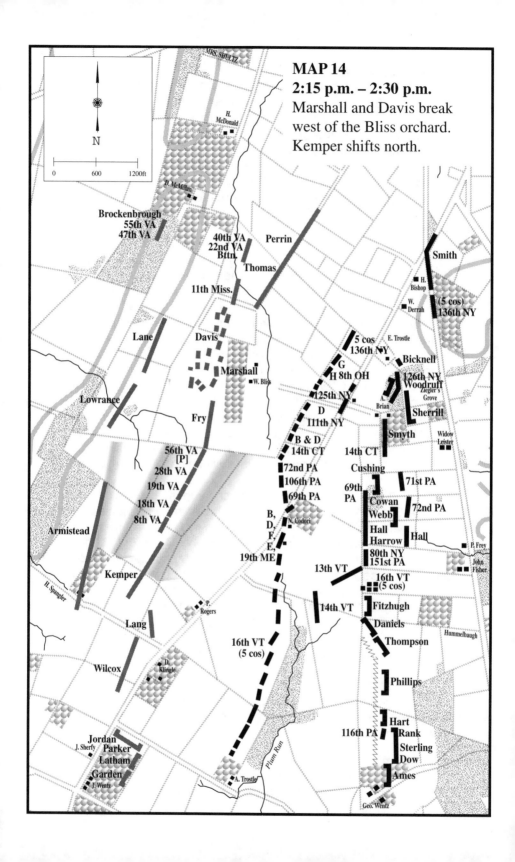

MAP 14
2:15 p.m. – 2:30 p.m.
Marshall and Davis break
west of the Bliss orchard.
Kemper shifts north.

MRS. SHULTZ

H. McDonald

D. McMillan

Brockenbrough
55th VA
47th VA

40th VA
22nd VA
Bttn.

Perrin

Thomas

11th Miss.

Smith

H. Bishop

W. Derrah

(5 cos)
136th NY

Lane

Davis

Marshall

W. Bliss

5 cos
136th NY

E. Trostle

Bicknell

G
H 8th OH

126th NY
Woodruff
Ziegler's Grove

Lowrance

Fry

125th NY

D
111th NY

A. Brian

Sherrill

Smyth

Widow Leister

56th VA
[P]

28th VA

19th VA

18th VA

8th VA

B & D
14th CT

72nd PA

106th PA

69th PA

14th CT

Cushing

71st PA

69th PA

Cowan

Webb

72nd PA

Armistead

B, D, F, E,
19th ME

N. Codori

Hall

Harrow

Hall

P. Frey

John Fisher

80th NY
151st PA

Kemper

13th VT

16th VT
(5 cos)

H. Spangler

P. Rogers

14th VT

Fitzhugh

Lang

Daniels

Hummelbaugh

Thompson

Wilcox

D. Klingle

16th VT
(5 cos)

Phillips

Hart

Rank

Sterling

Dow

Jordan

J. Sherfy

Parker

Latham

Garden

J. Wentz

116th PA

Ames

A. Trostle

Geo. Wentz

Plum Run

N

0   600   1200ft

125th New York and Company D of the 111th New York peeled back toward the main line. Companies B and D from the 14th Connecticut retired toward their own lines. In hurrying across the road, Privates James Inglis and William H. Hall (Company B) realized that Private Augustus Guild was not dead. Picking up Guild between them, they staggered toward the stone wall on Cemetery Ridge. Their comrades yelled at them to drop him and run before they lost their own lives. They refused. Rifle balls zipped about them. Every now and then other members of Companies B and D turned to pop off rounds at the Confederates who were closing in on them. Under their protection, Hall and Inglis safely brought in Guild.[80]

The contingent from the 69th, 106th, and the 72nd Pennsylvania regiments did not take to their heels. Their fierce resistance forced Garnett's skirmishers back into the brigade line, temporarily stalling the charge.[81] At the same time, the eight front companies of the 71st Pennsylvania at the western wall of the Angle emptied their rifles at long range into the 56th Virginia on the left of the brigade line.[82] Some of the Virginians returned fire.[83]

Farther to the south, the four companies from the 19th Maine and the battalion of the 16th Vermont, in the hollow southeast of Codori's, remained at their posts. From where he lay in the low ground to the left of the barn, Private Silas Adams (Company F, 19th Maine), who was facing southwest, could see nothing. The ridge along the Emmitsburg Road blocked his line of sight toward the Confederate lines. The sun had "cooked" him as he put it. He felt nearly dead from the suffocating heat, and like a hunter who had lain too still for too long in one spot waiting for his game to appear, he suddenly became aware of the heaviness of his own legs. They had gone completely numb. He feared he would not be able to stand when the Rebs hit their line.[84]

Kemper's Brigade

Kemper, glancing north, quickly realized that the distance between him and Garnett had expanded to over 200 yards and that Garnett was taking a pounding from the skirmishers west of the Codori House. He had to do something to restore the line and to drive the Federals back across the road. Placing Colonel Mayo in command of the brigade's left wing, he ordered the 3rd Virginia to flank to the left and to connect with Garnett's men as soon as they came on line. With that he rode toward Garnett's brigade, to warn him to rectify his alignment.[85] Pinned against the fence on the western side of the Emmitsburg Road, the bloodied Virginians filed quickly to the north, into the hollow in front of the third ridge.

The 3rd Virginia, while executing the maneuver under a terrifying flank fire from the Yankee guns on Little Round Top, and from McGilvery's guns on Cemetery Ridge, maintained its formation.[86] Pickett, who was supervising the division's alignment by himself, noticed that Kemper's men had not yet connected with Garnett's brigade. He instructed Mayo for the second time to maintain the proper interval with Garnett. Mayo turned to his men, and Pickett commanded the brigade to double-quick and to give the Yankees a cheer. While the regiments began straightening themselves out by quickstepping into the swale above the Rogers house, the general galloped along the eastern face of the ridge toward the center of the line.[87]

Mayo watched Pickett go into the hollow. Without warning, a large group of men turned about and surged toward the rear. Pickett and his aides, who had finally joined him, spurred in among them, futilely urging them back into the ranks.[88] Turning to his brother, Charles, Pickett sent him galloping to the rear to find Longstreet. The division needed vigorous and immediate support.[89] At the same time, Kemper dashed to the front of Armistead's brigade as it descended the slope. Prancing his frisky sorrel along the line, with their cheers resounding through the low ground, he ordered the brigade forward to close the gap created by Garnett's rapidly shrinking line.[90]

Garnett pranced his horse along the front of his command. "Cease firing," he shouted.[91] Colonel Eppa Hunton (8th Virginia) found Captain Michael P. Spessard (Company C, 28th Virginia) on the ground cradling a young man's head in his lap. Looking up at Hunton, Spessard plaintively drawled, "Look at my poor boy, Colonel." Hunton assumed that the mortally wounded boy had already died by the way Spessard sat there. Presently, the battle-hardened captain gently kissed his Hezekiah and rested his head on the ground. Rising, Spessard shouldered his sword and charged after his company, crying, "Forward, boys!"[92] Loading as they advanced, the Virginians reformed and swept toward the remaining Federal skirmishers around the Codori orchard.[93] Second Lieutenant W. Nathaniel Wood (Company A, 19th Virginia) noticed how much the line had shrunk in all of the confusion and naturally attributed it to combat attrition.[94] By then, even with Kemper's brigade on its flank, the two brigades covered only about a 1,400-foot front—a loss of over fifty percent of their original strengths.

Pettigrew's Division

Simultaneously Brigadier General Isaac Trimble, who was riding in front of the colors of the 7th North Carolina, saw Pettigrew's line stumble into the creek bottom which cut through the swale east of Bliss' orchard. To his astonishment, a great many of the 11th North Carolina and the 26th North Carolina on the left of Marshall's line remained behind, while the right wing (the 47th and the 52nd North Carolina) charged toward the front under a terrible plunging fire of shell and case shot.[95] About 800 feet of Pettigrew's original 3,300-foot line remained intact. He did not have enough men to smash the Federal right.

Meanwhile, Colonel William S. Christian and his two regiments from Brockenbrough's brigade, having run from Seminary Ridge, caught up with the right of their brigade as is neared the Long Lane and the security of the

Confederate line stationed in there. Rather than halt, Christian took the 47th and the 55th Virginia regiments over the road bank into the fields southwest of the small 8th Ohio and immediately came under a horrendous, but inaccurate skirmish fire. The regiments halted in formation and did nothing.[96] With his men closing rapidly upon the creek, Trimble deliberately studied Pickett's advance to his right front, where the artillery fire had seemed to have subsided. Squads of Virginians turned back from Garnett's line without having reached the Emmitsburg Road.[97]

Armistead's Brigade

Their unsteadiness affected Armistead's regiments as well. Prior to the charge, Captain Richard Logan, Jr. (Company H, 14th Virginia) personally instructed his file closers to assign themselves to the company's chronic "playouts" and to "take them into the fight or kill them." It did not matter to him whether the Yankees killed them or the file closers did. Logan said he would take personal responsibility for any who died from friendly fire. Fifth Sergeant Drewry B. Easley singled out Private James L. White, a former classmate of his, the biggest shirk in the company. During the last stage of the charge before reaching the Emmitsburg Road, White fell to the ground with a cry about being wounded. While the regiment continued forward, Easley leaned over White and demanded he show blood. At that, the teenage private sprang to his feet, and sprinting forward, dodged between the space separating the 14th Virginia from the 57th Virginia. Third Sergeant Calvin Garner, the file closer to Easley's left, immediately cocked his weapon and took off at a dead run behind the 57th while Easley broke through the ranks and dashed along the front of the regiment. The elusive White evaded them in all of the confusion. By the time they stopped running, the 14th Virginia had crossed the Emmitsburg Road.[98]

Spangler's Woods

While Pickett attempted to restore Garnett's shattered line, Captain Robert Bright found himself riding among the stragglers from his own division who had quit the field before it reached that last hollow. At one point he halted a rather large squad and asked them if they would right about face and assist those brave men who were carrying the charge forward. "What are you running for?" he plaintively asked. An enlisted man with a very confused expression upon his face stared back at the aide and exclaimed, somewhat astonished, "Why, good gracious, Captain, ain't you runnin' yourself?" Taken aback by the man's unabashed honesty, Bright realized that for all appearances he seemed to be leaving the field also. Without saying another word, he spurred his horse toward Woolfolk's silent battery on the crest of the first ridge.

He found Longstreet sitting on the fence along the northern edge of Spangler's Woods, staring blankly into the trees to the south. Swarms of men, some lame and many sound limped or meandered across the open

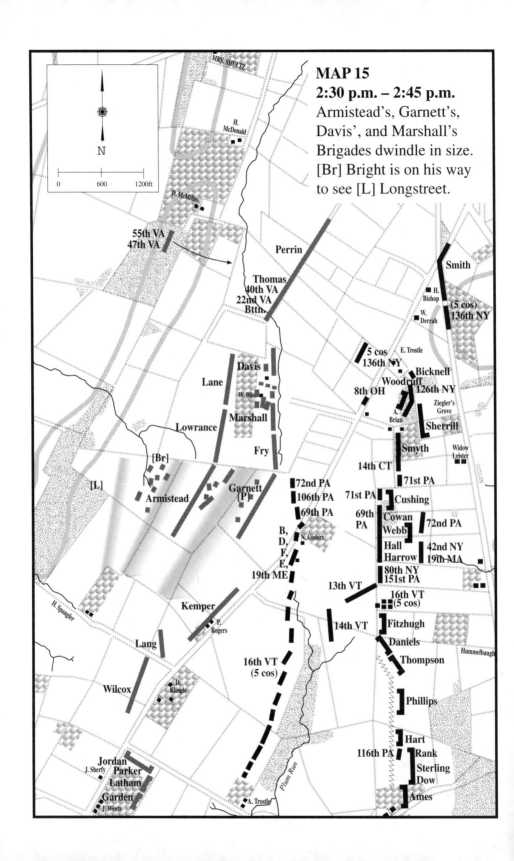

MAP 15
2:30 p.m. – 2:45 p.m.
Armistead's, Garnett's,
Davis', and Marshall's
Brigades dwindle in size.
[Br] Bright is on his way
to see [L] Longstreet.

ground behind the general. Bright rode up to the general, and after exchanging amenities, delivered his message from Pickett. "Where are the troops that were placed on your flank?" Longstreet asked. "Look over your shoulder and you will see them," Bright replied. Longstreet calmly twisted about but said nothing. Before he had turned south again, Colonel Arthur Fremantle spurred to a halt near the two officers. "I wouldn't have missed this for anything!" he exclaimed. "The devil you wouldn't," Longstreet shot back with a snide laugh. "I would have liked to have missed it very much! We've attacked, and been repulsed. Look there!"

Fremantle glanced in the direction of the general's nod. The field to the east was filled with Pickett's men who were sullenly walking to the rear. Pickett took the guns, Longstreet mistakenly asserted, but in twenty minutes had been forced to retire. "The charge is over," the amazed Bright heard him say. He could not understand how the general could make such an assertion when Pickett's regiments had not yet crossed the Emmitsburg Road, but were in the last hollow west of the road. [99] Major James Dearing, who remained on the first ridge throughout the advance, could have verified Longstreet's assertion. Pickett's division started losing men to desertion from the moment Garnett's brigade crested the second ridge. The whole affair had been unraveling since it began.[100] "Captain Bright," Longstreet matter-of-factly continued, "ride to General Pickett and tell him what you have heard me say to Colonel Fremantle." The captain wheeled about and had run about ten feet when the general called out, "Captain Bright!" Turning half around in the saddle he heard the general yell, while pointing, "Tell General Pickett that Wilcox's Brigade is in that orchard, and he can order him in to his assistance."[101]

The Ridge West of the Emmitsburg Road

Bright spurred his horse into a gallop and found Pickett about 100 yards west of the Emmitsburg Road on the western slope of the rise behind Kemper's right rear. Upon receiving Longstreet's order to send in Wilcox, Pickett immediately dispatched Captain Edward R. Baird to the hillside south of the Rogers house to fetch the brigade. Seconds later, he repeated the same directive to Lieutenant W. Stuart Symington and sent him clattering toward Wilcox. The lieutenant had barely left before Pickett turned to Robert Bright with the emphatic directive, "Captain Bright, you go." Running a hellish gauntlet of small arms and artillery fire from the southern end of the Federal line, the young aide raced for the top of the Rogers' hill.

Wilcox, his arms raised to stop Bright, waved him aside with, "I know; I know." The captain, while struggling with his heaving mount shouted back, "But, General, I must deliver my message."[102]

The Peach Orchard

Pickett, rather than wait for his officers to return, moved south along the west side of the road. Accompanied by Private Thomas R. Friend (Company C, 9th Virginia), who carried the division colors, he stopped on the high ground near the Sherfy barn, across from the Peach Orchard.[103] Major John C. Haskell, on his way across the Emmitsburg Road to his batteries in the Peach Orchard, saw the general standing near the barn, but did not have time to exchange amenities. Passing behind Jordan and Parker's guns, the major reined to a halt behind Latham's and Garden's guns on the eastern face of the orchard and immediately ordered Latham's three Napoleons and Garden's section of 12-Pounders to assist the charge from the flank.[104] The crews had limbered the five guns and moved them toward the front before Pickett's division crossed the Emmitsburg Road.[105]

The Angle

The 69th Pennsylvania remained prone along the western wall of the Angle. The officers bawled the regiment to its knees. Admonishing them not to fire until they could see the whites of the Rebels' eyes, Colonel Dennis O'Kane continued by reminding them they were defending their home soil. The Rebs were going to make a determined charge, but he knew that his boys were as brave as the Rebs. They had nothing to gain but the praise of the nation for holding their posts until the death or a quick death from the man standing next to them should they show the white feather and run. "And let your work this day be for victory or death," he further warned them. While the colonel tended to the right wing of the regiment, General Webb delivered a similar brave up talk to the left wing.[106] "Boys," he said, "don't fire until they get over that fence [pointing toward the Emmitsburg Road]. If you do as well today as you did yesterday, I will be satisfied."[107]

Pettigrew's Division

In coming out of the low ground onto the rise west of the Emmitsburg Road, Pettigrew's division presented its entire front to the Federal guns on Cemetery Hill while simultaneously walking into the picket fire from the Yankee skirmishers along the Emmitsburg Road. Second Lieutenant John H. Moore (Company B, 7th Tennessee) never forgot how the intense smoke from the bursting projectiles obscured everything around him with a "darkened magnificence."[108]

A bullet found its mark in Sergeant Major Thomas Davidson, who bore the flag of the 14th Tennessee. He shouted to Sergeant Robert Mockbee (Company B), "Bob, take the flag. I am shot." Several feet later, Private Columbus Horn (Company G) took the flag from him because he insisted it belonged to his company. Hardly fifty feet beyond, Horn got hit and Mockbee took the colors back. Color Corporal George B. Powell (Company C) took them from Mockbee and carried them forward.[109]

Kemper's Brigade

By the time Kemper connected with Garnett's right flank, they walked into the Mainers who were on the skirmish line in the Emmitsburg Road in front of the Codori house. The New Englanders did not stand on orders as the companies on the right of the line stood up and fell back.[110] Having left his skirmish line on its own hook east of the Rogers house, Kemper fronted his men. Small detachments sprang from the right of his line and rushed the Emmitsburg Road. Private Silas Adams (Company F, 19th Maine), who was lying in the field about 135 feet east of the road, watched those men tear down the fence on both sides of the road from the Codori house south along the Federals' front.[111]

Pettigrew's Division

When Fry's brigade reached the last post and rail fence west of the Emmitsburg Road, the concussions from the Federal guns and from their own, which were then sporadically firing over their heads, had become so loud that the officers could not hear shouted commands above the din.[112] The 14th Tennessee made short work of the obstruction and pressed forward.[113] The 71st Pennsylvania laid a devastating fire into the brigade's front. According to Second Lieutenant John H. Moore (Company B, 7th Tennessee) volley after volley culled the ranks in large numbers before the regiment ever reached the road. The 7th Tennessee hit the plank fence on their side of the road and spilled into it like cattle falling off a precipice. What was left of the brigade pressed itself onto the packed dirt. The very frightened lieutenant twisted his head around in time to see two mounted officers, one of whom was covered with blood, race along the rear of the line. His eyes never let go of them until one of them went down with his horse in a heap and the other disappeared along the Bliss farm lane. Rifle fire and canister pattered the rails like rain striking a roof in a down pour.[114] Private John McLeer (Company F, 1st Tennessee) moved in close to the color bearer, Wiley Woods, Thom Denson (Company F) having gone down before reaching the road. Woods told him to keep his eyes on the colors and take the flag if the Yankees cut him down.[115]

The 11th Mississippi, having lost so many men to the horrendous deluge of canister for the last hundred yards, did not have enough men to form a company at full strength. Second Lieutenant John V. Moore (Company A) ran to the front of Company D, trying to hold the line back to preserve its alignment with the rest of the division. Sergeant Andrew J. Baker (Company A) screamed at him, "John, for heaven's sake, give the command to charge." He yelled back he did not have the authority to take such a responsibility to which the impetuous Baker took it upon himself to order the charge. Those who could dropped into the road to catch their wind for the final advance. A round knocked Baker down before he reached the middle of the road.[116]

The 14th Connecticut

As the Rebels neared the Emmitsburg Road someone noticed a number of men in the 14th Connecticut praying. Another stared vacantly ahead,

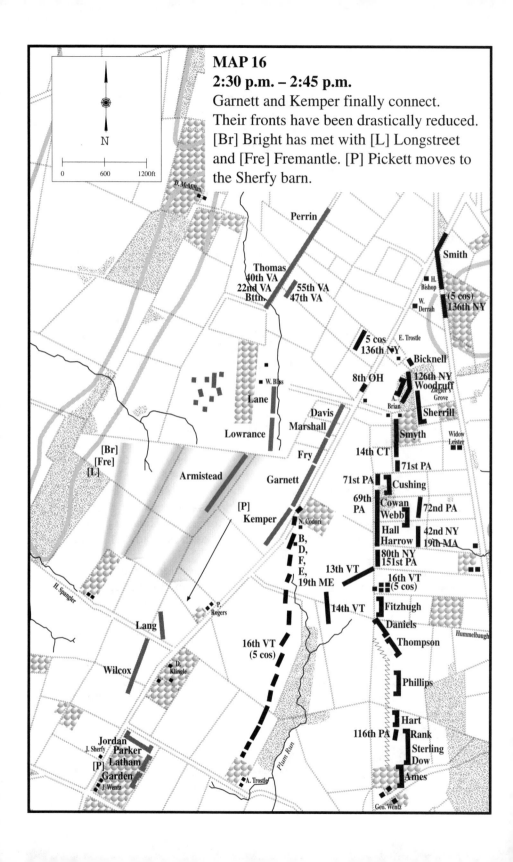

MAP 16
2:30 p.m. – 2:45 p.m.
Garnett and Kemper finally connect.
Their fronts have been drastically reduced.
[Br] Bright has met with [L] Longstreet
and [Fre] Fremantle. [P] Pickett moves to
the Sherfy barn.

N

0   600   1200ft

D. McMillan

Perrin

Smith

Thomas
40th VA
22nd VA
Bttn.
55th VA
47th VA

H. Bishop

W. Derrah

(5 cos)
136th NY

5 cos
136th NY

E. Trostle

Bicknell

8th OH

126th NY
Woodruff

Ziegler
Grove

W. Bliss

Lane

A. Brian

Sherrill

Davis
Marshall

Smyth

Widow
Leister

Lowrance

Fry

14th CT

71st PA

[Br]
[Fre]
[L]

Armistead

Garnett

71st PA

Cushing

69th
PA

Cowan
Webb

72nd PA

[P]
Kemper

N. Codori

Hall
Harrow

42nd NY
19th MA

B,
D,
F,
E,
19th ME

80th NY
151st PA

H. Spangler

13th VT

16th VT
(5 cos)

P. Rogers

14th VT

Fitzhugh

Lang

Daniels

Hummelbaugh

D. Klingle

Thompson

Wilcox

16th VT
(5 cos)

Phillips

Hart

Jordan
J. Sherfy
Parker

116th PA

Rank
Sterling
Dow

[P]
Latham
Garden

J. Wentz

A. Trostle

Ames

Plum Run

Geo. Wentz

absorbed in thought, while another dumped his cartridge box and laid his rounds out in a neat row along the base of the stone wall.[117]

Stevens Knoll

General Meade arrived at the signal station on Stevens Knoll and ordered the signal man there to inform the signal officer he had left at the Leister house of his whereabouts. When he did not receive any response, he assumed that the station had been abandoned there and decided to return to the Taneytown Road.[118] With his orderlies, Captain Charles E. Cadwallader, and Captain James Starr (Company I, 6th Pennsylvania Cavalry) and Second Lieutenant Louis H. Carpenter (Company L, 6th U.S. Cavalry) in tow, he started down the low hill toward his former headquarters. Musketry reverberated across the road from Cemetery Ridge. The general immediately dispatched his three officers to the VI Corps to bring up reinforcements. While they rode away, he passed through the northern tip of the woods west of the Leister house, where he met his son on foot. Before riding away, he told his son to take one of the orderlies'

Major General George G. Meade
Throughout the entire engagement he fought the battle as a commanding general should have by personally being on the field with his men.
Miller, *Photographic History*

horses, and added that he could be found later at headquarters or on the line. [119]

The artillery bombardment, the suffocating heat, and the continual exodus of disheartened soldiers from the ranks destroyed any hopes Lee may have entertained of actually taking and holding Cemetery Ridge. An estimated 3,000 of some 5,700 men in the front wave either never reached or crossed the Emmitsburg Road.

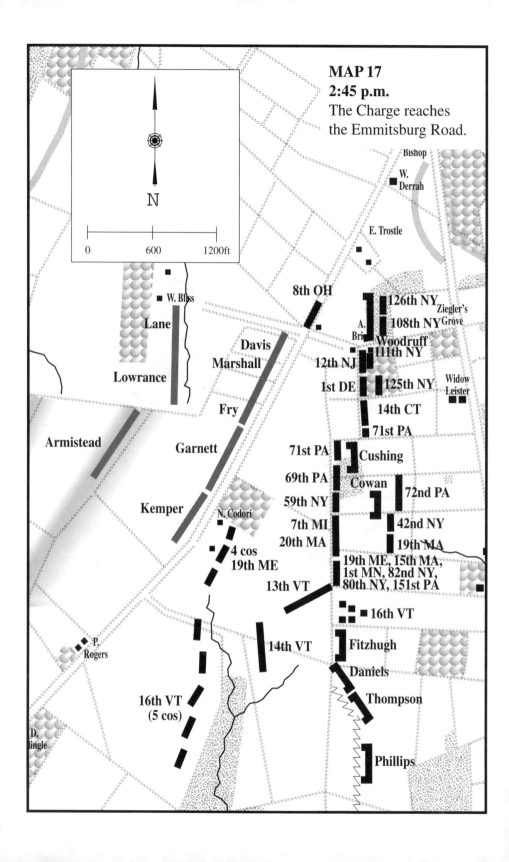

MAP 17
2:45 p.m.
The Charge reaches
the Emmitsburg Road.

2:45 p.m. through 3:00 p.m.

Garnett's Brigade

Before reaching the Emmitsburg Road, Garnett's frontage shrank about 700 feet—an average of one man from the ranks missing for every five feet of advance. As the Confederate regiments successively climbed over the high board fence and dropped into the road bed, their lines naturally swung facing southeast, thereby changing the direction of the advance away from Cemetery Hill toward Cemetery Ridge.[1] Lieutenant William Lochren (Adjutant, 1st Minnesota) could not believe what he was seeing. The road's deep banks provided not only a natural earthwork from the incoming artillery fire it was also a good place for the Rebels to reform their ranks for the final push.[2] A considerable number of Garnett's men did not leave the road bed. Throwing themselves prone, they let their comrades continue forward.[3] Despite his misgivings of ever surviving, Private William P. Jesse (Company F, 28th Virginia) braved the exploding shells and whizzing minie balls and climbed over the fence with his regiment.[4] Garnett's brigade, in crossing the road, ran into the southeasterly running fence on the north side of the orchard, which separated the right wing of the 18th Virginia (Companies A, B, C, and E) from the rest of the regiment. With the 8th Virginia, they marched on the south side of the fence.[5]

These are two views of the Codori barn. The photo on the left is looking west from the swale south of the orchard. The photo on the right is looking east-south of the orchard. Note the depth of the Emmitsburg Road in the foreground.

MOLLUS, USAMHI

111

**Colonel Eppa Hunton,
8th Virginia**

Wounded in the leg near the Codori barn, he had to quit the field before reaching the High Water Mark.

Miller, *Photographic History*

Glancing to the north, Colonel Eppa Hunton (8th Virginia) saw Fry's and Marshall's brigades show signs of breaking. Then he felt something slam into his right leg just below the knee. His horse shuddered under the impact too, as the bullet passed through its body. Blood gushed down the colonel's pant leg. Fearing the colonel would bleed to death before he could get him back to Seminary Ridge, Private George W. F. Hummer (Company H) grabbed the dying horse by the bridle and led the colonel out of the fight.[6]

Pettigrew's Division
    Fry's brigade, followed quickly by Marshall's and what was left of Davis' command, scrambled over both fences along the road and reformed in the drainage ditch on the eastern side.[7] The respite in the road-bed passed too quickly for Lieutenant John H. Moore (Company B, 7th Tennessee). While climbing over the top rail of the second fence, he glanced to both sides. Not over two thirds of the men who reached the pike crossed over to the eastern side. The regiment, in his estimation, had not halted at all. Those few who did leave the protection of its banks seemed to have lingered momentarily before clawing their way over the opposite fence. The 7th Tennessee, having lost half of its men before reaching the road, left most of what remained behind the cover of the two-foot-high berm. About fifty officers and men followed Colonel John A. Fite over the second fence.[8] Color Corporal George B. Powell (14th Tennessee) went down during the advance. Boney Smith, a black man attached to the regiment, took the colors and carried them forward.[9]

    The right of the division had caught up with Garnett's Virginians. A stone's throw north of the 11th Mississippi, Corporal Thaddeus Potter (Company H, 8th Ohio) incredulously watched the Rebel line claw out of the three-foot-deep road bed without paying any attention whatsoever to its left flank. Turning to the regiment, the adjutant, First Lieutenant John W. DePuy, cried out, "Will you follow me, boys?" Leaping to the top of the embankment, Captain Wells W. Miller shouted, "This way, Company H." With that the company-sized regiment clawed up the road bank, executing a left wheel against the fence on the Confederates' left rear.[10] Longstreet spied them from his position near Woolfolk's battery and immediately sent Colonel Osmon Latrobe galloping across the field to warn Trimble of their advance. At the same time, he dispatched Major G. Moxley Sorrel to Pickett with word to watch his right.[11]

Fry saw Garnett mouth something but could not understand him above the racket. Private Jonas Cook (Company I, 47th North Carolina), on the colonel's left, watched Fry salute the general with his sword, indicating that he did not understand. "I am dressing on you!" both heard Garnett scream.[12] The Confederates swiftly restored their lines and moved from the quick step to the double quick step.[13] From its elevated position at Ziegler's Grove, Woodruff's battery tore the left flank of the brigade to shreds, forcing it to close drastically to the right.[14]

Captain Jacob B. Turney (Company K, 1st Tennessee) saw his colonel, Newton J. George, go down with Captain Williams nearby. Thirty paces beyond them, Colonel Fry dropped, shot through both thighs. A number of the men, turning about in the ranks, ran back to assist him off the field, but Fry waved them away. "Go on," he grimaced. "It will not last five minutes longer." The brigade disappeared in the smoke-obscured field beyond Fry.[15] He lay alone until he spied Turney approaching him from behind. Beckoning the captain to his side, he asked for Colonel George. The colonel was hit, Turney replied. "Captain, take command of the regiment. Proceed with the charge, but don't stop to fire a gun," Fry admonished him. Turney disappeared to the front, trying to catch up with the line which had veered toward the northwest corner of the Angle.[16] Private John McLeer (Company F, 1st Tennessee) died before getting very far from the road, leaving the very lucky Wiley Woods, the color bearer, on his own again.[17] From where he lay, Captain Winfield Scott (Company C, 126th New York) could distinctly hear the Confederates' foot falls. The Rebels halted, despite the pounding they were getting from the Federal artillery.[18]

East of the Rogers House
Kemper's Skirmishers

In all of the confusion, First Lieutenant John Thomas James, commanding Company D, 11th Virginia on the skirmish line, continued pushing his extended formation east toward the Irish Brigade and McGilvery's artillery line. He could not understand why his men were not taking any hits from the Yankee skirmishers. Looking behind him, while descending into the creek bottom east of the Emmitsburg Road, he noticed the brigade had shifted too far north—beyond the protective screen of his company. The Yankees were generally aiming over the heads of his men to concentrate on the massive line cresting the ridge behind him.[19]

Northeast of the Rogers House
Kemper's Brigade

Because of the southwesterly course of the Emmitsburg Road, Kemper's right regiments crossed it ahead of the rest of the brigade. Within moments, the line materialized along the ridge, marching in perfect order—

as well drilled as any veteran Northern regiment. On the left of the Yankee skirmish line, the overheated New Englanders stood up. Silas Adams (Company F, 19th Maine) feverishly rubbed his legs to get the circulation going. Rising to his full height, he retired upon command toward Cemetery Ridge. Keeping their regulation fifteen pace intervals, the skirmishers turned twice to pepper the Confederates.[20] Phillips' Battery E, 5th Massachusetts Artillery continued to hammer the Confederates in the flank as they descended into the creek bottom.[21]

Company G, 11th Virginia took a number of hits. A Yankee skirmisher put a ball through Captain John H. Smith's right thigh. Staggered but not knocked down, he yelled at Fourth Corporal James R. Kent, "Take charge of the company; I am shot." Stopping to examine the wound, he soon realized he had no broken bones and stumbled after the company.[22] Just then Kent fell forward into the drainage ditch on the eastern side of the road. "How are you hurt, Kent?" Smith asked him. "Shot through the leg," came the reply. The captain helplessly watched the Yankees cut down Fifth Sergeant Martin V. B. Hickok (Company D) then Fifth Corporal Charles W. Simpson (Company E) with the colors before the regiment finished its descent into the valley. Canister knocked down the third color bearer on the way into the swale. Adjutant Harris grabbed the staff and carried the flag forward.[23]

Meanwhile, the 3rd Virginia, on the left flank, ran into heavy canister from the guns south of the copse of trees while it maneuvered through the Codori orchard. As the regiment neared the eastern face of the trees and started to realign itself, a shell whined in on top of Colonel Joseph C. Mayo. He instinctively jerked his head aside as the projectile whipped past his nose. Orderly Sergeant J. "Waddy" Forward (Company A) burst out laughing at the stunned expression upon the colonel's face. With the sergeant's laughter rolling off his back, Mayo trooped his line. He spied the lazy, extremely laid back Captain Thomas J. Lewis herding his Company C into line as if he were meandering to a country social. Carrying his sword over his shoulder by the point, he disinterestedly drawled, "Don't crowd, boys; don't crowd." "Pretty hot, Captain," Mayo shouted at him while passing behind the company. "It's redicklous, Colonel," Lewis drawled back in reference to the entire combat situation, "perfectly redicklous."[24] Farther to the right, Private Jacob Polak (Company I, 1st Virginia) caught up with Colonel Lewis Williams and returned his horse to him.[25]

The Field East of the Klingle House

Lieutenant C. H. C. Brown's section of the Washington Artillery rolled into battery on the high ground northeast of Sherfy's barn about 300 yards from Plum Run. He immediately opened fire on the right end of McGilvery's artillery line. Overshooting Captain Patrick Hart's 15th New York Battery, he dropped round after round among the Yankee limbers and caissons, inflicting tremendous casualties among the teams. Hart, who had been wounded during the artillery bombardment, immediately directed the center section to respond. To his delight the two shots blew two caissons near the Sherfy barn into splinters. They effectively silenced Brown's section and sent the gunners from Latham's 12-pounder, which had just unlimbered, scurrying for safer ground, leaving their gun by itself on the hillside. Demoralized, the Confederates left the seriously wounded Lieutenant Brown upon the field.[26]

The guns had barely fallen silent when the remaining four Napoleons, under Major John C. Haskell's personal direction, unlimbered farther to the east and zeroed in on Hart's battery. Hart along with Phillips' Massachusetts Artillery and Thompson's Pennsylvanians brought their sixteen guns to bear upon the outgunned Confederates. In short order, they killed the six horses to one of Garden's limbers and killed or maimed most of its gun crew, including First Lieutenant William A. McQueen, who went down with a shell fragment in the thigh. Within minutes, the Yankees dismounted two of the four Napoleons, making it impossible to withdraw them from the field.[27] His ammunition gone, Haskell ordered the surviving artillerymen to drag out as many wounded as they could. Calling to Garden and Latham, he told them to bring up limbers and ropes to retire the guns and to evacuate their crippled. While the company commanders spurred back to the Peach Orchard, the fearless Haskell rode into the open ground to mark the rendezvous point. Without warning, a spent piece of shrapnel hammered Major John C. Haskell on the sword hilt. Knocking the one-armed officer from the saddle, he thudded to the ground, dazed, unable to walk under his own power. The rescue party managed to bring the severely jarred officer out of the line of fire. They took him to the Sherfy barn, where to his dismay he spied General Pickett with his staff. The impression never left him. He never forgave Pickett for not having proved himself upon the field.[28]

The Angle
Cushing's Battery

Forcing himself to stand upright, Cushing raised his glasses to his eyes. Number Four, commanded by Acting Sergeant James Murphy, sent a canister round toward Garnett's line, which was crossing the Emmitsburg Road at a range of less than three hundred yards.[29] It decapitated two enlisted men in Company I, 69th Pennsylvania.[30]

The report had barely died away when Murphy collapsed, dead behind the gun. Private Christopher Smith, on Number Five, whose piece had only canister left, twisted his head to the right and saw the glasses fall from the lieutenant's face. The bullet, striking Cushing under the nose, whirled him around to the right. Sergeant Frederick Fuger, dropping his revolver, caught the lieutenant with his right arm as he collapsed face forward toward the rear of the battery.[31] One of the Pennsylvanians in

Company I, in noticing that Cushing was no longer on the field, yelled, "That artillery officer has his legs knocked from under him."[32] Fuger ordered Smith and Private John J. Wright to take the body to the limbers.[33] With his corpse clear of the trail, gun Number Four fired again.[34] The Number Five (ammunition runner) attached to Miles F. Newbury's limber raced back to the chest to get a round of ammunition. He shouted to Newbury, "Cushing is killed. See, they are carrying him off the field yonder."[35] The two enlisted men placed the lieutenant's torn body behind a rock outcropping between the Number Three and the Number Four teams, then returned to their guns.

While they were gone, Private Rody Landregan took over the center section of the battery. Glancing southwest, he saw Kemper's men converging into the low ground east of the Codori farm, moving as it seemed to him, by the left oblique. With the sergeant down, he took it upon himself to command the rifle. "Left oblique!" he screamed. "Boys, give them canister as quick as you can! Elevate your pieces so it will reach them." The gun violently recoiled as the double canister left the muzzle.[36]

First Lieutenant Samuel Canby, having assumed Cushing's position, stood alongside the Number Four gun studying the Confederate lines when a bullet ricocheted off his field glasses and struck his wrist.[37] Stunned and bleeding, Canby headed toward the Taneytown Road. Second Lieutenant Joseph S. Milne, an officer whom the men intensely disliked, stepped into Canby's place. Before he could issue any orders, a sniper dropped him with a fatal wound through his left lung.[38]

With the last officer out of action, General Webb stepped up to Sergeant Fuger. "Save your guns. Draw them by hand to the rear," Webb ordered him as he passed to the left, closer to the copse of trees. Fuger nodded and returned to what remained of the battery.[39] "Men, by hand to the front," he called out.[40] Going to Number Five, which was still manned by Privates Christopher Smith, Pat Glascott, and Corporal Ed Hurley, he assisted them in moving the piece to within twenty-five to thirty feet of the stone wall.[41] Landregan rolled his gun to the wall also.[42] They pushed them into position behind Company I, the right company of the 69th Pennsylvania.[43]

At about the same time, Sergeant Major William S. Stockton (71st Pennsylvania), who was with the two right companies on the left of the 14th Connecticut, peeked over the stone wall and saw Armistead's Confederates descending into the low ground west of the Emmitsburg Road. Without orders, he dashed south along the wall, gathering men as he moved. Reaching Cushing's silent Number One gun, he and his unauthorized detachment rolled it to within a few feet of the Angle. The infantrymen crammed it with everything they could get their hands on. Rocks, broken pieces of muskets, and a bayonet—they jammed the tube clear to the muzzle.[44]

Before long, Sergeant Fuger walked to the Angle and found the Number One gun, with the bayonet protruding from its muzzle, loaded and manned. Before returning to the two guns on the left, he told the Pennsylvanians to sight it in on the Emmitsburg Road and not to fire it until the Confederates reached that point. As Fuger walked away, Sergeant Major Stockton, who was standing between the gun and the Angle, noticed some of his men muscle the Number Two gun into battery to his left.[45] By then, most of Armistead's brigade was clambering over the fences on the road. The 38th Virginia, on the left of his line, however, having lost over 300 of its 480 effectives in the advance, did not get past the road bed. They halted between the two fences to return fire, some of which, undoubtedly hit the Confederates to their front.[46] The Pennsylvanians fired their artillery pieces, watched the rounds tear holes through the Virginians, then crouched behind the wall to await the onslaught which they knew would follow.[47]

Stannard's Brigade

Kemper's advance drove in the skirmishers of the 16th Vermont upon their own. The Rebels steadily marched toward Plum Run, heading straight toward the 14th Vermont which lay concealed in the growth and outcroppings along the base of the ridge. Colonel William T. Nichols (14th Vermont) ordered his wing of the regiment to its feet, attempting to rearrange his battle line.[48] A solid shot hissed into Company E. Striking Corporal Wesley C. Sturtevant squarely in the chest, it killed him instantly. His death premonition had proved mournfully true.[49] The Vermonters shouted at the skirmishers from the 19th Maine, who had not yet cleared their front, to hurry up and get out of their line of fire. Before the Mainers could move one way or the other several rounds of "friendly fire" zipped through Company F. They immediately broke to the east and rallied in Stannard's line.[50]

Garnett's Brigade

As the brigade pressed farther into the swale east of the Emmitsburg Road, Sergeant Francis W. Wilson (Company C, 18th Virginia), marching behind his captain, Henry T. Owen, called over the captain's shoulder, "What troops are those on our right? Are they our men or Yankees?" Owen shot a worried stare to the south, turned his head to the east and kept marching without saying a word. Presently, in a subdued, barely audible voice, he replied, "Yankees. March straight ahead and say nothing." Major Edmund Berkeley (8th Virginia) saw them also but kept his attention focused upon his disorganized regiment. In the short distance between them and the top of the hill Owen heard Garnett urge the men to increase their speed. "Faster, men! Faster!" he shouted at them until the front rank broke into a double quick step. "Steady, men! Steady," Garnett admonished them. "Don't double quick. Save your wind and your ammunition for the final charge."[51] At the base of Codori's knoll, along the eastern face of the orchard, the right wing of the 18th Virginia and the 8th Virginia filed left through the opening in the fence and turned southeast with the fence on their flank.[52] The commands became entangled as the two merged into a throng fifteen

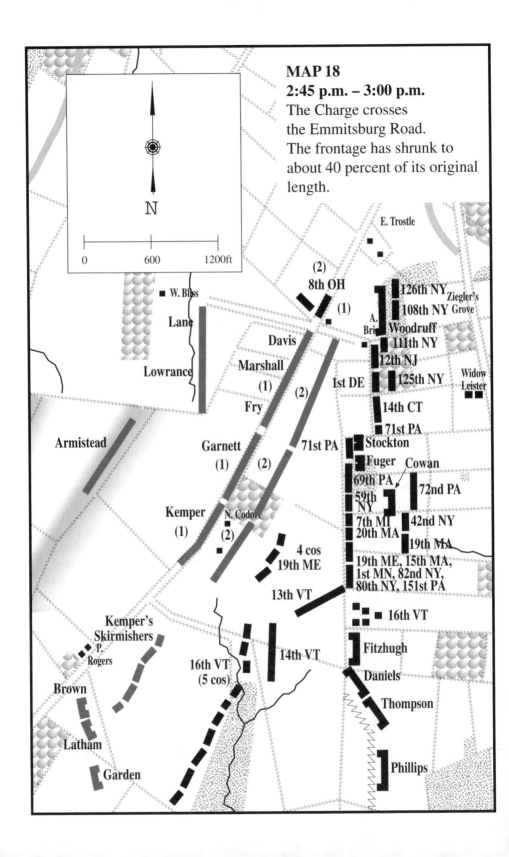

MAP 18
2:45 p.m. – 3:00 p.m.
The Charge crosses
the Emmitsburg Road.
The frontage has shrunk to
about 40 percent of its original
length.

N

0   600   1200ft

E. Trostle

W. Bliss

(2)
8th OH
(1)

126th NY   Ziegler's
108th NY   Grove
A.   Woodruff
Bri
111th NY
12th NJ
Lane

Davis
Marshall
(1)   (2)
1st DE   125th NY   Widow
                                    Leister
14th CT
Lowrance

Fry

Garnett   71st PA   71st PA
(1)   (2)   Stockton
                                  Fuger   Cowan

Armistead   69th PA   72nd PA
                                  59th
Kemper   N. Codor   NY   42nd NY
(1)   (2)   7th MI   19th MA
                                  20th MA
                                  19th ME, 15th MA,
              4 cos   1st MN, 82nd NY,
              19th ME   80th NY, 151st PA

              13th VT
                                  16th VT
Kemper's
Skirmishers
        P.   Fitzhugh
    Rogers   16th VT
                     (5 cos)   14th VT   Daniels
Brown
                                             Thompson
Latham

Garden   Phillips

to twenty ranks deep. They surged to within about fifty yards of the stone wall.[53] The movement precipitated a reaction on the southern end of the line. With a Yankee regiment popping from cover a couple of hundred yards away Kemper's line abruptly halted then left obliqued.[54]

Stannard's Brigade

Before the Virginians could react, General Stannard ordered the 13th Vermont and the rest of the 14th Vermont to their feet.[55] Both regiments volleyed into Kemper's men. The Confederates halted, and filed left toward the upper end of the Codori field.[56] The Vermonters fired repeatedly into them while they desperately tried to outmaneuver them.[57]

Kemper's Brigade

While their right flank cleared Stannard's front, their left flank crossed through the opening in the fence on the northern side of Codori's orchard and began to fall in behind Garnett's right rear.[58] The movement caused a great deal of consternation among the ranks of the small 1st Virginia because the 11th Virginia got tangled in their right flank. A very irate Colonel Lewis B. Williams (1st Virginia), his sword still resting against his shoulder, trotted over to Captain James R. Hutter (Company H, 11th Virginia). "Captain Hutter, can you do nothing with your men? They are crowding me out of line." With his men trying to clear the front of the Federals south of the Angle and with the 24th Virginia pushing him from behind, the younger Hutter was not in any mood to tolerate Williams' demands. "If you will go and attend to that little squad of yours, and let my regiment alone we will get along better," he nastily retorted.[59] Rebuffed, Williams turned his horse back toward his regiment and walked a few steps when a bullet struck him in the shoulder. The impact knocked him from the saddle. He impaled himself on his sword in the fall and died. His horse limped down the slope, following the 3rd Virginia into action.[60] Major Francis H. Langley immediately took command and just as quickly, a bullet dropped him—wounded.[61]

Company D of the 1st Virginia did not shift to the left quickly enough, thereby forcing Company C, to its right, to give ground to let it pass. First Lieutenant John Dooley (Company C) turned to Captain George F. Norton (Company D) and asked him to move his company farther north. Norton yelled the command when a shell burst lifted him off his feet and dropped him to the ground.[62] Captain Thomas H. Davis (Company B) stepped to the front of the regiment to assume command and was hit.[63]

South of the Angle
Harrow's Brigade

General Gibbon saw the Rebs crossing his front. The six companies of the 19th Maine, which had not gone out as skirmishers, also silently watched the Confederates sweeping by them. Spurring his horse over the slight works between the 20th Massachusetts and the 19th Maine, Gibbon

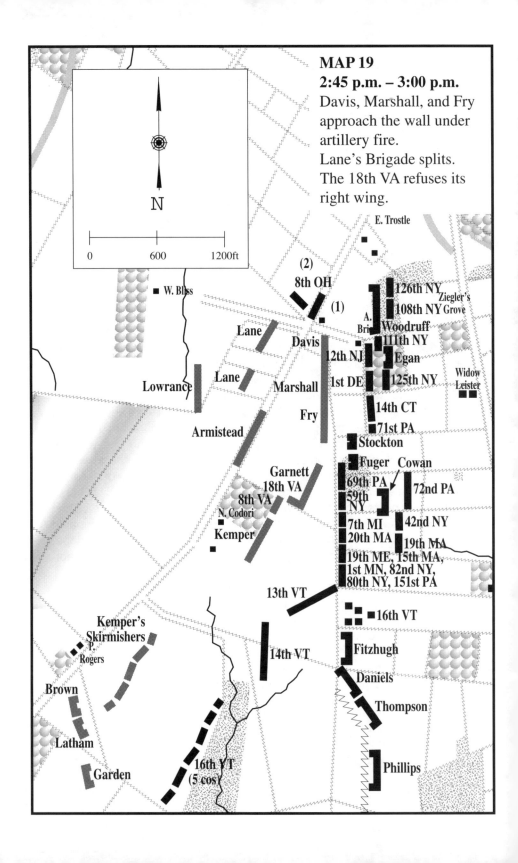

MAP 19
2:45 p.m. – 3:00 p.m.
Davis, Marshall, and Fry approach the wall under artillery fire.
Lane's Brigade splits.
The 18th VA refuses its right wing.

rode over along their front to their left flank and rashly waved them forward. To his astonishment, the New Englanders leveled their weapons to fire. Quickly gouging his spurs into the horse's flanks, he dashed around the southern end of the line, and rejoined his aides, Lieutenant Edward Moale and Captain Francis Wessels (106th Pennsylvania) and his lone orderly. Engulfed in the smoke from the small arms fire, he immediately sent Moale to the 13th Vermont with a directive for the regiment to change front forward on the right company. Colonel Francis V. Randall refused to comply. He insisted he was not under Gibbon's command. The exasperated lieutenant raced back to Gibbon who sent him to Colonel Norman Hall, on the right of the line, with instructions to get his regiments moving north.[64]

Meanwhile, Stannard had already commanded the 13th Vermont to change its front forward to flank Kemper from the south while calling the 16th Vermont into line on its left.[65] The 13th Vermont double quicked 100 yards to the front when Colonel Randall ordered Captain John Lonergan (Company A), "Change front, forward on first company." The company, being on the right of the line, halted. Sergeant James B. Scully, positioning himself as guide, marked the point for the regiment to pivot from. With each company coming on line successively to the right, the 13th double quicked toward the Confederates' exposed flank.[66]

As the 13th obliqued to the right front on its right company, Colonel Wheelock Veazey ran back to his regiment (16th Vermont) to get it moving by the right flank behind the 14th Vermont.[67] To the right rear of the 13th Vermont Colonel Theodore B. Gates (commanding the 151st Pennsylvania and the 80th New York) also decided to flank with the Rebels.[68] Executing an innovative maneuver, his men fired as they marched across the front of the II Corps. The Confederate artillery immediately opened fire to support their infantry. The New Yorkers and Pennsylvanians, despite the incoming case shot and solid shot, continued to dog the Rebels in their northerly advance. An enlisted man in the 80th New York unthinkingly propped his rifle upon Captain John D. S. Cook's shoulder and snapped off a round. The rifle cracked. Cook leaped into the air and whirled to give the man a verbal thrashing but was stopped mid-motion when he noticed how hard his men were laughing at him.[69] Having never been so unnerved, he swiftly realized it would not be very sporting of him to spoil their fun. Turning around, he continued with his company. Within moments, he felt something jolt the outside of his leg just below the hip. Stepping away from the formation he hurriedly stripped naked from the waist down. Fearing a fracture, he discovered instead a severe bruise. When he realized the extent of his injury, the captain put his clothes back on and rejoined his regiment.[70]

The Ridge West of the Emmitsburg Road

The tremendous crash of small arms fire greeted Colonel E. Porter Alexander as he with McCarthy's and Motes' guns passed through the openings in the fence onto the crest of the second ridge. In the distance he could see Stannard's Vermonters moving out to take Kemper on the flank. As soon as the pieces deployed they opened fire, catching the 13th Vermont on the left front. Within minutes, small arms smoke completely obliterated the Angle and everything to the north from view.[71]

Northeast of the Angle
Hays' Division

As the Confederate batteries shifted their fire from the Union right to the south, the 12th New Jersey unfurled its colors. The Federal guns at the Cemetery cut loose over the heads of their own infantry. The shells knocked holes in the Confederate brigades but the Rebels closed up and kept advancing.[72] The line literally melted away, Lieutenant William Peel (Company C, 11th Mississippi) recalled.[73] Private Billy O'Brien died, taking the colors to the ground with him. Private Joseph Smith (Company H) plucked the flag from the ground before his comrade, Private James Griffin (Company H) could get to them. A few paces beyond, Federal fire dropped them both—wounded. Private William P. Marion (Company H), who took them up, was killed by the bullet which snapped the staff in half. Private Joseph G. Marable (Company H) retrieved the upper half of the staff and led the regiment forward.[74]

At Ziegler's Grove, Captain Winfield Scott (Company C, 126th New York) watched some of the Federal skirmishers file off to the right of the main battle line and wheel south to take the Rebels on the flank.[75] Woodruff ordered his four guns, which had moved to the crest of Ziegler's Grove to open with canister.[76] Lieutenant Jonathan Egan broke his section to the left and went into battery twenty yards behind the left rear of the 12th New Jersey, south of the Brian house. At that instant a bullet struck Woodruff in the back as he turned his horse to move to the right of his battery.[77]

Kemper's Brigade

Colonel Joseph Mayo (3rd Virginia) and Captain Thomas M. Hodges (Company A) simultaneously spied a beautifully mounted Federal officer spurring his horse at a full gallop across the front of the regiment, not 100 yards off. Pointing him out as he proceeded, Hodges, then the colonel, yelled at the skirmishers who were closing in from the south, "Don't shoot him! Don't shoot him!."[78] Riding back to the center of Armistead's line at the Emmitsburg Road to within five feet of First Corporal James T. Carter (color guard, 53rd Virginia), Kemper called out to Armistead, "General, I am going to storm those works, and I want you to support me." "Did you ever see anything better on parade?" Armistead asked Kemper in reference to the formation of his own command. "I never did," Kemper replied.[79] Riding back to the front of his own brigade, Kemper rose in the stirrups. Pointing his sword toward the stone wall, he yelled, "There are the guns, boys, go for them." Colonel Joseph Mayo (3rd Virginia) thought it an "injudicious"

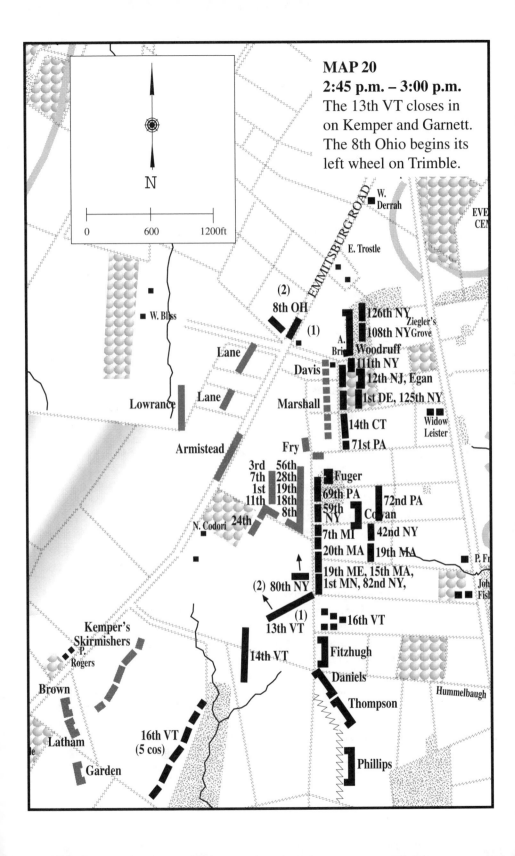

MAP 20
2:45 p.m. – 3:00 p.m.
The 13th VT closes in
on Kemper and Garnett.
The 8th Ohio begins its
left wheel on Trimble.

N

0   600   1200ft

W. Derrah

EVE
CEN

E. Trostle

(2)
8th OH
(1)

W. Bliss

126th NY
108th NY   Ziegler's
Grove
A.
Bri   Woodruff
Davis   111th NY
12th NJ, Egan
Marshall   1st DE, 125th NY
14th CT
Widow
Leister
Fry   71st PA

Lane

Lane

Lowrance

Armistead

3rd 56th   Fuger
7th 28th
1st 19th   69th PA   72nd PA
11th 18th   59th   Cowan
24th 8th   NY
N. Codori   7th MI   42nd NY
20th MA   19th MA
P. Fr
19th ME, 15th MA,
(2) 80th NY   1st MN, 82nd NY,   Joh
Fish
(1)
13th VT   16th VT

Kemper's
Skirmishers
P.
Rogers
14th VT   Fitzhugh

Brown   Daniels
Hummelbaugh
Latham   Thompson

Garden
16th VT
(5 cos)   Phillips

command.[80] Apparently a considerable number of the brigade's enlisted men thought the same thing, because they began dropping out of the formation while it advanced. To Captain John Holmes Smith's dismay and disgust the break evolved quickly from a trickle to a general break before it proceeded very far.[81]

Garnett's and Fry's Brigades

Despite the orders to hold their fire, the 56th Virginia, on the left of the line, under the independent authority of the company captains cut loose with a ragged volley.[82] Toward the center of the brigade line, Lieutenant W. Nathaniel Wood (Company A, 19th Virginia) felt something thump against his right leg. "Am I wounded?" flashed through his mind as he leaned against a large rock to inspect his wound. Finding himself only bruised, he rushed after his company.[83]

Meanwhile, the 1st Tennessee, Fry's regiment of direction on the right of the brigade line, surged ahead. Halting within fifteen feet of the Angle, to Garnett's left front, Captain Jacob B. Turney ordered them to give fire. Rifle balls zipped and slapped into the 71st Pennsylvania at point blank range, throwing the left wing of the regiment into confusion.[84] Sergeant Major Stockton (71st Pennsylvania) noticed a couple of men from his regiment take to their heels.[85] Turney's men dropped their weapons to "charge bayonets." The 1st Tennessee, with about twenty-five officers and men from the 7th Tennessee closing in from the left, rushed into a melee. Turney parried a saber thrust from a Yankee officer just as the bulk of the Pennsylvanians abandoned their end of the Angle.[86]

The Pennsylvanians hunkered down behind the wall, shouting, "We surrender!" "Crawl over to our side," Private Wiley Woods (Company F) called back, "and you shant be hurt."[87] With the enemy streaming over the brow of the ridge, Turney stepped on top of the wall to see what was happening around him. To the south, the Federal line appeared to be weakening, but to the north, the center and the left of Fry's brigade seemed to falter. Without any thought for their own safety, he, with his own Company K and a squad from other companies crossed onto the Federal side of the wall and formed a firing line on the northern face of the Angle.[88] As one of the Rebels passed by the prone Sergeant Major Stockton (71st Pennsylvania), the sergeant heard his canteen slosh. He asked for a drink of water, but the Rebel ignored him.[89]

To Lieutenant George W. Finley's astonishment, the left wing of the 71st Pennsylvania disintegrated. Most of the Yankees peeled back from the line in a panic and not as prearranged. "I thought it was all up," Private William J. Burns (Company G) wrote.[90] Completely unaware of Turney's presence at the apex of the Angle, the 56th Virginia bolted toward the wall. Frightened Pennsylvanians, rushing the Virginians with their hands above their heads, disrupted the line. "Don't shoot! We surrender!" they screamed. "Where shall we go?"[91]

The Angle

The 69th Pennsylvania waited for Garnett's and Kemper's advance with two to five captured muskets loaded with twelve buck shot by each soldier's side. Garnett's men moved by the left oblique, with Kemper's 3rd, 7th, and 1st Virginia regiments trailing to their right rear, toward the point of the Angle to close the gap between them and Fry's brigade. They were also trying to clear the rock ledge which blocked their view of Federal line south of the copse of trees. The 11th and the 24th Virginia, still trying to negotiate the opening in the fence north of the orchard, got cut off from the rest of the brigade.

At twenty yards, the Pennsylvanians unloaded the first volley into their flank knocking handfuls of Garnett's and Kemper's soldiers to the ground.[92] Major Edmund Berkeley (8th Virginia) went down with a severe leg wound. The bullet, striking him above the knee, traveled a full twenty inches along the bone, before stopping near his groin. His men hurriedly evacuated him to the west side of the Codori house.[93] The Rebels fronted and returned a south to north rolling volley with just as much deliberation.[94] A Rebel yell erupted in the smoke. At the same instant a minie ball bored through Lieutenant John Dooley's thighs, knocking him down. A second later, his good friend, Second Lieutenant William A. Kahoe (Company I, 1st Virginia) went down with a bullet wound in his left thigh. He lay next to Dooley in a great deal of pain and bleeding profusely.[95]

Having caught up with the 19th Virginia, Lieutenant W. Nathaniel Wood (Company A) abruptly stopped to examine the mess in which he found himself immersed. Only a skirmish line remained of the brigades' combined ranks. Six hundred feet to the south, he saw the 80th New York with the Vermonters to their left, swinging out on a hinge west of the earthworks and realized he faced but two options—stay put and be captured or run and probably catch a round in the back. He did not deliberate longer than it took him to turn about and take off as fast as his bruised leg could carry him. He skirted behind the right wing of the 18th Virginia, passed behind the 8th Virginia, and headed for the pile of rails north of the 11th Virginia before the second volley hit him. Something stung him in the side. A wad of coat fabric and vest burst from his front. The thought he had been wounded again slowed him to a walk. With every step, he expected to feel his own warm blood soaking through his clothes.[96]

Kemper found Major Berkeley (8th Virginia) lying in a great deal of pain near the Codori house. When asked if he was severely wounded, the major said yes, but it did not matter because they were all going to be captured soon. Why did he think that? Kemper asked. "Didn't you see those flanking columns the enemy are throwing out on our supports to sweep the field?" Berkeley queried. "Those are our men," the general reassured him. "You will soon see your mistake," Berkeley snorted before Kemper rode off, leaving the major to the care of Acting First Lieutenants

Thomas R. Harrison (Garnett's A.D.C.) and Thomas B. Hutchison, Berkeley's adjutant. They evacuated him from the field.[97]

Kemper left Berkeley to search out Armistead, whose regiments had closed to within seventy-five yards of the stone wall. "General," Kemper pleaded, "hurry up, my men can stand no more." Turning to Lieutenant Colonel Rawley Martin, he commanded, "Colonel, double quick." At that, Armistead pulled his black hat from his head and stuck it on the end of his sword. "Forward, double-quick!" he bellowed.[98]

Meanwhile, Kemper inadvertently rode so close to the Federals' line that he could clearly distinguish their facial features. For a second, the vivid image of an enlisted man sighting in on him flashed through his mind. Before he had time to react, a bullet tore into his groin, knocking him from the saddle. Captain Charles McAnally and several enlisted men from Company D, 69th Pennsylvania, surrounded him. They rolled him onto a blanket. The captain assured him they were taking him to a field hospital. Relinquishing his personal valuables, including his sword, to the captain, Kemper gave his address to McAnally with the request they be sent to his wife. As they hoisted Kemper off the ground to take him to their surgeon, a group of Kemper's men fired over him into his captors. The general never knew whether his men killed the Yankees or not. He only recollected his soldiers carrying him back toward Seminary Ridge on the same blanket. [99]

Upon seeing Kemper go down, Colonel William R. Terry (24th Virginia) sent Captain William T. Fry (A.A.G. to Kemper) on his wounded horse, toward the left of the line. He found Colonel Mayo (3rd Virginia) shaking hands with Garnett and congratulating him for having gotten so close to the wall with his men. Fry cried out to Mayo, who turned to hear what he had to say. Stop the movement to the left, the captain shouted, the Yankees had penetrated the rear of the line in force. Kemper shot—mortally wounded, he feared. The brush-covered, tree-lined fence row to the south had pressed Kemper's right flank (the 11th Virginia and the 24th Virginia) back on an acute angle to the rest of the brigade. The 11th Virginia lost all cohesion in the movement, Captain John Holmes Smith (Company G) recalled. To the front, he saw the Yankees behind a low earthwork masked by brush.[100] Mayo reacted immediately. With Kemper's fall, the brigade's command devolved upon him. Leaving Garnett in the melee at the wall, he rushed to Colonel Henry A. Carrington (18th Virginia, Garnett's brigade), with whose regiment his men had merged and asked him to pull as many men as he could from the firing line to turn the Yankees back.[101]

11th Virginia

Something struck Captain James R. Hutter (Company H, 11th Virginia) in the body with a jarring thud. Nevertheless, he continued to form his line until Adjutant Harris (who carried the regimental colors) yelled at him, "You are wounded." "Yes, but not much," Hutter shot back. At that, the adjutant rubbed his free hand over the captain's back until it stopped at a hole in his tunic. "The ball entered here," he said matter-of-factly. A quick glance at the blood saturating the front of his coat confirmed the worst. "I am a dead man," the captain calmly replied. Before he could say another word, a bursting shell prostrated him and several of the men standing nearby.[102]

Cushing's Guns

Back at the Angle part of the 56th Virginia charged the works. Three Confederates, breaking over the wall, killed Privates Simon Malinger and William Patton on Cushing's Number Four gun at the muzzle of the piece and wounded Rody Landregan before Company I of the 69th Pennsylvania brought them down.[103] At the same time, Fuger screamed "Men, run for your lives."[104] Landregan did not wait to be told a second time. Dropping the lanyard, he turned on his heels, and skittered back toward the ridge line. While Fuger stooped over to pick up the lanyard, General Webb collared Landregan in an attempt to force him back into the line.[105] The general demanded he stand where he was. "My God, General," Private William H. Porter (Company E, 72nd Pennsylvania) heard the artilleryman scream, "I can do nothing here alone! There is no use going back, all the men are gone, killed." "You stay here and I will get you help," Webb cried back, at which point a nearby caisson went up in smoke and flame.[106]

The Pennsylvanians quickly emptied their spare weapons.[107] Webb rushed over to the center of the 72nd Pennsylvania and grabbed the flag staff. Color Sergeant William Finnessey instinctively tugged back on the colors but the general would not relinquish them.[108] Unable to drag the sergeant and the flag from the line, Webb released his grip and stormed into the right wing of the 69th where he ordered Companies F, A, and I to fall back at right angles to the rest of the line. With the trees behind them, Companies A and I successfully back stepped until the northern face of the copse touched them. Company F, which was supposed to have been the hinge of the formation, did not execute the command. When the Confederates killed Captain George Thompson before he had time to relay the command to his company, his lieutenants—John Ryan and John Eagan—sent their men over the wall into the Confederates' ranks. For a few seconds, they engaged the Rebels with bared muzzles and with rifle butts until the Rebels captured or wounded the entire company.[109]

While Turney's small group of diehards peppered the stone wall along the crest of the ridge, a company from the 7th Tennessee and Captain N. J. Taylor with his company from the 13th Alabama, along with a few stalwarts from the 5th Alabama Battalion rushed into the open ground behind them. Captain Turney shot a worried glance over his shoulder in time to see the 69th Pennsylvania refuse its right wing. He immediately recalled the entire party to the Confederate side of the west wall.[110] As they retreated, they dragged Sergeant Major William Stockton and his four men from the

71st Pennsylvania with them. The Rebels ordered the Yankees to the rear but Stockton told his "boys" to stay put. A Confederate sergeant took over the prisoners but could not get them to leave the wall. Crouching down behind the large boulder at the corner of the fence, the Pennsylvanians decided to wait out the fight.[111]

A short distance to the south, Lieutenant George W. Finley (Company K, 56th Virginia) suddenly noticed their presence. He darted over to the Tennesseeans and Alabamians to determine their identity before running back to his own company. Grabbing a musket from one of his men, intent upon picking off one of Hays' men, he looked behind him and latched his eyes upon Garnett. For a moment, which seemed much longer, the general stared at Hays' line behind the wall to the left front.[112]

Within seconds the front evolved into a kaleidoscopic whirlpool. Turney and his band leaped the wall again, followed by a few of the 56th Virginia.[113] As they did so, the Number One man on the Number Two gun ran toward the crest, carrying the rammer with him. Private Robert B. Damron (Company D, 56th Virginia) and a number of his men swarmed around the piece, jubilant over its capture.[114] The 72nd Pennsylvania along the ridge between the copse of trees and the wall opened a horrendous fire upon them and the west face of the Angle as the Tennesseeans attempted to enfilade the far wall again.[115] One of their rounds slammed into Damron's right shoulder, forcing him to retreat to the wall.[116] The Confederates returned the fire. Captain Andrew McBride (Company D, 72nd Pennsylvania) dropped dead not two feet away from Captain Charles Banes. Banes noticed confusion toward the south of the regiment. Riding to the left wing, behind the copse of trees, he found the men doubling up. What was the matter? he asked. "This man's horse is crowding us out of our place." Looking around, he spied Lieutenant Frank Haskell and immediately sent him packing.[117] Color Sergeant William Finnessey died in the blast and Corporal Frank O'Donnell (Company D) took the flag from his hands. Seconds later, he went down and Corporal Charles Giberson (Company F) replaced him in the guard. Before the smoke cleared, Wills of the color guard also perished.[118]

Lieutenant Frank Haskell

Haskell's personal account of Longstreet's charge became famous before he died in battle in 1864.

MOLLUS, USAMHI

First Sergeant Frederick Fuger (Battery A, 4th U.S. Artillery) snapped the lanyard on Number Four gun then threw himself to the ground and played dead, while the rest of his artillerymen abandoned the pieces. "Stop, you Yankee devils!" the Confederates called as they poured over the wall. Private Miles F. Newbury, finding himself between two fires, dove behind a pile of small stones, hoping not to get killed by either side. Private Christopher Smith heard Ed Hurley let out a shriek as a ball struck him in the back, hurling him into the air. Smith swore he never had seen a man jump so high. Being so close to the crest of the hill, the surviving artillerymen hated returning to pick him up. His plea, "For God's sake, don't leave me here," brought them back. [119] The muzzle blast singed Lieutenant Finley's face.[120] Canister balls struck Garnett and his black horse at the same time. The general, shot through the waist, reeled and fell to the ground. His horse, responding to the tug on the reins, turned about and raced from the field, bleeding from a terribly gouged shoulder. In its headlong flight it leaped over a rock outcropping, nearly striking two wounded Confederate soldiers who had taken cover there. The semiconscious Private James W. Clay (Company G, 18th Virginia), partially blinded by the blood from a head wound, lay there with First Lieutenant Archer Campbell (Company G), whose arm had been shattered during the attack on the 69th Pennsylvania.[121]

Brigadier General
Richard B. Garnett

Dying within sixty feet of the Angle, his riddled body remained upon the field among other unidentifiable corpses.

Miller, *Photographic History*

Kemper's and Garnett's Brigades

Time stopped momentarily for Private Jacob Polak (Company I, 1st Virginia). The field seemed to quiet down when the Federal gunners abandoned their pieces. Perhaps he was stunned by the last blast of canister. He remembered standing in the line with Second Lieutenant Paul C. Cabell (Company H) discussing how the Federals were massing on the ridge line east of the wall. Seconds later he saw Colonel W. Tazwell Patton (7th Virginia) fall to the ground. Running over to the colonel, he asked him if he were hurt. Patton tried to reply, but could not. Lung shot, he gurgled blood with each attempt to speak. Polak left him where he fell and returned to his place in the line. (While Patton lay there, a second bullet tore away his lower jaw.)[122] A rifle ball struck Private James R. McPherson (Company C,

28th Virginia) in the right arm. He went down, unable to keep up the fight.[123] Colonel Robert C. Allen (28th Virginia), the colors of the regiment in his grasp, died in front of the wall.[124] Lieutenant John A. Lee (Company C) grabbed the flag and started to take it over the wall when a bullet knocked it from his hands. He picked it up again only to get dropped by a round. Falling on the west side of the wall, he continued to wave the colors to and fro.[125]

Pettigrew's Division

On the left of the 14th Connecticut, Sergeant Major William B. Hincks and Second Lieutenant William H. Hawley (Company B) worked as a team. Each being armed with Sharp's breech-loading rifles, they decided that Hincks would fire while Hawley loaded. The moment Fry's brigade swarmed into the Angle and over the fence paralleling their position, the two New Englanders opened with a continuous fire which a man armed with a muzzle loader could never match.[126] The rest of the regiment, being armed with several loaded muskets each, slaughtered the Rebels. With men dropping around him faster than he could tally, Major A. S. Van de Graaf (5th Alabama Battalion) threw himself down in the wagon tracks too overheated to go any farther.[127] Close by, Colonel John A. Fite (7th Tennessee) also went to ground. Dirt, kicked up by Yankee bullets, stung him about the face as he lay there, expecting to breathe his last at any moment.[128] Privates Jim Hale (Company K) and Tom Holloway (Company H) flopped down together. "Let's surrender," someone suggested. "Let's never surrender," Holloway shot back, while inadvertently raising his head into the path of an incoming bullet.[129] The Confederate color guards advanced, alone, in spite of the horrendous small arms fire, beyond the fence, converging to the right around the apex of the Angle toward the north wall. The color bearer of the 5th Alabama Battalion died before reaching the wall. Private Bullock (Company C) momentarily raised the standard before a bullet cut him down. Private Benjamin L. Manning (Company B) picked them up but a round snuffed him out. Private Thomas J. Gilbert (Company A) snatched the colors and carried them back to the farm lane.[130]

A portion of the 14th Tennessee, braving the horrendous small arms fire from the east wall of the Angle, went over the fence with the regimental colors and Lieutenant Colonel James Lockert. Men went down by the handfuls. About fifty feet beyond the slab fence, Private Theodore Hartman stepped up to the right of Orderly Sergeant June Kimble (Company A) and suggested they stay together. Twenty-five feet farther on, Private Billy McCulloch came up on Kimble's left. "Billy, stay with us," Kimble shouted. "I am with you," he screamed back. A second later, a minie ball cracked into McCulloch's skull. He collapsed face first onto the ground. Kimble and Hartman immediately veered to the right and took cover on the north side of the Angle.[131] The colors of the 14th Tennessee got within fifty feet of the east wall before Boney Smith hit the dirt—wounded. Jabbing the flagstaff in the ground, he momentarily urged the regiment forward until the intense pressure forced the men to lie down to save their lives. Nearby lay Colonel Lockert, shot through both thighs. The terrible fury of the initial contact having expended itself, an eerie lull settled over that last fifty yards of the killing ground.[132]

To the north, simultaneous with Fry's charge, Captain Scott (126th New York) peered through a crevice in the stone wall behind which he was lying as Pettigrew's first line leveled their weapons, then volleyed.[133] With an unexpected energy, they bolted forward, loading and shooting while they ran.[134] A sergeant from the 26th North Carolina, turning south toward Company G of the 47th North Carolina, caught Captain Joseph J. Davis' attention by pointing north and complaining about the collapse of that end of the line. A quick look by the captain verified the dissolution of Brockenbrough's brigade. Glancing behind him, however, Davis took heart in what appeared to be the determined advance of Lowrance's and Lane's brigades. "Our supports are coming up and we can whip them yet," he told the sergeant. To his right Lieutenant Colonel John A. Graves had the right wing well under control. Numbering around 150 officers and men, they could not hope to make much of an impact; nevertheless, the colonel continued to cheer the line forward.[135]

The 1st Delaware withheld its fire until the Confederate infantry crossed the farm lane paralleling the east wall of the Angle and climbed over the post and rail fence which bordered its eastern side.[136] As soon as the Rebels scrambled over that fence, Hays' division rose to its feet, and he belted out the command, "Fire!" A veritable sheet of smoke and fire enveloped the field, knocking the Confederate regiments into a shambles. Their lines melted.[137] The 47th North Carolina, on the western side of the fence, went to the ground to a man—killed, wounded, or too scared to stand up.[138] Captain Benjamin F. Little (Company E, 52nd North Carolina) fell in the blast while some of his men crossed over the fence. He lay on the field, fully conscious, watching his company get slaughtered in the open ground in front of him. Few who passed over the fence came back. Only the slightly wounded or the fast runners on his side managed to escape the maelstrom. Screams, curses—nothing could be heard above the din of small arms fire. The wounded Colonel James K. Marshall died in the fury and the brigade command devolved upon Lieutenant Colonel John T. Jones (26th North Carolina).

In the 52nd North Carolina, a bullet crashed through Lieutenant Colonel Marcus A. Parks' thighs.[139] A very short distance beyond the fifty-yard mark, Captain Albert S. Haynes (Company I, 11th North Carolina) spasmodically quaked as three rounds found their mark. Bleeding from the shoulder, with his right fibula shattered, he crumbled to the ground senseless. Lieutenant O. A. Ramseur, having seen Haynes fall, took over the regiment and led about 150 men toward the wall. Only two men from Company I managed to get back to Seminary Ridge unscathed.[140] Company F went in with Sergeant Robert Hudspeth and a handful of survivors from the fight on July 1. Private Tom Cozart carried the colors to within fifty feet of the Yankees before they snuffed him out.[141] An enlisted man from the equally decimated Company C snatched up the flag, but a bullet also killed him. Captain Francis W. Bird (Company C, 11th North Carolina) picked up the staff and stumbled to the rear with them.[142] Few of the Confederates got any closer than fifty feet from the Federal line.[143] By the time Company F reached that point, only Hudspeth remained on his feet. A shell burst knocked him down. (He managed to crawl off the field.)[144] A handful of the 52nd North Carolina, among them Major John Q. Richardson, who was mortally wounded, struggled to within a few feet of the Federals before going down.[145]

The 14th Connecticut and 1st Delaware, having stockpiled loaded weapons from the previous day's fight, kept up a continuous, unrelenting fire.[146] Despite orders to stay behind the wall, many of the men stood up to volley into the disorganized Rebels.[147] Pettigrew pranced his horse in front of his disintegrating division without getting hit. Lieutenant John Brady (1st Delaware), having just missed the general, hastily reloaded and was handing the rifle to Corporal Adam Huhn (Company A), who was next to him, when a minie ball thudded into the corporal's right temple, killing him instantly. From the corner of his eye, Brady saw the regimental colors go down. Dropping the rifle, he raced to the center of the line to retrieve them. Snatching them up, he handed them to Sergeant Thomas Seymour (Company B) and ordered him to kneel down to protect himself and the flag.[148]

"Come on; come on; come to death!" Captain Winfield Scott (Company C, 126th New York) heard someone taunt the Rebels.[149] The 12th New Jersey was waiting for them. Numbering about four hundred men, they had loaded their buck and ball loads with extra buckshot. Buck and ball was a cartridge designed for close work and Hays had not intended to have the men waste their lethal charges at long range.[150] He ordered the regiment to its feet. Officers futilely yelled at the men to "aim low." The 12th New Jersey volleyed without command, the men triggering the fusillade of their own accord. The Rebels in front of Colonel Thomas Smyth's brigade went down en masse.[151] About fifty to seventy-five Confederates pressed to within twenty feet of the regiment. Frantic Jerseymen, unable to reload fast enough, picked up large rocks out of the stone wall and hurled them at the Rebels.[152]

The 11th Mississippi lost four successive color bearers within a few yards; nevertheless, when Private Joseph Marable (Company H) picked up the upper half of the bullet-snapped staff, Lieutenants William Peel (Company C) and Robert A. McDowell (Company H) and eleven enlisted men gathered around them and closed to within thirty yards of the Federals.

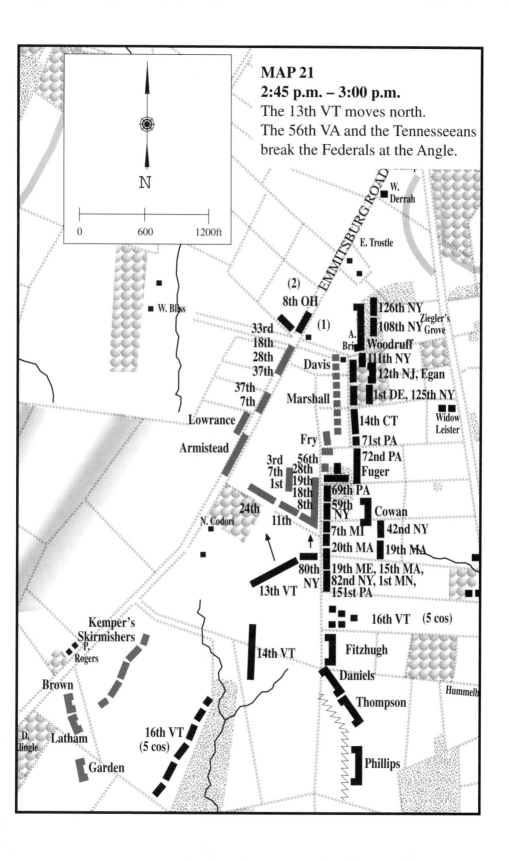

MAP 21
2:45 p.m. – 3:00 p.m.
The 13th VT moves north.
The 56th VA and the Tennesseeans
break the Federals at the Angle.

N

0   600   1200ft

W. Derrah

E. Trostle

(2)
8th OH

W. Bliss

33rd
18th
28th
37th

(1)

126th NY
108th NY   Ziegler's Grove
A.   Woodruff
Bri
Davis   111th NY
12th NJ, Egan

37th
7th

Marshall   1st DE, 125th NY

Lowrance   14th CT   Widow Leister

Armistead   Fry   71st PA

3rd   56th   72nd PA
7th   28th   Fuger
1st   19th
18th   69th PA
8th   59th
24th   NY   Cowan

N. Codori   11th

7th MI   42nd NY

20th MA   19th MA

80th   19th ME, 15th MA,
NY   82nd NY, 1st MN,
13th VT   151st PA

16th VT   (5 cos)

Kemper's
Skirmishers
P.
Rogers   14th VT   Fitzhugh

Brown   Daniels   Hummelb

D.   Latham   Thompson
lingle

16th VT
(5 cos)   Phillips

Garden

EMMITSBURG ROAD

Rushing forward, they took cover behind the west wall of the Brian barn and began popping off rounds at the 12th New Jersey and the 111th New York at point-blank range.[153]

The Emmitsburg Road
Trimble's Division

The blasts from Woodruff's and Egan's guns momentarily stalled Lowrance's and Lane's brigades which were approaching the Emmitsburg Road.[154] Lane's brigade split, with part of it heading toward the left flank to fill a gap created by Marshall's and Davis' advance across the road. The 33rd, 18th, 28th, and part of the 37th North Carolina regiments veered northeast while the 7th with the remainder of the 37th North Carolina guided to the southeast, crowding Lowrance's line.[155]

Trimble followed the left of the division, believing that Lowrance's brigade was still coming up on his right. Lane's left wing scrambled over the fence into the road bed and, contrary to orders, began shooting.[156] A ball hit Union brigade commander Colonel Eliakim Sherrill in the abdomen. A few very eager volunteers from the 39th New York carried him from the field before word could reach any of the regimental officers of his wounding.[157] The color guard of the 28th North Carolina with the 33rd North Carolina crossed into the field on the eastern side of the road. Rushing forward, they merged with the survivors of Marshall's brigade.[158]

On the right of the division, Major J. McLeod Turner, seeing the left wing of the 71st Pennsylvania abandon the wall, commanded the 7th North Carolina to knock down the fences bordering the pike. The North Carolinians hit the west fence with a vengeance and pushed it over; however, they lost momentum in their descent into the road bed and failed to budge the one on the east side.[159]

Behind him Lowrance's regiments, however, did not get beyond the Emmitsburg Road. The fences across their line of advance, having deranged their formations severely, created a great deal of confusion in the ranks. According to Third Lieutenant Henry C. Moore (Adjutant, 38th North Carolina), men dropped with fearful rapidity. The Yankee artillery and small arms fire reduced his front to a skirmish line before he reached the Emmitsburg Road. Reforming along the fence on the western side of the road, he attempted to rally the jumbled commands from his own brigade as well as from those fleeing from Marshall's regiments. He asked Captain Abel S. Cloud, commanding the 16th North Carolina, what he should do. "We will hold here until we get help," came the reply. Turner looked behind him and in the distance could see troops (Brigadier General William Mahone's brigade) maneuvering along Seminary Ridge. When they disappeared from sight on the western side of the crest, he realized that no help would arrive. The men returned a sporadic rifle fire into the smoke along their front.[160]

At that Turner, leading by example, climbed over the top rail and the few men who could, followed him. The attack dragged the right wing of the 37th North Carolina with it.[161] The 16th, 22nd, and the 38th North Carolina followed them over.[162] The charge lasted ten yards. A bullet bounced off his instep and knocked the major down. Rather than face slaughter, his squad turned about and raced back to the Emmitsburg Road. Those who survived the gauntlet, threw themselves onto the road and returned fire with the rest of the regiment.[163] The colors of 16th surged ahead toward the plank fence north of the Angle while those of the 22nd North Carolina and the 38th North Carolina, with their squad-sized regiments, continued to the stone wall.[164] Major John C. Timberlake (53rd Virginia) upon seeing the Tar Heels falter and retreat leaped upon the wall and screamed as loudly as he could, "For God's sake, come on!"[165]

As he approached the Angle, Lieutenant Thomas L. Norwood (Company A, 37th North Carolina) saw what was left of Cushing's crews abandon their position along the stone wall. Accompanied by a few officers, he leaped over the plank fence near the apex of the Angle, elated with the prospect of actually breaking the Union line.[166]

Major Turner, when he realized the bullet had not punctured his boot, raised himself to his feet and painfully hobbled back to the road. Once over the fence, he continued to the left of the regiment where he found Captain James G. Harris (Company H), his second in command and turned the regiment over to him. Scarcely had he done so than a minie ball thudded into his waist. Striking the spinal column in its exit, it dropped the major unconscious in the dirt. He regained his senses within seconds only to discover himself paralyzed from the waist down.[167]

Hays' Division

From where his men lay concealed behind the crest of the knoll on the northwestern side of Ziegler's Grove, Lieutenant L. Emerson Bicknell (Andrews' Sharpshooters) and his twenty riflemen carefully selected their targets. In quick order they shot down three mounted officers.[168] One of them was Trimble.[169]

Hays ordered the 39th New York to reinforce the flank along the Brian lane. "There was considerable shirking," Captain Samuel C. Armstrong (Company D, 125th New York) wrote later.[170] The New Yorkers did more than shirk. The Federal line along the 33rd North Carolina's left front became ominously silent. About sixty yards from the stone wall, Major Joseph H. Saunders (33rd North Carolina) noticed a Federal color bearer leap to his feet, drop the lance head of the standard to the ground, and take off at a trot toward the orchard on the crest of the ridge. With the National flag dragging in the grass behind him, he led a considerable number of his comrades in a headlong flight to safety.[171] Some of the 111th New York did not behave any better. One of their officers lay face first on the ground trying to protect his skull with a hard cracker box. Lieutenant John Brady (1st Delaware) was going to rally that officer's men when he noticed his own regimental colors fall again. Scrambling over to the center of the line, he found them with Sergeant Thomas Seymour, who had been literally cut in half by a 12-pounder ball. Brady picked up the flag, determined not to relinquish it until the action ended.[172]

To the north, Captain Morris Brown's Company A, 126th New York and Captain Samuel C. Armstrong's Company D of the 125th New York charged into Brian's lane from the Trostle house, and caught Davis' and Lane's brigades on the flank.[173] Colonel Osmon Latrobe, braving the hellish fire between the road and the stone wall, clattered up to General Lane, whom he found behind his brigade. He had just warned him of a possible flanking movement west of the Emmitsburg Road when a bullet bored into the general's horse, throwing it into a panic. At the same time, a round killed Latrobe's mount. Officer and horse went down in a heap. Freeing himself, Latrobe retrieved his saddle and staggered back toward Spangler's Woods.

With the horse bucking madly, Lane freed himself from the saddle and ran over to Colonel Clark M. Avery (33rd North Carolina), whom he ordered to face left to meet the troops. "My God, General," Avery hollered, "do you intend rushing your men into such a place unsupported, when the troops on the right are falling back?" Realizing how hopeless the situation had become, Lane gave the order to withdraw.[174] A round struck Major Joseph Saunders through his open mouth while he shouted at his wing of the 33rd North Carolina to close to the south. The bullet crashed through the back of his skull, knocking him unconscious. He tumbled into the grass, seemingly more dead than alive.[175] The 26th North Carolina, having less than sixty officers and men on the line, found itself in an untenable situation. The 12th New Jersey cut down the regimental color bearer within yards of the stone wall.[176] At the same time Lieutenant Emerson Bicknell and his sharpshooters joined in the rush to make the surprise more complete.[177] At the Brian barn, Lieutenant Peel of the 11th Mississippi anxiously looked behind him only to see Confederates streaming from the field. It did not take him long to order his men to throw down their arms. Within seconds, a white flag jutted out from the corner of the back wall.[178] Those Rebels who were not dead or wounded either ran for their lives or threw themselves behind stones, folds in the ground, the bank of the Emmitsburg Road, and Confederate corpses—anything that would provide some kind of cover.[179] Seconds later the pinned Rebels semaphored with their handkerchiefs or white strips of cloth that they had taken enough. They had no fight left in them.[180] At that the New Yorkers sprang over the fence and started rounding up prisoners. Captain Brown picked up the colors of the 28th North Carolina while his men brought in four other stands of colors.[181] A Yankee sergeant rushed in upon Peel and his squad and marched them back through the gate on the north side of the barn. As they passed through the 111th New York, one of the Federals leveled his weapon and jabbed the muzzle against one of the Rebels' chest, but the sergeant sprang between them and with an exclamation knocked the barrel skyward. Did he not see that those men had surrendered and were unarmed? he asked.[182]

The Peach Orchard

Having left Wilcox to make his own advance, Captain Robert A. Bright galloped into the Peach Orchard looking for Pickett. Unable to find him, he wheeled about to continue his search when, in the distance, he spied Hays' movement into the fields north of the Angle. The forces, being so much larger than what remained of Pickett's division, led him to estimate them to be about 7,000 strong. The sight of the division flag drew him toward the Sherfy barn where he found Pickett, too close to the road to see the flanking party. He quickly apprised the general of the situation and suggested Pickett pull the division out before the Yankees gobbled it up. "I have been watching my left all the time, expecting this, but it is provided for. Ride to Dearing's Battalion; they have orders to follow up the charge and keep their caissons filled; order them to open with every gun and break that column and keep it broken." With that, Bright again set off for the ridge west of Spangler's Woods.

Riding into Captain Robert M. Stribling's Virginia Battery, he found First Lieutenant William C. Marshall in command. When he told Marshall to pass the order to the rest of the batteries to return fire, the lieutenant replied, "The battalion has no ammunition. I have only three solid shot." Why did no one obey the order to keep the caissons full? Bright demanded to know. "The caissons have been away three quarters of an hour," the lieutenant explained, "and there is a rumor that General Pendleton has sent the reserve artillery ammunition more than a mile in rear of the field." Knowing the Federals would carry the field, Bright told the lieutenant to use his three rounds. The first ball missed. The second thudded into the ground in front of the Yankee formation. The third also missed. As the guns ceased fire, the captain spurred through the settling smoke and hunted for Pickett.[183]

Seminary Ridge

From his position on the ridge north of Spangler's Woods, Major William T. Poague carefully studied the charge. The moment he saw Pickett's men top the rise east of the Emmitsburg Road, he issued the order to limber up and prepare to advance. Within minutes, however, he noticed groups of men streaming from the field—first in small clusters then in alarmingly larger numbers. Without warning, Pickett rode alone into the battalion line. Stopping near one of the guns, the general studied the front with his glasses. Riding over to him, the major saluted. "General, my orders are that as soon as our troops get up the hill I am to move as rapidly as possible to their support. But I don't like the looks of things up there." Pickett, who did not even acknowledge Poague's presence, kept his eyes fastened upon the Federal lines. His expression seemed sad and hurt. In the distance, Poague spied a Virginia battle flag being trailed along the crest of Cemetery Ridge by a mounted soldier. "General," he asked, "is that Virginia flag carried by one of our men or by the enemy?" The general did not reply. Poague queried, "What do you think I ought to do under the circumstances? Our men are leaving the hill."

"I think you had better save your guns," Pickett shot back. Before the major could respond, the general took off at a gallop to the southeast. Poague responded as he had been trained. He ordered up his six howitzers to prepare to meet a counterattack.

Very shortly after Pickett left, General Robert E. Lee approached the major, calling him by name. "How are you off for ammunition, Major?" he asked. About one quarter of his original issue but the howitzers would come up soon, came the reply. "Ah! that's well; we may need them," Lee sighed. The general remained next to Poague to watch the retreat.[184]

Near the Leister House

Captain Meade reached the low ground on the eastern side of Cemetery Ridge about the time Pickett's men crossed the Emmitsburg Road. Looking in the direction of the firing, in the distance, he recognized his father alone in an open field. Presently, Lieutenant Ranald S. McKenzie, the general's A.D.C., galloped up to Meade, delivered a report and rode off. The captain did not catch his father's attention until he reined up alongside him. "Hello George, is that you?" the general said with a smile. "I am glad you are here." It was a pretty "lively" place, the general added before advising his son, "Let's go up here and find out what is going on." The closer they got to the crest, the less they could see through the smoke. Turning to the right to get away from the batteries, the general and his son headed toward the orchard behind the Brian barn. "Look out for Hays," Meade advised the captain.[185]

The Angle

Major Moxley Sorrel, failing to find Pickett, followed after Garnett and Armistead but never reached them. An artillery shell exploded under his chestnut mare, ripping its hind legs off. Angered over the death of his best horse, the staff officer quickly confiscated another horse from another mounted soldier who stood nearby. Before he left, he secured the other man's promise to retrieve the major's saddle.[186]

With the destruction of Garnett's brigade and the minimal silence which followed its demise, Armistead rushed his reduced brigade toward the 650-foot gap along the front of the 69th Pennsylvania. On the way, a minie ball whistled into Company I, 9th Virginia. Striking First Lieutenant

John C. Niemeyer in the head, it killed him instantly.[187] Color Sergeant Leander C. Blackburn (53rd Virginia) went down—wounded—in the hail of rifle fire from the wall. First Corporal James T. Carter grabbed the colors from his hands and attempted to carry them forward but Fourth Corporal John B. Scott wrenched them from his grasp. Rushing fifteen feet ahead of the brigade, he waved them back and forth until a bullet killed him. First Corporal Robert Tyler Jones, grandson of former President John Tyler, darted from the line and picked them up just as a round knocked Carter to the ground and another struck Jones in the arm.[188]

Armistead's men streamed to the lip of the rock ledge to within sixty feet of the 69th Pennsylvania, where his men went prone among the survivors of Garnett's brigade. The general slipped back to the rear of the line as the command traveled along the ranks to open fire. All the while, the Virginians were taking tremendous casualties. As the report of the volley died away, Armistead elbowed his way through the ranks to the front of the brigade, his hat now resting on the sword hilt, and led his Virginians across the front of the 69th Pennsylvania toward the stretch of wall abandoned by the 71st Pennsylvania.[189] The very few men who reached the wall stopped temporarily in front of it, unsure as to what course to follow. A quick scan of his own regiment told Second Sergeant Francis M. Baily (Company F) that only a skirmish line remained of the 9th Virginia.[190] "Colonel," Armistead called to Lieutenant Colonel Rawley Martin, "we can't stay here." "Then we'll go forward," Martin replied.[191] "Now give 'em the cold steel, boys!" Armistead yelled.[192] Corporal Jones leaped upon the top of the wall with the flag when a second bullet knocked him head first onto the Federal side. First Lieutenant Hutchings L. Carter (Company I, 53rd Virginia) picked the colors up and with Colonel Martin and three men from Company I—Third Sergeant Thomas Tredway, Second Lieutenant James W. Whitehead, and Private James C. Coleman—followed him over the top.[193]

Sergeant Drewry B. Easley (Company H, 14th Virginia), having failed to catch his deserter, plowed past the first rank of the 57th Virginia, which had overlapped the rear of his regiment. In the process, he ran into Company F of the 69th Pennsylvania. Instinctively, he dropped his bayoneted weapon to "charge bayonets" only to discover the Federals had their hands above their heads. "The day is ours," Major John C. Timberlake (53rd Virginia) cried aloud. Pushing through them, Easley found himself on top of the stone wall to the right of Cushing's Number Five gun. Glancing to the left, he saw Armistead crossing over to the left of Number Four.[194] "Turn the guns!" Armistead bellowed.[195] Major Timberlake (53rd Virginia) immediately leaped upon the rock wall as Armistead cleared it. "Look at your general!" he shouted. "Follow him!."[196] The moment Armistead stepped over the wall with a few men from the 28th Virginia, something shattered Private Calvin P. Dearing's rifle. Plucking a Mississippi rifle from the side of a nearby corpse, he immediately loaded it without springing the rammer. He pulled the trigger. The piece discharged with terrible force. The blast ripped the gun from his hands and sent him into a double somersault behind the line. In a daze, the private from Company G, believing he had been hit by a solid shot, watched the rifle land like a spear, muzzle first in the ground nearby.[197]

Private William P. Jesse (Company F, 28th Virginia) watched Captain Waller M. Boyd (Company G, 19th Virginia) cross over the wall. When he called for more men to follow, Jesse and a number of men from the 28th Virginia responded. A bullet struck Jesse in the thigh. He turned about and limped back toward Seminary Ridge.[198] The Virginians exploited the gap and poured into the copse between the rear of Company A and the right flank of Company D.[199] Private Erasmus Williams (Company H, 14th Virginia) nearly tore his left forefinger in two when he snagged it while trying to bring Number Four to bear east.[200]

Rounds slammed into the two right companies of the 69th Pennsylvania from the southwest. Lieutenant Colonel Martin Tshudy (69th Pennsylvania), his head bandaged from a wound received the day before, died behind Company I. Colonel O'Kane (69th Pennsylvania) went down—mortally wounded. Lieutenant Michael Mullen (Company G) perished in the hand-to-hand fighting to the left of Company D. Private Anthony McDermott (Company I) shot a frightened glance to his right toward Webb who was futilely yelling at the 72nd Pennsylvania to come to their assistance.[201] Second Lieutenant Henry Russell (Company A, 72nd Pennsylvania), who stood not ten feet from the general, knew the men could not hear Webb above the din shouting at them to flank to the right to clear the copse of trees. He took it upon himself to literally push his men to the north so they could safely return fire to the front.[202] Captain Charles H. Banes (A.A.G. of the Second Brigade) trooped the rear of the reluctant Pennsylvanians, slapping the men with the flat of his sword, but they would not budge.[203]

Company D turned back on itself and took the Rebels on in a vicious hand-to-hand fight. Private Hugh Bradley, gripping his rifle by the muzzle, swung it around him like a mace until a Confederate stove in his skull with a rifle butt. Private Thomas Donally when ordered to give up, shouted back, "I surrender," while knocking his assailant off his feet. That company's stubbornness saved Companies A and I from capture.[204] On the left of the regiment, Corporal John Buckley (Company K) pulled Private Henry W. Murray (Company H) to his feet. A bullet having taken away both of his eyes, the horribly mutilated man begged his corporal to kill him on the spot rather than live a life without his sight. Buckley ignored him and led him to the rear.[205]

The Confederates pushed toward the stone wall on the left of the 69th Pennsylvania. Private Robert T. Whittick (Company E) with the regimental flag retreated with the color guard about eight feet until the slashings in the copse of trees stopped him. In the process, he grabbed a Confederate by the collar and pulled him upright across the stone wall where he decked him. With the Rebs on top of them the Pennsylvanians fought with clubbed

muskets and fists.[206] The suddenness of the attack caught General
Hunt with Cowan's battery. He emptied his revolver into the Confederates, all the while shouting, "See
'em. See 'em. See 'em," before they
killed his mount. Horse and rider
went down as one. Cowan, who
stood to the general's left, and Sergeant Orasmus Van Ettan hurriedly
pulled Hunt free of the corpse.
Cowan immediately handed the
reins of Van Ettan's large bay to him.
Swinging into the saddle, Hunt called
over his shoulder as he galloped
away, "Look out, or you will kill our
men."[207]

Brigadier General Henry Hunt

The general nearly lost his life when the
Confederates shot his horse down near
Cowan's guns.

Battles and Leaders, III

The 59th New York, which was
lying down behind the cover of a
slight earthwork on line with the
Pennsylvanians, leaped to its feet
and streamed to the rear, uncover-
ing the front of Cowan's guns, which
were on the ridge behind them.[208] The majority of the Confederates went
to ground behind the wall, but Colonel James G. Hodges (14th Virginia),
with several officers behind him, leaped upon the wall and, waving his
sword, urged his men forward with "Take the guns." Some of the Confederates spilled over the works and were almost on top of the battery, shooting
as they advanced. Lieutenant William P. Wright collapsed with a bullet
through the lungs as he stood by Cowan's side.[209] The 7th Michigan refused its right flank, facing north and catching the Rebels in a very effective crossfire.[210]

The captain instructed his men to retire the guns as soon as they
fired. Private Jake McElroy, on the Number Two gun, having rammed canister down the tube, turned to Cowan and yelled, "Captain, this is my last
round." "I know it, Jake," the captain replied. McElroy collapsed on his face
the moment he stepped outside the wheel of the gun, with three bullet
wounds in his head. At thirty feet, the five pieces slammed double canister
into Armistead's men, pulverizing them. The right wing of the 18th Virginia
had just halted to fight it out with Stannard's Vermonters at a distance of
fifty yards when Cowan's last salvo caught them square on the flank. Not
giving the Rebels time to rally, the artillerymen retired their pieces by hand
to another rise of ground about fifty yards to the east.[211] The 13th Vermont
shot the Confederates to pieces as they closed in for the kill. As they did

so, the 16th Vermont, having caught up with them filed to the left behind their line and extended the formation farther west.[212]

Cowan and Private James Plunkett remained on the crest as the guns were run back. Fleeing Federal infantry swarmed all around them. A captain, his sword tucked under his arm, dashed past Cowan, his head bobbing like a turkey's with Cowan's curses echoing off his back. Plunkett jumped from one spot to the next, trying to pummel the infantrymen back into the ranks but to no avail. Out of exasperation, he slammed a coffee pot over a man's head with enough force to break the bottom out of it. The frightened infantryman kept on going, with the pot hanging around his ears.[213]

Southeast of the Angle

While Lieutenant Edward Moale was away, Gibbon looked to his left and noticed men trickling from the short line of works held by the 143rd Pennsylvania. Riding over to them, the general hurried them back into line and rode back to the 19th Maine, which had still not advanced beyond its works.[214]

Colonel Norman Hall's brigade, south of the copse of trees, under Lieutenant Moale's directive, was one of the first commands to respond to the rout of the 59th New York. Sergeant Major George W. Leach ran down the line to Lieutenant Colonel George N. Macy (20th Massachusetts), who was on the ground behind his regiment. Shouting above the din, the sergeant major cried, "Colonel Hall directs that you move the 20th in rear of the line and attack the flank of [the] enemy as they come in, at once." Calling to Captain Henry Abbott, on the right of the line, he commanded him to move his men en masse toward the copse of trees and that he would follow immediately with the rest of the regiment. Abbott, at the head of Company I, with Company A close behind, faced his men about. They started at a run toward the Federal center, losing their formations as they advanced. They fronted near the copse of trees when small arms fire spattered into the regiment. Three bullets slammed into Macy. One snatched his sword from his right hand. Another, striking him in the left shoulder, ripped the shoulder strap off his blouse and knocked him down. As he gained his feet, a third round shattered his left hand.[215] The charge dragged in the 7th Michigan and the 19th Maine. Private William Deming (Company F, 7th Michigan) got a bead on the color bearer of the 18th Virginia and killed him. Rushing forward, he grabbed the colors, stuck them in the ground by his side and started shooting into the Rebels at point-blank range. Without warning, Lieutenant Charles E. Hunt (59th New York) rode up to him. With his sword drawn, he threatened to cut the private down if he did not surrender the flag to him. In the general confusion, the soldiers who witnessed the shameful act swore the officer wore a colonel's shoulder boards.[216]

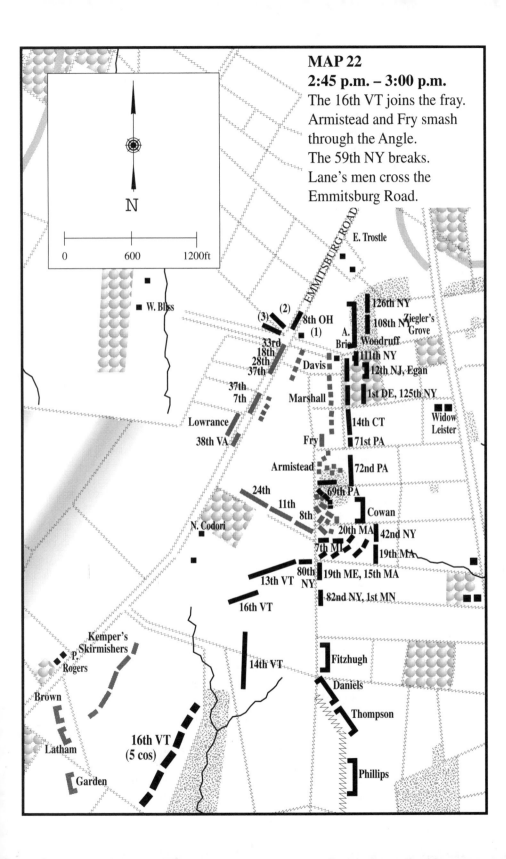

MAP 22
2:45 p.m. – 3:00 p.m.
The 16th VT joins the fray.
Armistead and Fry smash
through the Angle.
The 59th NY breaks.
Lane's men cross the
Emmitsburg Road.

N

0   600   1200ft

EMMITSBURG ROAD

E. Trostle

W. Bliss

(3) (2) 8th OH
        (1)

126th NY
108th NY   Ziegler's
A.   Grove
Bri   Woodruff

33rd
18th
28th   Davis
37th

111th NY
12th NJ, Egan

37th
7th   Marshall

1st DE, 125th NY

Lowrance
38th VA   Fry

14th CT   Widow
                   Leister

71st PA

Armistead   72nd PA

24th   69th PA
    11th
        8th   Cowan

N. Codori   20th MA   42nd NY
                   7th MI   19th MA

            80th   19th ME, 15th MA
    13th VT NY

    16th VT   82nd NY, 1st MN

Kemper's
P. Skirmishers   Fitzhugh

Rogers   14th VT
                            Daniels

Brown
                            Thompson

Latham   16th VT
          (5 cos)

Garden   Phillips

The 15th Massachusetts rushed into the fray resembling a mob more than a regiment. The moment they arrived at the southwestern side of the copse of trees, the New Englanders opened fire at point blank range at the Rebels, who had thrown themselves down behind the stone wall. For five minutes they took a terrible beating from the Rebels. Finally Private George H. Cunningham (Company B) screamed, "For God's sake let us charge; they'll kill us all if we stay here." At the sight of the Yankees surging forward en masse, the Confederates leaped up and bolted for their own lines. When they attempted to take their flag with them, the 15th Massachusetts halted and volleyed into them. The surviving Rebels flopped behind the wall again, and begged the Yankees to stop shooting and let them come in. The New Englanders complied. While a few of the Virginians leaped over to the Federal side of the wall, the rest hightailed it toward the Emmitsburg Road. The Bay Staters instantly leveled their weapons and cut loose, indiscriminately gunning down skedaddlers and prisoners alike.[217]

Moale had hardly met Gibbon there when something stung the general behind the left shoulder. The impact stunned him. Blood rolled down the inside of his sleeve and trickled over this left hand. He grew faint. Realizing that he could no longer effectively continue on the field, he told Moale to inform Brigadier General William Harrow that he had to take command. With Captain Francis Wessels at his side, Gibbon headed toward the rear.[218]

The Southern End of the Angle
The Angle

The Confederates swarmed around Cushing's abandoned field pieces, cheering the whole while.[219] Lieutenant Colonel Rawley Martin (53rd Virginia), his blood up, refused to surrender. Back at the Number Four rifle, which the Virginians had swung about, Private Erasmus Williams (Company H, 14th Virginia) shouted at him, "Look, Colonel, the Yankees are flanking us; we must get out of here." "No," Martin yelled back, "hold on, men, rally, rally, right here."[220]

Captain Jacob B. Turney (1st Tennessee) called back to what remained of his regiment to cross the wall and enfilade the Yankees on the left as soon as their supports came up. That fire would provide cover for the relief to break the center. Upon seeing part of Trimble's division advancing to their support, the captain ordered the regiment forward. The color bearer, Wiley Woods, and a few men climbed over the wall and followed him toward Cushing's Number Three gun.[221]

Sergeant Drewry B. Easley (Company H, 14th Virginia) kept pace with Armistead to within a few feet of Number Three gun when he noticed about twenty-five or more Federals, surrounding a stand of colors, closing in on their left. A volley slammed into the men around Armistead.[222] Private Anthony McDermott (Company I, 69th Pennsylvania) watched the general double over and clasp his stomach with his left hand. Dropping his sword, he clamped his right hand to his wounded left arm and staggered toward Cushing's Number Three gun. Reaching out with his hands, he flailed at the muzzle. His left hand slapped the tube as he dropped to his knees into Captain Turney's arms who momentarily snagged him before lowering him full length onto his right side. Turney did not wait to be cut down. As quickly as possible, he ordered the men within shouting distance to withdraw to the protection of the wall.[223] Orderly Sergeant June Kimble (Company A, 14th Tennessee) sprang over the north wall and made for the slab fence extending from the apex of the Angle.[224] Lieutenant George W. Finley (56th Virginia) did not stay in the killing ground for long either. He also retreated to the western face of the wall.[225]

The Codori House

The wounded Captain William Berkeley (Company D, 8th Virginia) and a half dozen injured Confederates, having taken shelter in the base-ment of the house with an equal number of Federal casualties heard the cheering also. The captain immediately told the Yankees they were Con-federate prisoners. Not at all, the Federals jeered, you are ours.[226]

Northeast of the Angle
The 14th Connecticut

Major Theodore Ellis (14th Connecticut), who wanted the colors of the 14th Tennessee as a prize, called for volunteers to get it. Sergeant Major William B. Hincks, Captain John Broatch (Company A), and Ser-geant George N. Brigham (Company D) leaped over the wall and charged pell-mell for the Rebel color guard. A Rebel turned while quitting the field and dropped Brigham with a bullet in his side. The screaming Hincks, through the corner of his eye, saw Cushing's lone Number Three gun to his left as he sped past the northern side of the Angle. Swinging his sword wildly over his head, he reached the flag ahead of Broatch. Still yelling like a madman and brandishing his sword, he pulled the flag from Boney Smith's hands. Hincks, who was more afraid of being hit by the buck and ball loads of the 12th New Jersey, wheeled about and raced back to the wall. A wild cheer went up from the 14th Connecticut which was carried along a good bit of the II Corps line. Major Theodore Ellis (14th Connecticut), seeing the Confederates retreating from the Angle, commanded the regiment to fire by the left oblique.[227]

Inside the Angle

Private Milton Harding (Company G, 9th Virginia), who was on Armistead's immediate left, ducked under the muzzle of the piece. Could he do anything for him? Harding asked. Get the brandy from his shoulder satchel, the general gasped. Armistead took a couple of swallows. Where was he hurt? the private asked. Hit in the breast and the arm, Armistead said. Harding offered to move the general but he refused. Watch out for yourself, Armistead

Captain John Broatch,   Lieutenant William B. Hincks,
Company A, 14th Connecticut   14th Connecticut

Broatch lost his race for the colors of the 14th Tennessee leaving them to, then, Sergeant Major Hincks, who in turn, won the Medal of Honor.

MOLLUS, USAMHI

told him.[228] Taking cover between the wheel and the tube, Easley returned fire until the Yankees sighted in on him. Gravel, kicked up by the low-striking bullets, stung him. One snapped off the tip of his ramrod at the forestock. Without any hesitation, the sergeant raced back to the stone wall, leaving Armistead, whom he presumed to be dead, where he had fallen. Harding was close behind.[229]

Artilleryman Miles Newbury, having been trod upon during the charge for the crest, lifted his head toward the southwest. To his relief, he saw Stannard's Vermonters closing in on Kemper's flank. "We have got that damn battery that cut us to shreds," he heard someone yell. Turning onto his side to face the voice, he defiantly retorted, "Yes, you have got it, but you look to the rear." Lieutenant Colonel Rawley Martin (53rd Virginia) twisted his body toward the right, hastily took in the situation and quick stepped back toward the wall. Newbury started for his own lines, only to be knocked unconscious by a Confederate shell burst.[230] Sergeant Major Stockton and his four Pennsylvanians, with Federal bullets slapping the rocks about their heads from the southwest, decided to make a run for it. Raising his head to see where the bullets came from, Stockton caught a glimpse of the Federals closing in on the Confederate right. At his command, he and his party leaped the wall, heading east.[231]

Armistead's downfall triggered an immediate response among the men in the Angle. Major Timberlake immediately ordered his men to the west side of the fence to fend off the Yankees as best as they could.[232] Hurling their weapons, then themselves to the ground, a great many of the Rebels gave up the fight, while others ran for their lives to the opposite side of the stone wall.[233] Someone shouted, "Hold on, boys, yonder comes our support."[234] Private Erasmus Williams (Company H, 14th Virginia) did not intend to stay. "We must get away from here, Colonel," he pleaded. Rawley Martin made a step to go over the wall when three bullets found their mark. One shattered his right thigh, another grazed his left leg, and a third slapped into his left thigh. Unable to stand, he toppled to the ground on the Federal side. Nearby lay First Lieutenant William H. Bray (Company E, 53rd Virginia) with a deadly thigh wound. Sergeant Thomas Tredway (Company I) rushed to Martin's assistance only to fall, mortally wounded, across the major's body. Williams broke into a run when a bullet bored through the meat of his left wrist. Despite the pain, he kept on going.[235] Drewry Easley (Company H, 14th Virginia) took a weapon from a wounded comrade. When trying to load it, the ball only passed about halfway down the bore. The exasperated sergeant slammed the rammer against the wall trying to load the piece when the man who handed it to him rolled over and belatedly said, "Don't load it; it's loaded." Welling up with anger, Easley demanded, "Where are you wounded anyhow? I don't see anything the matter with you." With a groan, the fellow rolled over, his face toward the ground. In a rage, Easley went to club the musket to bash the man's brains out but instead raised the piece as high as he could and let the butt drop full force upon the back of the man's skull. The man moaned as if hit by a shell.[236]

The Ridge West of the Codori Farm

The very busy Captain Robert Bright caught up with Pickett on the crest of the ridge southwest of the Codori farm. From where they stood they could see Armistead's men struggling at the wall and what was left of the right flank of the division literally fighting for its survival. No help could be expected, the captain informed the general. The Yankees were enveloping the division. Nothing could save them now. Seconds later, they helplessly watched the left of the line at the stone wall give way and collapse. When the reality of the fiasco dawned upon him, Pickett turned his horse toward the rear and Bright followed.[237]

The Angle

Without any warning, the small arms fire suddenly died away. On the northern end of the Angle, Captain Turney called together Captains James H. Thompson (Company F), Henry J. Hawkins, Thomas P. Arnold (Company H), and Thom Alexander to decide what to do. A courier reined to a halt behind the brigade, yelling for the commanding officer. Turney faced him. General Lee wanted the men to hold their position. Ewell had carried the left of the line, he said.[238]

Fry's Brigade

Falling off the top rail of the slab fence, Sergeant June Kimble (Company A, 14th Tennessee) landed behind a large rock. To his right, a man from the 38th Virginia had taken cover behind another rock. Glancing to his left, Kimble noticed that the fence ran along an outcropping of sorts. Everywhere he looked to either side, he noticed men singly or in pairs behind boulders plugging away at the Federals. Fifty to sixty yards to the northeast, he noticed a Yankee, conspicuous in his blue trousers and red shirt, standing with his left foot on a low spot in the wall and plinking away at the Confederates near the Angle. Five times, he unsuccessfully tried to pick off the man. Turning to the young Virginian on his right, he said, "Shoot that fellow in the red shirt to the left." "Why, damn him," the boy spat, "I have shot at him four times. I am getting out of here." Jumping to his feet, he turned on his heels to run. Kimble heard the distinctive crack of the bullet penetrating the Virginian's head. The "beardless youth," as he referred to him, fell like a spent shot onto his face—dead.[239]

The West Wall of the Angle

A panicked soldier raced along the back of the 56th Virginia shouting, "General Lee says fall back from here." A considerable number of soldiers broke for the rear. Lieutenant George W. Finley kept the men in his immediate vicinity in their places. Telling them he did not believe the authenticity of the report, he tried to reassure them by having them look to the west for supports.[240]

A rifle ball shattered Sergeant William M. Lawson's right arm, knocking the colors of the 1st Virginia from his hand. Private Jacob R. Polak (Company I) tried to pick them up when two bullets found their marks. One nicked his left arm. The other whacked his nose without carrying any of it away. Dropping the flag against the stone wall, he decided to make a run for it. (He had little trouble clearing the fence along the Emmitsburg Road, despite his injuries.)[241]

Southeast of the Angle
Hall's Brigade

General Winfield Scott Hancock (II Corps commander) and his orderly, Corporal Uriah N. Parmelee (Company D, 6th New York Cavalry) passed within fifty yards of the Confederates on their way to see Stannard. To Parmelee it seemed like the II Corps' right was folding up. As the two rode over a tumbled down section of stone wall near the right rear of the 42nd New York a bullet slapped Parmelee's hat brim within an inch of his head, and his horse kicked under the impact of another round. For a moment he thought the horse was done for. Forgetting about how close he came to dying, he fretted the entire time about how he had almost lost the easiest riding mount he had ever had.[242] Hancock rode up to Colonel Arthur F. Devereaux (19th Massachusetts), who motioned him aside to point at the Confederate flags inside the Angle. The colonel asked for permission to turn his men loose. "Get in God Damn quick," Hancock fired back. Turning to Colonel James E. Mallon, commanding the 42nd New York, he directed him to move his regiment by the right oblique. The two regiments took off in echelon, striking the copse of trees between the 20th Massachusetts and the immovable 72nd Pennsylvania. Breaking through the copse on the north side, Major Edmund Rice hollered, "Follow me, boys!" when a bullet in the hip sent him crashing to the ground. The National colors of the 19th Massachusetts went down. Lieutenant Moses Shackley (Company B) quickly picked them up. Within seconds, First Lieutenant Herman Donath (Company C), carrying the state flag, was killed and Shackley was wounded. Sergeant Benjamin Jellison (Company C), without thinking, raised both flags and charged, dragging the regiment behind him.[243] Formations fell apart as the ranks became tangled and jumbled. Men fired through any available openings, undoubtedly wounding some of their own in the smoke-clogged trees and open ground to their front.[244]

**Major Edmund Rice,
19th Massachusetts**

Wounded during the final charge against the copse of trees, the major used a captured Confederate battle flag as his crutch.

MOLLUS, USAMHI

Lieutenant William Lochren (Adjutant, 1st Minnesota) never heard anyone yell the regiment into a charge. Before he had time to restrain his men, Color Bearer Henry D. O'Brien dashed toward the backs of Webb's regiments as they charged into the melee. A bullet snapped off the staff two feet below the flag. Grasping the upper half of the staff, he continued on until two bullets struck him, with one of them smashing his hand. When the colors went down Corporal W. Newell Irvine (Company D) took them from him. The 1st Minnesota chased after him. The Rebels killed Captain Nathan S. Messick, commanding the regiment.[245] A ball struck First Lieutenant William Lochren in the belt and knocked him off his feet, whereupon Sergeant John Cole assumed command of his company.[246]

By then Captain John D. S. Cook (Company I, 80th New York) had rejoined his company on the southern side of the Angle. The fighting had become particularly vicious. The New Yorkers in the front rank, rather than use their bayonets, went into the melee with clubbed rifles while those behind them fired blindly over their heads into the confused mass in front of them.[247] After enduring about five minutes of volleying, the Confederate formations began dissolving by squads. Most of the Rebels in front of the 80th New York threw themselves to the ground rather than risk being shot in the backs by the Yankee rifle fire which swept the field west of the Angle. Captain Cook's men yelled at them to put their hands up and come in, saying they would not hurt them if they surrendered. Literally hundreds of the Virginians dropped their weapons, raised their hands, crouched over, and scurried into the Federal lines. They feared being killed by their own guns which still pummeled the area.[248] Captain George G. Benedict (A.D.C. to Stannard) swore that at least two thirds of the living Confederates surrendered. The Confederate dead littered the ground in front of the two Vermont regiments.[249]

The Angle

Private Anthony McDermott (Company I, 69th Pennsylvania) immediately wheeled about, and tapping General Webb on the shoulder, told him that the Rebels' commander was down and they were running. The general, who was bleeding from a bullet wound along the inside of his right thigh, turned and hollered at Lieutenant Colonel Theodore Hesser (72nd Pennsylvania), "Yes, boys, the enemy is running, come up, come up."[250] Webb, waving his sword in a circular motion toward the front, yelled something at the 72nd Pennsylvania which Private William H. Good (Company K) could not hear in the din. Lieutenant Henry Russell, on the left of the line ordered his Company A to fix bayonets. The command traveled up the line to the right to within a short distance of the colors. With Corporal Charles Giberson (Company F) leading the way with the regimental flag, Companies E and K bolted into the fray for the first time.[251] The regimental formation devolved into a disorderly mob. A bullet tore into Private William H. Porter's abdomen. Sergeant Thomas Murphy (Company G) of the color guard instinctively stooped to help Porter to his feet when a bullet hit Murphy's fingers. Seeing Porter wounded, Giberson, instead, handed the flag to Murphy, who continued the charge while he and another man dragged Porter to the rear. Close by, Second Sergeant Frederick Mannes (Company B) crouched down behind a large rock and tied off his bleeding ankle with leather straps.[252] A bullet struck Private James Wilson (Company K) as he came to within ten feet of the north wall. Major Samuel Roberts, commanding the right wing, ordered him to drop the color bearer of the 56th Virginia as he crossed the wall, about sixty yards to the west. The wounded private fired only to see the Rebel continue forward, uninjured.[253]

Without warning, a Confederate color bearer burst from the trees, heading for one of Cushing's forward guns. A round killed him as he planted the flag near the piece. Just as quickly, another Reb made a dash for the flag but died in the rifle fire before reaching it. Within quick order, two more flags were seen near the gun. Corporal Joseph H. DeCastro (Company I, 19th Massachusetts) charged into the fray with some men from the 72nd Pennsylvania. He struck down the color bearer of the 14th Virginia with his flag staff and handed the captured colors to Devereaux, despite the protest from the Pennsylvanians that they had captured the flag.[254]

Sergeant Drewry B. Easley (Company H, 14th Virginia) had just managed to load a second rifle when he became acutely aware of three bayonets being leveled at his head. He surrendered.[255] Twenty-nine-year-old Junior Second Lieutenant John H. Lewis (Company G), the senior uninjured officer of the 9th Virginia, after ordering his men to look out for their own safety, stood up as the Federals spilled over the wall, and was taken prisoner.[256] Three Federal soldiers, cowering behind the wall in front of Captain Michael P. Spessard (Company C, 28th Virginia) stood up in front of him. Wrenching the sword from his hand, they ordered him to give up. Spessard, angered by his son's death, responded with a barrage of stones. While the Yankees ducked to protect their skulls, the elder Spessard escaped.[257] During the resulting melee, Private Marshall Sherman (Company C, 1st Minnesota) took the flag of the 28th Virginia from Lieutenant John A. Lee (Company C) at the point of his bayonet.[258] Captain Robert McBride (Company F), 72nd Pennsylvania, grabbed the colors of the 56th Virginia from the standard bearer's hands and herded him to the rear. He stopped momentarily to put his name on the flag staff before sending the colors back. To his right, Private James Wilson (Company F), who had gone down with a leg wound, watched in horror as Second Lieutenant Alexander McCuen (Company K, 72nd Pennsylvania) decapitated the color bearer of the 3rd Virginia with his sword and took the flag.[259] At about the same time, Corporal Benjamin Falls (Company A, 19th Massachusetts) reached for the flag of the 19th Virginia, which he saw leaning against the west side of the wall. When it did not budge, he peeked over the wall to see it firmly clutched in the standard

**Private Marshall Sherman,
Company C, 1st Minnesota**

He won the Medal of Honor for capturing a Confederate battle flag at the Angle. He later lost his left leg in battle.

MOLLUS, USAMHI

bearer's hands. Holding his bayoneted rifle like a spear, he warned the Rebel, "Hut, Tut! Let go of that or I'll run ye through." With the flag and the Johnny in tow, he headed toward the crest of the hill. Finding the injured Major Rice hobbling along, he handed the flag to him to give him something to use as a crutch.[260]

Leaving the bullet-torn regimental flag resting against one of the guns, Lieutenant Hutchings L. Carter (Company I, 53rd Virginia) raised his hands and surrendered. Private John H. Robinson (Company I, 19th Massachusetts) claimed the capture.[261] Nearby, Sergeant Benjamin Jellison (Company C, 19th Massachusetts) jabbed the staffs of his two flags into the ground about nine feet from the wall and assisted in the mop-up. He brought in about one dozen dejected Confederates and the flag of the 57th Virginia. He turned the colors over to the wounded Second Lieutenant Joseph Snellen (Company C).[262] Second Lieutenant J. Irving Sale (Company H, 53rd Virginia) found himself cut off and very quietly handed over his sword.[263] When the Yankees closed to within twenty yards of the wall, Major Timberlake ordered his Virginians to cease fire. Some refused to do so until the Federals threatened to bayonet them to death.[264] Lieutenant George W. Finley (Company K, 56th Virginia), while surveying the ground to his rear, realized there was no way to escape. Federal rifle fire continued to drop fleeing Confederates in their race toward the Emmitsburg Road. After they loosed a final volley into the Yankees' faces, he ordered his men to lay down their arms.[265] The Federals cornered the stalwart Major John C. Timberlake (53rd Virginia) at bayonet point while he cut the clothing away from one of his soldiers' shattered arm. Glancing up to find about a dozen weapons leveled at him, he heard the Yankee captain demand his surrender. Timberlake defiantly said he would give up once he had tended to his man's wound. Standing up, he handed his sword to the captain who said something to him which he would never forget. "You are a damned brave set of fellows," the captain complimented him, "but you couldn't come it this time." "Do you see those supports yonder?" the major responded with a nod. "If they had come we would have come it, but it's too late now." With that, Timberlake sat down at the stone wall and watched unwounded Confederates rise up from the ground and run for their lives toward Seminary Ridge. He recognized the wounded Lieutenant Colonel William White (14th Virginia) pick himself up not fifty yards from the Yankees and make off toward the Confederate lines.[266]

Sergeant Thomas Murphy (Company G, 72nd Pennsylvania), while waving his hat about his head, took up the shattered flag staff of the 72nd Pennsylvania. With Private William H. Good and a squad or two from Companies E and K of the 72nd Pennsylvania, he climbed over the wall, breaking the Confederate line in half. Private Good left his best friend, Metz, lying dead across the stones as he slipped and fell on the sloping "blue rocks" behind the Confederate line.[267] Lieutenant Henry Russell (Company A) heard a Rebel, who lay across the wall, pleading to be dragged to safety. The officer grabbed him by the shoulders and pulled him over to the Federal side. As he did so, another moaned, "If we's known it was you'ns we'd never come across." Close by, Colonel Rawley Martin sat with his chin lowered to his chest, believing he was going to die. Colonel Theodore Hesser of the 72nd Pennsylvania stood next to him and, at his gesturing, handed him a pencil and a piece of paper. About ten yards east of the wall, Private Thomas Read (Company F, 72nd Pennsylvania) restrained an infuriated private from the 69th Pennsylvania from bayoneting an unarmed Rebel.[268]

Captain Jacob B. Turney (1st Tennessee), seeing the Virginians hoisting a white flag, knew the game was up. Bleeding from a flesh wound on his neck, with his clothes riddled with bullet holes, he recognized the futility of fighting to the last man. He commanded his men to give up.[269] Captain Thompson (Company F) waved his handkerchief, attracting the attention of a small Yankee from the 14th Connecticut. Going over the wall, the New Englander grabbed the colors by the staff and tried to wrench them from Private Woods' grasp. Lieutenant Foster told the stubborn soldier that Turney had ordered them to give up. The little Yankee said he reckoned Wiley would hand over the flag to which Woods snapped back he would go with the standard. The moment Woods stepped onto the Federal side of the field, the Tennesseans grabbed the Federal and pummelled him. Two more Connecticut soldiers rushed in on the stranded Wiley Woods. Both of them demanded the flag of the 1st Tennessee, with the second one trying to enforce his will with a bayonet. The obstinate Confederate refused to let them have the standard. He said they belonged to the brave little fellow who had laid his hands on them the first time and gone over the wall to get them. At that, the battered Federal rejoined Woods on the eastern side of the wall, and the Rebel promptly handed him the colors. One of the Connecticut officers rushed up to the two, telling the short soldier he did not know how to handle that Confederate rag. He ordered the man to drag it in the dirt.[270]

Lieutenant John H. Moore (Company B, 7th Tennessee) decided to make a break for it. He feared death every second during the frenzied run across the body-strewn field toward the Emmitsburg Road.[271] Orderly Sergeant June Kimble (Company A, 14th Tennessee), putting his Mississippi Rifle down, arched his back, reached under himself, and unbuckled his cartridge belt. Midthought he rebent his back and rebuckled his belt, having decided he did not want to rot in a Yankee prison.

He also made a break for it. Fearing a wound in the back which would be hard to explain, he turned around in mid-flight and quick stepped backwards to the Emmitsburg Road.[272] Major A. S. Van de Graaf, despite his severe heat exhaustion, forced himself to his feet and staggered off the field.[273]

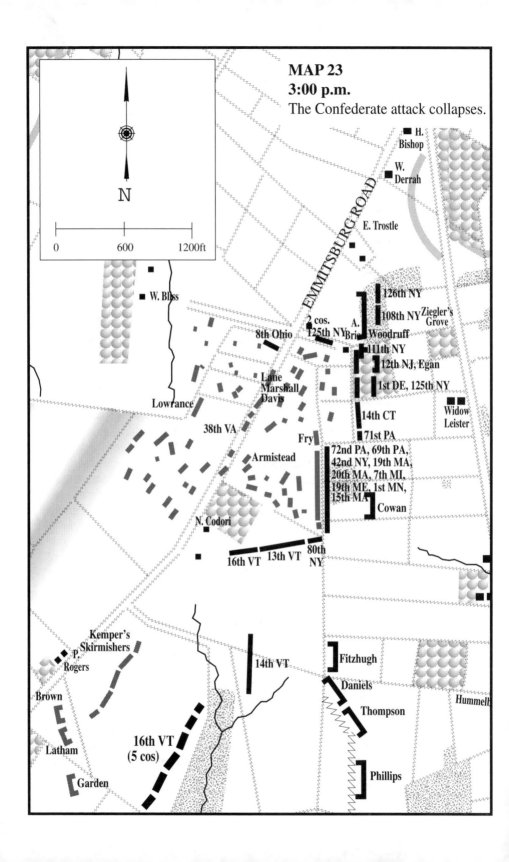

MAP 23
3:00 p.m.
The Confederate attack collapses.

N

0   600   1200ft

H. Bishop

W. Derrah

E. Trostle

EMMITSBURG ROAD

126th NY

108th NY

Ziegler's Grove

2 cos.
125th NY

8th Ohio

A. Brie

Woodruff

111th NY

12th NJ, Egan

Lane
Marshall
Davis

1st DE, 125th NY

W. Bliss

Lowrance

14th CT

Widow
Leister

38th VA

Fry

71st PA

Armistead

72nd PA, 69th PA,
42nd NY, 19th MA,
20th MA, 7th MI,
19th ME, 1st MN,
15th MA

Cowan

N. Codori

16th VT   13th VT   80th NY

Kemper's
Skirmishers

P.
Rogers

14th VT

Fitzhugh

Brown

Daniels

Hummel

Thompson

Latham

16th VT
(5 cos)

Garden

Phillips

East of the Codori Orchard
The 24th Virginia

Colonels Henry Carrington and Joseph Mayo with a small contingent of men from the 18th and the 3rd Virginia regiments rushed to the aid of the 24th Virginia, which they found on the hillside immediately north of the orchard. In all of the confusion, Captain William W. Bentley (Company E, 24th Virginia) managed to rally the few men he could find to keep the Vermonters from enveloping them. While the enlisted men and officers alike frantically fired discarded rifles to increase their rates of fire, a soldier standing nearby irritated Mayo by methodically rattling off the list of officer casualties from Kemper's brigade—Patton, Collcote, Phillips, Williams— too many for Mayo to keep track of. The Federals' flags had gotten too close to worry about who had died and he had become too engrossed in staying alive to worry about the deceased.

At that moment, Mayo's ears picked up a disconcerting hiss followed by an horrendous explosion which prostrated him. A sharp pain registered somewhere on his body; then everything went black for a few moments. He quickly regained his feet, his uniform plastered with shattered bone and globs of flesh. Nearby First Lieutenant W. Tell Taliaferro (Adjutant, 24th Virginia), screaming epithets which damned the Yankees with every other word, hopped about on both feet with his hand clamped on his butt. Junior Second Lieutenant Osceola T. White (Company A, 3rd Virginia) tapped Mayo on the shoulder. Pulling his hat off, he pointed to a nasty welt across the top of his head where a minie had clipped a swath through his thick blonde hair. Looking to the left Mayo saw Colonel William R. Terry of the 24th standing with Private George A. Harris (Company G) and Adjutant H. Valentine Harris (11th Virginia), with the colors of both regiments planted between the flanks. Terry, his face contorted in a grimace which looked almost like a smile, pointed his sword toward the rear.[274]

By then, Kemper's A.A.G., Captain William T. Fry, had returned to the 11th Virginia on foot. Many of the officers, including Captain Robert W. Douthat (Company F) gathered around the regimental flag on the right of the line. For a moment, the field seemed quiet. From his position behind the brush-covered fence, they could see little to the south. For a moment, they lied to themselves, believing the Yankees had fled the works to the east. Captain John H. Smith studied the ground behind them. Corpses, wounded men, dead horses blanketed the area. The reinforcements he expected to see never materialized. "...my heart never in my life sank as it did then," he sadly remembered. A murmur ran through the 300 or so men along the fence row. What were they to do? What were they to do? After a hasty consultation, the officers decided to send Private George "Big Foot" Walker (Company C) back to Seminary Ridge for reinforcements. Walker had hardly departed when they sent out another courier. He was insurance should Walker fall prey to the random artillery fire between the two lines.

"Look here, Captain." Smith turned about to see Private J. M. "Blackeyed" Williams (Company G), with his shirt pulled up to his shoulders, showing him where a bullet had cut a track across the width of his back.[275]

8th Virginia

To the left of the 11th Virginia, the 8th Virginia hunkered down behind the overgrown fence and peppered the advancing Federal flankers. First Lieutenant Charles F. Berkeley (Company D), having taken cover behind a large rock in the fence row with three enlisted men, realized they could not hold out against the numerically superior Federal forces. Pulling his hand-kerchief from his pocket, he handed it to First Corporal Benjamin R. Lunceford (Company C) with orders to tie it to his ramrod to signal their surrender. The corporal, who was firing through a crevice between their large rock and the one next to it, refused to comply. "Hold on awhile, Lieutenant. I am getting two at a crack," he called back.[276] (They were all captured when the Federals got too close for them to run away.)

Emmitsburg Road

While one aide eased Trimble from the saddle, another approached the general and asked, "General, the men are falling back, shall I rally them?" Looking to the south, Trimble observed large numbers of men streaming from the road bed. To the rear, he saw the bulk of Lowrance's brigade right about face in nearly perfect order and march off the field. "No!" he winced. "Let them get out of this. It's all over." With that, his aide assisted him onto his wounded horse and turned him rearward.[277]

Chaos reigned in the road. Lieutenant John H. Moore (Company B, 7th Tennessee) looked about him. Only seven of his forty-seven man company remained uninjured. Gathering his few survivors about him, he consulted with his lieutenant colonel, Samuel G. Shepard. When someone suggested giving up, Sergeant "Black" Dunn (Company E) defiantly replied, "They've got to get more blood out of me than they have before I ever surrender." They decided to run the gauntlet. Clawing their way over the riddled slab fence on the west side of the road, they hurried across the blackened, scorched grass without looking back. Less than twenty steps from the road, a parting shot severely injured Dunn. Lieutenant Furgerson S. Harris, propping himself up on two discarded muskets also hobbled off the field until Sergeant John Lanier (Company F) came to his assistance. Harris noticed Private Jim Martin staggering rearward nursing his mangled arm.[278]

Captain James G. Harris (Company H, 7th North Carolina) and several other North Carolinians ran over to Major J. McLeod Turner, who lay in the road, to tell him they had to retreat. The Yankees were closing in on the right of the regiment. They offered to take the major with them but he told them to leave him. He had not long to live, he informed them. He did not want to endanger their lives by slowing them down. They took off without him.[279]

Simultaneous with the flank movement, Company A, 2nd U.S. Sharpshooters reached the high ground behind the 14th Connecticut. Captain Abraham Wright maneuvered his Minnesotans from column of four into a single line and ordered them to open fire with their breech-loading rifles into the Confederates west of the wall. Watching his men cut down the Rebels like targets at a shoot, the captain sadly reflected that it "...really tried humanity to look on."[280]

Sixty feet from Hays' line, Second Lieutenant William N. Mickle (Company K, 37th North Carolina) hailed over First Lieutenant Thomas L. Norwood (Company A) and Second Lieutenant Iowa M. Royster (Company G) to tell them that the rest of the brigade had quit the field. Before they could respond, a hail of bullets killed Mickle, mortally wounded Royster, and brought down Norwood with a round in the chest.[281] With the troops abandoning the field to his right and to the left, Pettigrew issued instructions for the division to retire from the fight. As he neared the Emmitsburg Road with Lieutenant William B. Shepard, his A.D.C., a canister round killed the general's horse from under him and simultaneously shattered his left hand.[282] Lieutenant Colonel John T. Jones ordered the few survivors of his brigade to retreat.[283] The fight was over.

West of the Emmitsburg Road

At this point, someone in the 8th Ohio ordered, "O'er the fence, boys! Give it to 'em! Go for their colors!" The feisty westerners clamored over the fence behind Trimble's left flank into a wall of small arms fire from the creek bottom on their right flank. One of those shots mortally wounded Private Silas Judson (Company K) as he attempted to scale the fence. The ball penetrated his right arm and shoulder before lodging in his chest.[284] The Confederates also wounded Captain Wells W. Miller and killed First Lieutenant Elijah Hayden (both from Company H). At the same time a large number of Lane's men, who were running from the Emmitsburg Road, stampeded into the 8th Ohio, and were "gobbled up" in a vicious hand-to-hand fight.[285] Private James Richmond (Company F) found the colors of a North Carolina regiment lying in the field and started back toward the Brian farm with them.[286]

Brockenbrough's Brigade

Farther to the northwest, the idle Colonel William S. Christian and his two Virginia regiments waited for something to happen. A staff officer had already approached him with orders to hold until the right of the line rallied and the charge renewed. It became quite evident that the charge had died in its tracks. With Pettigrew demolished, the Yankee skirmishers shifted their attentions with renewed vigor toward his men. Christian commanded his soldiers to scatter and get back to their lines as quickly as possible. The colonel, who had been severely lamed during the Seven Days' Battles, limped off the field with the help of the color bearer of the 47th Virginia.

Unfortunately, a shell severely wounded the standard bearer which forced the colonel to assist him to the rear—a case of the halt leading the crippled.[287]

Northeast of the Angle
Egan's Section
General Hays, having ridden into Lieutenant Jonathan Egan's section (Battery I, 1st U.S. Artillery) from the right, jumped his horse over the wall moments after Captain Morris Brown captured the Confederate colors. His singular act of bravery inspired his adjutant general, Captain George P. Corts, his aide, Lieutenant David Shields, and a considerable number of his men to follow him into the melee. The 111th New York, to Egan's amazement, trailed the general into the field south of the Brian barn.[288] Riding up to Brown, he hailed, "Boys, give me a flag." Brown handed him the colors of the 28th North Carolina. Turning to his junior officers, Hays exclaimed, "Get a flag, Corts; get a flag, Dave, and come on." The two officers dashed away and quickly returned with captured colors which they had taken from some startled enlisted men.[289]

Hays' Division
During all of the commotion General Meade trotted into Egan's section. Calling Egan by name, he asked if he knew where General Hays could be found. The startled lieutenant, who had never seen the commanding general before, suddenly looked up at Meade, amazed that he knew him by name. Quickly recognizing his friend, Captain Meade, Egan merely pointed over to the spot where Hays had crossed the wall. For a very long thirty seconds, the general stared into the melee around the Brian barn.[290] The Yankees were jubilant. Hays, with his two officers behind him, trooped his line, his horse foaming at the mouth, while all three dragged their captured flags through the dirt behind them. "The act was significant and symbolic," Captain Scott (Company C, 126th New York) later wrote, "From that hour the glory and victory of the one, and the overthrow and disgrace of the other was settled."[291] Meade also witnessed the incident. Egan distinctly heard him snarl with the same breath, "I don't care for their flag. Have they turned?" "Yes, sir," Egan replied. "They are just turning."[292]

With bullets zipping in from the vicinity of the Angle, Meade wheeled his horse south and left his son with Egan. The captain shook hands with the artillery officer, while asking how he was faring in this fight and about Woodruff's whereabouts. He was over in the grove, Egan said while pointing. With that the younger Meade mounted and rode off after his father.[293]

Very few of Longstreet's men recrossed the Emmitsburg Road to safety. Of the original force of about 11,500 officers and men, an estimated 6,900 escaped injury. Of the 4,600 or more casualties, some 2,800 (about 68 percent) were captured or wounded and captured. The majority of those were incurred east of the Emmitsburg Road.

5   *3:00 p.m. through 5:00 p.m.*

Northeast of the Angle
Hays' Division

With everything growing relatively quiet on his end of the line, Lieutenant John Brady (1st Delaware) stood up to see what was going on. A lone battle flag attracted his attention. It stood in the southwest corner of the field where the northwest corner of the Angle joined the slab fence. Handing the 1st Delaware's flag to Sergeant John M. Dunn, he yelled for First Lieutenant William Smith (Company A) to follow him.[1] In crossing the wall, they inadvertently triggered a general advance.

Hays' Division

General Hays intercepted the two as they cut diagonally across the field. The general called Brady aside while Smith continued after the flag. Smith defiantly ripped the colors of the 5th Alabama Battalion from its staff and trooped back to Brady. After waving the trophy at them, he recrossed the stone wall and tramped toward the rear. The moment he reached the top of the hill in Brian's orchard, a solid shot cut him in half.[2]

Color Sergeant John M. Dunn (1st Delaware), flag in hand, leaped over the stone wall, dragging the rest of his regiment with him.[3] Wright's sharpshooters (Company A, 2nd U.S.) had barely fired a handful of rounds when the 14th Connecticut stood up and crossed the wall with the 1st Delaware. Corporal Christopher Flynn (Company K) was in the forefront. While chasing the Rebels toward the Emmitsburg Road, he came across the discarded colors of the 52nd North Carolina. He picked the flag up and turned it over to his colonel. Private Elijah W. Bacon (Company F) carried off the standard of the 16th North Carolina, while other members of his regiment picked up the 38th North Carolina.[4] With leveled bayonets and rifle butts, the enraged Federal infantry rounded up a large number of prisoners and herded them back into their lines.[5]

Captain Abraham Wright's men (Company A, 2nd U.S. Sharpshooters) did not participate in the mopping up. Retreating Rebels blanketed the ground between the board fence and the Emmitsburg Road. He and his men had every opportunity to get clean shots at their backs, but they did nothing. "We could have picked off many of them," he later recalled, "but our bullets would have gone very close to the heads of our own men, and,

somehow, we did not have much desire just to kill someone."[6] The 14th Connecticut captured forty Confederates, including ten regimental officers.[7] An enlisted man rushed in upon the prostrate Colonel John A. Fite (7th Tennessee). "You are my prisoner," he said. He recognized that fact, the colonel bluntly responded. Did the private want his sword? he continued. "I'll take you to my officer," the soldier replied before asking the colonel to identify himself and his regiment. Colonel John A. Fite handed his sword to Captain Samuel A. Moore, who was standing next to Major Ellis. When Ellis remarked, "I'll take that scabbard too," Fite told him all right. He had no use for the damn thing.[8] The Andrews Sharpshooters, after losing two men in hand-to-hand combat, bagged one hundred thirty stranded Rebels.[9]

Captain Samuel Moore, Company F, 14th Connecticut

Colonel John Fite (7th Tennessee) surrendered his sword to Moore at the wall north of the Angle.

MOLLUS, USAMHI

While the 1st Delaware scoured the bloodied field, picking up casualties, they came under fire from Confederate sharpshooters who had taken cover in the smoldering ruins of the Bliss barn. First Lieutenant John Dent (Company G), having assumed command of the regiment, led a detail against the noisome skirmishers. Driving them away, he rallied his regiment and led it back to the security of the stone wall.[10]

Close to the wall Captain Richard S. Thompson (12th New Jersey) came across the lifeless bodies of a North Carolina color bearer and the smooth-faced boy who died next to him. His men dragged in the desperately wounded Major John Q. A. Richardson (52nd North Carolina)—a victim of buckshot. At the major's insistence they laid him on the ground where a surgeon administered an opiate to him. Glancing at the Yankees' division flag, he noticed the blue club on the white field. The commanding officers told them they were going to be attacking green Pennsylvanians, he gasped, "But when we saw that old clover-leaf unfurled, we knew what kind of green militia we had to contend with." With that, he became more quiet. Turning his head to one side, with his eyes dulling and becoming fixed in their sockets and the death pall settling over his face, he noticed a stand of U.S. colors. His gaze saddened a little. "After all, after all," he muttered as if continuing a conversation, "that is the glorious old flag." He died. The men laid a blanket over Richardson's face and returned to the ranks.[11] A sergeant pulled the severely wounded Lieutenant Thomas L. Norwood (Company A, 37th North Carolina) over the stone wall. Glancing feebly about, he spotted several other Confederate prisoners before blacking out.[12]

Nearby, Lieutenant Colonel Newton J. George (1st Tennessee), as he stepped into the ranks of the 14th Connecticut, asked where all of their men were, and was told he was looking at them. The astonished George, when he realized how understrength the Yankee regiments were, blurted in disgust, "Oh! that I had known it a half hour since."[13]

The Angle
With the firing having ceased, Private Christopher Smith returned to the field with Sergeant Frederick Fuger. While wandering near Gun Three, a wounded officer caught the sergeant's attention by calling out his name. The sergeant leaned closer to the fellow and recognized him as General Armistead. "I thought it was you, sergeant," Armistead said weakly, "and if I had known that you were in command of that battery I never should have led the charge against you." Fuger coldly left the general where he lay, while telling Smith that he had served under Armistead in the Mormon Expedition in Utah.[14]

Not too long after that, Captain John C. Brown (Company K, 20th Indiana) meandered over the bloodied ground to inspect the carnage when he happened upon a wounded Confederate officer. He lay on his right side, with his head resting upon his right palm on a rock outcropping surrounding a small tree. The captain asked him how badly had he been wounded. Shot through the body twice and bleeding profusely, the officer replied. The captain tendered his condolences when the Rebel queried, "Are you a mason?" "I am." At that Armistead petitioned him as a "brother" to assist him. Reassuring him he would return, the captain hurried over the ridge to his own company and brought back two enlisted men with a stretcher. They picked up the general and carried him to the rear.[15] On the way, they were joined by another enlisted man, who helped them with the stretcher.

Captain Charles Banes noticed three enlisted men carrying a general officer from the front. As they passed him, the captain stopped them to find out who the officer was. He identified himself as General Armistead and surrendered his revolver to the captain. While the soldiers hauled the general away, the captain inspected the chambers and found them all loaded. Handing the pistol to a nearby orderly to keep for him, he tended to his present duties.[16]

East of the Angle

While the fighting near the Angle subsided, and the Federals mopped up, the wounded Captain Henry H. Bingham, II Corps Judge Advocate, came upon a party of enlisted men who were carrying a wounded Confederate off the field. The impatient captain told them to put the man down and return to their regiments. They had an important prisoner, they shouted back. Longstreet himself, they insisted as they struggled to get him over into the rock outcroppings behind Cushing's guns. A glance at the braid on the writhing officer's uniform convinced Bingham that they had someone of rank. He dismounted and asked the officer his name. General Armistead, Confederate Army, came the pained response.

"General," he said, "I am Captain Bingham of General Hancock's staff, and if you have anything valuable in your possession which you desire taken care of, I will take care of it for you." Was the General Hancock he spoke of a General Winfield Scott Hancock? the Confederate asked. Yes, he was, Bingham replied. Hancock was "an old and valued friend," Armistead said. "Tell General Hancock for me that I have done him and done you all an injury which I shall regret the longest day I live."

At that, Armistead authorized Bingham to remove his watch, chain, spurs, wallet, and seal from him. The captain complied. After telling the enlisted men to get the injured general to a hospital, he mounted and headed south, looking for Hancock.[17] They carried the general to Doctor Daniel G. Brinton, who with a Doctor Harvey, tended Armistead's wounds. He had been hit twice by rifle balls—one in the fleshy part of the left arm, the other in the right leg. Brinton judged neither as life-threatening because no arteries had been severed, no bones broken or nerves cut.[18]

Cowan's Battery

Farther to the north, Cowan's New Yorkers stopped hurling percussion shells into Confederates west of the Angle. Captain John G. Hazard (commanding the II Corps artillery brigade) rode up with Hunt. The general congratulated Cowan for taking such an advantageous position. As the smoke cleared, Cowan saw the Confederates retreating. Ordering his guns back to his original position, he rolled into line on the right of Captain Robert H. Fitzhugh's Battery K, 1st New York, which had just swung into battery moments before.[19] From there, Cowan hurriedly looked toward the Codori farm. To his surprise four Confederate Napoleons wheeled into battery on the last ridge west of the Emmitsburg Road. In short order, they sent four shells whirling toward his six guns. The exasperated Cowan ripped his tunic off and threw it to the ground. With Sergeant Van Ettan commanding one piece, the captain personally sighted another one. The two guns fired. Seconds later, two of the Confederates' ammunition chests burst into flame and the guns quit the field.[20]

The smoke had hardly cleared when the captain and his men started cutting the harnesses from their dead horses. Webb loaned him twenty volunteers from the 20th Massachusetts. Nearby, he heard a civilian ask for the identity of the battery. One of the workers pointed to Cowan. The civilian walked over and introduced himself as Wilkeson, a reporter. The captain, having seen him before on the field at Gaines Mill, allowed him to stay. His son was Bayard Wilkeson, an artillery commander who had died during the first day's fighting, the reporter interjected. With a "heavy heart" he had to do his job, he added. Unable to find his coat, some scoundrel having taken it, Cowan walked Wilkeson down to the wall, amid the human carnage, to explain the action to him.[21]

South of the Angle

The field grew quiet excepting for the piteous cries of the wounded and the dying. The veterans of the 80th New York regrouped themselves and took the time to see what they had done. Twenty yards to their front they spotted a pile of Confederate officers—four to five bodies deep. The man on the top of the heap was dying. The Yankees waited until he breathed his last before they approached him. He was lying across a full colonel. Rolling his corpse away, the enlisted men searched the dead colonel's body, took his diary and his map of Virginia, and turned it over to Colonel Theodore B. Gates. His scabbard and sword being too riddled by small arms fire to be of any use, a sergeant stripped him of it and handed it to Captain John Cook (Company I). The belt buckle was designed after the seal of Virginia with the inscription "Sic semper tyrannus." (Forty years later Cook returned it to the widow of Colonel James G. Hodges, 14th Virginia.)[22] Not too long after that Cook's New Yorkers cornered First Lieutenant James B. Miller (Garnett's Provost Marshal) who had been shot in the hip. Colonel Gates ordered the wounded Cook to escort the Rebel to the rear. On the way back Miller told the captain that Longstreet had been killed at the very muzzle of one of the Yankee guns.[23]

Just to the southwest of the copse of trees, Private Amos C. Plaisted (Company B, 15th Massachusetts) called the quaking Major John C. Timberlake (53rd Virginia) a coward because he crawled over the stone wall and dropped at the enlisted man's feet. Timberlake snapped that he feared no Yankees but did not care to be under the artillery fire of the guns which covered the Confederate retreat.[24] Private Robert N. Tolbert (Company B, 7th Virginia), having just taken the colors from the wounded Color Corporal Jesse Young, found himself surrounded by members of the 19th Maine and surrendered.[25] Two of the New Englanders came away from the wall with the colors of the 1st and the 7th Virginia regiments but did not get very far. Sergeants Martin McHugh (Company D) and Hugh Carey

(Company E) of the 82nd New York accosted the Mainers. The New Yorkers ripped the standards from their staffs and made for the rear, but not before rifle fire wounded Carey in the left side and the arm.[26]

Captain James C. Lynch (Company B, 106th Pennsylvania), having stepped on a dead Confederate in crossing the wall west of the copse of trees, encountered Colonel Henry Carrington (18th Virginia). The colonel immediately offered his sword to the captain. "I will give you my parole," he said. Lynch brusquely told him he did not have time for that and kept on going, leaving Carrington on his own hook.

After delivering his Confederate officer to the field hospital near Meade's Headquarters, Captain John D. S. Cook (Company I, 80th New York) decided to let a doctor take a look at his injured leg. It was swollen and terribly bruised but the doctor had nothing he could do to relieve the captain's distress. Cook decided to rejoin his regiment.[27]

East of the Codori Orchard
11th Virginia

Having not been under fire for several minutes, and having heard nothing from the two runners they sent out, the officers of the 11th Virginia and the 24th Virginia decided they had to do something. Rather than be overrun in a counterattack, they decided it was time to retreat. With artillery rounds coming in from the north, they ordered the men to retire singly or in small groups to avoid attracting the gunners' attention.[28] Yelling at his men to spread out, Colonel Joseph Mayo (3rd Virginia) started leading them back across the Emmitsburg Road to safety.[29] The other officers and men followed suit.

Captain Robert W. Douthat (Company F, 11th Virginia) stayed behind in the shade of the trees along the fence with his wounded friend, Captain John H. Smith (Company G), to dress Smith's bleeding thigh. Pulling a towel from his haversack, Smith ripped it into strips and tied off his wound. While Smith wrapped his leg, Douthat picked up a discarded rifle. He fired it, reloaded and fired again, and again. All the while he insisted he could see the Yankees. Rising up on his elbow, Smith spotted a Federal column, about seventy-five yards away, moving at the oblique toward their right front. A surge of adrenaline sent him to his feet. "What are you doing?" he shouted in horror. Douthat immediately let his piece fall to the ground as he realized how foolish he had been to bring the wrath of what appeared to be a regiment down upon them. "It's time to get away from here," he said.

He broke into a run with the wounded Smith staggering after him. The Yankees shot at them without scoring any hits. The two kept running, with rifle shots pocking the earth around them and with stamina produced by genuine fear, they safely scaled the fences along the Emmitsburg Road. Once in the fields to the west, they slowed down, flotsam in a rippling sea of defeated soldiers.[30]

1st Minnesota

Sergeant John Cole (Company C), expecting to round up as many of the uninjured Confederates as possible, formed a skirmish line with the few effectives he could find from the regiment. He held the left of the formation with Privates Charles I. Clark, John Brown, Marshall Sherman, and R. M. Eastman completing it to his right. Thirty feet west of the wall where Armistead's men broke through, the sergeant spied a Confederate, hidden behind a row of brush, wigwagging a white rag from the tip of a ramrod. Telling the rest of the men to go forward, he walked over to the ground cover and brought in about fifty uninjured Confederates.[31] Close by, First Lieutenant William Harmon (Company C), having regained his wind, followed after his regiment in the mop-up. A Confederate unsuccessfully tried to get the lieutenant to leave his officer alone so he could escape. At the same time another Rebel tried to sight in on Harmon, but he "got the drop on him" with his revolver before the fellow could discharge his weapon. The lieutenant had to physically keep his men from killing the scoundrel.[32]

Meanwhile the remaining five men continued on toward the Emmitsburg Road. On the way, they brought in a few prisoners. Passing north of the orchard they discovered what looked like an entire battle line lying in the road bed. The Westerners ordered the Rebs to climb over the fence, but they refused, fearing the Yankee artillery would murder them en masse. The Federals assured them they would be safe if they all dropped their guns. Rising in unison, the Rebels climbed over the fence at which point a Confederate gun back on Seminary Ridge sent a round screaming overhead. The frightened Rebels refused to advance on a front. Eastman led them by files to the right into the hollow toward an opening in the stone wall at the Angle.[33]

The Emmitsburg Road

Despite his crippling injury, Major J. McLeod Turner (7th North Carolina) pulled himself onto his rear in time to see the Federals south of him herding prisoners and assisting the slightly wounded. A member of the major's former company, bleeding profusely from a wound above the ankle, hobbled up to Turner. The major pulled a tourniquet from his pants pocket and tied off the man's leg.[34] A short distance to the south, Second Lieutenant Daniel F. Kinney (Company F) found himself and his company completely surrounded by Yankees who had crossed into the field west of the road and had swung north.[35]

To the south, Colonel Edward C. Edmonds (38th Virginia), seeing the 8th Ohio moving in from the north, attempted to refuse his left wing, but a bullet struck him in the head and left him bleeding to death in the road bed. Major Joseph R. Cabell looked around to see if he should take over the regiment only to discover Lieutenant Colonel Powhatan B. White down in the road with a thigh wound. As the one-armed White propped himself up on his right arm to give a command, two minie balls thudded into his good shoulder and arm, knocking him senseless. Major Cabell tried to refuse the left wing only to find out that the fence row foiled the maneuver. He immediately had the regiment pull back to the cover of the western side of the road. Looking behind, he believed he saw supports coming forward. Once again he sent the regiment into the road. This time they crossed into the open ground west of the Angle. To the left wounded North Carolinians began waving white flags. Cabell's Virginians jerked the flags from their hands, but the Tar Heels rehoisted them. With the Yankees closing in from both flanks, the major gave up the fight and ordered his few men to quit the field.[36]

Presently two Yankees moved the paralyzed Major Turner (7th North Carolina) into the field west of the road and laid him among the wounded from the 11th and the 26th North Carolina, who in their suffering bore terrible witness to the effectiveness of the Federal fire.[37]

The Rogers House
The Confederate captain in command of the detachment guarding the Federal prisoners at the Rogers house, having watched the charge from the beginning, slammed his field glasses to the ground. "My God, we're beaten!" he exclaimed, at which point Second Lieutenant Frank Moran (Company H, 73rd New York) and his fellow captives rent the air with the "manly" huzzahs of the Army of the Potomac.[38] Meanwhile, Pickett's survivors streamed over the prone Floridians. An officer suddenly materialized from the dense smoke among the ranks of the 5th Florida, bleeding profusely from a shattered left arm. Captain James Johnson (Adjutant, 5th Florida), noticing the bone protruding from the man's elbow, saw blood spurting from the man's severed artery. Taking his handkerchief, the captain quickly tied a bayonet between the arm and the bandage and twisted the wound shut. The lieutenant, who was fully conscious, kept listening to the firing to the front, rather than paying any attention to his serious condition. How was the battle going? Johnson asked. "The front line is fighting as bravely as men ever fought, but the second, damn them, are not, and I belong to the second line."[39]

Southwest of the Angle
Stannard's Brigade
The color sergeant of the 8th Virginia regiment pitched his flag into the bushes near the Vermont line spitting that he would not fight with that flag in his hands. A Vermonter picked it up where the color sergeant had left it, only to get wounded and drop the colors. Private Piam Harris (Company E, 16th Vermont) found it and carried it from the field.[40] Not too far away, Captain John D. S. Cook (Company I, 80th New York) noticed a white cloth hanging from a clump of bushes very close to the regiment's

front. At first he glanced away but the rag seemed to move. It was a Confederate signaling to surrender. "Come in, Johnnie; come in; we won't hurt you," one of his New Yorkers cried out. To everyone's surprise nearly a dozen Confederates dashed from the brush. As soon as the Rebels were in his ranks, Cook sent out a skirmish line which bagged those who had not surrendered.[41]

11th Virginia

Very shortly after the shell's explosion knocked Captain James R. Hutter off his feet, Captain John C. Ward (Company E) crawled over to him and offered him a swing from his double-barreled canteen. Water or whiskey? he asked. No whiskey, but water, the dazed Hutter responded. While he took the drink, Ward exclaimed, "Just see how the prisoners are coming in." Looking to the south, Hutter noticed about ten Confederate infantrymen, their weapons at the shoulder, escorting in about three times their number of Federals. When they came to within hailing distance, a Federal sergeant approached them from behind. "Gentlemen," he said, "you are prisoners of war."

"By God six, that remains to be seen," Ward snarled. Hutter, who had not completely regained his senses, gave Private Glenmore Turner (Company G) a confused top to bottom stare. "Glenmore, are you a prisoner of war with a gun on your shoulder?" "Captain, I haven't a round of ammunition, nor have my com-

Captain John C. Ward, Company E, 11th Virginia

The captain escaped capture east of the Emmitsburg Road only to be "gobbled up" by Federal cavalry later in the day.

Dennis Kazee collection

rades; they are picking us up one or two at a time." Struck with the reality of being a prisoner of war, Hutter told the Yankee sergeant he was a terribly injured captain and he would not surrender his sword to him. The sergeant, accepting the captain as a gentleman at face value, agreed to get his officer to make the surrender proper. He walked off without posting a guard on the two gentlemen.

Ward used the time to examine Hutter's back. He had not been hit there. Ward then opened Hutter's tunic and pulled up his shirt. A minie ball had scraped the meat off both sides of his chest near the nipples without striking the breastbone. Neither one of them waited on protocol. Rather than stay where they were, Ward helped Hutter back through the orchard to the Emmitsburg Road. From there, they hobbled south toward the Rogers house.[42]

Seminary Ridge
North of Spangler's Woods

The exhausted remnants of Pettigrew's division met General Robert E. Lee as they returned to their former positions along Seminary Ridge. The general trotted his horse back and forth desperately trying to rally his demoralized soldiers. Spying Sergeant Billy Young (Company I, 7th Tennessee), he commanded him to take command of Heth's division and re-form the men. Young screamed at the men to stop but they ignored him. Frustrated beyond endurance, he took his rifle and knocked soldiers down with the butt to force them to comply. When that failed he returned to Lee who, when he realized the hopelessness of the situation, immediately changed the subject. Did any of his officers come out? Lee asked. Young scanned the first rise of ground west of the woods and spied a familiar face among the defeated. "There comes Colonel Shepard now," he replied.

Lieutenant Furgerson S. Harris (Company H, 7th Tennessee), with John Lanier's assistance, had just reached the top of the ridge when his eyes latched onto Longstreet standing under a tree by the northwest corner of the woods. Federal artillery shells had bracketed the area, making it extremely dangerous to be anywhere near the crest. An enlisted man, named Grissom, whom the Tennesseeans referred to as "Black Ram" was helping the dangerously wounded Captain Robert Miller (Company E, 7th Tennessee) past Longstreet when the sound of a particularly large incoming round sent everyone scurrying for cover. The scream of the projectile filled the air. Black Ram dropped the captain and leaped ten feet to his left toward the cover of a large tree stump. The shell exploded in his right shoulder. The explosion left a tremendous crater in the ground and splattered Grissom's body into pieces too small to identify.

Lee rode over to Colonel Shepard with Young trailing behind. Extending his hand to Shepard, he said, "Colonel, tell your men it is my fault; the fault is mine." Releasing his grip Lee continued, punctuating his directives by deliberately pointing to each objective, "Take command of these men, form them, and drive those people back if they come over here." Turning to Billy Young, he gently patted the boy on the shoulder and complimented him with, "My brave boy, if I had an army like you this would not have happened."

By then the exhausted Lieutenant John H. Moore (Company B, 7th Tennessee) had staggered onto the ridge. "Colonel," he gasped in disgust, "if them damned fellows hadn't broke on the right we could have held that ridge."[43] Again, a visibly shaken Lee said, "Colonel, rally your men and protect our artillery. The fault is mine, but it will be all right in the end." The words had barely left his mouth when Pettigrew, his arm blackened, his wrist shattered by canister, assisted by Captain Thomas J. Cureton (Company B, 26th North Carolina), walked up to the general. Lee repeated what he had told Shepard and added, "General, I am sorry to see you wounded. Go to the rear."

The colonel, with Lieutenant Moore's help, gathered what he could find of Fry's brigade around Poague's Battalion on the brow of the ridge.[44] Thirteen men, among them the badly wounded Lieutenant Furgerson S. Harris (Company H), did not comprise a regiment.[45] Orderly Sergeant June Kimble (Company A, 14th Tennessee) threw himself into a four-man rifle pit along the ridge, crowding the four men who were already there.[46] Lee remained mounted, with his field glasses to his eyes and studied the Federal lines for a short time. He then turned south. Encountering Longstreet not too far off, they rode out to the ridge east of the woods and studied the Federals in the distance. Incoming shells still exploded periodically overhead. Lieutenant Moore, who expected both of them to get hit at any moment, thought their bravado unnecessary. The mere thought of either of the generals getting killed made him quiver as if suddenly chilled.[47] Longstreet, braving the artillery fire, spurred toward Eshleman's Battalion along the Emmitsburg Road.[48] Lee trailed after him at a walk.

Wilcox's and Lang's Charge

While the Yankees were mopping up the Confederates at the Angle, Brigadier General Cadmus Wilcox's brigade moved by the left oblique to cross the Emmitsburg Road north of the Rogers house. The 9th Alabama held the southern end of Wilcox's line, followed respectively by the 10th, 11th, 8th, and 14th regiments.[49] On the crest of the hill, west of the house, Lang's Floridians got to their feet as the command "Attention" echoed along the line. With the Rebel Yell renting the air around them, the brigade moved east, slightly behind Wilcox's men, intent upon driving back the Federals whom they saw moving into the low ground along Plum Run. The 5th Florida had barely reached the Emmitsburg Road when the Yankees abruptly halted, right about faced and headed back to their works along Cemetery Ridge. The Confederates pressed across the road into the hollow toward Plum Run under a horrendous fire from McGilvery's Artillery.[50] A canister ball slammed into Captain George Clark (Company B, 11th Alabama), leaving him unconscious on the ground.[51]

Colonel E. Porter Alexander, having ordered his guns to temporarily cease fire, watched in disbelief as the two brigades charged over the ridge toward the Emmitsburg Road. Judging the time to be about ten minutes after Pickett's assault had died in its tracks, he sadly watched Lang's small brigade sweep by his right flank.[52] McGilvery's Artillery, east of Plum Run and Cowan's battery east of the Angle saw them before the infantry did. As he turned his guns to meet the attack, Captain Charles Banes (Webb's staff) rushed a section from Lieutenant William Wheeler's 13th New York

Independent Battery into the position formerly held by Rorty. The pair of 3-inch rifles unloaded a few rounds into Wilcox's flank and limbered up.[53] The remaining pieces in the line mercilessly pummelled the Alabamians and Floridians.[54]

Hancock and Parmelee found Stannard and his aides, Lieutenants George G. Benedict and George W. Hooker, on a knoll a little in advance of the II Corps line. Benedict could not hear anything Hancock said to Stannard above the racket of the fighting. He considered Hancock to be "the most splendid man I saw on horseback, and magnificent in the flush and excitement of battle." Without warning, Hancock cried out and reeled.

Hooker and Benedict jumped to the general's side and caught him as he fell from the saddle. Stannard leaned over him while the two officers laid him out on his back. Hancock, too shocked to speak, slapped his hand to the right side of his groin. Stannard pulled the general's fingers aside and opened the torn cloth around the wound. He found a hole big enough to stick three fingers into on the inside of the right leg close to the trunk.

"Don't let me bleed to death," Hancock gasped. "Get something around it quick." Stannard whipped out his handkerchief and with Benedict's help adjusted it around the leg above the wound. Noticing that the blood neither spurted nor was bright red, the lieutenant tried to comfort Hancock. "This is not arterial blood, General; you will not bleed to death." "That's good," Hancock sighed, "thank you for that, Doctor."

Using a pistol barrel in the handkerchief's knot, the officers twisted the tourniquet until the blood flow stopped. Major William G. Mitchell and Captain Henry H. Bingham, Hancock's aides, rode up while the others applied the bandage.[55] Hancock did not give either of them an opportunity to do more than express their condolences. With an exclamation the major dashed off to hunt up a commissioned surgeon.[56] Bingham was dispatched, still carrying Armistead's personal effects, to order Stannard's two regiments to flank Lang and Wilcox.[57] Wilcox, who saw them coming at his left rear commanded his regiments to stand firm and to hold their own until he could get artillery to bear upon the Yankees. Riding back to the ridge, he ruefully discovered that the guns had no more ammunition. He started back to his brigade to order a retreat.[58]

The 14th Vermont slammed an accurate and devastating fire into the Confederates, disrupting their formations. A shell burst prostrated Second Lieutenant James H. Wentworth (Company D, 5th Florida), leaving him unconscious among the dead and wounded.[59] Captain Council A. Brian ordered the 5th Florida back to its breastworks, leaving the rest of the brigade to the south on its own.[60]

Colonel Wheelock Veazey (16th Vermont), looked over his shoulder toward the crest in front of the Rogers house. Commanding the 16th Vermont to face by the rear rank, he rushed the line about twenty rods south, to the right rear of the 14th Vermont. He flanked the Vermonters by the right for a distance equal to the front of the regiment, then faced them southeast. As he ordered them to fire into Wilcox's and Lang's left flank on the oblique Stannard sent word to him to throw his regiment between those Confederates to the south and the Federal guns below the Angle by returning to his old position behind the 14th. Running over to the knoll, Colonel Veazey asked for permission to charge the Confederates instead. Stannard reluctantly assented to the move, which he considered extremely dangerous. The Vermonters swept across the front of the 14th Vermont, catching the Floridians in the marshy, over-grown creek bottom along Plum Run. With his small regiments broken by the rocky terrain, and with the noise too loud for any spoken command to be effectively heard, Colonel David Lang yelled for those who could possibly hear him to retreat. The New Englanders killed, captured or wounded the majority of the Floridians in Lang's brigade, and Captain Charles Brink bagged the colors of the 2nd Florida.[61]

Upon reaching the line, Colonel David Lang turned to Captain James Johnson (adjutant) and told him matter-of-factly they could never hold the hill if attacked. "There are some officers on horseback over to our right," he added with a gesture. "See if you can't explain to them the situation and get us some support." The captain took off at a run, north across the farm lane to the high ground on its south side.[62]

Brigadier General Cadmus Wilcox
Wilcox cried violently over the loss of his brigade in the final forlorn hope against the southern end of Cemetery Ridge.

Battles and Leaders, III

Wilcox, with tears streaming from his eyes, spurred back to his original position along the Emmitsburg Road, where he found Lee scanning the field with his glasses. He reached the general and his staff about the same time that the wheezing Captain Johnson arrived with Lang's message. "General Lee," Wilcox blubbered, "I came into Pennsylvania with one of the finest brigades in the Army of Northern Virginia and now my people are all gone. They have all been killed." Lee, with the pain of the loss evident upon his face, turned toward Wilcox. "It is all my fault, General," he quietly replied. At that, Johnson interrupted the moment with his plea for help. Before his eyes, Lee's demeanor instantly changed from a compassionate, warm man to the professional soldier he really was. With a totally

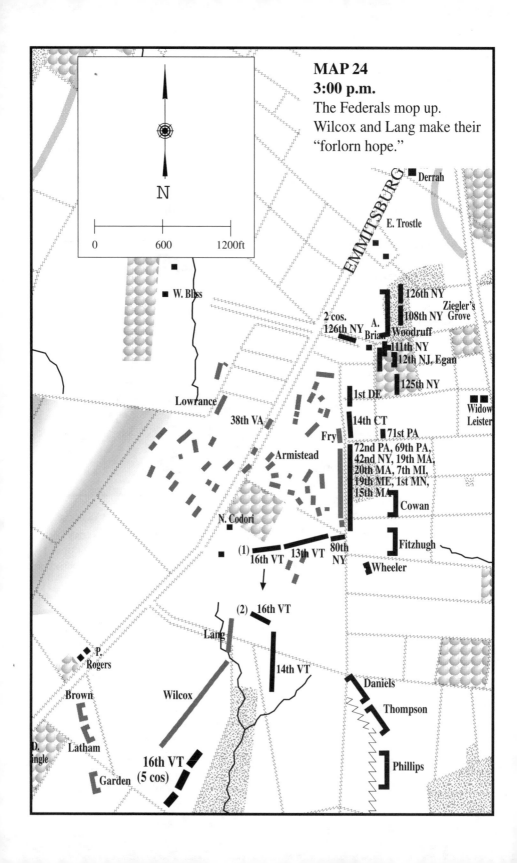

MAP 24
3:00 p.m.
The Federals mop up.
Wilcox and Lang make their
"forlorn hope."

N

0   600   1200ft

EMMITSBURG

Derrah

E. Trostle

W. Bliss

126th NY
108th NY
Ziegler's Grove
2 cos.
126th NY
A. Brian
Woodruff
111th NY
12th NJ, Egan
125th NY

1st DE
Lowrance
Widow
Leister
38th VA
14th CT
Fry
71st PA
72nd PA, 69th PA,
42nd NY, 19th MA,
20th MA, 7th MI,
19th ME, 1st MN,
15th MA
Armistead

N. Codori
Cowan

(1)
16th VT   13th VT   80th NY
Fitzhugh
Wheeler

(2)   16th VT

Lang
14th VT

P. Rogers
Daniels
Brown
Wilcox
Thompson

D. ingle
Latham

16th VT
Garden   (5 cos)
Phillips

different demeanor and tone, he commanded an aide, "Go to those woods and order support to them." Running as fast as his exhausted legs would carry him, the captain returned to the 5th Florida and awaited the supports which never materialized.[63]

The Ridge West of the Emmitsburg Road

Very shortly after the Alabamians and Floridians quit the field, General Lee, without any staff, rode up to Colonel E. Porter Alexander. He said nothing to either the colonel or Lieutenant Fred M. Colston, who had accompanied Alexander onto the field. Alexander believed Lee intended to rally the men in person should Meade decide to counterattack. For a brief time he actually wanted the Yankees to attack just to see the commanding general in the middle of the fight. Several minutes lapsed when Colonel Arthur Fremantle rode out to join them. He spoke freely to Alexander, questioning him about details of the action. Alexander responded without being formally introduced by Lee. (The colonel thought that the general did not approve of him being in his gray shirt sleeves and sporting a torn knee in his pants.) Cheering broke out from the left of the Federal line. Lee ordered Colston to check out what was going on. When the lieutenant's horse balked at having to go out without Alexander's horse, Colston harshly spurred its flanks. "Oh, don't do that," Lee remonstrated him. "Use gentle measures. I had a foolish horse once, and gentle measures always had the best result."

Lieutenant F. M. Colston

Robert E. Lee, despite the utter failure of Longstreet's assault, took the time to chastise Colston for roughly spurring a fractious horse during the retreat.

Miller, *Photographic History*

All the while Pickett's refugees streamed around the officers. Lee quietly, yet firmly, urged them, "Form your ranks again when you get back to cover. We want all good men to hold together now." Repeatedly, Alexander heard him say, " It was all my fault this time." Presently, four litter bearers, carrying a blanket-draped officer upon their shoulders, approached the general. He spurred over to them. "Whom have you there?" he asked. "General Kemper." At hearing Lee, Kemper feebly pulled the blanket away from his head. "General Kemper," Lee began, "I hope you are not badly hurt." "Yes, General, I think they have got me this time." "Oh, I trust not! I trust not!" Lee replied while the litter bearers headed south with Kemper.[64]

Not too far to the south, Longstreet halted behind Captain Merritt Miller's section of the 3rd Company, Washington Artillery. The captain, puffing his pipe, strode back and forth, commanding his men to fire over the heads of their retreating men. The beaten Confederates walked without panic toward the rear where their general knew they would rally.[65]

Stannard's Brigade

While the Vermonters finished off Lang's and Wilcox's brigades, Major William Mitchell arrived with the II Corps Medical Director, Doctor Alexander N. Dougherty, to assist the downed Hancock. Untying the tourniquet the doctor poked his forefinger into Hancock's leg up to the first finger joint. He deftly pulled a bent ten-penny iron saddle nail from the wound and showed it to the exhausted general. "This is what hit you," he said, "and you are not so badly hurt as you think."[66] Hancock called to Mitchell, "Tell General Meade that the troops under my command have repulsed the enemy's assault and that we have gained a great victory. The enemy is now flying in all directions in my front." With that, Mitchell galloped away.[67]

Stannard dispatched Benedict to deliver an order to Lieutenant Colonel Charles W. Rose of the 14th Vermont to cease fire and take four of the companies from his wing to the support of the 16th Vermont.[68] Seconds later a case shot burst over the little knoll on Cemetery Ridge, from which Stannard was supervising the final actions of his three regiments. It killed Private George H. White (Company G, 2nd U.S. Sharpshooters), whose New Hampshire company supported Daniels' 9th Michigan Battery.[69] A cast iron ball from the same round struck Stannard in the upper part of his right leg, penetrating downward for three inches into his thigh. Despite the intense pain he remained upon the field. Surgeon Dougherty, who had just treated Hancock, immediately examined the wound. He extracted the ball and bandaged the injury. Stannard still would not retire. (General Abner Doubleday personally asked him to leave but he would not. He remained at his post until the last of his wounded was brought in, at which point he collapsed and was carried to a field hospital.)[70]

Lieutenant George G. Benedict (A.D.C. to Stannard) barely reached the 14th Vermont and the 16th Vermont. In passing down the western slope of Cemetery Ridge he had to go between the artillery fire of both armies—the Federals' hounding Pickett's survivors and the Confederate guns trying to cover Wilcox's retreat. A spent case ball struck his pistol cartridge box without touching him. (It did buckle a Smith and Wesson cartridge in half.) By the time he found the 14th, the order had been given to cease fire. A couple of the excited Yankees did not hear the command and coldly continued to fire until Major Nathaniel B. Hall literally grabbed them by their tunics and shook them into submission.[71] With Wilcox's Confederates effectively controlled, the lieutenant returned to Stannard's side. Hancock, having just sent his report of Pickett's defeat to Meade, seemed in better spirits. Benedict helped to lift him into an ambulance, then returned to his brigade duties.[72]

East of the Angle

A mob of Confederate prisoners swarmed rearward in the wake of the 72nd Pennsylvania's charge. The wounded Sergeant Frederick Mannes (Company B) watched the Rebels calmly looting the Federal casualties of haversacks, canteens, and blankets on their way to the rear. He called Captain Charles Banes' attention to the possibility that the enemy could turn captured Federal weapons upon them if they were not watched more closely. Banes and two men rushed into the herd, only to find themselves overwhelmed by superior numbers. As Mannes lay there, the captured Lieutenant Colonel Henry Carrington (18th Virginia) walked up to him and asked, "Sergeant, where's your second line?" "We can lick you with one line these days, Colonel," the Yankee impudently replied.[73]

The Confederates continued rearward, surrounding Meade as he approached the copse of trees. Shells from Motes' and McCarthy's guns screamed overhead. One of the guards yelled at the Rebs to move faster because they were all in sight of the gunners. Private Eli Cox (Company F, 1st Tennessee), at six feet tall being one of the tallest men in the company, calmly said to Wiley Woods (Company F), "Them's our shells." Woods knew whose they were and he did not feel like getting killed by them.[74] Where should they go, they queried. Meade, with unsuppressed jubilation pointed east toward the low ground near the Leister house. "Go along that way," he laughed, " you will be well taken care of." His son, having rejoined him, heard several guns open to the west. They were Alexander's reserve pieces along the Emmitsburg Road. As the shells screamed overhead, the prisoners raced for cover. "Why, it's hotter here than it was in front," one of them shouted at the captain as he trotted by him. Before the Confederates had completely gotten away, Lieutenant Frank Haskell (Gibbon's staff) rode up to Meade.[75]

"How is it going here?" the general asked. Haskell replied, "I believe, General, the enemy's attack is repulsed." Meade's white face grew brighter. "What! Is the assault already repulsed?" he exclaimed. "It is, sir." "Thank God," the general sighed.[76]

Captain Cook staggered into the conversation on the way back to his regiment. Meade talked loudly about the rumor that Longstreet had died in the assault. Cook butted into the conversation with the report that the Rebel officer had given him. Meade cast aside the captain's intelligence. He doubted the veracity of the Rebel's story. He said, "Any army must be in a desperate condition when a corps commander led a charge like that."[77]

Major William G. Mitchell (Hancock's aide) finally joined the gaggle of officers. When informed that Hancock was terribly wounded, Meade removed his kepi, and rising slightly in the stirrups, he leaned toward Mitchell. With genuine compassion, he told the major, "Say to General Hancock that I regret exceedingly that he is wounded and that I thank him for the Country and for myself for the service he has rendered today."[78]

With that, Mitchell spurred away and the general continued on his tour of the lines.[79] Meade immediately sent Haskell south with orders to bring up reinforcements as they were needed.[80]

The Copse of Trees

While the firing subsided, General Webb, Colonel Norman Hall, and Colonels Devereaux and Mallon gathered on the east side of the trees. The general was livid. Embarrassed at nearly losing his command when the Rebels forced it back from the wall, he raged against the 72nd Pennsylvania for failing to advance when he wanted them to go in.[81]

Stannard's Position

Lieutenant Henry A. Battles' Company of the Washington Artillery harassed the Federals with several solid shot and case to cover their own men's retreat.[82] Lieutenant George G. Benedict (A.D.C. to Stannard) was hurrying past the 13th Vermont on his way to the rear with an order. He had just yelled something lighthearted to Sergeant Major Henry H. Smith when in quick succession he heard a "thud," horrifying screams, and the bursting of a shell. He wheeled about and discovered a gaping hole in the regimental column. The unexploded shell had taken out three of four men in a file from Company K and the two officers who were marching next to them before exploding. The shot jarred the outside man, Private James M. Hogaboom, knocking him to the ground. It smashed Private Clark H. Butterfield, killing him instantly. Cutting the third man, Corporal William Church, nearly in half, it ripped one leg from his body and hurled it, without the pants leg, several feet away. The column temporarily doubled back upon itself, then straightened out. Stepping over the gory remains of their friends, the men closed ranks and kept marching to the rear. At that point it burst, killing Sergeant Major Smith and knocking Lieutenant Colonel William D. Munson to the ground unconscious.[83] Lieutenant Stephen F. Brown (Company K) immediately dropped down beside the dying Corporal Church to see what he could do for him when a second burst knocked him on his face, severely dazing him.[84]

Another shell gave Major General Abner Doubleday a very close call. Having reined in beside Major General John Newton, he immediately sent out stretcher bearers to bring in the Confederate wounded when the Confederate artillery seemed to deliberately fire upon his position. A hot fragment, about an inch and one-half long, tore through his hat brim and struck him in the back of the neck. The impact hurled him over his horse's neck onto the ground with an unceremonious thud. Instinctively feeling his head and neck to see if they were still attached, he plucked the chunk of metal from his velvet collar. Had the piece hit him with the ragged edge as opposed to the rounded side of the shell he would not have been alive to recover the souvenir. Picking himself up, his head ringing from the blow, he quietly walked to and fro for several minutes to get his bearing.[85]

General Meade

In the meantime, Meade, after trotting to a point behind Cowan's former position and having decided his men had control of the field, turned to his son and said matter-of-factly, "Well, everything seems to be all right here; we ought to be hearing from Howard; I think I will go over there." Wheeling his horse counterclockwise, he headed rapidly north toward Cemetery Hill. His son reined his mount about to follow him when a shell exploded over his head. A fragment imbedded itself in the horse's flank. Plunging and pitching wildly, it thudded to the ground, leaving the hapless captain on foot for a second time that day.

Picking himself up, he started meandering toward the Widow Leister's house, hoping to procure another mount when Brigadier General Alexander Webb caught his attention. Webb was trying to get men to man Cushing's remaining guns. First Sergeant Fuger and three or four of the remaining artillerymen had rolled a piece into the rocky outcropping near the crest of the ridge. Webb yelled at Meade to take command of the piece and to keep it firing before the Rebs could silence it. The jarred captain ordered a number of infantrymen to go forward with him when an artillery lieutenant, his head bandaged and his left arm in a sling, approached him. Samuel Canby, having just returned from the field hospital, said the battery was his and he would take command of the gun. Meade managed to borrow a replacement mount from one of Webb's orderlies and returned to the Leister house.[86]

After conferring with Howard, Meade proceeded down the hill toward the Leister house. On the way, he ran into Colonel Charles H. Tompkins' VI Corps artillery battalion on the way to the front. Meade personally ordered Captain William McCartney's Battery A, 1st Massachusetts into the line on the western side of the hill.[87] The captain rolled his six Napoleons into the space vacated by Captain Frederick M. Edgell's Battery A, 1st New Hampshire Artillery.[88]

The Angle

Back at the Angle, the victorious Federal regiments began mopping up. Private McDermott (Company I, 69th Pennsylvania) walked down to the wall where he declined to help the bespectacled Captain Theodore L. Wright (Company G, 72nd Pennsylvania) and Captain Benjamin J. McMahon (Company C, 71st Pennsylvania) drag one of Cushing's guns back toward the ridge. He had more humane work to do—gather in his regiment's wounded and dead and find his messmate.[89] Several feet from the wall he spied his friend's corpse and, close by, he noticed a Confederate battle flag leaning against the wall in front of Company I's former position. Without warning, two soldiers, each with a brass "42" on his cap, rushed past him. One snatched up the flag. As the fellows brushed by him, McDermott admonished them by saying he saw nothing honorable in what

they had done. Private Michael McDonough (42nd New York) nevertheless could claim he took the colors of the 22nd North Carolina at
Gettysburg.[90]

The 8th Ohio

Having been sent to the rear of Cemetery Ridge by Meade in person,
Colonel Franklin Sawyer ordered his battered regiment to stack arms and
rest. As they dispersed, an enlisted man from another regiment walked up
behind Second Lieutenant David S. Koons (Company C) and insubordi-
nately slapped him on the shoulder, exclaiming, "By Jinks, I got 100 myself." The exhausted lieutenant ignored him. Shortly after they stacked
their weapons, Colonel Samuel Carroll, their brigadier, walked his horse
into their bivouac. He greeted Sawyer with, "I suppose you have been
raising hell again." Looking around, he continued, "Where's your gunstacks?"
"There's what is left," the weary Sawyer replied while pointing. "Where is
Pierce? Where is Captain Nickerson? Where is Captain Miller?" Carroll
shot back. "All wounded and taken off the field," Sawyer told him. "Where
is Lieutenant Hayden?" Carroll inquired with considerable emotion. "Dead
on the field," came the reply. Unable to restrain himself any longer, Carroll
burst into tears.[91]

The Rogers House

Captain John C. Ward (Company E, 11th Virginia) and his badly jarred
friend, Captain James R. Hutter (Company H) sheltered themselves in the
basement among the Yankee prisoners and their guards. Ward was beside
himself, thrilled with having escaped. Hutter did not share his enthusiasm.
He did not like being so far below grade, too much like a trap being ready
to be sprung. At his insistence they crawled out through a window on the
western side of the house only to find the desperately wounded Kemper
lying unattended upon a blanket in the back yard. Ward gave him some
water to drink before they walked into the hollow below the house.

Ward wanted to get back to their own lines as quickly as possible.
Hutter wanted to wait until it got dark. They stopped at a rail fence somewhere south of the Spangler house to get their bearings. Hutter was not
sure of their exact location. Ward was too confident for the colonel's liking.
Under the captain's direction, they inadvertently meandered south for some
distance. From the crest of a hill they spied troops milling about a short
distance ahead. "Didn't I tell you so?" Ward taunted the colonel. "Hello,
boys, is that Pickett's Division?" "Yes; come on Mr. Johnnies, we want
you." Without warning, they found themselves surrounded by dismounted
cavalry who promptly escorted them to the road at the base of the hill to a
mounted contingent of the 2nd Pennsylvania Cavalry.[92]

West of the Spangler Farm

Private Erasmus Williams (Company H, 14th Virginia) returned to
the hole which he had dug for himself prior to the bombardment to pick up

his haversack and case knife. Turning west parallel with Spangler's farm lane, he started for the reverse slope of Seminary Ridge a few paces ahead of an ambulance in the lane. Without warning, a Federal shell ripped the canvas cover off the wagon, jarring it so hard that it bounced the lone, blanket-wrapped passenger into the dirt. Leaping from the seat, the driver blurted, "Come here and help me to carry this man off." "I am shot myself and unable to help anybody," Williams protested. "You must help me," the driver pleaded in a more reconciliatory tone. "Take hold, and let's carry this wounded man along the road beyond." Glancing eastward, Williams knew they were in a direct line with the Federal artillery on the southern end of Cemetery Ridge. "No," Williams insisted, "but if you take him around this hill I will try to help him with my right hand."

Grabbing the blanket with his good hand while the driver gripped the opposite end, Williams helped drag the wounded man around the back-side of the ridge to a field hospital. On the way, Williams griped about the futility of saving a corpse. "I believe he is already dead; it is not worthwhile carrying him anywhere," he added after examining the soldier's graying face. Who was it they were hauling off? Williams asked. "It is Kemper," the driver replied. Leaving the desperately wounded general with the doctors, Williams had his own wounds looked after. To his relief, the ball had not struck any bones. He would keep his left hand.[93]

Spangler's Woods
The Southern End

A very dejected General George Pickett, with Captain Robert A. Bright close behind, rejoined what he could find of his command along the stream in the southern end of Spangler's Woods. About an hour had elapsed since the charge failed. As he approached a stand of colors, the color bearer, Third Corporal Charles P. Belcher (Company B, 24th Virginia), waved them back and forth, shouting, "General, let us go to them again!" His cry fell on unlistening ears, the general's attention being distracted by litter bearers carrying Kemper past him. At the sight of his terribly injured friend, Pickett broke down and cried.

Lee suddenly rode up alone. "General Pickett," Lee began in a con-cerned tone, "place your division in rear of this hill and be ready to repel the advance of the enemy should they follow up their advantage." His eyes filled with tears, his chin lowered to his chest, Pickett sobbed, "General Lee, I have no division now. Armistead is down, Garnett is down, and Kemper is mortally wounded." Taking Pickett by the hand, the command-ing general tried to soothe his shattered nerves. "Come, General Pickett," he said, "this has been my fight, and upon my shoulders rests the blame. The men and officers of your command have written the name of Virginia as high as it has ever been written before."

Turning away from the grieving Pickett, Lee asked Bright, "Captain, what officer is that they are bearing off?" "General Kemper." "I must speak to him," Lee said while spurring Traveler after the stretcher. Bright followed. Pickett did not.

The moment they recognized Lee, the four stretcher bearers halted, the slight jolt causing Kemper to open his eyes. Looking down at Kemper, Lee spoke from the heart, "General Kemper, I hope you are not very seriously wounded." His body roaring with pain, Kemper replied, "I am struck in the groin and the ball has ranged upward; they tell me it is mortal." "I hope it will not prove so bad as that. Is there anything I can do for you, General Kemper?" Lee asked while Kemper propped himself up on one elbow. "Yes, General Lee," he grimaced, "do full justice to this division for its work today." "I will," Lee said, while bowing his head. He then rode off. At that, Pickett turned to the 300 or so men who had gathered around him. "You can go back to the wagons and rest until you are wanted," he told them.[94]

Pickett spurred his horse into the open ground east of the woods and futilely attempted to reform more of his men as they came back. His brother, Charles, having failed to locate Longstreet, found him on the southern end of the first ridge, with tears streaming down his face.[95] Without saying anything to his brother, the general suddenly galloped north to find his corps commander. "Where is General Longstreet?" he shouted as he spurred his horse. Longstreet, who saw him coming, dispatched his courier, William Youngblood (15th Alabama), to intercept him. The private never forgot how very distressed Pickett looked, with his long hair streaming behind him. As the two approached Longstreet, Pickett literally cried out, "General, I am ruined; my division is gone—it is destroyed." The unflappable Longstreet, knowing the condition of the division better than its commander, told Pickett the situation was not as bad as he believed. In a few hours, he would be able to find an impressive number of his men.[96]

The Northern End of Spangler's Woods

A familiar voice—Lucien Jones' (Company F)—greeted Lieutenant W. Nathaniel Wood (Company A, 19th Virginia) the moment he reached the shade of Spangler's Woods. Was the lieutenant's wound serious? the sergeant asked. "I think I am shot through," Wood grimaced. How was the sergeant faring? the lieutenant inquired. "I am mortally wounded," the gut-shot enlisted man replied, "but fell in the discharge of duty near the cannon's mouth."

Wood quickly opened his tunic, fully expecting to find it holding most of his insides in place. The front of the jacket was badly torn. Removing his vest, he discovered it in similar shape. Finally, he took off his sweaty shirt and found a hole in it. As he threw it to the ground, he noticed a small blood stain on it. The ball had merely broken the skin on his side, nothing more.[97]

Appendix

The Confederate Artillery Placement

A Reassessment of the Confederate Artillery Deployment Prior to the Charge

At 3:00 p.m., July 3, 1863, following a two-hour bombardment of unprecedented proportions, fifteen thousand Confederates, on a one-mile front, assaulted a waiting Federal position of infantry and artillery. The attack was a forlorn hope, doomed to failure from the start.

This author, intent upon improving prior studies, has used new material and has explained the tactical situation in greater detail than has been done in previous works. He has reevaluated materials which have always been at the historians' fingertips but which they have routinely overlooked or have not explored closely enough. The consequence of such oversights is that myth and often repeated tales have supplanted the accurate accounting of what actually transpired on that momentous afternoon.

The Dispositions of the Confederate Artillery

Colonel Edward Porter Alexander wrote explicitly about his part in the charge during and after the war. According to his supplemental after action report, dated August 10, 1863, he said that he had seventy-five guns to deploy along the eastern face of Seminary Ridge and an additional nine howitzers under the command of Major Charles Richardson (Lieutenant John J. Garnett's Battalion) in reserve. He made no mention of placing any guns on his flank.[1] He repeated that information in "The Great Charge and Artillery Fighting at Gettysburg" in *Battles and Leaders of the Civil War*.[2] He said virtually the same thing in a letter dated March 17, 1877 in *The Southern Historical Society Papers*, the notable variation being that he said that Brigadier General William N. Pendleton (Chief of Artillery, Army of Northern Virginia) loaned him seven instead of nine 12-pounder howitzers.[3] His recollections changed slightly in his *Military Memoirs of a Confederate* (1907) when he added that besides his seventy-five guns and Pendleton's nine howitzers, he had deployed eight of the First Corps' guns

181

on the right flank to cover Lee's right and rear from attack. In all, Alexander had ninety-two field pieces—a tremendous amount of armament—at his disposal. In his memoirs he asserted "...the remaining 75 [guns] were posted in an irregular line beginning in the Peach Orchard and ending near the northeast corner of the Spangler wood."[4] In his edited reminiscences, *Fighting for the Confederacy* (1989), which he used as the basis of his *Memoirs*, he also said that he had seventy-five guns and Pendleton's nine howitzers.[5]

What specific guns did his battalions use on the field and how were they deployed? In *The Official Records of the War of the Rebellion* there is an undated memo from Pendleton which identified the numbers and types of guns in Lieutenant General James Longstreet's Corps by battalion. According to Pendleton, the First Corps had eighty-three guns which agreed exactly with Alexander's accounting.[6] It seems evident that Alexander consulted *The Official Records* when writing his memoirs.

The Official Records and a marvelous resource compiled by David G. Martin, *Confederate Monuments at Gettysburg: The Gettysburg Battle Monuments*, Volume I, specifically enumerated the types of guns which participated in the cannonade.[7]

Batteries and Guns under Alexander's Command[8]

P: Parrott   R: ordnance rifle
H: howitzer   N: Napoleon

Battalion	Battery	State	20# P	10# P	3" R	12# N	24# H	12# H	Total
Alexander	Jordan	Va.			4				4
Alexander	Moody	La.					4		4
Alexander	Parker	Va.		1	3				4
Alexander	Rhett	S.C.						4	4
Alexander	Taylor	Va.				4			4
Alexander	Woolfolk	Va.	2			2			4
Cabell	Carlton	Ga.		2				2	4
Cabell	Fraser	Ga.		2	2				4
Cabell	Manly	N.C.			2				2
Cabell	McCarthy	Va.			2	2			4
Dearing	Blount	Va.				4			4
Dearing	Caskie	Va.		1	1	2			4
Dearing	Macon	Va.		2		2			4
Dearing	Stribling	Va.	2			4			6
Eshleman	Miller	La.				3			3
Eshleman	Norcom	La.				2		1	3
Eshleman	Richardson	La.			1	2		1	4
Eshleman	Squires	La.				1			1
Total			**4**	**8**	**15**	**28**	**4**	**8**	**67**

According to Pendleton's memo Cabell had fifteen guns present but he could only deploy fourteen of them on July 3. Alexander officially had twenty-two pieces while the battlefield plaques said he had twenty-four guns present. Dearing deployed eighteen guns as Pendleton noted. Eshleman had eleven pieces present, one more than recorded in the memo.[9] When the numbers are compared, Pendleton's memo asserted that there were sixty-five pieces among the four battalions while the battlefield markers account for sixty-seven pieces. Alexander erred by including Major Mathias W. Henry's four batteries (Latham, Bachman, Garden, and Reilly) in his tally. Pendleton credited the battalion with eighteen guns which would have brought Alexander's total to the traditional eighty-three guns.[10] If Alexander had placed the eight guns on the flank as he insisted he did, he would have had seventy-five field pieces remaining to support the charge.

The battlefield markers said that Henry had nineteen guns. The tablets clearly place Henry's Battalion on the extreme Confederate right flank on July 3, where it assisted in repelling Colonel Elon J. Farnsworth's cavalry foray.[11] Alexander erred, as did everyone who cited him, when he recorded that he put eight instead of eighteen guns on the right to protect the flank and the rear of the army. Captain M. W. Hazlewood in "Gettysburg Charge," which appeared in *The Southern Historical Society Papers* (XXIII), created more confusion when he included a schematic of the charge in which he placed Henry's Battalion on the right of Alexander's line as part of the supporting artillery for the attack, rather than on the right flank along the Emmitsburg Road.[12]

Of the sixty-seven field pieces which Alexander actually had present for action from the Peach Orchard to the northeast corner of Spangler's Woods, he kept twelve of them (four 24-pounder howitzers and eight 12-pounder howitzers) in reserve behind his main line. He deployed the fifty-five longer range guns on his 1,300-yard front.

A minor discrepancy over the number of howitzers which Alexander borrowed from Pendleton also appeared in his battle accounts. In his article for *The Southern Historical Society Papers*, Alexander reported that he had seven howitzers on loan from Pendleton. A careful check of the armaments and a crossreferencing with Pendleton's memo and a footnote in *Fighting for the Confederacy* substantiated neither nine nor seven as the correct number of 12-pounder howitzers detached to Alexander's command.

Colonels William T. Poague's and John J. Garnett's battalions were the ones closest to Longstreet's left flank. Their battalion and battery markers indicate that one of the howitzers came from Captain George Ward's Mississippi Battery. Two more were detached from Captain Joseph Graham's North Carolina artillery. Captain James V. Brooke's Virginia Battery (Lieutenant Addison W. Utterback, commanding) sent two additional 12-pounders. Captain James W. Wyatt sent one howitzer from his battery, making Poague's contribution six howitzers. Captain Charles R. Grandy (Garnett's Battalion) detached two howitzers from his Virginia light artillery battery to Alexander, bringing the total number of loaned guns to eight. Poague's

Battalion tablet (MN 632) identifies the reserve position of Poague's six guns. (The position is south of McMillan Woods, .05 mile north of the Virginia monument on the west side of West Confederate Avenue.) Grandy's post is not marked. The tablet states that the two howitzers were south of McMillan's Woods.[13] With these eight additional pieces, Alexander had fifty-five long-range field guns and twenty of the short-range howitzers, which brings his total to seventy-five guns—the exact number cited by Alexander in his writings. Gary Gallagher in *Fighting for the Confederacy* identified the Major Richardson, who commanded the eight loaned howitzers, as Charles Richardson from Garnett's Battalion.[14]

The Specific Locations of the Confederate Artillery for Ewell's and Hill's Corps

In his article for *The Southern Historical Society Papers* (XXIII), Captain Martin W. Hazlewood placed the supporting artillery battalions from north to south in the following order: McIntosh, Lane, Garnett, Pegram, Poague, Cabell, Dearing, Eshleman, Alexander, and Henry, which would lead one to believe that the Army of Northern Virginia had a phenomenal 171 guns involved in the entire bombardment.[15] The key to understanding where the batteries were placed and which particular pieces from Lieutenant Generals Ambrose P. Hill's and Richard S. Ewell's Corps took part in the cannonade can be found in Martin's *Confederate Monuments* and in *The Official Records* (XXVII, part 2). The few existing reports from Ewell's Artillery commanders—Lieutenant Colonels Thomas H. Carter and William Nelson—clearly indicate that his gunners were to draw fire from the Federal guns on Cemetery Hill away from the infantry during their charge toward Cemetery Ridge.[16] It can be inferred, therefore, that any Second Corps guns were positioned to perform the same function—to draw the fire of the XI Corps guns on Cemetery Hill away from Pickett's/Pettigrew's charge.

Captain Charles I. Raine's Virginia Battery (Latimer's Battalion, Ewell's Corps) anchored the far left of the Confederate artillery line with two 20-pounder Parrotts on Benner's Hill, 1,320 yards northeast of MN 623.[17] From that position the two guns could fire directly into Cemetery Hill.

About one and one-half miles to the northwest on the southern edge of the woods on the crest of Oak Hill Captain William B. Hurt (McIntosh's Battalion, Hill's Corps) put the two breech-loading Whitworth rifles from his Alabama Battery. (The guns near the Peace Light mark the section's correct location.) From there, they could overlook the town and fire directly into the Federal positions along Cemetery Hill and Cemetery Ridge.[18]

About one mile to the southwest, immediately north of the railroad cut on Seminary Ridge, Captain William P. Carter (Carter's Battalion, Ewell's Corps) placed his section of 10-pounder Parrotts. Captain William J. Reese's map of the battle shows an artillery position north of his battery which agrees with MN 609 which places the two guns near the railroad cut. A problem arises, however, when trying to determine whether Carter was north or south of the cut. His battalion commander, Lieutenant Colonel Thomas H. Carter, stated that he ordered the ten rifled guns of the battalion into battery north of the Chambersburg Pike on both sides of the railroad cut.[19] The woods on Seminary Ridge stopped about one hundred sixteen feet north of the cut—not enough room for a battery which would require one hundred ninety-two feet to properly deploy. A section required ninety-six feet to go into battery.[20] The logical place to put the two Parrots was on the north side of the cut.

The four rifled pieces (Captain Charles W. Fry's Virginia Battery) consisted of the two 10-pounder Parrotts and two 3-inch rifles. They went into battery on the open ridge south of the cut between the railroad bed and the Chambersburg Pike.[21] There was enough room there to adequately place the guns.

Captain William J. Reese (Carter's Battalion, Ewell's Corps) put his four 3-inch rifles into battery on Seminary Ridge about 1.25 miles southwest of the Whitworths on Oak Hill. According to Reese's map of the battle, the battery was along the ridge road which ran south from the Chambersburg Pike to the Seminary. Its left flank was near the Pike.[22]

Lieutenant John M. Cunningham (Dance's Battalion, Ewell's Corps) rolled his four 3-inch rifles into battery just north of the Fairfield Road, south of the Lutheran Seminary.[23] McIntosh's Battalion of Hill's Corps held the ridge to the south. One tenth of a mile to the right, Lieutenant Samuel Wallace's four 3-inch rifles of the 2nd Rockbridge Artillery remained in their July 2 position with Captain William B. Hurt's two rifles to his immediate right. Captain R. Sydney Rice's Virginia Battery of four Napoleons and Captain Marmaduke Johnson's two rifles and two Napoleons finished out the battalion line.[24]

Captain Willis J. Dance (Ewell's Corps) deployed the rest of the battalion along Seminary Ridge south of McIntosh's Battalion. Captain David Watson's 2nd Company, Richmond Howitzers (four 10-pounder Parrotts), Lieutenant Charles B. Griffin's Virginia Battery (two 3-inch rifles), then Captain Benjamin H. Smith, Jr.'s 3rd Company, Richmond Howitzers (four 3-inch rifles) extended the battalion's front a little over one-half of a mile below the Fairfield Road.[25]

Major William J. Pegram's Battalion (Hill's Corps) extended the artillery position toward Spangler's Woods with five of his six batteries. Captain Thomas A. Brander (Letcher Artillery) held the left of the line with two Napoleons and two 10-pounder Parrotts. Captain Joseph McGraw's Virginia Battery (four 12-pounder Napoleons) and Lieutenant William E. Zimmerman's four 3-inch rifles (Pee Dee Artillery) followed next. Lieutenant Andrew B. Johnston with his section of Napoleons then Captain

Edward A. Marye's two Napoleons and two 10-pounder Parrotts finished the battalion line.[26]

Two batteries from Major John Lane's Georgia Battalion held the McMillan Orchard and woods. Captain Hugh M. Ross' Company A (one 12-pounder Napoleon, three 10-pounder Parrotts, and one 3-inch naval Parrott) set up in the orchard with Captain John T. Wingfield's three 3-inch naval Parrotts and two 20-pounder Parrotts continuing the formation along the east side of the farm lane which ran south along the crest, bordering McMillan's Woods (to the west).[27]

Major William T. Poague completed Hill's artillery formation along the eastern face of the woods with a section of Napoleons from Captain Joseph Graham's North Carolina Battery, then a 10-pounder Parrott and two 3-inch rifles from Captain James W. Wyatt's Virginia Battery. Lieutenant Addison W. Utterback (Brooke Artillery) with two Napoleons continued the line to the south. Captain George Ward and his Mississippi Battery put his three Napoleons into the line to within a few feet of Spangler's Woods.[28]

A close examination of the armament shows that Lee was utilizing every available long-range field piece he had to support his grand charge on July 3. Contrary to many modern accounts, he used artillery from all three of his corps, not just Hill's and Longstreet's. His eighty guns and Alexander's fifty-five guns bring the number of guns actively employed in the cannonade to one hundred thirty-five field pieces. (If the twenty howitzers which Alexander had at his disposal are added to that total, one will discover that there were one hundred fifty-five guns present on the field.)

Battalions and Batteries from Ewell's and Hill's Corps

P: Parrott   NP: Naval Parrott
N: Napoleon   R: ordnance rifle
W: Whitworth

Corps	Battalion	Battery	20# P	2 W	10# P	3" R	12# N	3" NP	Total
Ewell	Latimer	Raine	2						2
Hill	McIntosh	Hurt		2					2
Ewell	Carter	Carter			2				2
Ewell	Carter	Fry			2	2			4
Ewell	Carter	Reese				4			4
Ewell	Dance	Cunningham				4			4
Hill	McIntosh	Wallace				4			4
Hill	McIntosh	Hurt				2			2
Hill	McIntosh	Rice					4		4
Hill	McIntosh	Johnson				2	2		4
Ewell	Dance	Watson			4				4
Ewell	Dance	Griffin				2			2
Ewell	Dance	Smith				4			4
Hill	Pegram	Brander			2		2		4

(continued)

Corps	Battalion	Battery	20# P	2 W	10# P	3" R	12# N	3" NP	Total
Hill	Pegram	McGraw					4		4
Hill	Pegram	Zimmerman				4			4
Hill	Pegram	Johnston					2		2
Hill	Pegram	Marye			2		2		4
Hill	Lane	Ross			3		1	1	5
Hill	Lane	Wingfield	2					3	5
Hill	Poague	Graham					2		2
Hill	Poague	Wyatt				1	2		3
Hill	Poague	Utterback					2		2
Hill	Poague	Ward					3		3
Total			**4**	**2**	**16**	**30**	**24**	**4**	**80**

The Deployment of Longstreet's Artillery

A number of problems exist when it comes to interpreting the positions of Longstreet's artillery. Unlike most of Ewell's and Hill's battery markers, the bronze tablets recording the positions of Longstreet's guns along West and South Confederate Avenues identify the sequential positions of the batteries but are not geographically close to their actual locations. Historians of the engagement have attempted to identify battalion positions but not battery positions, and, it appears, some of them have not paid close attention to either the terrain or to the details available through the *Official Records* and the many memoirs and reminiscences about the battle. Captain Martin W. Hazlewood in "Gettysburg Charge" while generally accurate about the overall northwest to southeast sequence of the battalions leaves the reader with no idea about where the guns were specifically located. He placed the battalions in the following order from left (northwest) to right (southeast): Cabell—Dearing—Eshleman—Alexander—Henry.[29]

In *Pickett's Charge*, Stewart used a very sketchy map with no terrain features on page 163, which accurately shows Pegram, Lane, and Poague along a northeasterly running line where Seminary Ridge and McMillan's farm would be were they on the map. Farther south the reader will find another part of Poague's Battalion and a section of guns marked "Alex." for "Alexander." The author also noted in the map's legend, "The position of Cabell's guns is uncertain; they may have been in line with Poague's and Alexander's in front of Garnett." From there one will find a north-south line of artillery labeled "Cabell" and "Dearing." They are facing the Emmitsburg Road with the Codori house directly east of Cabell. The right end of Dearing's line crosses the Emmitsburg Road.[30]

Kathy Georg Harrison's and John W. Busey's *Nothing But Glory* has a map on page 22 showing artillery positions by battalion. Cabell and

Alexander are on a north-south line with its left flank near the long fence row which runs northeast toward the Federal lines and with its right flank near the northeast corner of Spangler's orchard. Dearing's Battalion is located west of the Rogers house with its right flank crossing Spangler's lane. The guns are facing east. From there Cabell and Alexander continue the line close to and parallel with the Emmitsburg Road to the Trostle farm lane. At that point Eshleman's and Haskell's Battalions cross the Emmitsburg Road on a northeasterly front east of the Sherfy house to the Peach Orchard.[31]

The logical way to proceed is to describe the guns' positions from Poague's left to the end of Alexander's line. Colonel Edward P. Alexander's place in the chain of command must be addressed first. Longstreet had appointed him acting Chief of Artillery for the First Corps. Colonel James B. Walton, the official Chief of Artillery and the former commander of the Washington Artillery, stayed with that battalion throughout the engagement. First Lieutenant William M. Owen, the battalion adjutant, confirmed that Walton was near the battalion and that Walton was given a written order from Longstreet to commence firing. From his position west of the Peach Orchard, Walton was expected to supervise the right wing of the Corps artillery, otherwise Longstreet would not have told him to direct the fire from the guns north of the Peach Orchard against Little Round Top if they could not be used effectively against the copse of trees.[32] To be accurate, Alexander should not have been cited as a battalion commander during Pickett's Charge. Major Frank Huger commanded Alexander's Battalion.

The key to understanding the correct alignment of Longstreet's batteries is in *The Official Records*, XXVII, part 2. Major Benjamin F. Eshleman reported his battalion position as follows: Captain Merritt B. Miller (3rd Company) and Captain Charles W. Squires (1st Company) with their four Napoleons went into battery along the Emmitsburg Road one hundred yards north of the Peach Orchard. Captain Osmond B. Taylor (Battery C, 12th Virginia Artillery Battalion) from Huger's command was to their immediate right with his four 12-pounders.

Lieutenant Henry A. Battles and the two Napoleons from his 4th Company fell in on Miller's and Squires' left with his guns on a northeasterly front. Battles had to refuse the line to counteract a possible enfilade along the southern end of the line.[33] At that point Captain Basil C. Manly (Colonel Henry C. Cabell's Battalion) with his two ordnance rifles and two 3-inch rifles from Lieutenant William J. Furlong's Pulaski Artillery (under Manly's Lieutenant J. H. Payne) went into battery in echelon, facing northeast.[34]

Lieutenant Robert M. Anderson of Captain Edward S. McCarthy's 1st Richmond Howitzers rolled into battery on Payne's left with the battery's two ordnance rifles. Furlong completed Cabell's line with his two 10-pounder Parrotts and connected with Eshleman's left battery, the 2nd Company

Washington Artillery Battalion—two 12-pounder Napoleons and a captured 3-inch rifle (Captain John B. Richardson, commanding).[35]

Taylor's battery, which belonged to Huger's Battalion, represented one-third of the command which supported the charge. Captain William W. Parker's Virginia Battery of one 10-pounder Parrott and three 3-inch rifles and Captain Tyler C. Jordan's Bedford Artillery (four 3-inch rifles) anchored the battalion's right flank. Jordan was to Taylor's right on a northeasterly line east of the Emmitsburg Road, with Parker to his right, facing north along Trostle's Lane—200 feet north of the Peach Orchard.[36]

Major James Dearing's Virginia Battalion went into position on the northwest-southeast ridge immediately east of Spangler's Woods. According to MN 577, MN 576, MN 575, and MN 574, he arranged his batteries in the following order from left to right: Captain Joseph G. Blount, Captain Miles C. Macon, Captain William H. Caskie, and Captain Robert M. Stribling.[37] Stribling recorded in his after-action report that the Washington Artillery (Eshleman) was about 200 yards to his right (east), which would place him on the southern end of the ridge closest to Spangler's Woods.[38]

Alexander finished out the First Corps' artillery position with Lieutenant James Woolfolk's Virginia Battery from his (Huger's) former battalion, and four guns from Captain Edward S. McCarthy's 1st Company Richmond Howitzers and Captain Henry H. Carlton's Troup Artillery from Colonel Henry C. Cabell's Battalion. Woolfolk went into battery, according to MN 563, near the northeast corner of Spangler's Woods, which Alexander confirmed.[39] In *Fighting for the Confederacy* he said that Woolfolk's battery was posted very close to the point from which he was observing the artillery barrage.[40] In a letter to his father dated July 17, 1863, Alexander said that he was standing in the corner of the woods behind a tree during the bombardment.[41] Carlton's 1st section of 10-pounder Parrotts were to Woolfolk's left. He positioned his section of 12-pounder howitzers in the hollow behind him.[42] McCarthy's section of 12-pounder Napoleons rolled into battery to Carlton's left.[43] To summarize, the artillery deployed in front of Pickett's division from northwest to southeast as follows: McCarthy, Carlton, Woolfolk, Blount, Macon, Caskie, Stribling, Richardson, Furlong, Anderson, Payne, Manly, Battles, Squires/Miller, Taylor, Jordan, and Parker.

The Length of the Cannonade

According to the preeminent historians on the subject of Pickett's Charge, the cannonade lasted from 1:00 p.m. until 3:00 p.m. Fairfax Downey, *The Guns of Gettysburg*, and Douglas Southall Freeman, *Lee's Lieutenants A Study in Command* (III), both say that the bombardment lasted two hours.[44] Kathy Georg Harrison and John W. Busey, *Nothing But Glory*, said that the artillery opened fire shortly after 1:00 p.m. and that

MAP 25
Confederate Artillery Positions

	Battery	Guns
1.	Raine	2
2.	Hurt	2
3.	Carter	2
4.	Fry	4
5.	Reese	4
6.	Cunningham	4
7.	Griffin	2
8.	Smith	4
9.	Wallace	4
10	Hurt	2
11.	Rice	4
12.	Johnson	4
13.	Watson	4
14.	Brander	4
15.	McGraw	4
16.	Zimmerman	4
17.	Johnston	2
18.	Marye	4
19.	Ross	5
20.	Wingfield	5
21.	Graham	2
22.	Wyatt	3
23.	Utterback	2
24.	Ward	3
25.	McCarthy	2
26.	Carlton	2
27.	Woolfolk	4
28.	Blount	4
29.	Macon	4
30.	Caskie	4
31.	Stribling	6
32.	Richardson	3
33.	Furlong	2
34.	Anderson	2
35.	Payne	2
36.	Manly	2
37.	Battles	2
38.	Miller	4
39.	Taylor	4
40.	Jordan	4
41.	Parker	4
42.	Latham	5
43.	Garden	4

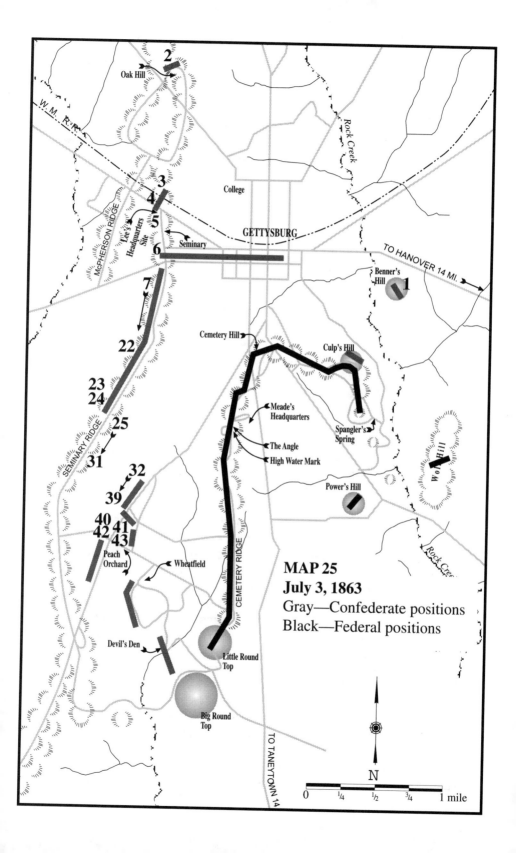

Oak Hill

2

W. M. R. R.

Rock Creek

3
4
5
Lee's Headquarters Site
6
Seminary

GETTYSBURG

College

McPHERSON RIDGE

7

TO HANOVER 14 MI.

Benner's Hill
1

22

23
24

25

31

Cemetery Hill

Culp's Hill

Meade's Headquarters

Spangler's Spring

SEMINARY RIDGE

The Angle
High Water Mark

Wolf Hill

32

39

Power's Hill

40 41
42 43

Peach Orchard

Wheatfield

CEMETERY RIDGE

Rock Creek

MAP 25
July 3, 1863
Gray—Confederate positions
Black—Federal positions

Devil's Den

Little Round Top

Big Round Top

TO TANEYTOWN 14

N

0   1/4   1/2   3/4   1 mile

after fifteen minutes of firing, the Confederates had forty-five minutes of ammunition left but used a map which clearly illustrated the troop positions during the cannonade from 1:00–3:00 p.m.[45] Glenn Tucker, *High Tide at Gettysburg*, cited reporter Samuel Wilkeson's timing of the cannonade at one hour.[46] Bruce Catton, *Glory Road*, said it lasted from half an hour to two hours rather than discuss the matter at all. George R. Stewart, *Pickett's Charge*, specifically stated that the artillery fighting lasted from 1:07 p.m. until 2:55 p.m.[47] Edwin Coddington, *The Gettysburg Campaign*, referred to and concurred with Alexander in regard to the 1:00 p.m. commencement of the firing but did not mention how long it lasted.[48]

Downey's work, while it might read well, is poorly cited and researched. He did not use a primary source when stating the time of Pickett's attack. In a footnote, he cited Freeman, *R. E. Lee* (III: 122), and Freeman, *Lee's Lieutenants* (III: 138). Freeman did not say where he arrived at the two-hour length of the bombardment. He seemed to have assumed that it lasted two hours. In a footnote he commented about the location of Pettigrew's deployment with no reference to the time at which the charge started.

Tucker, when using Wilkeson's watch to time the length of the cannonade, cited in footnote 1 Alexander's article from *The Southern Historical Society Papers* (IV: 107) in which there is no reference to the reporter. Stewart dismissed Alexander's assertion that the cannonade lasted about one hour as "some quirk." To support his belief that the bombardment continued for at least forty-five minutes beyond that, he cited Major General Winfield S. Hancock's and Brigadier General Albion P. Howe's reports in the *Official Records* as the most accurate in regard to the duration of the artillery duel.

All of these historians either ignored or dismissed what Alexander had to say about how long the cannonade lasted. In all of his accounts except *Battles and Leaders*, III, his supplemental report, and a July 17, 1863, letter to his father, Alexander said that he specifically sent a note to Pickett to advance at 1:25 p.m. According to his supplemental report, he wrote Pickett his first request to march at 1:30 p.m. At 1:35 p.m., he notified Pickett that the Federal fire had slackened and that he had silenced eighteen of the enemy's guns. At 1:45 p.m., Longstreet rode out to his position and at 1:50 p.m., Pickett's men were advancing toward the guns.[49]

(In the *Battles and Leaders* article he wrote that he waited twenty-five minutes before sending Pickett the first message, which would have made the time 1:25 p.m.) According to his *Military Memoirs*, he sent his second message at 1:40 p.m., followed by two verbal messages to start the attack. (In *Fighting for the Confederacy*, he said he sent the second note at 1:40 p.m. Keep in mind that the *Battles and Leaders* article preceded *Fighting for the Confederacy*, which preceded *Military Memoirs*. As time went on, Alexander tried to fine-tune his previous writings, which, as he gathered more information, can account for the five-minute time variation in the several accounts.)

All three sources agree that sometime between 1:40 p.m. and 1:50 p.m. Longstreet joined Alexander at the left end of the artillery line and that between 1:50 p.m. and 2:00 p.m. Pickett's men passed through the guns in their charge upon Cemetery Ridge.

Coddington remains the only recent author to have addressed the time in his footnotes. He stated that in Alexander's letter to his father, Alexander mentioned that he observed the Federal position for forty minutes from behind a tree in Spangler's Woods before sending for Pickett and that it made sense that this was the more accurate time than those recorded in his later accounts. It is important to note, however, that Alexander could have been referring to the time at which he sent the second note to Pickett, which would not contradict his statements in *Military Memoirs* or his August 10, 1863 report, of the battle.

Traditionally, historians have discounted Alexander's time references in favor of the times cited in the reports in the *Official Records*. After compiling twenty-seven reports from the *Official Records*, Coddington confirmed that the artillery bombardment began at 1:00 p.m. and he concurred that Alexander's time, as he recorded it, was accurate. He disregarded Colonel Walton's statement that he received orders to fire at 1:30 p.m. because, "...It is impossible to reconcile this evidence with Alexander's statement, which is substantiated by an overwhelming majority of reliable witnesses."[50]

Coddington did not apply the same standard when determining when the infantry charge actually began. He used Winfield S. Hancock's, Colonel Norman J. Hall's, Brigadier General Alexander Webb's, First Sergeant J. Walker's, and Lieutenant Frank Haskell's accounts to substantiate that the charge began at 3:00 p.m. Hancock and Webb both said the artillery fight lasted one hour and forty-five minutes. Walker (Company K, 9th Virginia) said the firing lasted one hour, thereby making the attack time 2:00 p.m. instead of 3:00 p.m. Haskell was the only witness who reported that the firing ceased exactly at 3:00 p.m.[51] This statement did not meet the criteria of being "...substantiated by an overwhelming majority of witnesses." It does not mean that the people whom Coddington cited were unreliable, but one out of the five is not a consensus of the majority of witnesses consulted.

Stewart, in what many have considered the classic microstudy of the charge, specifically wrote that the artillery ceased fire "...at about five minutes before three o'clock." He proved his assertion by referring to the time in Hancock's after-action report. The remainder of his notes are about the number of Confederate rounds expended and their rate of fire.[52]

Here, presented in tabular form, are what the participants said about the length of the artillery assault.

The following tables are organized by armies.

Army of the Potomac
abt.: about   hr: hour   min.: minutes

Name	Regiment/Rank	Time
Abbott, Henry L.	20th Massachusetts	probably 2 hours
Adams, Silas	19th Maine	about 2 hours
Bassett, Richard A.	126th New York	about 2 hours
Benedict, George G.	12th Vermont	1 hour 30 minutes
Coates, Henry C.	1st Minnesota	5 hours
Cole, Jacob H.	57th New York	1 hour
Regimental Committee	19th Massachusetts	1 hour 40 minutes
Cook, John D. S.	20th N.Y.S.M.	3–5 hours
Cowan, Andrew	1st N.Y. Light Arty.	1 hour
Curtis, Sylvanus	7th Michigan	3 hours
Davis, William	69th Pennsylvania	about 2 hours
Devereaux, Arthur	19th Massachusetts	about 2 hours
Dow, Edwin B.	6th Maine Arty.	abt. 1 hour 30 min.
Fuger, Frederick	B, 4th U.S. Arty.	1 hour 30 minutes
Galwey, Thomas F.	8th Ohio	1 hour 40 minutes
Gates, Theodore	80th N.Y.	about 2 hours
Gibbon, John	General, U.S.A.	2 hours
Haines, William P.	12th New Jersey	abt. 1 hour 30 min.
Hall, Norman J.	Colonel, U.S.A.	2 hours
Hancock, Winfield	General, U.S.A.	abt. 1 hour 45 min.
Harrow, William	General, U.S.A.	about 2 hours
Haskell, Harry L.	125th New York	ends about 2 p.m.
Hays, Alexander	General, U.S.A.	abt. 2 hrs. 30 min.
Hazard, George	1st Minnesota	little over 1 hr.
Hazard, John G.	Capt., U.S. Arty.	1 hr. 15 min.
Hincks, William B.	14th Connecticut	little over 1 hr.
Hunt, Henry J.	General, U.S.A.	abt. 1 hr. 30 min.
Hyde, Thomas	7th Maine	about 1 hour
McDermott, Anthony	69th Pennsylvania	1–2 hours
McGilvery, Freeman	Col., Vol. Arty.	abt. 1 hr. 30 min.
McMahon, Andrew R.	15th N.Y. Arty.	about 2 hours
Meade, George G.	General, U.S.A.	over 2 hours
Morgan, Charles H.	I.G., II Corps	45 minutes
Newbury, M. F.	B, 4th U.S. Arty.	1 hour 35 minutes
Phillips, Charles	E, 5th Mass. Lgt. Arty.	1 hour
Rhodes, John H.	B, 1st R.I. Artillery	abt. 1 hr. 30 min.
Rice, Edmund	19th Massachusetts	2 hours
Sawyer, Franklin	8th Ohio	about 2 hours
Seely, A.P.	111th New York	about 2 hours
Smith, Christopher	B, 4th U.S. Arty.	little over 1 hr.
Smyth, Thomas A.	General, U.S.A.	3 hours
Stannard, George J.	General, U.S.A.	1 hour 30 minutes
Tyler, Cyril H.	7th Michigan	2 hours
Veazey, Wheelock G.	16th Vermont	about 2 hours
Ward, Joseph R. C.	106th Pennsylvania	2 hours
Webb, Alexander S.	General, U.S.A.	1 hour 45 minutes

over 2 hours: 6 (13%)   about 2 hours–2 hours: 18 (39%)
1.5–1.75 hours: 12 (26%)   a little over 1 hour–1.25 hours: 4 (9%)
about 1 hour–1 hour: 6 (13%)

Army of Northern Virginia

Name	Regiment/Rank	Time
Anderson, Richard	General, C.S.A.	1 hour
Aylett, William R.	53rd Virginia	1 hour
Cabell, H. C.	Artillery	over 2 hours
Carter, James T.	53rd Virginia	1 hour 30 minutes
Coxe, John	2nd South Carolina	about 30 minutes
Crocker, James F.	9th Virginia	2 hours
Davis, Joseph R.	General, C.S.A.	about 2 hours
Dearing, James	Artillery	about 1 hour
Dooley, John	1st Virginia	1 hour
Eshleman, Benjamin	Artillery	about 30 minutes
Finley, George W.	56th Virginia	over 1 hour
Fite, John A.	7th Tennessee	1–2 hours
Fremantle, Arthur	British observer	over by 2:30 p.m.
Galloway, Felix R.	Artillery	50 minutes
Haskell, John C.	Artillery	several hours
Johnston, David E.	7th Virginia	about 2 hours
Jones, J.	26th North Carolina	ends about 2 p.m.
Kimble, June	14th Tennessee	about 1 hour
Lang, David	Col., Fla. Brigade	about 2 hours
Loehr, Charles T.	1st Virginia	about 2 hours
Lowrance, William	34th North Carolina	about 1 hour
Manly, Benjamin C.	Artillery	ends about 3 p.m.
Martin, Rawley	53rd Virginia	little over 1 hour
McCarthy, E. S.	Artillery	1 hour 40 minutes
McCulloch, Robert	18th Virginia	2 hours
Mitchie, H. C.	28th Virginia	ends about 2 p.m.
Moore, James H.	7th Tennessee	about 1 hour
Peyton, Charles S.	19th Virginia	1 hour
Pickett, George	General, C.S.A.	about 2:45 p.m.
Sorrel, G. Moxley	CIS, ANV	ends about 2 p.m.
Turney, J. B.	1st Tennessee	2 hours
Walton, Joseph B..	Artillery	over 2 hours
Wilcox, Cadmus	General, C.S.A.	50 minutes

over 2 hours: 3 (9%)   about 2–2 hours: 9 (27%)
1.5–1.75 hours 4 (12%)   a little over 1 hour–1.25 hours: 2 (6%)
about 1–1 hour: 15 (46%)

Forty-eight percent of the Federals believed that the cannonade lasted from under one hour to one hour forty-five minutes—nine percent more than said that it lasted about two hours. An impressive sixty-four percent of the Confederates said that the artillery fire lasted from under one hour to one hour forty-five minutes. Therefore, out of the seventy-nine men in the survey, fifty-four percent (forty-three) said that the bombardment did not last longer than one hour forty-five minutes.

Of those forty-three, twenty-one (forty-nine percent), most of them Confederate, wrote that the cannonade ended after one hour. Sixteen (thirty-seven percent) timed the artillery fight at one hour and one-half to one hour forty-five minutes. Only six (fourteen percent) said it ended after one and one-quarter hours.

Numbers and percentages can be argued forever. Would it not be logical to accept the testimony of the officer who was directly responsible for ordering the infantry assault? The entire timing for the attack rested upon Colonel E. Porter Alexander—upon his sense of the combat situation and his timing. There is no logical reason to disregard his time citations other than the fact that they are contrary to the accepted timetables established by tradition.

In *Fighting for the Confederacy* Alexander tried to rationalize how some authors could say that the cannonade lasted over one hour. When writing about the 11:00 a.m. skirmish between A. P. Hill's Artillery and the Federal guns on Cemetery Ridge, he concluded, "This duel made a great deal of noise while it lasted, & many writers have imagined it to have been part of the cannonade to prepare the way for Pickett." He also wrote, "Now, I could not hope to bombard effectively with anything less than the whole force of artillery at my disposal...& I had not the ammunition to make it a long business. It must be done inside of an hour if ever."[53]

Both John Gibbon in his 1863 *The Artillerist's Manual* and the Board of Artillery Officers' 1861 *Instruction for the Field Artillery* said that gunners could fire two or three rounds per minute.[54] By Alexander's own admission, he expected to and did have his men fire fast at Cemetery Ridge and Cemetery Hill. Captain Justis Scheibert, a Prussian observer with the Confederates, described the artillery fight as a "waste of powder."[55] Lieutenant Colonel Freeman McGilvery (commanding the 1st Volunteer Brigade, U.S.A.) wrote, "This fire was very rapid and inaccurate, most of the projectiles passing from 20 to 100 feet over our lines."[56] Captain Charles A. Phillips (Battery E, Massachusetts Light Artillery) concurred in his July 6, 1863, report. "About 1 o'clock," he stated, "the enemy opened a heavy fire from a long line of batteries, which was kept up for an hour, but beyond the noise which was made no great harm was done."[57] Private Felix R. Galloway (Battery A, Cutts' Battalion) indirectly affirmed that the Confederate guns on his end of the line did fire at a very fast rate. According to Galloway, the battery was ordered to fire one hundred rounds per gun, then to cease fire to let the infantry advance. His crew expended forty rounds before the Federals responded.[58] Brigadier General Henry Hunt ordered his artillerists to wait fifteen to twenty minutes before replying to the Confederate guns, which they did.[59] To have expended forty rounds in twenty minutes, Cutts' men would have been firing at a rate of two rounds per minute. The seriousness of the Confederate attack became quite evident to the Federals at the Angle. Haskell and Gibbon said it was the most vicious they had ever experienced.[60] Miles F. Newbury, who served with Lieutenant Alonzo Cushing's Battery A, 4th U.S. Artillery at the time, counted six rounds per minute dropping into his position.[61] First Sergeant Frederick Fuger in the same battery reported that he lost eighty-three out of ninety horses that day.[62] After the war, Alexander heard that one of the Federal batteries lost twenty-seven out of thirty-six horses within ten minutes during the cannonade.[63]

Apparently, Alexander's battalions came under criticism for firing too fast and for wasting ammunition. Major Benjamin F. Eshleman defended his battalion's ammunition expenditure when he wrote that his artillerymen "...by their steady and judicious firing caused immense slaughter to the enemy."[64] The word "judicious" implies that a possible charge of wild firing had circulated among the upper echelon officers in the Army of Northern Virginia. Major James Dearing recorded in his report that his guns "... commenced firing slowly and deliberately. To ensure more accuracy and to guard against the waste of ammunition, I fired by battery." Despite his efforts, his men ran out of ammunition for all but his rifled guns before Pickett charged.[65] Captain B. C. Manly (Battery A, 1st North Carolina Artillery) affirmed that his pieces fired "...slowly and with deliberation."[66]

The majority of the evidence indicates that the artillery fire lasted from one hour to one hour forty-five minutes. Nevertheless it is possible to reconcile the statements of those who said the cannonade stopped after two hours. The traditional interpretations of the charge lead one to believe that the Confederate artillery ceased fire entirely during the Confederate advance.

Alexander, Lieutenant Edwin Dow (6th Maine Battery), Private Christopher Smith (Battery A, 4th U.S. Artillery), Major B. F. Eshleman, and Colonel Alfred H. Belo (55th North Carolina) all testified that the Confederate artillery fired over their own troops during the charge. Alexander specifically ordered all of his guns with less than fifteen rounds of ammunition to fire over the heads of their own infantry. Major Eshleman in *The Official Records* complained that his guns were left alone on the field to support the infantry attack after the batteries on both flanks exhausted their ammunition and had withdrawn from the fight. Dow noted that the Confederate infantry charged under the cover of their own artillery fire, which Smith corroborated. According to him, during the charge, a Confederate shell killed two horses and one of the battery's artillerymen. Belo saw Captain Howell G. Whitehead (Company E) struck on the chest by a Confederate shell at the stone wall.[67]

This is the author's scenario of the charge. At 1:50 p.m. the Confederate artillery ceased fire and the infantry advanced through the guns toward the front. Moving into the hollow east of the guns on the first ridge, they aligned ranks and moved forward. With Pettigrew joining their left, the combined forces of Pettigrew and Pickett ascended the second ridge under a tremendous fire from Ziegler's Grove and Little Round Top. In the next hollow they closed again on the center. As they crested the third ridge, they came under small arms fire from Federal skirmishers and canister from McGilvery's, Cowan's, and what was left of Cushing's batteries. In the third hollow, they closed up a third time on the center with their ranks terribly thinned. After crossing the Emmitsburg Road, they reached and held onto the Federal works for another twenty minutes before being driven back. They retreated under a harassing fire. Manly's battery kept up its fire until 3:00 p.m. when he exhausted his ammunition supply. It is this author's conclusion that Pickett's Charge lasted from the cannonade until the final shots were fired from 1:00–3:00 p.m. and not 1:00 p.m. until 4:00 p.m. as currently believed.

Appendix

The Confederate Infantry Strengths and Casualties

Pickett's Division

Brigades	Present	KIA	WIA	WIA/CIA	CIA	Total	%
Kemper[1]	1781	114	223	214	127	678	38.1
Garnett[2]	1851	181	213	286	225	905	48.9
Armistead[3]	2188	196	199	333	329	1057	48.3
Total	5820	491	635	833	681	2640	
Ave./Pres.		8.4%	10.9%	14.3%	11.7%	45.4%	

Pettigrew's Division

Brigade	Present	KIA	WIA	WIA/CIA	CIA	Total	%
Fry[4]	900	51	163		321	535	59.4
Marshall[5]	1205	69	137	248	156	610	50.6
Davis[6]	1143	119	207		114	440	38.5
Brockenbrough[7]	500	1	3		3	7	1.4
Total	3819	240	510	248	594	1592	
Ave./Pres.		6.3%	13.4%	6.5%	15.6%	41.7%	

Trimble's Division

Brigade	Present	KIA	WIA	WIA/CIA	CIA	Total	%
Lane[8]	1076	60	65	113	143	381	35
Lowrance[9]	840	10	27	40	112	189	22.5
Total	1916	70	92	153	255	570	
Ave./Pres.		3.7%	4.8%	8%	13.3%	29.8%	

R. H. Anderson's Division

Brigade	Present	Casualties	%
Wilcox[10]	1200	204	17
Lang[11]	400	155	38.8
Total	1600	359	
Ave./Pres.		22.4%	

Notes

Chapter 1

1. Napier Bartlett, *Military Record of Louisiana* (Baton Rouge: Louisiana State University Press, 1992), 187.

2. E. P. Alexander to J. William Jones, March 17, 1877, Southern Historical Society Papers (hereafter, SHSP), IV:97.

3. See Appendix A for the footnoted details explaining the individual batteries' actual placements.

4. The standard story is that Alexander put 75 guns on line out of 83 under his command. In an undated Addenda in *OR*, vol. XXVII, pt. 2, 355, Pendleton reported that the First Corps had 90 guns in the battle and brought off 83 of them. Alexander apparently got his figures from this report. It is important to note that there were 90 guns with the corps during Gettysburg. The "83" is the number of guns present *after* the battle. According to the after-action reports and the interpretive tablets on the battlefield, the following numbers of guns were present: Cabell 14, Eshleman 10, Alexander 24, for a total of 48 guns, not including Henry's Battalion of 19 guns nor Dearing's Battalion of 18 guns. Before the 1:00 p.m. cannonade he would have Dearing's 18 guns, 1 captured 3" rifle, with 9 more from Garden's and Latham's Batteries, and his original 48 pieces, giving him a total of 76 guns of which he would put his twelve howitzers in reserve to follow up the charge.

    Robert N. Scott, comp., *The Official Records of the War of the Rebellion*, XXVII, pt. 2 (Washington, D.C.: U.S. Government Printing Office, 1887), 375, 379, 380, 384, and 434. Reports of B. F. Eshleman, H. C. Cabell, B. C. Manly, W. J. Furlong, and C. W. Motes. Edward Porter Alexander, *Military Memoirs of a Confederate* (New York: Da Capo Press, 1993), 418. David G. Martin, *Confederate Monuments at Gettysburg*, I (Highstown, N.J.: Longstreet House, 1986), 65, 68, 71–75, 83–87, 90–93, 97, 100, 109, 111, 118, 124.

5. Gary Gallagher, ed., *Fighting for the Confederacy* (Chapel Hill: University of North Carolina Press, 1989), 245.

6. George Clark, "Wilcox's Alabama Brigade at Gettysburg," *Confederate Veteran* (hereafter, *CV*) (XVII:230). *OR*, XXVII, pt. 2, 619. Report of Brig. Gen. Cadmus M. Wilcox.

7. Alexander and Bartlett said the two horses were wounded.

    OR, XXVII, pt. 2, Report of Maj. B. F. Eshleman, 434. Gallagher, *Fighting for the Confederacy*, 245. William Miller Owen, *In Camp and Battle with the Washington Artillery of New Orleans* (Boston: Ticknor and Co., 1885), 247. Bartlett, *Military Record of Louisiana*, 187–88.

8. *OR*, XXVII, pt. 2, 434. Report of Maj. B. F. Eshleman.

9. George Grenville Benedict, *Army Life in Virginia* (Burlington: Free Press Association, 1895), 171–72.

10. Ibid., 172.

11. A close examination of the number of guns present from the monuments and the battle-field markers indicate that Osborn had only two of his batteries in position at the time. Wheeler's 13th New York Light was with the reserve. Heckman's Battery K, 1st Ohio Light was not on the hill. Bancroft's Battery G, 4th U.S. was on the eastern side of the hill and did not come up until the attack began.

    Edmund J. Raus, Jr., *A Generation on the March–The Union Army at Gettysburg*, 1st Edition. (Lynchburg, Va.: H. E. Howard, Inc., 1987), 87–89, 102, 103, 165–66.

12. Ibid., 90–91. *OR*, XXVII, pt. 1, 891, 892–93. Reports of Capt. Elijah D. Taft and Frederick Edgell.

13. Raus, *The Union Army at Gettysburg*, 82, 98–99, 100. See also Map II.

14. The map to delineate the troop positions which follow come from the text cited below.

    Kent Masterson Brown, *Cushing of Gettysburg, The Story of a Union Artillery Commander* (Lexington, Ky.: University of Kentucky Press, 1993), 232. David L. Ladd and Audry J. Ladd, ed., *The Bachelder Papers*, II (Dayton: Morningside Bookshop, 1995), 964. Letter, Emerson L. Bicknell, Aug. 6, 1883.

15. Raus, *The Union Army at Gettysburg*, 156.

16. Col. R. Penn Smith, "The Part Taken by the Philadelphia Brigade in the Battle," The Philadelphia *Weekly Times*, May 28, 1887.

17. Edwin B. Coddington, *The Gettysburg Campaign, A Study in Command* (New York: Charles Scribner's Sons, 1984), maps between 504 and 505.

18. John H. Lewis, *Recollections from 1860–1865* (Washington, D.C.: Peake & Co., 1895), 81.

19. William N. Wood, *Reminiscences of Big I*, edited by Bell I. Wiley (Wilmington: Broadfoot Publishing Co., 1987), 43.

20. Robert McCulloch, "About the Charge of Pickett's Division," CV (XXI:474).

21. John E. Dooley, *John Dooley Confederate Soldier His War Journal*, edited by Joseph T. Durkin, S.J. (Washington, D.C.: Georgetown University Press, 1945), 98-100.

22. Please note that Daniel, apparently, corrected the title in his own hand to read "11th Virginia."

    J. Risque Hutter, "Ninth Virginia, Kemper's Brigade," The Richmond *Times*, Sept. 10, 1905, John W. Daniel Papers, Box 28, Newspaper Clippings, Accession # 158, Folder (1905 Aug. 20–Nov. 12), Manuscripts Dept., Alderman Library, University of Va.

23. Lewis, *Recollections*, 80.

24. Joseph C. Mayo, "Pickett's Charge at Gettysburg," SHSP (XXXIV:328).

25. In their tremendous account of Pickett's Division on July 3, Harrison and Busey established that Kemper's brigade led the column, followed by Garnett and Armistead, respectively.

    Kathy Georg Harrison and John W. Busey, *Nothing But Glory: Pickett's Division at Gettysburg* (Gettysburg: Thomas Publications, 1993), 15.

26. Robert B. Damron, 56th Virginia, "Recollections of Some of the Incidents of the Battle of Gettysburg, Pa., July 3, 1863," John W. Daniel Papers, Box 23, Accession #158 5383, A–E, Folder, Civil War Material: Gettysburg, 3 July 1863 (Pickett's Charge), 1903–05, n.d., Manuscripts Dept., Alderman Library, University of Va.

27. Dooley, *John Dooley*, 101.

28. See map, Harrison and Busey, *Nothing But Glory*, 13–14. Robert B. Damron, 56th Virginia, "Recollections of Some of the Incidents of the Battle of Gettysburg, Pa., July 3, 1863," John W. Daniel Papers, Box 23, Accession #158 5383, A–E, Folder, Civil War Material: Gettysburg, 3 July 1863 (Pickett's Charge), 1903–05, n.d., Manuscripts Dept., Alderman Library, University of Va.

29. Wood, *Big I*, 43.

30. Robert McCulloch, "About the Charge of Pickett's Division," CV (XXI:474). Wood, *Big I*, 43.

31. Ladd and Ladd, *The Bachelder Papers*, I, 96. Letter, George G. Benedict, March 16, 1864.

32. O. P. Blaisdell, "Gettysburg: Memories of Several Comrades—Stannard's Brigade—the Cavalry," *The National Tribune*, July 17, 1904, 3. *OR*, XXVII, pt. 1, 349. Report of Brig. Gen. George J. Stannard. Ladd and Ladd, *The Bachelder Papers*, I, 48–50, 55, 59. Letters, George G. Benedict, Dec. 24, 1863, and Wheelock Veazey (undated). Diary, July 2, 1863, George J. Stannard.

33. Parker opened fire at around 4:00 a.m. at the Federal skirmishers, then continued firing at intervals throughout the morning. This agrees closely with McCarthy's statement that his and another battery fired for about 5–10 minutes (20 rounds) at the Federals. Eshleman mistook Taylor's battery for Parker's, and Parker "thought" that Taylor rather than McCarthy helped him in suppressing the Federal skirmishers. Taylor did not fire until 1:00 p.m.

    OR, XXVII, pt. 2, 379, 431–32, 434. Report of Capts. E. S. McCarthy and Osmond B. Taylor, and Col. B. F. Eshleman. Silas Adams, "The Nineteenth Maine at Gettysburg," *Papers Read Before the Commandery of the State of Maine, Military Order of the Loyal Legion of the United States* (Wilmington: Broadfoot Publishing Co., 1992), 259. Janet B. Hewett, Noah Andre Trudeau, and Bryce A. Suderow, ed., *Supplement to the Official Records of the Union and Confederate Armies*, V, pt. 1 (Wilmington: Broadfoot Publishing Co., 1995), 367. Report of Capt. William W. Parker.

34. Frank E. Moran, "A Fire Zouave: Memoirs of a Member of the Excelsior Brigade," *The National Tribune*, Nov. 13, 1890, 3. Ladd and Ladd, *The Bachelder Papers*, II. Letter, Frank E. Moran, Jan. 24, 1882.

35. Richard S. Thompson, "A Scrap of Gettysburg," *Gettysburg Papers*, II, Ken Bandy and Florence Freeland, ed. (Dayton: Morningside Bookshop, 1978), 957.

36. Kent Masterson Brown, in his biography of Alonzo Cushing, asserts that the Confederate artillery deliberately opened upon Battery A, 4th U.S. Artillery at the copse of trees. No evidence from the battery indicates that it was subjected to fire at this time. It is evident, however, that the 14th Connecticut's skirmishers along the Emmitsburg Road were fired upon this early in the morning.

    Captain E. S. McCarthy (First Richmond Howitzers) said that early in the morning, probably before 4:00 a.m., his section and another battery drove back a line of Federal skirmishers after firing twenty rounds at them. He evidently erred as to the time.He said he was posted 300–400 yards in front of the skirmishers, which would have placed him on the third ridge east of Spangler's Woods.

    OR, XXVII, pt. 2, 379. Report of Capt. E. S. McCarthy. Brown, *Cushing of Gettysburg*. 223–25.

37. Charles D. Page, *History of the Fourteenth Regiment, Connecticut Vol. Infantry* (Meriden, Conn.: Horton Printing Co., 1906), 142, 150.

38. *OR*, XXVII, pt. 2, 379. Report of Capt. E. S. McCarthy.

39. Page, *14th Conn.*, 142–43.

40. Thompson mistakenly said that he was next to Battery K, 4th U.S. Artillery. The battery beside him, some distance to the right, was Rorty's B, 1st New York Artillery. At first, I thought it was Evan Thomas' C, 4th U.S., but according to Gulian Weir, he was with the reserve near Cemetery Hill along the Taneytown Road.

    OR, XXVII, pt. 1, 238 and 890. Reports of Gen. Henry Hunt and Capt. James Thompson. Ladd and Ladd, *The Bachelder Papers*, I, 55, 96. Diary, July 3, 1863, George J. Stannard. Letter, George G. Benedict, March 16, 1864. Raus, *The Union Army at Gettysburg*, 164. Rollins, *Pickett's Charge*, 301.

41. *OR*, XXVII, pt. 1, 888. Report of Capt. Patrick Hart.

42. Ibid., 885. Report of Capt. Charles A. Phillips. Ladd and Ladd, *The Bachelder Papers*, I, 169, Letter, Charles A. Phillips.

43. McGilvery's report would lead one to think that he had deployed 39 guns, and not the 15 he actually had in place on the morning of July 3. His report is misleading. Capt. Nelson Ames (Battery G, 1st New York Artillery) said that he was near the Frederick and Gettysburg Pike at 10:00 a.m. when "the cannonading from the rebel lines commenced." He remained there until around noon when he was ordered from the cover of a woods to repulse the Confederate infantry were moving forward, under the cover of their guns, to charge the Federal lines. He was told to go into line wherever there was room.

    The cannonade began at 1:00 p.m. (10:00 a.m.), according to Ames. He was moved forward around 2:00 p.m. just as the Confederates began their attack and not the noon hour as he asserted. This coincides with Dow's account, in which the commander of the battery asserted that at 11:00 a.m. (actually 1:00 p.m.) the cannonade began and lasted for an hour and a half, at which time the Rebels advanced under the cover of their own guns. This would mean that the battery commenced firing about 2:30 p.m. (12:30 p.m. by Dow's time).

    If Ames did not get going until around 2:00 p.m. it is fair to assume that he could have used half of an hour to get into battery. Dow said that he was between Ames' New York and the 2nd Connecticut. That being the case, they probably approached the field at the same time from the Artillery Reserve Division near the Taneytown Road.

    In his official report, Henry Hunt said that between 1:00 p.m. and 2:30 p.m. he went to the Artillery Reserve Park and "ordered all of the batteries to be ready to move at a moment's notice." More than likely he erred on his time. He was at Little Round Top when the artillery barrage began. It would not have taken him 1.5 hours to ride to the Artillery Reserve near the Taneytown-Granite School House Road intersection. Enough evidence exists to show that the Federal fire slackened by 1:45 p.m. (not 2:30 p.m. as Hunt asserted) and that the Confederate infantry began its advance at around 2:00 p.m. and not 3:00 p.m. as Hunt said.

    Dow, Ames, and Sterling (2nd Connecticut) could not have been on the ridge south of Stannard's brigade during the bombardment. McGilvery's three batteries (Thompson's, Phillips' and Hart's) were the only ones ordered to open fire by Hancock and before being told to cease fire during the bombardment by Hunt, then McGilvery. Dow said that his men ceased fire and lay behind the earthworks throughout the bombardment, which implies that they were on the field at the same time as McGilvery's three batteries. They probably ceased fire at McGilvery's request. Had the other batteries been given such contradictory orders during the cannonade, they would have mentioned it in their reports. Rank's guns, according to the National Park Service plaque, were present during the early morning, which I believe to be an error. The other horse artillery battery, Daniel's 9th Michigan, came on the field around 1:15 p.m. at which time Rank probably arrived. It does not make sense that the cavalry would have split two batteries in the same brigade. Daniel's battery was not on the field until the artillery fight began.

    OR, XVII, pt. 1, 238–39, 883–84, 898, and 901. Reports of Hunt, McGilvery, Phillips, Dow, and Ames. NPS markers on southern Hancock Avenue. Rollins, *Pickett's Charge!*, 114–15.

44. St. Clair A. Mulholland, *The Story of the 116th Regiment, Pennsylvania Infantry* (Gaithersburg, Md.: Olde Soldier Books, Inc.), 145 and 377.

45. At 16 yards per gun there was enough room, according to the regulations, to place the 26 guns which eventually occupied that line.

46. *Supplement to the OR*, vol. 5, 348 and 353. John Cheves Haskell, Memoirs, 1861–1865, Special Collections Dept., William R. Perkins Library, Duke University, Durham, N.C., 33.

47. Sergeant Hitchcock makes it clear that his company had been on the skirmish line before the Bliss buildings were burned. It was customary to send two companies at a time out on skirmish duty.

    Ladd and Ladd, *The Bachelder Papers*, II, 1183. Letter Charles A. Hitchcock, Jan. 20, 1886.

48. Thompson's account would have placed the regiment on the field before the 125th New York occupied that spot.

    Benjamin W. Thompson, "Personal Narrative of Experiences in the Civil War, 1861–1865," *Civil War Times Illustrated* (October 1973), 20.

49. Benedict, *Army Life in Virginia*, 173.

50. Ibid.

51. The only Confederate guns firing at the time were McCarthy's and Parker's. McCarthy pinned the 14th Connecticut. Parker's were firing at maneuvering infantry "at intervals" throughout the morning.

    Supplement to the OR, V, pt. 1, 367. Report of Capt. William W. Parker.

52. Ladd and Ladd, *The Bachelder Papers*, I, 55, 96. Diary, July 3, 1863, George J. Stannard. Letter, George G. Benedict, March 16, 1864.

53. Benedict mistakenly reported this incident as occurring during the main artillery bombardment.

    Benedict, *Army Life in Virginia*, 173. Ladd and Ladd, *The Bachelder Papers*, I, 59, Letter, Wheelock Veazey (undated).

54. Benedict, *Army Life in Virginia*, 173–74. Ladd and Ladd, *The Bachelder Papers*, I, 55. Diary, July 3, 1863, George J. Stannard.

55. Benedict, *Army Life in Virginia*, 174–75.

56. John D. S. Cook, "Personal Reminiscences of Gettysburg," *Gettysburg Papers*, II, 926.

57. Benedict, *Army Life in Virginia*, 174–75.

58. Map insert and the Report of Col. R. M. Mayo, 47th Virginia, Aug. 14, 1863, Henry Heth Collection, Eleanor S. Brockenbrough Library, Museum of the Confederacy as cited in Richard Rollins, *Pickett's Charge: Eyewitness Accounts* (Redondo Beach, Calif.: Rank and File Publications, 1994), 241.

    In the average brigade, the approximate strength of line infantry to frontage to field and staff was about 78–80 % muskets and 20–22% field and staff, and sergeants. This frontage is an assumption on my part. The frontages for all of the brigades in Pettigrew's assault are similarly estimates of approximate frontage.

59. The troop positions for the regiments of Pettigrew's and Trimble's are listed from left to right (north to south) as they are listed on an untitled diagram in Box 23, Accession #23 158 5383 A–E, Folder: Civil War Material: Gettysburg, 3 July 1863 (Pickett's Charge), 1903–05 n.d., John W. Daniel Papers, Manuscripts Dept., Alderman Library, University of Va.

    According to Weymouth T. Jordan, Jr., Davis' brigade had 1,713 men present on July 1, not counting the 11th Mississippi which did not take part in the first day of battle. The brigade lost, according to the official statements, 897 officers and men in the total battle. According to Steven H. Stubbs in his manuscript, "They Suffered the Most," (p.43) the 11th Mississippi lost 337 men on July 3. A nominal tabulation of the casualties for the 55th North Carolina equaled 109 casualties for a total loss of 446 men between the two regiments. That number, while 42 men higher than Clark's count in his North Carolina history, is more accurate and precludes the possibility of the 2nd and the 42nd Mississippi of suffering any casualties on July 3. 1,713 plus the 387 men in the 11th Mississippi totals 2,100 effectives. The brigade lost 1,397 effectives during the entire battle, 446 of whom fell on July 3. By deducting 446 from 1,397 one arrives at a total of 951 casualties on July 1 and 2. By subtracting 951 from 2,100, one arrives on a July 3 strength of 1,149 officers and men.

    Walter Clark, ed., *Histories of the several Regiments and Battalions From North Carolina in the Great War 1861–'65*, II (Wilmington: Broadfoot Publishing, 1991), 367. Weymouth T. Jordan, Jr., comp., *North Carolina Troops 1861–1865 A Roster*, XIII, Infantry. (Raleigh, N.C.: Div. of Archives and History, 1993), 375, 386, 430–532. (See the footnotes.) S. A. Ashe, "North Carolinians at Gettysburg, A Critical Review of the famous Confederate Charge on July 3, 1864 [sic]," *The National Tribune*, Oct. 31, 1901, 2.

60. According to Captain S. A. Ashe, Pettigrew went into action on July 1 with about 1,700 officers and men and he lost 1,100. Walter Clark in "Twenty-Sixth Regiment" said that Pettigrew's brigade lost 528 officers and men on July 3. Robert U. Johnson and Clarence C. Buel, *Battles and Leaders of the Civil War*, III (Secaucus, N.J.: Castle) states that Pettigrew lost 1,105 total for the three days.

The most accurate accounting comes from the brigade marker at Gettysburg. The brigade lost 1,405 from about 2,000 engaged during the battle. A nominal tabulation from the rosters show that the brigade suffered 610 casualties on July 3 which means 795 men were hit on July 1 and 2. By subtracting 795 from 2,000 one arrives at an approximate strength of 1,205 on July 3.

Lowrance had 1,250 present on July 1. He lost 599 during the three days of battle. A nominal check shows that 189 fell on July 3, which means 410 went down between July 1 and 2. 410 subtracted from 1,250 equals 840 present on July 3.

Clark, *North Carolina in the Great War 1861–'65*, II, 367. S. A. Ashe, "North Carolinians at Gettysburg, A Critical Review of the famous Confederate Charge on July 3, 1864 [*sic*]," *The National Tribune*, October 3, 1901, 3. *Battles and Leaders*, III, 439. Jordan, Jr., *A Roster*, V:6–105, and 283–385; VI:10–117, and 463–601; VII:10–132; IX:253–353; X:8–104; XI:244–363; XII: 415–521. Martin, *Confederate Monuments*, I, 197.

61. For the brigade positions see Clark, *North Carolina in the Great War 1861–'65*, II, 363. Troop strength for Fry's brigade comes from George R. Stewart, *Pickett's Charge* (Boston: Houghton Mifflin Co., 1987), 173. The frontage for Pettigrew's division is estimated as follows: Archer: 900 present less 22% F&S, Sgts., non-combatants = 702 on line, less 10% as skirmishers = a frontage of about 630 feet. Marshall: 1,205 present, less 22% = 940 on line less 10% skirmishers = 845 feet. Davis: 1,149 present, less 22% = 896 on line, less 10% skirmishers = 807 feet. Brockenbrough: 500 present less 22% = 390 on line, less 10% skirmishers = 351 feet. 630 feet + 940 feet + 896 feet + 351 feet = division frontage of 2,817 feet.

62. Lane had 1,355 present on July 1. He lost 381 of 660 casualties on July 3. By deducting the 279 lost on July 1 and 2 one arrives at a July 3 strength of 1,076 officers and men.

S. A. Ashe, "North Carolinians at Gettysburg, A Critical Review of the famous Confederate Charge on July 3, 1864 [*sic*]," *The National Tribune*, October 3, 1901, 3. *B & L*, III, 439. Report of Brig. Gen. James Lane, *OR*, XXVII, pt. 2, 666. Martin, *Confederate Monuments*, I, 195. Jordan, *A Roster*, IV:405–514; V: 305–424; VIII:110–231; IX:118–244; XI:468–604.

63. According to Col. Edwin Porter Alexander, Longstreet knew during the night of July 2 that Pickett would be in an assault during the early morning of July 3 and nothing more.

Gallagher, *Fighting for the Confederacy*, 244.

64. From where he stood on Seminary Ridge, Lee could not have seen any Federal guns in the low ground immediately east of the Rogers house where McGilvery had placed his twenty-five guns.

65. James Longstreet, *From Manassas to Appomattox* (New York: DaCapo Press, 1992), 385–86.

66. A. L. Long, *Memoirs of Lee*, as cited in Alexander, *Military Memoirs of a Confederate*, 416.

67. If Longstreet heard Ewell's guns that would have placed the time of the meeting sometime between 5:00 a.m. and 6:00 a.m.

Longstreet, *From Manassas to Appomattox*, 386–87.

68. Ralph Orson Sturtevant, *Pictorial History of the Thirteenth Regiment Vermont Volunteers, War of 1861–1865* (Burlington: Self-Appointed Committee of Three, 1911), 290–91.

69. Franklin Sawyer was not a very good writer. His sentences appear fragmented, more like thoughts which he expected the reader to interpret. He credited Captain Lewis with commanding the picket line. Galwey said that Capt. Pierce was on the picket line. More than

likely, both companies were on the front. The regiment had about 164 officers and men present for duty on the morning of July 3. Each company had approximately 17 men present for duty. Two companies could have been on the picket line without any trouble.

Thomas Francis Galwey, *The Valiant Hours*, W. S. Nye (ed.) (Harrisburg: Stackpole, 1961), 108. Thaddeus S. Potter, "On Skirmish: Gallant Behavior of the 8th Ohio at Gettysburg," *The National Tribune*, January 31, 1895, 3. Franklin Sawyer, *A Military History of the 8th Ohio Vol. Inf'y* (Huntington, W.Va.: Blue Acorn Press, 1994), 129.

70. Galwey, *The Valiant Hours*, 108.

71. Sawyer, *8th Ohio*, 129.

72. Galwey, *The Valiant Hours*, 108.

73. William P. Seville, *History of the First Regiment, Delaware Volunteers, from the Commencement of the "Three Months' Service" to the Final Muster-Out at the Close of the Rebellion.* (Highstown, N.J.: Longstreet House, 1986), 81.

74. The historian of the 14th Connecticut placed the time at about 7:30 a.m. which would have made it three hours and three minutes after sun up.
Ladd and Ladd, *The Bachelder Papers*, III, 1394–95. Letter, John L. Brady, May 24, 1886.

75. Thomas Galwey said that the charge occurred before 8:00 a.m. which coincides with the attack by the charge by the 1st Delaware. When reading his account it is quite easy to get confused as to the actual time of the charge because Galwey inserted a statement about the later raid by the 14th Connecticut in the middle of his account of the morning charge. Sawyer insists that the charge took place early in the morning. Galwey's time is accurate. He carefully noted times of day right down to his timing of the opening shots of the artillery duel preceding Pickett's Charge—12:50 p.m.
Galwey, *The Valiant Hours*, 108. Sawyer, *8th Ohio*, 129. Thaddeus S. Potter, "On Skirmish: Gallant Behavior of the 8th Ohio at Gettysburg," *The National Tribune*, January 31, 1895, 3.

76. Ladd and Ladd, *The Bachelder Papers*, III, 1394–95.

77. Galwey, *The Valiant Hours*, 109.

78. Martin, *Confederate Monuments*, I, 82–83, 88–89.

79. Galwey, *The Valiant Hours*, 109.

80. Sawyer, *8th Ohio*, 129.

81. See map. It indicates that the 125th New York was on the line by 8:30 a.m. It makes sense that those companies would have advanced at the same time as the 108th and the 126th New York. The sight of several companies coming on the run toward the Emmitsburg Road at the same time would have provoked a strong Confederate response.
Ladd and Ladd, *The Bachelder Papers*, III, 1752. Letter, Sebastian D. Holmes, July 10, 1890. Elwood W. Christ, *"Over A Wide, Hot...Crimson Plain," The Struggles for the Bliss Farm at Gettysburg* (Baltimore: Butternut and Blue, 1994), 60.

82. Arabella M. Willson, *Disaster, Struggle, Triumph, The Adventures of 1000 Boys in Blue From August, 1862, to June, 1865* (Albany: The Argus Co., 1870), 180. George H. Washburn, *A Complete Military History and Record of the 108th Regiment N.Y. Vols. From 1862 to 1894* (Rochester, N.Y., 1894), 52.

83. W. F. Beyer and O. F. Keydel, ed., *Deeds of Valor*, I (Woodbury, N.Y.: Longmeadow Press, 1992), 249.

84. Willson, *Disaster, Struggle, Triumph*, 180.

85. Ibid. Scott wrote that his companies fought in the forenoon and ran into a strong body of Confederates. Galwey did not report any Confederates on the right flank but did say that the Ohioans ran into a heavy line of Confederates during the company's attack and were driven back to the rail fence parallel with the Emmitsburg Road. It makes sense, even though that it is not recorded that the 126th did come up on the 8th's right and drove

Confederates from the Emmitsburg Road. It is interesting to note that the 126th was relieved at 11:00 a.m., the same time that Galwey cited for the arrival of the 55th Ohio (actually the 136th New York) on the right of Co. B. It does not make sense that the road would not be secured north of the 8th Ohio. Christ's maps 5, 6, and 7 show Cos. A & C on the right of the 8th Ohio and on Von Steinwehr's left. Thaddeus Potter, Co. H, 8th Ohio also said that a company from the XI Corps came out to support the 8th Ohio.

Winfield Scott, " Pickett's Charge As Seen From the Front Line," *The Gettysburg Papers*, II, 903. Thaddeus S. Potter, "On Skirmish: Gallant Behavior of the 8th Ohio at Gettysburg," *The National Tribune*, Jan. 31, 1895, 3. Galwey, *The Valiant Hours*, 111.

86. Washburn, *108th New York*, 52.

87. Ladd and Ladd, *The Bachelder Papers*, I, 316. Letter, Charles A. Richardson, Aug. 18, 1867.

88. Sergeant Fuger, who commanded the battery by the end of the battle, stayed in the army into the 20th century and retired as a colonel. He testified and/or wrote about his Gettysburg experience at least three times—1891, 1907, 1909. His story changed with each successive telling. Like Mr. Christ, I concur that the sergeant misstated the day on which the battery fired to silence skirmishers.

Frederick Fuger, "Cushing's Battery at Gettysburg," *Journal of Military Service Institution of the United States*, vol. 41, Nov.–Dec. 1907, 404–10. Christ, *Bliss Farm*, fn. 162: 189. John Reed, et al. v. The Gettysburg Battlefield Memorial Association, et al., Supreme Court of Pennsylvania, Middle District, May Term, 1891, Nos. 20 and 30, 228. Testimony of Capt. Charles Banes, A.A.G., 2nd Brig., 2nd Div., II. Hereafter cited as Reed, et al.

89. In his various accounts of the battery's role at Gettysburg Fuger got the dates of the action mixed up. According to Fuger the battery set the Bliss barn on fire on the morning of July 2 in response to sharpshooters' annoying the battery from the farm. Mr. Christ in his book on the Bliss Farm states that Fuger was mistaken because Federal troops occupied that area until the evening attack by the Confederates on July 2, which means that Cushing was not being harassed by anyone on the morning of July 2. The barn was fired on July 3. That being the case the battery responded to the sharpshooters on July 3 and not July 2. The sergeant said that at 8:00 a.m. the three caissons were exploded while the ammunition carriers were *getting ready* for firing. Therefore, I have interpreted the chain of events to be as follows. 1) Cushing orders the guns to silence the skirmishers. 2) Hunt rides up to confer with Cushing while the men are loading the pieces. 3) The Confederates hit limbers 1, 2, and 3.

Frederick Fuger, "Cushing's Battery at Gettysburg," *Journal of Military Service Institute of the U.S.* (Nov.–Dec. 1907), 41:406–7.

90. Fuger said the shell hit Limber 1 and spread to Numbers 2 and 3. Aldrich who was facing the front with the lead team of Arnold's Number 6 limber saw Cushing's Number 1 explode after his Number 2 went up.

Thomas M. Aldrich, *The History of Battery A First Regiment Rhode Island Light Artillery in the War to Preserve the Union 1861–1865* (Providence: Snow & Farnham, Printers, 1904), 210. Frederick Fuger, "Cushing's Battery at Gettysburg," *Journal of Military Service Institute of the U.S.* (Nov.–Dec. 1907), 41:407.

91. Aldrich, *History of Battery A*, 210.

92. In his account for the *Journal of Military Service Institute of the U.S.*, Fuger said that only the horses' tails were singed. He also said that infantry men caught the horses which ran away. Having walked the ground and paced off the approximate location of Limber Number Three, it is very unlikely that Fuger actually saw what happened to the team on the first limber. He would have been standing in a hollow below the line of sight of Limber Number One.

Aldrich, *History of Battery A*, 210.

93. Frederick Fuger, "Cushing's Battery at Gettysburg," *Journal of Military Service Institute of the U.S.* (Nov.–Dec. 1907), 41:407.

94. Ibid. *OR*, XXVII, pt. 2, 674. Report of Maj. William T. Poague.

95. There are two typographical errors or transcription errors in this text. "Fuger" is recorded as "Huger" and "limbers" are written as "timbers." Fuger in his testimony said that the guns were on the highest point of the ridge and used the back of his flattened hand to illustrate his point, whereby the index finger rises slightly above the level of the other fingers. He stated that the noses of the lead horses were 27 feet to the rear of each gun trails and, in turn, the noses of the lead horses for each of the caissons were thirty feet behind the rear of each limber chest and were behind the ridge in a hollow. That hollow is very evident today. Placing the caissons in the hollow kept them below the line of sight of the Confederate gunners. Fuger erred when he said the guns were 100' from the west wall of the Angle. Brig. Gen. Alexander Webb placed the battery at the beginning of the 1:00 p.m. cannonade. (The material in the brackets are my additions.) "...it was on the line which would join the angle with the rear portion [eastern side] of the clump of trees." Under cross examination, Pvt. Anthony W. McDermott, Company I, 69th Pennsylvania, said the following in regard to Cushing's six guns: "They were on the crest of the hill, in our rear, at the time of the artillery firing....They were back a little of what might be called an imaginary line drawn from the rear of the angle to the clump of trees." Sgt. Maj. William S. Stockton, 71st Pennsylvania, testified that the regiment lay behind the crest of the hill near the northeast corner of the stone wall and that Cushing's guns were on the actual crest.

   Reed, et al., 128, 159, 225, and 242–43. Testimony of Frederick Fuger, Alexander Webb, respectively.

96. *OR*, XXVII, pt. 2, 632. Report of Col. David Lang.

97. Beyer and Keydel, *Deeds of Valor*, I, 248–50.

98. Christ, *Bliss Farm*, 58.

99. Frederick Fuger, "Cushing's Battery at Gettysburg," *Journal of Military Service Institute of the U.S.* (Nov.–Dec. 1907), 41:407.

100. According to Fuger, the battery fired at the Confederates for one-half of an hour and then resumed firing three or four times later that morning but for a few minutes each time. During the morning, Cushing was reprimanded for wasting shells. That would probably have happened during this first firing because of its duration. He also unhorsed a Confederate officer with a deliberately aimed shot. There is no evidence that the guns were being severely hit, if at all, by the Confederates. This would have allowed the Federals time to run through the drill with precision. During the bombardment preceding Pickett's Charge the gunners did not resight their guns. They fired without "training" their pieces. Pvt. William P. Haines, Company F, 12th New Jersey, said the firing began about 9:00 a.m. and that Woodruff's battery took part in the artillery duel.

   Christopher Smith, "Bloody Angle, The Story of Cemetery Ridge From the Blue and Gray, Buffalo *Evening News*, May 29, 1894, 5. William P. Haines, *History of the Men of Co. F, with Description of the Marches and Battles of the 12th New Jersey Vols.* (Mickleyon, N.J.: 1897), 39.

101. Alexander did not state the time that this happened. It had to have been while Alexander was forming his defense along Spangler's Woods. Evidence indicates that McCarthy and Carlton were in position prior to Pickett's and Dearing's arrival.

   Gallagher, *Fighting for the Confederacy*, 253. Report of Col. H. C. Cabell, SHSP, X:166.

102. Frederick Fuger, "Cushing's Battery at Gettysburg," *Journal of Military Service Institute of the U.S.* (Nov.–Dec. 1907), 41:407.

103. Smith said they unhorsed Jubal Early during the morning. Rody Landregan said that it was Pickett and that it occurred during the height of the charge. Both "believed" that the officers were the ones they "heard" they were. Landregan probably saw Pettigrew go down

with one of his horses. Members of the 8th Ohio recalled seeing a Confederate officer on a white horse on the northern end of the field.

Christopher Smith, "Bloody Angle, The Story of Cemetery Ridge From the Blue and Gray," Buffalo *Evening News*, May 29, 1894, 5. Rody Landregan, "Battery A, 4th U.S.–Its Savage Work on Pickett's Column," *The National Tribune*, Sept. 2, 1909, 7.

104. Fremantle does not mention the color of Walton's horse but he does say right after writing about being fired at with two or three shells that Walton's horse was killed and that it did happen during the morning of July 3, 1863.

Rollins, *Pickett's Charge!*, 6.

105. Christopher Smith, "Bloody Angle, The Story of Cemetery Ridge From the Blue and Gray," Buffalo *Evening News*, May 29, 1894, 5. Rody Landregan, "Battery A, 4th U.S.—Its Savage Work on Pickett's Column," *The National Tribune*, Sept. 2, 1909, 7.

106. Henry J. Hunt, "Artillery," *Military Historical Society Papers*, 1918 (13:94).

107. Reed, et al., Testimony of Capt. James C. Lynch, Co. B, 106th Pennsylvania, 303.

108. Joseph R. C. Ward, *History of the One Hundred and Sixth Regiment Pennsylvania Volunteers* (Philadelphia: F. McManus, Jr. & Co., 1906), 199.

109. Reed, et al., Testimony of George Hansell, Pvt., Co. K, 72nd Pennsylvania, 49.

110. Ladd and Ladd, *The Bachelder Papers*, II, 967. Letter, Samuel Roberts, Aug. 18, 1883.

111. Map 5, establishes the time of the assault from 8:30 a.m.–9:30 a.m.

Christ, *The Bliss Farm*, 60. Ladd and Ladd, *The Bachelder Papers*, III, 1394–95, 60.

112. Letter, John L. Brady, 24, May 1886, John B. *Bachelder Papers*, New Hampshire Historical Society (microfilm GNMP/LIB), OR, XXVII, pt. 1, 470. New Jersey Battlefield Commission 1886–1892, *Final Report of the Gettysburg Battlefield Commission of New Jersey* (Trenton: John T. Murphy Publishing Co., 1891), 110 and 115 as cited in Christ, *Bliss Farm*, 58.

113. On May 3, 1997, I met with historian Scott Hartwig at the Cyclorama building at Gettysburg National Battlefield. He told me that at the time of the battle, the uncut grass and the unharvested wheat was about chest high—3–4 feet tall.

Haines, *Company F*, 39.

114. Thompson, "Scrap of Gettysburg," *Gettysburg Papers*, III, 957–58.

115. Haines, *Company F*, 39–40.

116. Ladd and Ladd, *The Bachelder Papers*, II, 962–63. Diary, July 3, 1863, Patrick H. Taylor.

117. J. H. Moore, "Heth's Division at Gettysburg," The Southern Bivouac, III, #9, May 1885, 389–90.

118. Thompson, "A Scrap of Gettysburg," *Gettysburg Papers*, II, 957–58. Page, *14th Conn.*, 144.

119. Haines, *Company F*, 40.

120. Christ, *Bliss Farm*, 59.

121. On July 4, 1863, Thompson said that his men captured one major and "some privates." In his article published in 1897, he said they captured one major and ten enlisted men.

Thompson, "A Scrap of Gettysburg," *Gettysburg Papers*, II, 958. Gerry Harder Poriss and Ralph G. Poriss, ed., *While My Country is in Danger: The Life and Letters of Lieutenant Colonel Richard S. Thompson, Twelfth New Jersey Volunteers* (Hamilton, N.Y.: Edmonston Publishing Co., 1994), 76.

122. Haines, *Company F*, 40.

123. Christ, *Bliss Farm*, 59.

124. Ibid., 61.

125. Ibid.

126. Thompson, "A Scrap of Gettysburg," *Gettysburg Papers*, II, 958.

127. Haines, *Company F*, 40.
128. This had to have occurred, otherwise it would not have been necessary to attack the barn later and to burn it.
129. Page, *14th Conn.*, 144.
130. See Appendix A for the documentation.
131. The frontage for a battery in line of battle could extend anywhere from 44–82 yards. Carlton's battery and McCarthy's section held the extreme left of Alexander's line north of the fence. Woolfolk was in battery north of the fence on the ridge immediately east of the northeast corner of Spangler's woods. Dearing's Battalion went into line immediately to Woolfolk's right. (In his letter to J. William Jones in SHSP, IV:103, he said that he had 7 guns as opposed to 9 guns.) Alexander said the howitzers were "under cover" behind the infantry. That hollow provided logical shelter by putting the guns below the line of sight of the Federal artillery.

     Gallagher, *Fighting for the Confederacy*, 249, 253. E. P. Alexander to J. William Jones, March 17, 1877, SHSP, IV:103 Alexander, *Military Memoirs of a Confederate*, 418. R. Snowden Andrews, *Andrews' Mounted Artillery Drill* (Charleston: Evans and Cogswell, 1863), 68. Martin W. Hazlewood, "Gettysburg Charge. Paper as to Pickett's Men," SHSP, XXIII, 231. Ladd and Ladd, *The Bachelder Papers*, I, 488. Letter, Edward Porter Alexander, May 3, 1876.
132. G. W. Finley, "Bloody Angle," Buffalo *Evening News*, May 28, 1894, 7.
133. According to Alexander, Dearing's battery arrived after he had taken the guns from Pendleton and while he was talking with Lee and Longstreet to discuss *where* Pickett was to march. That would place the time after 9:00 a.m.

     Gallagher, *Fighting for the Confederacy*, 253.
134. Harrison and Busey, *Nothing But Glory*, map, 22. John W. Daniel Papers, Box 23, Accession #158 5383, A–E, Folder, Civil War Material: Gettysburg, 3 July 1863 (Pickett's Charge), 1903–05, n.d., Manuscripts Dept., Alderman Library, University of Va.
135. George Clark, "Wilcox's Alabama Brigade at Gettysburg," CV (XVII: 230).
136. Letter to Hal, Sept. 4, 1863, Raymond J. Reid Papers, Saint Augustine Historical Society. James B. Johnson, "Limited Review of What One Man Saw of the Battle of Gettysburg," Bill Walker Collection.
137. Harrison and Busey, *Nothing But Glory*, 185 and 226.
138. "Captain John Holmes Smith's Account," SHSP, XXXII, 190.
139. The information which I collected indicates that Kemper's brigade spent a couple of hours in the open fields southeast of Spangler's Woods.

     Dooley, *John Dooley*, 102. Rollins, *Pickett's Charge!*, 144. Harrison and Busey, *Nothing But Glory*, 452–56.

     Using the same method as with Garnett's frontage, I arrived at the following numbers for Kemper's brigade. 3rd Virginia: 280 feet; 7th Virginia: 287 feet; 1st Virginia: 130 feet; 11th Virginia: 324 feet; 24th Virginia: 298 feet. With the left of the 3rd Virginia on the northern end of the orchard, the 1st Virginia would have been in the orchard as Dooley described it in his journal. Brigade frontage: 1,319 feet.
140. Dooley's account does not imply that the action got out of hand or that it involved the entire regiment. Such an action would have brought the regimental officers into the ranks to restore order. His writing intimates that this "action" was a localized, spontaneous affair which did not attract any superior officer's notice. Therefore I surmised that the men stayed in ranks. The "very small green apples" he speaks about sound like the crab apples.

     Dooley, *John Dooley*, 102.
141. Robert McCulloch, "About the Charge of Pickett's Division," CV, XXI, 1913:474.
142. Harrison and Busey, *Nothing But Glory*, 457–66.

143. George W. Finley, "Bloody Angle," Buffalo *Evening News*, May 29, 1894, 7. Robert B. Damron, 56th Virginia, "Recollections of Some of the Incidents of the Battle of Gettysburg, Pa., July 3, 1863," John W. Daniel Papers, Box 23, Accession #158 5383, A–E, Folder, Civil War Material: Gettysburg, 3 July 1863 (Pickett's Charge), 1903–05, n.d., Manuscripts Dept., Alderman Library, University of Va.

144. June Kimble, "Tennesseeans at Gettysburg—the Retreat," CV (XVIII:460).

145. Moore said that Lee, Longstreet, and Pickett rode the line but Col. B. D. Fry, the brigade commander, said that the group consisted of Lee, Longstreet, and A. P. Hill. Fry delivered the plan for the assault to Pickett after the conference adjourned.

   J. H. Moore, Co. B, 7th Tennessee, "Heth's Division at Gettysburg," The Southern Bivouac, III, #9, May 1885, 389.

146. Birkett D. Fry's earliest account, from which he copied any further reports is in the *Bachelder Papers*, I.

   Robert D. Damron. "Recollections of Some Incidents of the Battle of Gettysburg, PA, July 3, 1863," 1, John W. Daniel Papers, Box 23, Accession #158 5383, A–E, Folder, Civil War Material: Gettysburg, 3 July 1863 (Pickett's Charge), 1903–05, n.d., Manuscripts Dept., Alderman Library, University of Va.) B. D. Fry, "Pettigrew's Charge at Gettysburg," SHSP (VII: 92). J. H. Moore, Co. B, 7th Tennessee, "Heth's Division at Gettysburg," The Southern Bivouac, III, #9, May 1885, 389. Ladd and Ladd, *The Bachelder Papers*, I, 518. Letter of Birkett D. Fry, Dec. 27, 1877.

147. Fry and Moore said that Lee rode the line in the forenoon. That is not the same time as the early morning. It makes sense that Lee would have trooped the line with Longstreet after he had approached him near Spangler's lane. If Pickett were preparing his line to advance he would have trooped the line from left to right to have been in the northeast corner of Spangler's Woods where both Alexander and Fry would have found him. Garnett rode through Carlton's two guns where Alexander had positioned himself which was near that corner of the woods. It was also the highest elevation from which Garnett could have observed the Federal lines without being conspicuous.

   Robert D. Damron, "Recollections of Some Incidents of the Battle of Gettysburg, PA, July 3, 1863," 1, John W. Daniel Papers, Box 23, Accession #158 5383, A–E, Folder, Civil War Material: Gettysburg, 3 July 1863 (Pickett's Charge), 1903–05, n.d., Manuscripts Dept., Alderman Library, University of Va. B. D. Fry, "Pettigrew's Charge at Gettysburg," SHSP (VII: 92). J. H. Moore, Co. B, 7th Tennessee, "Heth's Division at Gettysburg," The Southern Bivouac, III, #9, May 1885, 389.

148. Wiley Woods, "The First Tennessee Flag at Gettysburg," *Confederate Veteran*, Battles, 1861–1932, n.d., box 1, Special Collections Department, William R. Perkins Library, Duke, University, Durham, N.C.

149. *Supplement to the OR*, vol. V, pt. 1, #5, 430. Postwar account of Capt. Thomas J. Cureton, June 15, 1890. From the John Randolph Lane Papers. Southern Historical Collection, UNC, Chapel Hill, N.C.

150. B. D. Fry, "Pettigrew's Charge at Gettysburg," SHSP (VII: 92).

151. Edmund Berkeley, "Rode With Pickett," CV (XXXVIII:175). Robert A. Bright, "Pickett's Charge at Gettysburg," CV (XXXVIII: 264).

152. Wood, *Big I*, 44.

153. Robert B. Damron, 56th Virginia, "Recollections of Some of the Incidents of the Battle of Gettysburg, Pa., July 3, 1863," John W. Daniel Papers, Box 23, Accession #158 5383, A–E, Folder, Civil War Material: Gettysburg, 3 July 1863 (Pickett's Charge), 1903–05, n.d., Manuscripts Dept., Alderman Library, University of Virginia. Ladd and Ladd, *The Bachelder Papers*, I, 484. Letter, Edward Porter Alexander, May 3, 1876.

154. George W. Finley, "Bloody Angle," Buffalo *Evening News*, May 29, 1894, 5.

155. Edmund Berkeley, "Rode With Pickett," CV (XXXVIII:175).

156. In his recollections of the event, Clark mentally reversed Pickett's formation by saying that the left of Pickett's line occupied the Alabamians' old position. It is interesting to note that Trimble, years after the war, insisted that the far right of the line was only a couple of hundred yards from the Emmitsburg Road. He had to have meant Kemper's brigade.

    Dooley, *John Dooley*, 102. George Clark, "Wilcox's Alabama Brigade at Gettysburg," CV (XVII:230). Ladd and Ladd, *The Bachelder Papers*, II, 933. Letter, Isaac Trimble.

157. Joseph C. Mayo, Jr., "Pickett's Charge at Gettysburg," SHSP (XXXIV:328–29).

158. Alexander said that Armistead was centered on Kemper and Garnett and 200 yards to their rear.

    Gallagher, *Fighting for the Confederacy*, 256.

159. Williams did not name the lieutenant. The officer would have been his company file closer which would explain why he was standing behind the line. Company H had two lieutenants—John A. Logan and Philip P. Guerrant. Logan was captured. Guerrant was "probably" wounded and was captured.

    Harrison and Busey, *Nothing But Glory*, 373. Erasmus Williams, "A Private's Experience in Gettysburg," 1, John W. Daniel Papers, Box 23, #158 5383 A–E, Folder Civil War Material: Gettysburg, 3 July 1863 (Pickett's Charge), 1903–05, n.d., Manuscripts Dept., Alderman Library, University of Virginia.

160. E. P. Alexander said that Dearing's guns were in place by 10:00 a.m. which meant that Pickett's men came upon the field about that time.

    Battles and Leaders, III, 362. OR, XXVII, pt. 2, 375, 379, 384. Reports of Col. H. C. Cabell, Capt. E. S. McCarthy, and Lieut. C. W. Motes.

161. The bronze tablet at the battle field places Woolfolk in this position as does a statement made by Robert Damron of the 56th Virginia.

    Martin, *Confederate Monuments*, I:91.

162. Miller in his history of the Washington Artillery said that only six of the guns were actively engaged. Alexander had twenty-four guns, eight of which were 24-pounder and 12-pounder howitzers which were not practical to use on the firing line. While he does not say so, it does not seem likely that he deployed them since none of his other batteries deployed them.

    OR, XXVII, pt. 2, 355, 380, 388, 434. Reports of Majors James Dearing, and B. F. Eshleman, Capt. B. C. Manly, and Gen. William N. Pendleton's addenda. John Cheves Haskell, "Memoirs," Special Collections Library, William R. Perkins Library, Duke University, Durham, N.C., 33. Miller, *Washington Artillery*, 249, fn. 1.

163. If Miller reports that his guns were 100 yards north of the Peach Orchard and that Taylor was on his immediate right Taylor could not have been .5 mile northeast of the Peach Orchard as believed by Mr. Martin. That would have put him near the Rogers house, which is too far north. Further, the tablets for Jordan and Parker state that they fought in the same area of the Peach Orchard in which they fought on July 2. Parker's tablet cites the position as 200 feet north of the Peach Orchard and east of the Emmitsburg Road. That means that the guns were in the vicinity of the Wentz house. Taylor's battery which would have occupied a front of sixty-four yards would have been thirty-six yards north of the Peach Orchard on the Emmitsburg Road, facing east.

    Martin, *Confederate Monuments*, I:92, 109.

164. Alexander said that he had 75 guns on the line without going into the specifics about how they were actually deployed. The numbers show that he had 55 guns on the ridge and 12 howitzers in reserve. At regulation intervals of 16 yards per gun, those 55 guns would have held a front of 880 yards.

165. See Appendix A.

166. Galwey, *The Valiant Hours*, 109–11. Thaddeus S. Potter, "On Skirmish: Gallant Behavior of the 8th Ohio at Gettysburg," *The National Tribune*, Jan. 31, 1895, 3.

167. Potter places Company H on the skirmish line when the XI Corps sent a company to reinforce it.

Thaddeus S. Potter, "On Skirmish: Gallant Behavior of the 8th Ohio at Gettysburg," *The National Tribune*, Jan. 31, 1895, 3.

168. George H. Hazzard, *History of the First Regiment Minnesota Volunteer Infantry 1861–1864* (Stillwater, Minn.: Easton & Masterson, 1918), 364 and 369. (Reprint Ron R. Van Sickle Military Books, Gaithersburg, Md., 1987). Ladd and Ladd, *The Bachelder Papers*, I, 285. Letter, William Colvill, Jr., Aug. 30, 1866.

169. William Lochren, "The First Minnesota at Gettysburg," *Gettysburg Papers*, II, 611.

170. Hincks said that Moore commanded the right wing of the regiment and that Ellis commanded the left wing.

　　Ladd and Ladd, *The Bachelder Papers*, I, 399. Statement of William B. Hinch (Hincks), Sept. 20, 1870. Christ, *The Bliss Farm*, 67.

171. Doten also said that Moore commanded the right wing of the regiment.

　　Ladd and Ladd, *The Bachelder Papers*, I, 401. Statement, Frederick P. Doten, Sept. 22, 1870. Page, *14th Conn.*, 143.

172. Page, *14th Conn.*, 146.

173. Ibid., 144–45.

174. Christ, *The Bliss Farm*, 70.

175. Ibid.

176. Page, *14th Conn.*, 145.

177. For Captain Broatch to have seen Brainard get hit Co. A had to have been with Moore. Co. I suffered casualties on the way to the barn under Moore's command. Moore took his Co. F along, and Co. G suffered losses in the barn. This makes the initial raiding party Cos. A, F, G, and I. Cos. B and D were on the skirmish line. That left Ellis to command Cos. C, E, H, and K.

178. Christ, *The Bliss Farm*, 72–73. Page, *14th Conn.*, 147–48.

179. Page, *14th Conn.*, 147–48.

180. Ibid., 146.

181. Christ, *The Bliss Farm*, 74. Page, *14th Conn.*, 145. Ladd and Ladd, *The Bachelder Papers*, I, 406–7. Letter, Theodore G. Ellis, Nov. 3, 1870.

182. Christ, *The Bliss Farm*, 74.

183. Herb S. Crumb (ed.), *The Eleventh Corps Artillery at Gettysburg: The Papers of Major Thomas Ward Osborn* (Hamilton, N.Y.: Edmontson Publishing Co., Inc., 1991), 69. From Philadelphia *Weekly Times*, Saturday, May 31, 1879, vol. III, No., 14, "The Artillery at Gettysburg."

184. According to Osborn, he had five batteries from the XI Corps in position on the ridge for a total of 26 guns. Of those 26 only two batteries were in position and actively engaged during the bombardment preceding the charge.

　　Crumb, *The Eleventh Corps Artillery*, 70. From Philadelphia *Weekly Times*, Saturday, May 31, 1879, vol. III, No., 14, "The Artillery at Gettysburg. Raus, *The Union Army at Gettysburg*, 87–89, 102, 103, 165–66.

185. The artillery accounts intimate that these guns were in the vicinity of Cemetery Hill and not along the Granite School House Road where Fitzhugh's and McGilvery's reserve volunteer artillery brigades were located.

186. Raus, *The Union Army at Gettysburg*, 157. Map II.

187. Huntington places Norton between Hill and Wheeler. This is an error.

　　Ibid., 102, 177. Map II. Ladd and Ladd, *The Bachelder Papers*, I, 622. Letter, James F. Huntington, June 6, 1878.

188. Doubleday's reluctance to draw fire with Cowan's Battery indicates that there were no other guns south of McGilvery's three batteries other than Dow's. Had they been there prior to the charge, the Confederates on the Emmitsburg Road would have seen them.

Andrew Cowan, "When Cowan's Battery Withstood Pickett's Splendid Charge," *New York Herald*, July 2, 1911. Ladd and Ladd, *The Bachelder Papers*, I, 281. Letter, Andrew Cowan, Aug. 26, 1866.

189. Scott, " Pickett's Charge," *The Gettysburg Papers*, II, 903. Washburn, *108th New York*, 52.

190. Gallagher, *Fighting for the Confederacy*, 250. B & L, II, 362. Alexander, *Military Memoirs*, 420. Alexander, Letter to J. William Jones, March 17, 1877, SHSP (IV:102).

191. Galwey said that the troops which came up on the picket line were from the 55th Ohio. The 55th was near the intersection of the Baltimore and Taneytown Pikes. To have put skirmishers west of the cemetery where Galwey said they were would have been too far from the regiment. The 136th New York was on picket duty that day in that area. Their regimental marker would put them on the Taneytown Pike northeast of Ziegler's Grove. Galwey said that a couple of XI Corps battalions came up on the 8th Ohio's right. They probably were several companies of the 136th New York.

John Michael Priest (ed.), *John T. McMahon's Diary of the 136th New York 1861–1864* (Shippensburg, Pa.: White Mane, 1993), 53, and fn. 33, 80. Galwey, *The Valiant Hours*, 111.

192. Thaddeus S. Potter, "On Skirmish: Gallant Behavior of the 8th Ohio at Gettysburg," *The National Tribune*, Jan. 31, 1895, 3.

193. Galwey, *The Valiant Hours*, 111.

194. Thaddeus S. Potter, "On Skirmish: Gallant Behavior of the 8th Ohio at Gettysburg," *The National Tribune*, Jan. 31, 1895, 3.

195. George P. Metcalf, "Recollections of Boyhood Days," Gregory A. Coco Collection, Harrisburg CWRT Collection, USAMHI, Carlisle Barracks, Pa., 93.

196. John W. Hand, "Gettysburg: A Graphic Account of the Battle by an Eleventh Corps Captain," *The National Tribune*, July 24, 1890, 3.

197. Had he been at the northern end of his position, Alexander would have seen that McCarthy's Napoleons had moved 200 yards farther east to assist one of Hill's sections in driving the 14th Connecticut from the farm. I inserted the story of the two officers and their drunken surgeon at this point because it would explain why Alexander would not have been present to see McCarthy take part in the fight.

Gallagher, *Fighting for the Confederacy*, 250–51, 253.

198. Postles was mistaken in regard to the day on which the event occurred and the time of day, which is not uncommon in so many reminiscences. His quotes sound believable. Since his details match virtually everything cited by the regimentals of the 1st Delaware and the 14th Connecticut except their assertions that he gave the order to fire the barn I have decided to take his testimony in that regard as the fact.

Beyer and Keydel, *Deeds of Valor*, 228–30. Ladd and Ladd, *The Bachelder Papers*, I, 398. Letter, Orsamus B. Sawyer, Sept. 20, 1870. Orsamus Sawyer was a corporal of the 14th who insisted that Postles told the major to burn the buildings.

199. Mr. Christ in his book says that neither Postles' nor Hitchcock's accounts can be taken as truthful. He is in error.

Christ, *The Bliss Farm*, 75. Ladd and Ladd, *The Bachelder Papers*, I, 1762; II, 1183. Letters, Clinton D. MacDougall, Aug. 27, 1890, and Charles A. Hitchcock, Jan. 20, 1886.

200. Moore swore in an affidavit that an aide from Smyth, the brigade commander, personally ordered him to fire the barn. Theodore Ellis asserted on Oct. 13, 1870, that a Captain Porters ordered them to set the barn and house ablaze. On Nov. 3, 1870, he identified that officer again—this time as Capt. J. P. Postles. Only one other man in the 14th Connecticut, Cpl. Orsamus B. Sawyer, said that he heard Postles give the order to Ellis to burn the house and barn and retreat. It is interesting that Sawyer heard the order delivered to Ellis when Moore testified that he was ordered by Smyth's aide to fire the barn. In his Official Report, Ellis did not identify the person who ordered him to torch the barn, neither did

Smyth or Alexander Hays. Colonel MacDougall (111th New York) and Sergeant Hitchcock (111th New York) both attested to the fact that Hitchcock carried the order to burn the buildings. Postles would have remembered giving an order such as that, despite the passage of 40 years. His statement and Hitchcock's cannot be dismissed or held suspect because they do not fit the generally told story of this incident. Mr. Christ argues that Hitchcock's account about hunting up matches is suspect because the men did not need them to accomplish their mission. All they had to do was ignite powder with their percussion caps. None of the accounts mention such a unique way of starting the fires.

Ladd and Ladd, *The Bachelder Papers*, I, 398, 402, 404, 407. Letters Orsamus B. Sawyer, Sept. 20, 1870; Theodore G. Ellis, Oct. 13, 1870, and Nov. 3, 1870. Statement, Samuel A. Moore, Oct. 5, 1870. Ibid., II, 1762. Letter, Clinton D. MacDougall, Aug. 27, 1890. Christ, *The Bliss Farm*, 74–75, 195–96. *OR*, XVII, pt. 1, 454, 465, 467. Reports of Brig. Gen. Alexander Hays, Col. Thomas A. Smyth, Maj. Theodore Ellis.

201. Ladd and Ladd, *The Bachelder Papers*, I, 403–5, 406–7. Statement, James A. Stroazzi, Oct. 5, 1870. Letter, Theodore G. Ellis, Nov. 3, 1870. Page, *14th Conn.*, 147–48.

202. Galwey, *The Valiant Hours*, 109.

203. Christ, *The Bliss Farm*, 76. Page, *14th Conn.*, 147–48, 162.

204. Christ, *The Bliss Farm*, 76–77. Ladd and Ladd, *The Bachelder Papers*, II, 1184. Letter, Charles A. Hitchcock, Jan. 20, 1886.

205. Thaddeus S. Potter, "On Skirmish: Gallant Behavior of the 8th Ohio at Gettysburg," *The National Tribune*, Jan. 31, 1895, 3.

206. Galwey, *The Valiant Hours*, 112.

207. Scott, " Pickett's Charge," *The Gettysburg Papers*, II, 903.

208. Page, *14th Conn.*, 148.

209. *OR*, XXVII, pt. 2, 379. Report of Capt. E. S. McCarthy.

210. Fuger said that the battery fired the barn on July 2 and that at 11:00 a.m. the battery got in a one-half-hour artillery duel. He apparently got his dates confused. Therefore his statement about the wounding of Lt. Samuel Canby is probably in error. Fuger seldom told the same statement the same way in his several accounts of the Battle of Gettysburg. No two statements are identical.

Frederick Fuger, "Cushing's Battery at Gettysburg," *Journal of Military Service Institution of the U.S.* (Nov.–Dec. 1907), 41:406. Frank A. Haskell, *The Battle of Gettysburg*, Bruce Catton (ed.) (Boston: Houghton Mifflin Co., 1958), 75. Aldrich, *History of Battery A*, map on 215. Robert Garth Scott (ed.), *Fallen Leaves: The Civil War Letters of Major Henry Livermore Abbott* (Kent, Ohio: Kent State University Press, 1991), 184.

211. Haskell, *Gettysburg*, 77–78.

212. John Gibbon, *Personal Recollections of the Civil War* (Dayton: Morningside, 1978), 146.

213. Haskell, *Gettysburg*, 77–79.

214. Gibbon, *Recollections*, 144–45.

215. Christopher Smith, "Bloody Angle," Buffalo *Evening News*, May 29, 1894, 5.

216. J. Risque Hutter, "Ninth Virginia, Kemper's Brigade," The Richmond *Times*, Sept. 10, 1905, John W. Daniel Papers, Box 28, Newspaper Clippings, Accession # 158, Folder (1905 Aug. 20–Nov. 12), Manuscripts Dept., Alderman Library, University of Virginia.

217. Erasmus Williams, "A Private's Experience in Gettysburg," 1, John W. Daniel Papers, Box 23, #158 5383 A–E, Folder Civil War Material: Gettysburg, 3 July 1863 (Pickett's Charge), 1903–05 n.d., Manuscripts Dept., Alderman Library, University of Va.

218. There is a variation in the quoted conversations between Alexander and Wright in these four sources but they are essentially the same. The one in the *Bachelder Papers* predates the others and is taken verbatim from Longstreet's notes.

B&L, II, 362–64. Alexander, *Military Memoirs*, 420–22. Gallagher, *Fighting for the Confederacy*, 254–55. Ladd and Ladd, *The Bachelder Papers*, I, 485–86. Letter, Edward Porter

Alexander, May 3, 1876. John Cheves Haskell Memoirs, 1861–1865, Special Collections Dept., William R. Perkins Library, Duke University, Durham, N.C., 34–35.

For Alexander's exact location see SHSP (IV:104).

219. Robert A. Bright, "Pickett's Charge at Gettysburg," CV (XXXVIII:263).

220. Haskell, *Gettysburg*, 80–81.

221. Harmon's account varies a little from Haskell's in that in the 1890s he asserted that Meade said the following: "Lee has concentrated his 160 guns in his center, and soon will open fire on our center. Our artillery will answer and for a while there will be a grand artillery duel. After it is over, Lee, having massed his infantry, will attack our center in force. There will be close and desperate fighting, so desperate that every available man must be used...." Harmon did say that at that point Company C was relieved from division provost duty.

William Harmon, "Company C at Gettysburg," *The Minnesota Journal*, June 30, 1897, 7.

222. Haskell, *Gettysburg*, 80–81.

223. Ladd and Ladd, *The Bachelder Papers*, III, 1752. Letter, Sebastian D. Holmes, July 10, 1890.

224. Sturtevant, *13th Vermont*, 291.

Chapter 2

1. Gallagher, *Fighting for the Confederacy*, 246 and 255. Alexander to his father, July 17, 1863, Alexander-Hillhouse Papers, UNC, as cited in fn. 2, Coddington, *The Gettysburg Campaign*, 787.

2. Owen, *Washington Artillery*, 248–49, 253. *Battles and Leaders*, III, fn. 362.

3. Too many reliable sources timed the opening shot at 12:50 p.m.–1:00 p.m. and stated that it came from a Whitworth or a gun with a similar distinctive sound. When one considers that the piece designated to fire misfired and had to be reprimed, it allows enough time for the Whitworth to have opened fire first.

Crumb, *The Eleventh Corps Artillery at Gettysburg*, 31 and 70. Ladd and Ladd, *The Bachelder Papers*, III, 1396. Letter, John L. Brady, May 24, 1886.

4. Galwey, *Valiant Hours*, 112.

5. Haskell, *Gettysburg*, 81.

6. William R. Driver, "Pickett's Charge at Gettysburg," *Gettysburg Papers*, II, 892.

7. Adin B. Underwood, *Three Years' Service of the Thirty-Third Mass. Infantry Regiment, 1862–1865* (Huntington, W.V.: Blue Acorn Press, 1993), 134.

8. Scott, " Pickett's Charge," *The Gettysburg Papers*, II, 904.

9. Ladd and Ladd, *The Bachelder Papers*, III, 1409. Letter of Lt. Anthony W. McDermott, 69th Pennsylvania.

10. Owen, *Washington Artillery*, 248–49, 253. *Battles and Leaders*, III, fn. 362.

11. The general consensus is that the cannonade started at 1:00 p.m. and lasted two hours. Most of the material which I have surveyed agree that the cannonade began at 1:00 p.m. with variations ranging from 1:30 p.m. (Owen, *Washington Artillery*) to after 2:00 p.m.(Longstreet, *OR*). I have decided to use Alexander's time schedule as the correct time. His account is the most consistent and logical.

Battles and Leaders, III, 363. Gallagher, *Fighting for the Confederacy*, 257. Alexander, *Military Memoirs*, 422.

12. Owen, *Washington Artillery*, 248–49, 253. *Battles and Leaders*, III, fn. 362.

13. Thompson, "Scrap of Gettysburg," *Gettysburg Papers*, II, 959.

14. Alexander, *Fighting for the Confederacy*, 257, 259. Ladd and Ladd, *The Bachelder Papers*, I, 430. Extract, Post War Account, Henry J. Hunt, Jan. 20, 1873.

15. History Committee, *History of the Nineteenth Regiment Massachusetts Volunteer Infantry 1861–1865* (Salem: Salem Press, 1906), 234–35.

16. Benedict, *Army Life in Virginia*, 175.

17. Benjamin W. Thompson, "Personal Narrative of Experiences in the Civil War, 1861–1865," CWTI, Oct. 1973, 21.

18. Ladd and Ladd, *The Bachelder Papers*, II, 1069. Letter, David Shields, Aug. 27, 1884.

19. Thompson, "Scrap of Gettysburg," *Gettysburg Papers*, II, 960.

20. See the Map.

Harrison and Busey, *Nothing But Glory*, 96. Benjamin W. Thompson, "Personal Narrative of Experiences in the Civil War, 1861–1865," CWTI, Oct. 1973, 21.

21. Thompson, "Scrap of Gettysburg," *Gettysburg Papers*, II, 959.

22. Ibid., 960. Ladd and Ladd, *The Bachelder Papers*, III, 1742–1743. Letters, Sebastian D. Holmes and Samuel B. McIntyre, June 26 and 27, 1890, respectively.

23. Haines, *Company F*, 41.

24. Benjamin W. Thompson, "Personal Narrative of Experiences in the Civil War, 1861–1865," CWTI, Oct. 1973, 21.

25. Ladd and Ladd, *The Bachelder Papers*, III, 1744. Letter, Samuel; Intyre, June 27, 1890.

26. Benjamin W. Thompson, "Personal Narrative of Experiences in the Civil War, 1861–1865," CWTI, Oct. 1973, 21.

27. Haines, *Company F*, 41.

28. Thompson, "Scrap of Gettysburg," *Gettysburg Papers*, II, 960.

29. Page, *14th Conn.*, 149.

30. Ladd and Ladd, *The Bachelder Papers*, II, 1068. Letter, David Shields, Aug. 27, 1884.

31. Gibbon, *Recollections*, 147.

32. Haskell, *Gettysburg*, 82. Gibbon, *Recollections*, 146–47. William Harmon, "Company C at Gettysburg," *The Minnesota Journal*, June 30, 1897, 7. The Robert Brake Collection, Box 10, Federal Units, Minnesota—New York, USAMHI, Carlisle Barracks, Pa.

33. Ladd and Ladd, *The Bachelder Papers*, III, 35–36. Report of Lt. Col. Charles H. Morgan.

34. Ibid., I, 352–53. Letter, Henry H. Bingham, Jan. 5, 1869.

35. Ibid., II, 852–53. Letter, George Meade, May 6, 1882.

36. Harmon, the 1st Lieutenant, Co. C, 1st Minnesota corroborated the descriptions as given by Gibbon and Haskell. He said that Gibbon's orderly was decapitated and that that shell frightened the horses into overturning the wagon.

Haskell, *Gettysburg*, 81–83. William Harmon, "Company C at Gettysburg," *The Minnesota Journal*, June 30, 1897, 7. The Robert Brake Collection, Box 10, Federal Units, Minnesota–New York, USAMHI, Carlisle Barracks, Pa.

37. Gibbon, *Recollections*, 147.

38. Ladd and Ladd, *The Bachelder Papers*, I and II , 432–33, 649, 755–56. Extract, Postwar Account, Henry J. Hunt, Jan. 20, 1873. Letters, Henry J. Hunt, July 24, 1879, and May 8, 1881.

39. *OR*, XXVII, pt. 1, 885, 888, and 890. Reports of Capts. Phillips, Hart, and Thompson. Ladd and Ladd, *The Bachelder Papers*, I, 167, 169, and 425. Letters, Charles A. Phillips. One is undated. The other is dated July 6, 1863. Extract, Postwar Account, Henry J. Hunt, Jan. 20, 1873.

40. Andrew Cowan, "When Cowan's Battery Withstood Pickett's Splendid Charge," *New York Herald*, July 2, 1911.

41. Letter, William A. Ewing to his mother, July 4, 1863, *Toledo Blade*, Saturday, July 11, 1863, 2.

42. Crumb, *The Eleventh Corps Artillery at Gettysburg*, 37–38.

43. According to Huntington, Battery H had nearly exhausted its ammunition supply and would have to be replaced. The captain of the battery would have reported that to the brigade commander. Huntington also said that Hill (Buell) had expended his ammunition and that he replaced him with Edgell's guns. Hill did not leave the hill at any time. When referring to Hill's battery, Huntington was more than likely referring to Norton's battery.

  Capt. James F. Huntington, "Notes of Service With a Light Artillery at Chancellorsville and Gettysburg," Marietta *Sunday Observer*, Aug. 11, 1918.

44. Ibid.

45. Crumb, *The Eleventh Corps Artillery at Gettysburg*, 34, 36, 37, 38, 39, 72.

46. Gallagher, *Fighting for the Confederacy*, 258.

47. Ibid., 248, 258.

48. The maps for July 2 and July 3, respectively, show the artillery at the southwest side of the Granite School House-Taneytown Road intersection and at the western base of Power's Hill. This would confirm what Ames said in his report when he placed the battery behind a woods and said that he did not move out until the Confederate infantry advanced under the cover of its guns.

  Battles and Leaders, III, 299, 308, 344. *OR* XXVII, pt. 1, 901. Report of Capt. Nelson Ames.

49. Andrew Cowan, "When Cowan's Battery Withstood Pickett's Splendid Charge," *New York Herald*, July 2, 1911.

50. Capt. Jabez Daniels said that his battery opened fire at 12:30 p.m., which evidently is an incorrect time citation. He was sent into position by Newton, who was close to the action and therefore had to have arrived on the field very shortly after the Confederates opened fire. Rank, who belonged to the same brigade, probably got his time wrong, as did Daniels. He would have been in the general vicinity during the early morning, as cited by the NPS marker, but he more than likely was deployed at the same time as Daniels.

51. Benedict, *Army Life in Virginia*, 175–76.

52. Ibid., 185.

53. In his account, Veazey said that the 14th Vermont crawled into line, unobserved by the Confederates on the right of his skirmishers. I cannot substantiate this particular statement and have chosen not to use it in this account. The regiment's line was along the western base of the ridge but not out in the field with the skirmishers.

  Benedict, *Army Life in Virginia*, 176. Ladd and Ladd, *The Bachelder Papers*, I, 60, Letter, Wheelock Veazey (undated).

54. Benedict, *Army Life in Virginia*, 176.

55. *Battles and Leaders*, III, 374.

56. Hazzard, *1st Minnesota*, 366.

57. Lochren, "1st Minn.," *Gettysburg Papers*, II, 612.

58. Benedict, *Army Life in Virginia*, 176–77.

59. Ladd and Ladd, *The Bachelder Papers*, I, 379. Letter, George G. Meade, Sr., Dec. 4, 1869.

60. Ladd states that Meade moved to Slocum's Headquarters at Powers Hill. That would have placed the general too far south to have had any control over the field. Meade said that the signal station and the headquarters were along the Baltimore Pike which would have placed them at the signal station on Stevens Knoll.

  Ladd and Ladd, *The Bachelder Papers*, II, 852–53. Letter, George Meade, May 6, 1882.

61. Page, *14th Conn.*, 149.

62. Ladd and Ladd, *The Bachelder Papers*, I, 341. Letter, Charles A. Richardson, May 8, 1868.

63. Page, *14th Conn.*, 149–50.

64. Scott, " Pickett's Charge," *The Gettysburg Papers*, II, 905.

65. Ibid.

66. Washburn, *108th New York*, 52. Ladd and Ladd, *The Bachelder Papers*, II, Letter, David Shields, Aug. 27, 1884.

67. Ibid., 50.

68. Ibid., 52.

69. George P. Metcalf, "Recollections of Boyhood Days," Gregory A. Coco Coll., Harrisburg CWRT Coll., USAMHI, Carlisle Barracks, Pa., 93–94.

70. John W. Hand, "Gettysburg: A Graphic Account of the Battle by an Eleventh Corps Captain," *The National Tribune*, July 24, 1890, 3.

71. George P. Metcalf, "Recollections of Boyhood Days," Gregory A. Coco Coll., Harrisburg CWRT Coll., USAMHI, Carlisle Barracks, Pa., 94.

72. The map shows Edgell to the right of Taft's four guns. Osborn said that he pulled the guns from his line and placed them to meet the threat from the right flank. He also said that he had fourteen guns involved in the fight. All of the guns mentioned were Ordnance Rifles or Parrotts.

    Crumb, *The Eleventh Corps Artillery at Gettysburg*, map on 30, 34 and 72.

73. McLaughlin does not appear in the battery's roster.

    Letter, Aug. 5, 1863, *Portage County Newspaper*.

74. The staff officer with Meade had to have been his son. He was the only officer which Meade identified as accompanying him anywhere on the field.

    Crumb, *The Eleventh Corps Artillery at Gettysburg*, 72–73.

75. Ladd and Ladd, *The Bachelder Papers*, I, 379. Letter, George G. Meade, Dec. 4, 1869.

76. The 111th New York was on the right of the brigade at the time, to the right of the 12th New Jersey.

    Washburn, *108th N.Y.*, 50.

77. Benjamin W. Thompson, "Personal Narratives of Experiences in the Civil War, 1861–1865," *CWTI* (Oct. 1973), 22.

78. Ladd and Ladd, *The Bachelder Papers*, III, 1752. Letter, Sebastian D. Holmes, July 10, 1890.

79. Ibid., III, 1754. Letter, Thomas Geer to C. D. MacDougall, July 28, 1890.

80. Washburn, *108th N.Y.*, 50.

81. Ladd and Ladd, *The Bachelder Papers*, I, 353. Letter, Henry H. Bingham, Jan. 5, 1869.

82. Gibbon, *Recollections*, 147.

83. Haskell could not have seen the destruction being done to Woodruff's battery in Ziegler's Grove. Having been in the hollow and behind the rock outcropping where Gibbon and Haskell were, I determined there was no way he could have seen over the ridge to the north. He had to have obtained that information second hand.

    Haskell, *Gettysburg*, 86–87.

84. Gibbon, *Recollections*, 148.

85. Haskell, *Gettysburg*, 87.

86. Gibbon places the limbers' bursting after he left the cover of the ridge. Haskell places it before they left cover. In all likelihood both happened. Frederick Fuger said that the battery lost nine ammunition chests. Three were blown up in the morning; two were hit while Haskell was nearby and three more were hit after he and Gibbon left the ridge. That leaves one unaccounted for.

    Frederick Fuger, "Cushing's Battery at Gettysburg," *Journal of Military Service Institution of the United States*, vol. 41, 1907, 409. Gibbon, *Recollections*, 148.

87. Christopher Smith, "Bloody Angle," Buffalo *Evening News*, May 29, 1894, 5.

88. John H. Rhodes, *The History of Battery B First Regiment Rhode Island Light Artillery in the War to Preserve the Union 1861–1865* (Providence: Snow & Farnham, 1894), 208.

89. In the magazine article, Rhodes said that Perrin had the right section. In the regimental, which is more complete, he said that Brown had the right section. Since Lieutenant Brown told Rhodes how the round got stuck and that the right section was his, I decided to go with the regimental history as opposed to the "Gettysburg Gun" article.

    John H. Rhodes, "The Gettysburg Gun," *Personal Narratives of Events in the War of the Rebellion, Being Papers Read Before the Rhode Island Soldiers and Sailors Historical Society*, VII (Wilmington: Broadfoot Publishing Co., 1993), 390, 392.

90. Rhodes, *Battery B 1st R.I.*, 208.

91. The regimental history has more detail in it than Rhodes' article for the RISSHS. It is much more precisely written.

    John H. Rhodes, *Battery B 1st R.I.*, 207, 208.

92. Rhodes, "The Gettysburg Gun," 393–98. Rhodes, *Battery B 1st R. I.* 209–10.

93. *19th Mass.*, 235.

94. Joseph C. Mayo, "Pickett's Charge," SHSP (XXXIV:329–30). David E. Johnston, *The Story of a Confederate Boy in the Civil War* (Radford, Va.: Commonwealth Press, Inc., 1980), 217.

95. Dooley, *John Dooley*, 103–4.

96. Ibid., 104.

97. Ibid.

98. J. Risque Hutter, "Ninth Virginia, Kemper's Brigade," The Richmond *Times*, Sept. 10, 1905, John W. Daniel Papers, Box 28, Newspaper Clippings, Accession # 158, Folder (1905 Aug. 20–Nov. 12), Manuscripts Dept., Alderman Library, University of Va.

99. "Captain John Holmes Smith's Account," SHSP (XXXII:189).

100. Johnston, *Confederate Boy*, 217. Johnston said he was sergeant major at that time.

101. Ibid., 216.

102. Johnston did not name the man. He said that he was close to him, which implies his immediate front or right front—as far as he could see from a prone position. His statement about a solid shot hitting thirty feet to his left from his prone position would probably have been gotten second hand after the fighting. The only enlisted man killed in Co. G was Private Dodson.

    Harrison and Busey, *Nothing But Glory*, 217. Johnston, *Confederate Boy*, 217.

103. Editors of Time-Life Books, *Voices of the Civil War: Gettysburg* (Alexandria, Va.: Time Life, 1996?) Not paginated. Account of Captain John T. James.

104. Wood, *Big I*, 44.

105. Erasmus Williams, "A Private's Experience in Gettysburg," John W. Daniel Papers, Box 23, #158 5383, A–A, Folder, Civil War Material: Gettysburg, 3 July 1863 (Pickett's Charge), 1903–05 n.d., Manuscripts Dept., Alderman Library, University of Va.

106. The road described by the surgeon; Doctor Holt is the one near the McMillan farm.

107. Maud Morrow Brown, *The University Greys, Company A, Eleventh Mississippi Regiment, Army of Northern Virginia, 1861–1865* (Richmond: Garrett and Massie, Inc., 1940), 38. I am deeply grateful to Steven H. Stubbs (Galveston, Texas), who graciously loaned me his Gettysburg chapter, from his manuscript copy of his regimental history on the 11th Mississippi. "They Suffered the Most, The Story of the Eleventh Mississippi Infantry Regiment" (28–29, 65) from which I received the following citations in reference to the incidents covered in this chapter: Andrew J. Baker, "Veterans Camps and Inquiries," *CV* (VI:436); Lt. William Peel, "Diary of Lieutenant William Peel," July 3, 1863, Mississippi State Archives.

108. The surgeon, who published his reminiscence in the *New Orleans Times Democrat* on June 22, 1913, said that the regiment was in front of the guns and that the farm lane which paralleled the crest ran for about 30 yards. There were no regiments in front of their guns until the charge began. The short lane which parallels the crest of the ridge is McMillan's

Lane. On July 26, 1913, a friend of Gage's, who was near him when he was hit, said that the regiment was 200 yards south of the field hospital. He got his directions mixed up. It had to have been north. The brigade marker, according to this veteran marks the place where Gage was hit. It is exactly .35 mile north of the Virginia Monument.

Brown, *University Greys*, 37–44. Martin, *Confederate Monuments*, 191 for citation of marker 175, Davis' Brigade. Stubbs, "They Suffered the Most,", Gettysburg Chapter, 29–30.

109. June Kimble, "Tennesseeans at Gettysburg—the Retreat," CV (XVIII:460).

110. B. D. Fry, "Pettigrew's Charge at Gettysburg," SHSP (VII:92).

111. F. S. Harris, "From Gettysburg," *Lebanon Democrat*, Aug. 10, 1899.

112. Felix Richard Galloway, Gettysburg—The Battle and the Retreat," CV (XXI:388).

113. Joseph C. Mayo, "Pickett's Charge at Gettysburg," SHSP (XXXIV:331).

114. Johnston, *Confederate Boy*, 217.

115. Joseph C. Mayo, "Pickett's Charge at Gettysburg," SHSP (XXXIV:331).

116. Harrison and Busey, *Nothing But Glory*, 193.

117. Johnston, *Confederate Boy*, 217–18. Joseph C. Mayo, "Pickett's Charge at Gettysburg," SHSP (XXXIV:33).

118. Christopher Smith, "Bloody Angle," Buffalo *Evening News*, May 29, 1894, 5.

119. Reed, et al., 228. Testimony of Pvt. Anthony W. McDermott, Co. I, 69th Pennsylvania Ladd and Ladd, *The Bachelder Papers: Gettysburg in Their Own Words*, III, 1410. Letter, Anthony W. McDermott to J. B. Bachelder, June 2, 1886.

120. Christopher Smith, "Bloody Angle," Buffalo *Evening News*, May 29, 1894, 5.

121. Ibid. *Battles and Leaders*, III, 390.

122. *19th Mass.*, 236. OR, XXVII, pt. 1, 242–45. Report of Col. Arthur F. Devereaux, 19th Massachusetts.

123. Rollins, *Pickett's Charge!*, 120.

124. *19th Mass.*, 236. OR, XXVII, pt. 1, 242–45. Report of Col. Arthur F. Devereaux, 19th Massachusetts.

125. *R*, XXVII, pt. 1, 242–45. Report of Col. Arthur F. Devereaux, 19th Massachusetts.

126. This is not exactly the way that the regimental historians reported the incident. They have a Lieutenant Brown calling to Devereaux for volunteers. The officer had to have been Stephen Brown (Co. K, 13th Vermont). It implies, however, that the captain who had originally asked for volunteers was no longer giving orders. At that point the twenty-seven men responded to the call. Devereaux in the *OR*, however, has the captain asking for volunteers and getting six, then at a second call getting the remaining twenty.

Ibid.; *19th Mass.*, 236.

127. OR, XXVII, pt. 1, 242–45. Report of Col. Arthur F. Devereaux, 19th Massachusetts.

128. *19th Mass.*, 236.

129. Galwey, *The Valiant Hours*, 114–15.

130. Benjamin W. Thompson, "Personal Narrative of Experiences in the Civil War, 1861–1865," *CWTI* (Oct. 1973), 22. Benjamin W. Thompson, "Pickett did not lead," *The National Tribune*, Jan. 25, 1915, 7.

131. Robert A. Bright, "Pickett's Charge at Gettysburg," CV, vol. 38:263 (1930).

132. The time at which he wrote the notes varies by five minutes between the *OR* and SHSP reports and the time cited in his other sources.

Supplement to the OR, vol. V, pt. 1, 361. Report of Col. E. P. Alexander. Alexander to William Jones, SHSP (IV:107). *Battles and Leaders*, III, 364. Gallagher, *Fighting for the Confederacy*, 258.

133. Robert A. Bright, "Pickett's Charge at Gettysburg," CV, vol. 38:263 (1930).

134. Linthicum delivered a preliminary order to Garnett's brigade to prepare to advance when the guns ceased fire, therefore he had to have gotten the orders from someone.

Longstreet, *From Manassas to Appomattox*, 392. Robert McCulloch, "About the Charge of Pickett's Division," CV (XXI:474).

135. Despite the time variances between Alexander's various accounts it is evident that sometime between 1:25 p.m. and 1:40 p.m., he sent Pickett two written notes to start his attack. According to Capt. Robert A. Bright (Pickett's staff), Alexander's note read, "Tell General Pickett we have silenced eight of the enemy's guns, and now is the time to charge."

Alexander, *Military Memoirs*, 423. Gallagher, *Fighting for the Confederacy*, 259. *Supplement to the OR*, vol. 5, pt. 1, 109. Alexander to William Jones, March 17, 1877, SHSP, IV:107–8. *Battles and Leaders*, III, 364. Robert A. Bright, "Pickett's Charge at Gettysburg," CV (XXXVIII:263).

136. Crumb, *The Eleventh Corps Artillery at Gettysburg*, 75–76.

137. Ladd and Ladd, *The Bachelder Papers*, I, 353. Letter, Henry H. Bingham, Jan. 5, 1869.

138. Crumb, *The Eleventh Corps Artillery at Gettysburg*, 75–76.

139. Raus, *The Union Army at Gettysburg*, 157.

140. According to Aldrich, *Battery A, First Rhode Island Light Artillery*, 216–17. Aldrich's gun fired double canister (the battery's last shot) into the 26th North Carolina at point-blank range. He also asserts that the guns fired by the oblique into Cushing's position to stop the Confederates from taking Cushing's gun. There is no corroborative evidence to indicate that this often repeated story actually occurred. Nor is it logical. If Arnold's guns had swept the Angle with canister, no Confederates would have been able to cross the wall and the Federal troops in the Angle would have been slaughtered by friendly fire. Sgt. Maj. William B. Hincks (14th Connecticut) said that the battery, having exhausted its ammunition before the charge began, retired from the fight. The July 10, 1863, report of Col. John T. Jones (26th North Carolina), the Feb. 10, 1864, report of 1st Lt. Louis G. Young (A.D.C. to Pettigrew), the postwar recollections of Capt. Thomas J. Cureton (26th North Carolina) and Lt. Gaston H. Broughton (26th North Carolina) make no mention of canister at close range. Surely to have survived that, they would have remembered the terrific carnage. Coddington in *The Gettysburg Campaign*, fn. 36, 790, identified the batteries which withdrew as Brown's and Arnold's.

Page, *14th Conn.*, 150. *Supplement to the OR*, vol. V, pt. 1, 410–14, 416–23, 426–31. *OR*, XXVII, pt. 1, 480. Report of Capt. John G. Hazard. *Battles and Leaders*, III, 374.

141. Bingham stated that he relayed Meade's order to three or four batteries. with Arnold, Cushing, and Brown's guns out of action that left Woodruff's, Cowan's, and Rorty's batteries in the II Corps line.

Ladd and Ladd, *The Bachelder Papers*, I, 353. Letter, Henry H. Bingham, Jan. 5, 1869.

142. Page, *14th Conn.*, 150.

143. bid., 151.

144. The Philadelphia *Weekly Press*. Account of Col. R. Penn Smith, as reported in the *Gettysburg Compiler*, June 7, 1887.

145. In his official report dated July 12, 1863, General Webb said that he sent his A.A.G., Capt. Charles Banes, to bring up two batteries and that he brought up Wheeler's 1st New York Artillery. The editors of the *OR*s corrected the error by noting in brackets that it was Cowan's 1st New York Independent Battery. Webb further stated that Cowan replaced Brown's R.I. Battery which had quit the field. The officer who delivered the order to hold their fire for the infantry had to have been Bingham. He said that he did not recall the exact words of the order to Hunt and Hancock but "Cease firing. Hold your fire for the infantry," could have been Bingham's interpretation of observing "great care with their ammunition and endeavor to preserve it and not fire so rapidly or extravagantly."

When Banes testified in 1890 in the lawsuit over the placement of the monument to the 72nd Pennsylvania, he muddled the sequence of events. He said that Webb sent him between 1:45 p.m. and 2:00 p.m. to find Brig. Gen. Henry Hunt to get permission to take two batteries to the front. He found Hunt near Little Round Top, discussed the issue "at length" and got permission to bring up the guns. He found Wheeler near the Artillery reserve and Wheeler offered to go to the front with him. Riding ahead, he found Webb who ordered him to get Brown's Rhode Island Battery. Banes rode down to Cowan and sent him to the Angle. Returning to Webb, Banes was ordered to put the 72nd Pennsylvania upon the field. As he executed that command, the colonel of the 72nd saw the Confederates at the Emmitsburg Road. Lt. William Wheeler (13th New York Battery) came to the support of the II Corps late in the attack. The Confederates according to his account were not more than 400 yards away. He went into line on Brown's (Cowan's) left and enfiladed the Confederate line.

When Alexander saw the Federal guns retire from the fight at 1:30 p.m. Banes was being dispatched south. Pickett's assault began at 1:50 p.m. By then Banes was near Little Round Top with Hunt. From there, he cut north to Cemetery Hill, where he picked up Wheeler's battery. While Wheeler went forward, Banes rejoined Webb and was told to put the 72nd Pennsylvania on the field. The colonel saw the Confederates at the Emmitsburg Road. It was about 2:08 p.m. When he retold his story in 1890, Banes, obviously, got the sequence of events confused. 38 minutes gave him enough time to cover the three-mile round trip from the Angle to Little Round Top to Cemetery Hill and back.

Rollins, *Pickett's Charge!*, 302. Wheeler's *OR* report. Reed, et al., Testimony of Charles H. Banes, 272–73. Hollingsworth and Cox, *The Third Day at Gettysburg*, 45. Andrew Cowan, "Cowan's New York Battery: Its Old Captain Tells of Its Glorious Share in Repulsing Pickett's Charge," *The National Tribune*, Nov. 12, 1908, 7. "Undated Remarks by Andrew J. Cowan," The Gettysburg Campaign, The Robert L. Brake Coll., USAMHI. These two accounts are identical. Ladd and Ladd, *The Bachelder Papers*, I, 281. Letter, Andrew Cowan, Aug. 26, 1866.

146. *OR*, XXVII, pt. 1, 480. Report of Capt. John G. Hazard.

147. Gibbon, *Recollections*, 147–48.

148. Cook, "Personal Reminiscences," *Gettysburg Papers*, II, 928. Gibbon, *Reminiscences*, 149–50.

149. Moe, *The Last Full Measure*, 284–85.

150. The colonel said that only half of the regiment fit at the wall and that the right wing was back at Arnold's former position. Stockton said that two companies remained back at the rear angle. The map on page 96 in *Nothing But Glory* shows that there was enough room from the right flank of the 69th Pennsylvania and the northwest corner of the Angle to accommodate about three hundred men. The 71st Pennsylvania had 331 effectives.

Reed, et al., Testimony of SGM William S. Stockton, 71st Pennsylvania, 243. The Philadelphia *Weekly Press*, Account of Col. R. Penn Smith as cited in *The Gettysburg Compiler*, June 7, 1887. Raus, *The Union Army at Gettysburg*, 121.

151. R. W. Martin, "Armistead at the Battle of Gettysburg," SHSP (XXXIX:186).

152. No one noticed the A.D.C. deliver the command but it may be inferred that the brigade stood up after the command came from Pickett's aide.

Letter, Capt. B. L. Farinholt to J. W. Daniel, April 5, 1905, John W. Daniel Papers, Box 23, 158 5383 A–E, Folder, Civil War Material: Gettysburg, 3 July 1863 (Pickett's Charge), 1903–05 n.d., Manuscripts Dept., Alderman Library, University of Va.

153. R. W. Martin, "Armistead at the Battle of Gettysburg," SHSP (XXXIX:186). "Rawley Martin's Account," SHSP (XXXII:184).

154. Letter, Capt. B. L. Farinholt to J. W. Daniel, April 5, 1905, John W. Daniel Papers, Box 23, 158 5383 A–E, Folder, Civil War Material: Gettysburg, 3 July 1863 (Pickett's Charge), 1903–05 n.d., Manuscripts Dept., Alderman Library, University of Va.

155. "Captain John Holmes Smith's Account," SHSP (XXXII:190).

156. George W. Finley, "Bloody Angle," Buffalo *Evening News*, May 29, 1894, 5.

157. Haskell in an incomplete report said that he took Latham's and Garden's batteries with him to the Peach Orchard. In a May 12, 1906, account he changed this statement to say

that he took Reilly's, Latham's, and Garden's batteries to the Peach Orchard. He placed Alexander at the right of the line when Longstreet rode out to talk with Alexander and said that Pickett and his staff were behind a large barn on the edge of the Peach Orchard. That would have placed Pickett too far to the right of his division. This particular source is not very reliable. In his memoirs at Duke, however, Haskell placed the barn on the left of his guns behind the line. It was a large stone barn. He also said that he took in five guns on the right of Pickett during the charge which conforms to the report Maj. B. F. Eshleman, who identified the guns.

OR, XXVII, pt. 2, 435. Report of Maj. B. F. Eshleman. John Cheves Haskell, "Memoirs," Special Collections Dept., William R. Perkins Library, Duke U., 34. *Supplement to the OR*, vol. V, pt. 1, 361,348 and 349, 354 and 355. Reports of Col. E. P. Alexander and Maj. John C. Haskell.

158. Robert D. Damron, "Recollections of Some of the Incidents of the Battle of Gettysburg, PA, July 3, 1863," John W. Daniel Papers, Box 23, #158 5383 A–E, Folder, Civil War Material: Gettysburg, 3 July 1863 (Pickett's Charge), 1903–05 n.d., Manuscripts Dept., Alderman Library, University of Va.

159. Gallagher, *Fighting for the Confederacy*, 261. *Supplement to the OR*, vol. V, pt. 1, 361. Report of Col. E. P. Alexander.

160. Gallagher, *Fighting for the Confederacy*, 261. *Supplement to the OR*, vol. V, pt. 1, 361. Report of Col. E. P. Alexander.

161. John Cheves Haskell, "Memoirs," Special Collections Dept., William R. Perkins Library, Duke U., 34.

162. Gallagher, *Fighting for the Confederacy*, 261.

163. George W. Finley, "Bloody Angle," Buffalo *Evening News*, May 29, 1894, 5.

164. Robert D. Damron, "Recollections of Some of the Incidents of the Battle of Gettysburg, PA, July 3, 1863," John W. Daniel Papers, Box 23, #158 5383 A–E, Folder, Civil War Material: Gettysburg, 3 July 1863 (Pickett's Charge), 1903–05 n.d., Manuscripts Dept., Alderman Library, University of Va. Randolph Shotwell, as cited in Rollins, *Pickett's Charge*, 172.

165. George W. Finley, "Bloody Angle," Buffalo *Evening News*, May 29, 1894, 5.

166. Robert D. Damron, "Recollections of Some of the Incidents of the Battle of Gettysburg, PA, July 3, 1863," John W. Daniel Papers, Box 23, #158 5383 A–E, Folder, Civil War Material: Gettysburg, 3 July 1863 (Pickett's Charge), 1903–05 n.d., Manuscripts Dept., Alderman Library, University of Va.

167. Robert McCulloch, "About the Charge of Pickett's Division," CV (XXI:474).

168. Letter, Hunton to John W. Daniel. July 15, 1904, George W. Jones Papers, 1832–1865, Special Collections Dept., William R. Perkins Library, Duke University, Durham, N.C.

169. Joseph C. Mayo, "Pickett's Charge at Gettysburg," SHSP (XXXIV:331). Robert D. Damron, "Recollections of Some of the Incidents of the Battle of Gettysburg, PA, July 3, 1863, John W. Daniel Papers, Box 23, #158 5383 A–E, Folder: Civil War Material: Gettysburg, 3 July 1863 (Pickett's Charge), 1903–05 n.d., Manuscripts Dept., Alderman Library, University of Va.

170. Robert A. Bright, "Pickett's Charge at Gettysburg," CV (XXXVIII:264).

171. Dooley, *John Dooley*, 105.

172. J. Risque Hutter, "Ninth Virginia, Kemper's Brigade," The Richmond *Times*, Sept. 10, 1905, John W. Daniel Papers, Box 28, Newspaper Clippings, Accession #158, Folder (1905 Aug. 20–Nov. 12), Manuscripts Dept., Alderman Library, University of Va.

Chapter 3

1. B. D. Fry, "Pettigrew's Charge at Gettysburg," SHSP (VII:92).

2. June Kimble, "Tennesseeans at Gettysburg—the Retreat," CV (XVII: 460).

3. B. D. Fry, "Pettigrew's Charge at Gettysburg," SHSP (VII:92).

4. *Supplement to the OR*, V, 429. Postwar account of Capt. Thomas J. Cureton, 26th North Carolina, June 15, 1890.

5. Davis did not say who gave the order to advance. Pettigrew probably gave the command. The Federals clearly saw him riding from one end of his division to the other during the charge. It seems very much like him to have had a personal hand in ordering the attack. *OR*, XXVII, pt. 2. Report of Brig. Gen. Joseph R. Davis.

6. June Kimble, "Tennesseeans at Gettysburg—the Retreat," CV (XVII:460).

7. J. H. Moore, "Heth's Division at Gettysburg," The Southern Bivouac (III:390).

8. Rollins, *Pickett's Charge!*, 254.

9. Ibid., 239–40. Account of William S. Christian.

10. Gallagher, *Fighting for the Confederacy*, 261.

11. Robert D. Damron, "Recollections of Some of the Incidents of the Battle of Gettysburg, PA, July 3, 1863, John W. Daniel Papers, Box 23, #158 5383 A–E, Folder: Civil War Material: Gettysburg, 3 July 1863 (Pickett's Charge), 1903–05 n.d., Manuscripts Dept., Alderman Library, University of Va.

12. Letter, Thomas R. Friend to Maj. Charles Pickett, Dec. 10, 1894. Virginia Historical Society, ViH MSS 2P5868b3.

13. *Supplement to the OR*, V, 312. Postwar Account of Maj. Edmund Berkeley, 8th Virginia.

14. Harris clearly states that Fry's brigade marched a very short distance to the front and formed on Garnett's left. The attack was not as staggered as some witnesses asserted. Captain William W. Bentley, Co. E, 24th Virginia, said that the first movement made by Kemper's brigade was to left flank the distance of a regiment before fronting and advancing. Col. Joseph Mayo (3rd Virginia) corroborated this. He said that very shortly after passing the batteries, the brigade moved left and received a flank fire during the entire movement. Kemper's brigade touched Garnett's right flank but was further advanced toward the southeast in the low ground near Spangler's house. When Garnett flanked left, he dragged Kemper with him. In his report, Maj. Charles Peyton (19th Virginia, Garnett's brigade) stated that his regiment crossed three high post and rail fences in getting to Cemetery Ridge. If Garnett followed the path indicated by many of the references to the battle, his men would have climbed over one worm fence and five post and rail fences. By flanking left over one worm fence and then moving east, Garnett would have encountered one worm fence and three post and rail fences—two of which were along the Emmitsburg Road.

   F. S. Harris, "From Gettysburg," *Lebanon Democrat*, Aug. 10, 1899. Robert D. Damron, "Recollections of Some of the Incidents of the Battle of Gettysburg, PA, July 3, 1863," John W. Daniel Papers, Box 23, #158 5383 A–E, Folder: Civil War Material: Gettysburg, 3 July 1863 (Pickett's Charge), 1903–05 n.d., Manuscripts Dept., Alderman Library, University of Va. Letter, W. W. Bentley to W. Fry, July 9, 1863, George Edward Pickett Papers, Manuscript Dept., William R. Perkins Library, Duke University, Durham, N.C. *OR*, XXVII, pt. 2, 386. Report of Major Charles Peyton, 19th Virginia. Report of the Committee, *Five Points in the Record of North Carolina in the Great War of 1861–5* (Farmville, Va.: Farmville Printing, 1995), Map between 26 and 27. Joseph C. Mayo, "Pickett's Charge at Gettysburg," SHSP (XXXIV:331).

15. J. R. McPherson, "A Private's Account of Gettysburg," CV (VI:149).

16. G. W. Finley, "The Angle," Buffalo *Evening News*, May 29, 1894, 7.

17. 1st Cpl. James T. Carter of the color guard stood immediately to Blackburn's left and heard the entire conversation. His rendition, while less dramatic than Colonel Rawley Martin's, sounds more genuine.

18. Rawley Martin, "Colonel Rawley Martin's Account," SHSP (XXII:184). "Armistead at the Battle of Gettysburg," SHSP (XXXIX:186).

19. Rollins, *Pickett's Charge!*, 171.

20. Wood, *Big I*, 46. Ladd and Ladd, *The Bachelder Papers*, I, 283. Letters, Andrew Cowan, Aug. 26, 1866, and Henry J. Hunt.

21. Scott, "Pickett's Charge," *Gettysburg Papers*, II, 906–7. Thompson, "Scrap of Gettysburg," *Gettysburg Papers*, II, 961. Cook, "Personal Reminiscences," *Gettysburg Papers*, II, 923 and 926.

22. Page, *14th Conn.*, 151.

23. Ibid.

24. Thompson, "Scrap of Gettysburg," *Gettysburg Papers*, II, 960.

25. Page, *14th Conn.*, 151.

26. Ladd and Ladd, *The Bachelder Papers*, III, 1397. Letter, John L. Brady, May 24, 1886.

27. William Harmon, "Company C at Gettysburg," *The Minnesota Journal*, June 30, 1897, 7; Box 10, Federal Units, Minnesota—New York, Manuscripts Division, USAMHI, Carlisle Barracks, Pa. *OR*, XXVII, pt. 1, 425. Report of Capt. Henry C. Coates.

28. T. S. Potter, "On Skirmish: Gallant Behavior of the 8th Ohio at Gettysburg," *The National Tribune*, Jan. 31, 1895, 3.

29. Ladd and Ladd, *The Bachelder*, III, 1750. Letter, John I. Brinkerhoff, July 9, 1890.

30. Robert D. Damron, "Recollections of Some of the Incidents of the Battle of Gettysburg, PA, July 3, 1863," John W. Daniel Papers, Box 23, #158 5383 A–E, Folder: Civil War Material: Gettysburg, 3 July 1863 (Pickett's Charge), 1903–05 n.d., Manuscripts Dept., Alderman Library, UVA, Charlottesville, Va.

31. Robert D. Damron, "Recollections of Some of the Incidents of the Battle of Gettysburg, PA, July 3, 1863," John W. Daniel Papers, Box 23, #158 5383 A–E, Folder: Civil War Material: Gettysburg, 3 July 1863 (Pickett's Charge), 1903–05 n.d., Manuscripts Dept., Alderman Library, UVA, Charlottesville, Va. Harrison and Busey, *Nothing But Glory*, 331 and 332.

32. G. W. Finley, "The Angle," Buffalo *Evening News*, May 29, 1894, 7.

33. Letter, H. C. Mitchie to Lt. Topscott, February 21, 1904, John W. Daniel Papers, Manuscripts Dept., Alderman Library, UVA, Charlottesville, Va.

34. Wood, *Big I*, 45–46.

35. Lochren, "1st Minn.," *Gettysburg Papers*, II, 612.

36. Cook, "Personal Reminiscences," *Gettysburg Papers*, II, 928.

37. "Letter from General Trimble, October 15th, 1875," SHSP (IX:33).

38. Ladd and Ladd, *The Bachelder Papers*, II, 933. Letter, Isaac Trimble.

39. The editor of the volume cited below indicates that Edgell replaced Norton on the line but that the monument for the battery was placed farther to the front because the batteries found the original position which they occupied too cramped. Norton had six guns. Edgell had four. He could easily have placed his guns in the spot held by Norton. The citation for Edgell states that the battery was "on this ground" which could loosely be interpreted the cemetery as opposed to the exact location for the monument. If they both occupied the same area at the same time, it is highly unlikely that both batteries would have placed their monuments on the same spot. Edgell's marker is probably where it is because it places it closer to the road leading into the cemetery.

    Crumb, *The Eleventh Corps Artillery*, 83, 84. Report of Capt. William McCartney, 1st Massachusetts Battery. Raus, *The Union Army at Gettysburg*, 48–49.

40. For the monumentation upon the field see Raus, *The Union Army at Gettysburg*, Map II. *OR*, XXVII, pt. 1, 239, 880. Reports of Gen. Henry Hunt and Capt. G. V. Weir.

41. Ladd and Ladd, *The Bachelder Papers*, II, 1153. Letter, Gulian V. Weir, Nov. 25, 1885.

42. *OR*, XXVII, pt. 1, 896, and 899. Reports of Capt. R. H. Fitzhugh and Lt. A. Parsons.

43. Mulholland asserts that the battery fired during the bombardment preceding the charge. In his official report he states that the artillery which remained "almost silent" during the artillery duel, did not fire until the Confederates charged. The infantry dug the works prior to Sterling's arrival on the field.

    OR, XXVII, pt. 1, 898. Report of Lt. E. Dow. Mulholland, *116th Pa.*, 140.

44. The captain's account places him on the field as the Confederate infantry are beginning their charge.

    OR, XXVII, pt. 1, 901. Report of Capt. N. Ames.

45. Christopher Smith, "Bloody Angle," Buffalo *Evening News*, May 29, 1894, 5.

46. He placed the regiment partly behind Cushing's caissons which would have put the regiment on the eastern slope of Cemetery Ridge.

    John Reed, et al., 149. Testimony of Adj. Charles W. West. 72nd Pennsylvania.

47. Ibid., 152. Testimony of Maj. Samuel Roberts, 72nd Pennsylvania.

48. Ibid., 171. Testimony of Brig. Gen. Alexander Webb.

    This is the author's reconstruction of how Webb reacted. Roberts heard Cushing ask for men.

49. According to Fuger, Webb came to Cushing and Cushing asked for permission to move the guns to the wall and to take all of the canister with it. In "Cushing's Battery," Fuger recalled that Webb replied, "Do so." Sixteen years earlier, the sergeant said that he could not recall what Webb said. Webb stated under oath that he did not see Cushing move the guns or go to the guns, which would be consistent with Major Roberts' testimony that he heard Cushing ask for volunteers. Cushing had to have received his second wound on the way to the guns after leaving Webb. Cowan, five years before the trial, wrote to Webb that he "always believed" that Cushing received "another" wound at that point, implying that Cushing had already received his shoulder wound. In his letter to Bachelder, written one month later, Cowan stated that Cushing was bleeding from the legs or thighs and that he received his fatal wound later.

    Frederick Fuger, "Cushing's Battery at Gettysburg," *Journal of Military Service Institution of the United States*, 41:408. Reed, et al., 128–29, 152, 171. Testimony of 1st Sgt. Frederick Fuger, Major Roberts, and Brigadier General Webb. Andrew Cowan to Alexander Webb, Nov. 6, 1885, Alexander Webb Papers, Select List of Correspondents, Historical Manuscripts Division, Yale University Library, New Haven, Conn. Ladd and Ladd, *The Bachelder Papers*, II, 1157. Letter, Andrew Cowan, Dec. 2, 1885.

50. Andrew Cowan, "Cowan's New York Battery: Its Old Captain Tells of Its Glorious Share in Repulsing Pickett's Charge," *The National Tribune*, Nov. 12, 1908, 7. Ladd and Ladd, *The Bachelder Paper*, I, 282. Letter, Andrew Cowan, Aug. 26, 1866.

51. Ibid. Andrew Cowan to Alexander Webb, Nov. 6, 1885, Alexander Webb Papers, Select List of Correspondents, Historical Manuscripts Division, Yale University Library, New Haven, Conn. Undated Remarks by Andrew J. Cowan, The Gettysburg Campaign, The Robert L. Brake Collection, USAMHI. Andrew Cowan, "Cowan's New York Battery: Its Old Captain Tells of Its Glorious Share in Repulsing Pickett's Charge," *The National Tribune*, Nov. 12, 1908, 7. Frederick Fuger, "Cushing's Battery at Gettysburg," *Journal of Military Institution of the United States*, 41:408. Reed, et al., 128–29. Testimony of First Sergeant Frederick Fuger.

52. Benedict when he said that the general's statement "brought every man's arms into his hands, and a many a man's heart into his mouth," undoubtedly was describing his own reaction as well.

    Benedict, *Army Life in Virginia*, 177.

53. Sturtevant, *13th Vermont*, 303.

54. Scott, "Pickett's Charge," *Gettysburg Papers*, II, 906.

55. Ibid.

56. Diary, July 3, 1863, Charles Wesley Belknap 125th New York, Diary, 14, Sept. 1862–21, Oct. 1863, Civil War Miscellaneous Collection, BEE–BER, Manuscripts Division, USAMHI, Carlisle Barracks, Pa., 41.

57. Gallagher, *Fighting for the Confederacy*, 262. Alexander, *Military Memoirs of a Confederate*, 424.

58. *OR*, XXVII, pt. 2, 375, 379, and 384. Reports of Captain McCarthy and Lieutenant Motes. Martin, *Confederate Monuments*, I 68, 69, 112.

59. Dearing said that two of the guns came from Norcom (Battle) of the 4th Company, Washington Artillery and that one each came from Miller's 3rd Co. Washington Artillery and Taylor's Virginia Battery. Lt. C. H. C. Brown, however, clearly stated that his two guns (Miller's) moved into the field on the right of Pickett's column and engaged the Federals. Martin, *Confederate Monuments*, I, 71, 74, and 75. Alexander, *Military Memoirs of A Confederate*, 424. *OR*, XXVII, pt. 2, 389. Report of Major Dearing. Owen, *The Washington Artillery*, 253.

60. B. D. Fry, "Pettigrew's Charge at Gettysburg," SHSP (VII:92–93).

61. Thompson, "Scrap of Gettysburg," *Gettysburg Papers*, II, 962.

62. June Kimble, "Tennesseeans at Gettysburg—the Retreat," CV (XVII: 460–61).

63. Woods said that he called to Denson. I have interpreted that as "yelled." The fact that he "missed" Stant Denson from his side implies that he did not know that Stant had been hit. Wiley Woods, "The First Tennessee Flag at Gettysburg," CV Battles, 1861–1932, n.d., box 1, Special Collections Department, William R. Perkins Library, Duke University, Durham, N.C.

64. Rollins, *Pickett's Charge!*, 254.

65. Scott, "Pickett's Charge," *Gettysburg Papers*, II, 907.

66. Scott said that the left half wheel occurred about one quarter of a mile into the charge which would have placed it in the hollow immediately west of the Bliss orchard. Ibid.

67. Robert A. Bright, "Pickett's Charge at Gettysburg," CV (XXXVIII:264).

68. The 14th Connecticut captured the flag of the 52nd North Carolina. The color bearer of the 26th North Carolina died near the wall in front of Hays' division. The colors of the 11th North Carolina were carried from the field. Only the flag of the 47th North Carolina remained, and Symington took a North Carolina battle flag from Marshall's brigade. It had to have been the 47th North Carolina though he later said it was allegedly the colors of the 11th North Carolina.. *Supplement to the OR*, V, pt. 1, 307. Letter, William S. Symington to James Longstreet, Oct. 26, 1892. Letter, W. Stuart Symington to Charles Pickett, Oct. 17, 1892. The Gettysburg Campaign, The Robert L. Brake Collection, USAMHI, Carlisle Barracks, Pa.

69. Rollins, *Pickett's Charge!*, 254.

70. Lt. Col. J. McLeod Turner , 7th North Carolina, mistakenly said the men which swarmed around his regiment came from Brockenbrough's Virginia Brigade. They did not. The Virginians were much farther to the north and did not flee in a southwesterly direction. Letter, J. McLeod Turner, 7th North Carolina, Oct. 10, 1877, printed in *The Raleigh Observer*, Nov. 30, 1877. For further reference see Michael W. Taylor, "North Carolina in the Pickett-Pettigrew-Trimble Charge at Gettysburg," *Gettysburg Magazine*, Jan. 1, 1993.

71. Letter, William B. Shepard, Sept. 18, 1877, printed in *The Raleigh Observer*, Nov. 30, 1877.

72. Letter, J. McLeod Turner, 7th North Carolina, October 10, 1877, printed in *The Raleigh Observer*, November 30, 1877.

73. This frontage is based upon the number of men present in Garnett's brigade when it went into position before the bombardment began. It is clear from testimony from the 24th

Virginia that the brigade did not flank left until after it cleared the guns on the top of the hill. When it did flank to the left, according to Colonel Mayo's accounts, the 3rd Virginia was on the left of the Codori house on the west side of the Emmitsburg Road directly in front of the orchard. By blending Mayo's account with those of Kemper, Hutter and Bentley, it becomes evident that the brigade cleared the front of the Rogers house, flanked left into the hollow to the north west of the Emmitsburg Road, fronted, then flanked again to connect with Garnett. By the time the 3rd Virginia reached the orchard north of the Codori house, Garnett's front had been cut down to less than one thousand feet. Fronting on the Emmitsburg Road, the two brigades charged southeast toward the Angle.

Joseph C. Mayo, "Pickett's Charge at Gettysburg," SHSP (34:332). Rollins, *Pickett's Charge!*, 134. *Supplement to the OR*, vol. 5, 328, 331. Reports of Lieutenant Colonel Hutter and Captain Bentley.

74. *Supplement to the OR*, vol. 5, pt. 1, 327–28. Postwar address of Lt. Col. James R. Hutter.

75. *Ibid.*, 331. Report of Capt. William W. Bentley. Charles T. Loehr, "The Old First Virginia at Gettysburg," SHSP (XXXII:36).

76. Rollins, *Pickett's Charge*, 164–65, James B. Johnson account.

77. *Supplement to the OR*, vol. 5, pt. 1, 327–28. Postwar address of Lt. Col. James R. Hutter.

78. Joseph C. Mayo, Jr., "Pickett's Charge at Gettysburg," SHSP (XXXIV:331).

79. Page, *14th Conn.*, 152.

80. *Ibid.*, 150–51, 152. Ladd and Ladd, *The Bachelder Papers*, III, 1745. Letter, Samuel B. McIntyre, June 27, 1890.

81. Ladd and Ladd, *The Bachelder Papers*, II, 967. Letter, Samuel Roberts, Aug. 18, 1883.

82. G. W. Finley, "Bloody Angle," Buffalo *Evening News*, May 29, 1894, 5.

83. Owen's account is disjointed and poorly written. He mentions the Federals firing on the column from a stone wall along the Emmitsburg Road after Kemper was hit. Kemper was hit after Garnett's brigade crossed the road, not before. The 71st Pennsylvania opened fire at long range upon the Confederates while their skirmishers pulled back. 1st Lt. George W. Finley, 56th Virginia, seems to indicate that this was the case. It is known that the skirmishers from the 72nd Pennsylvania did throw up a small work. More than likely, Owen is describing the brigade's first contact with these Pennsylvanians.

H. T. Owen, "Pickett at Gettysburg," Philadelphia *Times*, NPS clippings, vol. 6:9. G. W. Finley, "Bloody Angle," Buffalo *Evening News*, May 29, 1894.

84. Adams, *War Papers*, IV, 260–61.

85. Kemper does not mention the Federal skirmishers in his account, but Capt. Robert Stewart (72nd Pennsylvania) testified that his men temporarily stalled the Confederate charge and forced them to form a line of battle with three brigades. The skirmishers would have been on Kemper's flank and had to be neutralized to keep the charge going.

Letter, James L. Kemper to W. H. Swallow, Feb. 4, 1886. GNMP. Ladd and Ladd, *The Bachelder Papers*, II, 967. Letter, Samuel Roberts, Aug. 18, 1883.

86. Joseph C. Mayo, Jr., "Pickett's Charge at Gettysburg," SHSP (XXXIV:331).

87. Joseph C. Mayo, Jr., "Pickett's Charge at Gettysburg," SHSP (XXXIV:331). Letter, Thomas R. Friend to Maj. Charles Pickett, Dec. 10, 1894. Va. Historical Society. ViH MSS 2P5868b3.

88. Joseph C. Mayo, Jr., "Pickett's Charge at Gettysburg," SHSP (XXXIV:331).

89. Letter, Charles Pickett to the editor, *Richmond Times*, Nov. 11, 1894, Virginia Historical Society, Richmond, Va. VIMSS2P5068B2.

90. Mayo mistakenly believed that he saw the North Carolinians retreating from the front, however, since he saw Kemper in front of Armistead's brigade and Pickett and his officers trying to rally men at the same time, they had to have been very close to one another. They were in the last hollow before reaching the Emmitsburg Road, where Bright said they were while he was with Longstreet. With those three premises in mind, Mayo had to have been looking into

the hollow and not on to the higher ground where the North Carolinians were. As an addendum to Mayo's observation, Kemper wrote in 1866, "I never saw any command or any troops on the Confederate side except the three brigades of Kemper's division."

Joseph C. Mayo, Jr., "Pickett's Charge at Gettysburg," SHSP (XXXIV:331). Letter, Thomas R. Friend to Maj. Charles Pickett, Dec. 10, 1894. Va. Historical Society. ViH MSS 2P5868b3. Ladd and Ladd, The Bachelder Papers, II, 1192. Letter, James Kemper.

91. H. T. Owen, "Pickett at Gettysburg," The Philadelphia Times, NPS clippings, vol. 6, 9.

92. While Hunton did not say exactly where the incident occurred, it does not seem logical that the captain would have abandoned his place in line and then ordered forward unless his line had been halted. The Federal skirmishers did halt the line in the last hollow, therefore I put this incident in this location.

Autobiography of Eppa Hunton, 100.

93. H. T. Owen, "Pickett at Gettysburg," The Philadelphia Times, NPS clippings, vol. 6, 9.

94. Wood, Big I, 46.

95. The nominal casualty returns from Marshall's brigade seem to substantiate Trimble's observation. The 11th North Carolina lost 97 officers and men, and the 26th North Carolina lost 104 casualties. The 47th North Carolina suffered 202 casualties, and the 52nd North Carolina accounted for an additional 287 more. Of those, the 11th and the 26th had 133 men wounded and captured, wounded and missing, while the 47th and the 52nd lost 351 effectives to the same causes. It is evident that not very many of the men in the left wing got as far as the Emmitsburg Road.

Supplement to the OR, V, pt. 1, 444. Letter, Isaac R. Trimble to John B. Bachelder. Letter, J. G. Harris, The Raleigh Observer, Nov. 30. 1877. Jordan, North Carolina Troops, V:6–105; VII:463–601; XI:244–363; XII:415–521.

96. Rollins, Pickett's Charge!, 240. William S. Christian's account.

97. Letter, Isaac R. Trimble, The Raleigh Observer, Nov. 30, 1877.

98. Easley did not say exactly where this incident occurred, except that it happened early in the charge. By the time he caught up with the regiment it was at the western face of the Angle where the regiment encountered Co. F, 69th Pennsylvania.

D. B. Easley, "With Armistead When He Was Killed," CV (XX:379).

99. Bright said the stragglers were from Pettigrew's division. To have been among the North Carolinians he would have had to have been on the north side of the fence which separated Pickett from Pettigrew and Trimble. The shortest distance between Pickett and Longstreet was a straight line to the west. Bright would not have gone out of the most direct line of approach to stop men on his flank, particularly when the two other aides were ordered to stop the rout.

Robert A. Bright, "Pickett's Charge at Gettysburg," CV (38:264). Rollins, Pickett's Charge!, 149.

100. W. R. Bond, "Pickett or Pettigrew: It Was Pettigrew's North Carolinians Rather Than Pickett's Virginians Who Bore the Brunt of the Charge at Gettysburg," The National Tribune, Oct. 31, 1901, 2.

101. Reading Fremantle's account aside from any other would lead one to believe that it occurred after the charge had ended. Bright said that the incident happened while he was with Longstreet before Pickett's division had reached the Emmitsburg Road. That being the case, two things had to have happened. First, Longstreet obviously misheard Bright's message and thought that Bright had said that Pickett had already taken the Federal works at the Angle. Second, men had to have been abandoning Pickett's division in large numbers before the line crossed the Emmitsburg Road. The men Fremantle and Longstreet saw coming toward them had to have come from Pickett's three brigades.

102. Robert A. Bright, "Pickett's Charge at Gettysburg," CV (XXXVIII:265). Letter, Robert A. Bright to Charles Pickett, Oct. 15, 1892, Virginia Historical Society, Richmond, Va. ViH MSS 2P5868b1.

103. Letter, Thomas R. Friend to Charles Pickett, Dec. 10, 1894, Virginia Historical Society, Richmond, Va., ViH MSS 2P5868b3.

104. John Cheves Haskell, Memoirs, 1861–1865, Special Collections Library, William R. Perkins Library, Duke University, Durham, N.C., 34–35.

105. Gregg S. Clemmer, *Valor in Gray, The Recipients of the Confederate Medal of Honor* (Staunton, Va.: Hearthside Publishing Co., 1996), 313.

106. Ladd and Ladd, *The Bachelder Papers*, III, 1410. Letter, Anthony W. McDermott, June 2, 1886. Anthony W. McDermott, *A Brief History 69th Regiment Pennsylvania Veteran Volunteers* (Philadelphia), 31.

107. Reed, et al., 259. Testimony of Joseph McKeever, Co. E, 69th Pennsylvania.

108. J. H. Moore, "Heth's Division at Gettysburg," The Southern Bivouac (III:391).

109. Richard Rollins, "Black Confederates at Gettysburg," *Black Southerners in Gray: Essays on Afro-Americans in Confederate Armies*, Richard Rollins (ed.), Journal of Confederate History Series (XI:135, 140). Richard Rollins, *"The Damned Red Flags of the Rebellion"* (Redondo Beach, Calif.: Rank and File Publications, 1997), 180.

110. This is the author's supposition. The right of the 19th Maine's skirmish line would have seen Kemper's approach before the companies in the hollow near Plum Run. Kemper's main line did not record running into any Federal skirmishers, therefore it is safe to assume that they did not run into any near Codori's buildings.

111. Adams, *War Papers*, IV, 260–61.

112. *Supplement to the OR*, V, 429. Postwar account of Capt. Thomas J. Cureton, 26th North Carolina, June 15, 1890.

113. June Kimble, "Tennesseeans at Gettysburg—the Retreat," CV (8:461).

114. J. H. Moore, "Heth's Division at Gettysburg," *The Southern Bivouac* (III:391).

115. Wiley Woods, "The 1st Tennessee Flag at Gettysburg," CV Papers, Battles, 1861–1932, n.d., Box 1, Special Collections Dept., William R. Perkins Library, Duke University, Durham, N.C.

116. Rollins, *Pickett's Charge!*, 254. Andrew J. Baker, "Tribute to Captain Magruder and wife," CV (VI:507).

117. Page, *14th Conn.*, 152.

118. Ladd and Ladd, *The Bachelder Papers*, I, 379. Letter, George G. Meade, Dec. 4, 1869.

119. Ibid., II, 853, 857. Letter, George Meade, May 6, 1882.

Chapter 4

1. When studying the alignment of the fence rows it became evident that Cemetery Hill had become the target of the attack and not the Angle. The Federal soldiers on the northern end of the field remarked how it seemed that the Confederates were heading toward their right flank. When one considers that Fry's brigade was the brigade of direction and that his original path would have taken him east, the only logical reason for swinging to the right (southeast) was that the Emmitsburg Road altered the direction of the brigade.

2. Lochren, "1st Minn.," *Gettysburg Papers*, II, 613.

3. R. M. Eastman, "Cemetery Hill: How the 1st Minnesota Gathered in the Prisoners," *The National Tribune*, Nov. 16, 1905, 3.

4. Letter, H. C. Mitchie to Lieutenant Topscott, Feb. 21, 1904, John W. Daniel Papers, Manuscripts Dept., Alderman Library, University of Va.

5. Capt. H. T. Owen said that the right wing of the regiment got to within 50 yards of the Federal works and that those four companies had turned into a column some 15 to 20 ranks deep. He did not say that the Federals coming in on the right forced the line to conform to that movement. There was no logical reason for the contraction of the line other than the fact that the fence destroyed the formation prior to the advance of the Federals.

Kemper's left passed through the orchard. The distance from Fry's right to the orchard was under 600 feet. I estimated that Garnett's right flank was about halfway across the western face of the orchard. It probably was smaller than that. The 8th Virginia was in the orchard on Kemper's left. Colonel Hunton (8th Virginia) was shot to the left of the barn.

Letter, Eppa Hunton to John W. Daniel, July 15, 1904, Special Collections Dept., William R. Perkins Library, Duke University, Durham, N.C. H. T. Owen, "Pickett at Gettysburg," The Philadelphia *Times*, NPS clippings, vol. 6, 9.

6. Letter, Eppa Hunton to John W. Daniel, July 15, 1904, Special Collections Dept., William R. Perkins Library, Duke University, Durham, N.C.

7. Veterans talked about finding Confederate dead piled up in a ditch along the road. It was quite common back then to put run-off ditches along the upper edge of a swale along a road bed. The eastern side of the road was higher than the ground to the east as opposed to the ground on the western side.

8. Mrs. N. G. Robertson, "In regard to My Father's capture at Gettysburg, he has this to say in his memoirs," Confederate Veteran Papers, Reminiscences, n.d., Box 8, Special Collections Dept., William R. Perkins Library, Duke University, Durham, N.C. J. H. Moore, "Heth's Division at Gettysburg," *The Southern Bivouac* (III: 391). Ladd and Ladd, *The Bachelder Papers*, II, 914. Letter J. H. Moore, Nov. 12, 1884.

9. Rollins, *"The Damned Red Flags of the Rebellion,"* 180.

10. Thaddeus S. Potter, "On Skirmish: Gallant Behavior of the 8th Ohio at Gettysburg," *The National Tribune*, Jan. 24, 1895, 3.

11. Longstreet, *From Manassas to Appomattox*, 393. G. Moxley Sorrel, *Recollections of a Confederate Staff Officer* (Wilmington: Broadfoot Publishing, 1995), 164.

12. Fry left two accounts behind. In *Confederate Veteran* (1910), Fry said that the incident with Garnett occurred just before Garnett was struck down near the stone wall. In SHSP, vol. 7, Fry made no exact mention of where the incident occurred. J. B. Turney in *Confederate Veteran*, vol. 8 (1900) asserted that the incident occurred before the brigade reached the plank fence on the Emmitsburg Road.

    B. D. Fry, "Pettigrew's Charge at Gettysburg," SHSP (VII:93). LeRoy Farrington, "Testimony About Battle of Gettysburg," CV (18:524.)

13. Lochren, "1st Minn.," *Gettysburg Papers*, II, 613.

14. Moore mistakenly said that a battery enfiladed the regiment from the right as it advanced from the Emmitsburg Road to the lane, fifty yards from Hays' line. There was no battery on the regiment's right which could have done that. He had to have meant the fire came in from the left which would have been from Woodruff's guns at Ziegler's Grove. He said that the battery had not been in action during the charge. Woodruff's guns could not fire during the charge because they had only canister left and therefore had to wait until the Confederates came within range.

    J. H. Moore, "Heth's Division at Gettysburg," *The Southern Bivouac* (III:392).

15. B. D. Fry, "Pettigrew's Charge at Gettysburg," SHSP (VII 93).

16. J. B. Turney, "The First Tennessee at Gettysburg," CV (VIII:536).

17. Wiley Woods, "The 1st Tennessee Flag at Gettysburg," *Confederate Veteran* Papers, Battles, 1861–1932, n.d., Box 1, Special Collections Dept., William R. Perkins Library, Duke University, Durham, N.C.

18. Scott, "Pickett's Charge," *Gettysburg Papers*, II, 909.

19. *Voices of the Civil War—Gettysburg* (Time-Life Books: Alexandria), 121.

20. Adams, *War Papers*, IV, 260–61.

21. Ladd and Ladd, *The Bachelder Papers*, I, 169 and 171. Letters, Charles A. Phillips. One is undated and the other is dated July 6, 1863.

22. John H. Smith, "Captain John Holmes Smith's Account," SHSP (XXXII:193).

23. Ibid. (32:191 and 194).

24. Joseph C. Mayo, "Pickett's Charge at Gettysburg," SHSP (XXXIV:332).

25. Charles T. Loehr, "The 'Old First' Virginia at Gettysburg," SHSP (XXXII:35).

26. Owen, *The Washington Artillery*, 253–54. *OR*, XXVII, pt. 1, 888. Report of Patrick Hart.

27. Clemmer, *Valor in Gray*, 308–9, 313. John Cheves Haskell, Memoirs, 1861–1865, Special Collections Library, William R. Perkins Library, Duke University, Durham, N.C., 34. *OR* XXVII, pt. 1, 885, 888. Reports of Charles A. Phillips and Patrick Hart.

28. John Cheves Haskell Memoirs, 1861–1865, Special Collections Library, William R. Perkins Library, Duke University, Durham, N.C., 34–35.

29. Thomas Moon, "The Heroic Cushing: A Plain Old Veteran's Story of the Fight at Gettysburg," *The National Tribune*, Dec. 3, 1908, 7. Rody Landregan, "Battery A, 4th U.S.—Its Savage Work on Pickett's Column," *The National Tribune*, Sept. 2, 1909, 7. Christopher Smith, "Bloody Angle," Buffalo *Evening News*, May 29, 1894, 5. Frederick Fuger to William H. Morgan, "Lieut. Cushing at Gettysburg: The Heroic Fight of His Battery Against Pickett's Charge," *The National Tribune*, Jan. 28, 1909, 7. Frederick Fuger, "Cushing's Battery at Gettysburg," *Journal of Military Service Institution of the United States*, 41:408.

30. Ladd and Ladd, *The Bachelder Papers*, III, 1410. Letter, Anthony W. McDermott, June 2, 1886.

31. Moon said that Cushing was hit beneath the nose. Fuger in both of his accounts said that Cushing was shot in the mouth. In his letter to Morgan, Fuger added the story of dropping his pistol to catch the lieutenant. Smith recorded that Cushing was looking through his glasses when he was hit.

    Thomas Moon, "The Heroic Cushing: A Plain Old Veteran's Story of the Fight at Gettysburg," *The National Tribune*, Dec. 3, 1908, 7. Rody Landregan, "Battery A, 4th U.S.—Its Savage Work on Pickett's Column," *The National Tribune*, Sept. 2, 1909, 7. Christopher Smith, "Bloody Angle," Buffalo *Evening News*, May 29, 1894, 5. Frederick Fuger to William H. Morgan, "Lieut. Cushing at Gettysburg: The Heroic Fight of His Battery Against Pickett's Charge," *The National Tribune*, Jan. 28, 1909, 7. Frederick Fuger, "Cushing's Battery at Gettysburg," *Journal of Military Service Institution of the United States*, 41: 408.

32. Ladd and Ladd, *The Bachelder Papers*, III, 1410. Letter, Anthony W. McDermott, June 2, 1886.

33. Christopher Smith, "Bloody Angle," Buffalo *Evening News*, May 29, 1894, 5. Frederick Fuger to William H. Morgan, "Lieut. Cushing at Gettysburg: The Heroic Fight of His Battery Against Pickett's Charge," *The National Tribune*, Jan. 28, 1909, 7.

34. Rody Landregan, "Battery A, 4th U.S.—Its Savage Work on Pickett's Column," *The National Tribune*, Sept. 2, 1909, 7.

35. Norton L. Newberry, "Cushing's Battery," *The National Tribune*, March 23, 1911, 3.

36. Rody Landregan, "Battery A, 4th U.S.—Its Savage Work on Pickett's Column," *The National Tribune*, Sept. 2, 1909, 7.

37. At first, I did not believe that Smith accurately reported the wounding of Lieutenant Canby because the traditional histories have him being wounded on July 2. However, Heitman cites Canby as being promoted to captain for bravery and meritorious service at Gettysburg on July 3, which would imply that he had to have been present on that day. Capt. George Meade, aide to George G. Meade (general commanding) said that after the action he was ordered to round up men by General Webb to assist a sergeant and several artillerymen man a couple of their guns which were on a slight elevation among some boulders. Webb said that all of the battery's officers had been killed or wounded and did not want the battery to be totally silent. At that point an artillery officer with his head bandaged and his arm in a sling said that it was his battery and he would take over for young Meade. Cushing's battery was on an elevation among some large outcroppings (boulders), and every officer had been hit. Only Sergeant Fuger and a few of the enlisted men remained. The officer who was hit in the head and in the arm (as described by Smith) had to have been Canby. He apparently returned to the battery after the fighting was dying down and resumed command, for which he was later promoted to captain.

Christopher Smith, "Bloody Angle," Buffalo *Evening News*, May 29, 1894, 5. Francis B. Heitman, *Historical Register and Dictionary of the United States Army*, I (Washington, D.C.: Government Printing Office, 1903), 279–80. Ladd and Ladd, *The Bachelder Papers*, II, 856. Letter, George Meade, May 6, 1882.

38. Christopher Smith, "Bloody Angle," Buffalo *Evening News*, May 29, 1894, 5. Rhodes, *History of Battery B*, 214. *OR*, XXVII, pt. 1, 480. Report of Capt. John G. Hazard, C.O., Artillery Brigade, II Corps. S. Bessette, "Memorial Day 1989," *Cannon Fodder, Battery B Newsletter*, July–August 1989, vol. 2, no. 2.

39. For Webb to have said that to Fuger, Fuger would have had to have followed Smith and Wright back to the limbers. Smith said that they placed Cushing behind some rocks. Those rocks are in a depression immediately east of Cushing's marker.
    Christopher Smith, "Bloody Angle," Buffalo *Evening News*, May 29, 1894, 5.

40. N. F. Newberry, "Cushing's Battery," *The National Tribune*, March 23, 1911, 3.

41. Landregan was on gun Number Four with Simon Malinger, James Murphy, William Patton, Patrick Mullen, and Edward McConnell. According to St. Clair Mulholland they were on the third gun (Four was the third from the left of the battery) when Cushing was killed. He also erroneously said that Malinger took Cushing's body to the rear. Malinger was killed at the wall. Landregan said that his Numbers One and Two were killed. Patton and Malinger were the only enlisted men killed after Murphy died. The other two fatalities occurred on July 2. They had to have been on Number Four Gun. Armistead's marker is near the spot occupied by the third gun. To see what he recorded, Smith had to have been on Number Five. Number Six apparently did not go to the wall. Number One was rolled down on the right by the 71st Pennsylvania. Sgt. Maj. William Stockton, 71st Pennsylvania saw another gun run down to the wall next to the one his men had rolled down. That must have been Number Two gun.
    Ibid.; Rody Landregan, "Battery A, 4th U.S.—Its Savage Work on Pickett's Column," *The National Tribune*, Sept. 2, 1909, 7;
    Christopher Smith, "Bloody Angle," Buffalo *Evening News*, May 29, 1894, 5; Mulholland, *116th Pa.*, 148–49. Reed, et al., 243. Testimony of SGM William S. Stockton, 71st Pennsylvania.

42. Rody Landregan, "Battery A, 4th U.S.—Its Savage Work on Pickett's Column," *The National Tribune*, Sept. 2, 1909, 7.

43. Reed, et al., Testimony of Pvt. Anthony W. McDermott, Co. I, 69th Pennsylvania, 220.

44. Ibid., 243. Testimony of SGM William S. Stockton, 71st Pennsylvania.

45. The sergeant did not identify the guns by the number. They had to have been guns One, Two, Four, and Five. Christopher Smith was on Number Five, Rody Landregan, on Number Four, and Stockton on Number One. The Crew of Number Two remains anonymous. Pvt. Anthony W. McDermott, Co. I, 69th Pennsylvania, said that Cushing had four guns at the Angle as did an enlisted man in the 14th Virginia.
    Reed, et al., 243. Testimony of SGM William S. Stockton, 71st Pennsylvania. Ladd and Ladd, *The Bachelder Papers*, III, 1411. Letter, Anthony W. McDermott, June 2, 1866.

46. Cabell mistakenly said his men got within thirty paces of the Federal line, yet he could not refuse his left wing because the regiment was trapped between the fence rows of the lane. He could not have gotten past the Emmitsburg Road, which would explain how the regimental colors were picked up by the 8th Ohio to his left rear.
    Supplement to the OR, V, pt. 1, 333. Report of Maj. Joseph R. Cabell. Reed, et al., 243. Testimony of William S. Stockton, 71st Pennsylvania.

47. According to a great deal of testimony, the field was blanketed with the heavy yellowish white sulfuric smoke of artillery fire. The 71st Pennsylvania did fire the guns at the Confederates, but more than likely it was not at Garnett's brigade. Cushing was killed during the left oblique as Garnett crossed the road. There would not have been enough time for the infantry to have rolled the guns down to the wall, load and fire them to catch Garnett as he crossed. They had to have fired at Armistead's line.

The reading tends to lead one to believe that the Number One gun was rolled down as the charge began, but that was not likely. Cushing was alive when the charge began. He was alive when the first two oblique rounds were fired at Kemper. He was low on crew members and apparently did not get them from the 71st until after he was dead. Therefore he had only four serviceable guns when Kemper started the oblique. He and his officers would never have allowed enlisted men to roll two unmanned pieces to the wall ahead of the other four guns. Therefore the Numbers One and Two guns had to have been rolled down after he and his officers were disabled and the command structure of the battery literally fell apart.

Col. Robert P. Smith of the 71st Pennsylvania named fourteen volunteers who assisted Cushing. Ironically that is enough men to man two guns. The artillerymen are careful to mention the names of the men who assisted them. None of them were the Pennsylvanians. The colonel further stated that the gun did not go down to the wall until the Confederates began their oblique movement.

Reed, et al., 243. Testimony of SGM William S. Stockton. The Philadelphia *Weekly Press* as cited in the *Gettysburg Compiler*, June 7, 1887. Account of Robert Penn Smith.

48. Benedict, *Army Life in Virginia*, 177.

49. Sturtevant, *13th Vermont*, 317.

50. Adams, *War Papers*, IV, 260–61.

51. H. T. Owen, "Pickett at Gettysburg," *The Philadelphia Times*, NPS clippings, vol. 6, 9. *Supplement to the OR*, V, pt. 1, 312. Letter, Edmund Berkeley to John W. Daniel , Sept. 26, n.d.

52. On the afternoon of July 2, the 15th Massachusetts had taken position in the hollow where Colonel Ward's monument now stands, facing west toward the Emmitsburg Road. They were in front of Brown's Rhode Island Battery. The 82nd New York was to their left. They built a breastwork of rails behind the fence (referring to the eastern fence of the orchard) and were attacked there. The rails for the breastwork were used to reinforce the fence already there. Those rails came from the fence to their right—the one which divided Garnett's command on the day. It is only logical that they tore out the fence section(s) to their immediate right so their line could form facing west. Smith did not see a lot of the fence because it was brush-covered. He talks about trees and brush obscuring his vision.

OR, XXVII, pt. 1, 423. Report of Lt. Col. George C. Joslin, 15th Massachusetts.

53. Letter, Henry T, Owen to H. A. Carrington, Jan. 27, 1878, as cited in Rollins, *Pickett's Charge*, 161–62.

54. Ladd and Ladd, *The Bachelder Papers*, I, 55, Diary, July 2, 1863, George J. Stannard.

55. Benedict, *Army Life in Virginia*, 177.

56. Sturtevant, *13th Vermont*, 303.

57. Ibid., 178. Ladd and Ladd, *The Bachelder Papers*, I, 55–56, Diary, July 3, 1863, George J. Stannard.

58. The account from Joseph Mayo indicates that the regiment was mingled with Garnett's line, in particular with the 18th Virginia. The 8th Virginia was bent back on itself, at first not because of the Vermonters, but because the fence on their right flank was forcing them to double back upon themselves. It seems that the 3rd, 7th, and 1st Virginia cleared the fence and that the 11th and the 24th were forced to refuse their line to meet the Vermonters' attack. The fence on the northern side of Codori's would have been a natural source of cover. The Confederates were moving at a left oblique also, which would indicate that they were behind Garnett at least a short distance.

59. In his account, Hutter referred to himself in the quote as colonel. He was a captain at the time. I changed the quote to agree with his correct rank. J. Risque Hutter, "Ninth Virginia, Kemper's Brigade," The Richmond *Times*, Sept. 10, 1905, John W. Daniel Papers, Box 28, Newspaper Clippings, Accession #158, Folder (1905 Aug. 20–Nov. 12), Manuscripts Dept., Alderman Library, University of Va.

60. Joseph C. Mayo, "Pickett's Charge at Gettysburg," SHSP (XXXIV:333).

61. Charles T. Loehr, "The 'Old First' Virginia at Gettysburg," SHSP (XXXII:35).

62. Dooley, *John Dooley, Confederate Soldier,* 106.

63. Charles T. Loehr, "The 'Old First' Virginia at Gettysburg," SHSP (XXXII:35).

64. Interestingly enough, Frank Haskell claims to have delivered the message to Hall. He also claimed to be the officer who forced the 72nd Pennsylvania back into line during the height of Armistead's advance into the Angle.

   Gibbon, *Recollections,* 152. Ladd and Ladd, *The Bachelder Papers,* I, 260, 263. Letter, John Gibbon, June 17, 1866 and letter, Edward Moale, June 25, 1866. Haskell, *Gettysburg,* 103–4, 108.

65. Benedict, *Army Life in Virginia,* 178. Ladd and Ladd, *The Bachelder Papers,* I, 55–56, Diary, July 3, 1863, George J. Stannard.

66. Sturtevant, *13th Vermont,* 304–5.

67. Contrary to the traditional images of the 13th and the 16th Vermont's' flanking movement which shows them going into action perpendicular to Kemper, Veazey argued that had the 13th right wheeled into line immediately, it would have walked into the right oblique fire of the 14th Vermont. In addition, the 13th would not have been facing any Confederates because their left flank would have been facing along the front of the Confederate line. He insisted that the two regiments attacked on an oblique line. The regimental historian of the 13th Vermont, Ralph Orson Sturtevant, stated that the 16th Vermont did not come up on the left flank of the 13th Vermont until the charge was about over because it took some time to get the regiment formed and moved off the ridge.

   Sturtevant, *13th Vermont,* 303–10. Ladd and Ladd, *The Bachelder Papers,* I, 60 and 61, Letter, Wheelock Veazey (undated). Benedict, *Army Life in Virginia,* 178.

68. Ladd and Ladd, *The Bachelder Papers,* I, 95–96, Letter, George G. Benedict, March 16, 1864.

69. Cook, "Personal Reminiscences," *Gettysburg Papers,* II, 928–29.

70. Ibid., 929.

71. Gallagher, *Fighting for the Confederacy,* 263–64.

72. Scott, "Pickett's Charge," *Gettysburg Papers,* II, 907–8. Thompson, "Scrap of Gettysburg," *Gettysburg Papers,* II, 963.

73. Rollins, *Pickett's Charge,* 254.

74. Baxter McFarland, "The Eleventh Mississippi Regiment at Gettysburg," *Publications of the Mississippi Historical Society* (II:551–52).

75. Scott, "Pickett's Charge," *Gettysburg Papers,* II, 909.

76. Tully McCrae, "Reminiscences About Gettysburg," March 30, 1904, 6. Manuscript, Private Collection of George Staley Smith, Sacketts Harbor, N.Y.

77. Tradition places Egan's section on the northern side of the Brian farm lane. However, Egan said he was "...a little to the right and front [rear] of Cushing's Battery and about fifteen or twenty yards in rear of the stone wall where Genl Hays Division of the 2nd Corps was posted." If he was behind Hays' line, he had to have been northeast of and not northwest of Cushing's original position. He would have been firing canister at the Confederates as they crossed the Emmitsburg Road while Hays' men were lying down to receive the charge.

   Letter, Egan to George Meade, Feb. 8, 1870. Peter F. Rothermal Papers, Pennsylvania Historical and Museum Commission, Harrisburg, Pa. Ladd and Ladd, *The Bachelder Papers,* III, 1977, 1980.

78. Joseph C. Mayo, "Pickett's Charge at Gettysburg," SHSP (XXXIV:332.)

79. James F. Crocker, "Gettysburg—Pickett's Charge," SHSP (XXXIII:132–33). James T. Carter, "Flag of the Fifty-Third Va. Regiment," CV (X:263).

80. Joseph C. Mayo, "Pickett's Charge at Gettysburg," SHSP (XXXIV:332).
81. John H. Smith, "Captain John Holmes Smith's Account," SHSP (XXXII:191).
82. G. W. Finley, "Bloody Angle," Buffalo Evening News, May 29, 1894, 5.
83. Wood, Big I, 46.
84. J. B. Turney, "The First Tennessee at Gettysburg," CV (VIII:536).
85. Reed, et al., 243. Testimony of SGM William Stockton, 71st Pennsylvania.
86. J. B. Turney, "The First Tennessee at Gettysburg," CV (VIII:536). J. H. Moore, "Heth's Division at Gettysburg," The Southern Bivouac (III:391).
87. Wiley Woods, "The 1st Tennessee Flag at Gettysburg," Confederate Veteran Papers, Battles, 1861–1932, n.d., Box 1, Special Collections Dept., William R. Perkins Library, Duke University, Durham, N.C.
88. J. B. Turney, "The First Tennessee at Gettysburg," CV (VIII:536). J. H. Moore, "Heth's Division at Gettysburg," The Southern Bivouac (III:391).
89. Reed, et al., 247. Testimony of SGM William Stockton, 71st Pennsylvania.
90. G. W. Finley, "Bloody Angle," Buffalo Evening News, May 29, 1894, 5. Diary, July 3, William J. Burns, Co. G, 71st Pennsylvania., "Civil War Diary, Sept. 27, 1861–Dec. 31, 1863, "Save the Flag Collection," USAMHI, Carlisle Barracks, Pa.
91. G. W. Finley, "Bloody Angle," Buffalo Evening News, May 29, 1894, 5.
92. A rock ledge parallels the western face of the Federal position toward the southern end of the Federal line. Garnett's men, to fire effectively, had to file to the left to see the troops around the copse of trees.
   Ladd and Ladd, The Bachelder Papers, III, 1403, 1410–11. Letters, John Buckley, n.d. and Anthony W. McDermott, June 2, 1886. Rody Landregan, "Battery A, 4th U.S.—Its Savage Work on Pickett's Column," The National Tribune, Sept. 2, 1909, 7. Dooley, John Dooley, 106.
93. Supplement to the OR, V, pt. 1, 312. Letter, Edmund Berkeley to John W. Daniel, Sept. 26, n.d.
94. Ladd and Ladd, The Bachelder Papers, III, 1403, 1410–11. Letters, John Buckley, n.d. and Anthony W. McDermott, June 2, 1886. Rody Landregan, "Battery A, 4th U.S.—Its Savage Work on Pickett's Column," The National Tribune, Sept. 2, 1909, 7. Dooley, John Dooley, 106.
95. Dooley, John Dooley, 107. "Recollections of Some of the Incidents of the Battle of Gettysburg, PA, July 3, 1863," Robert B. Damron, John W. Daniel Papers, Box 23, #158 5383 A–E, Folder Civil War Material: Gettysburg, 3 July 1863 (Pickett's Charge), 1903–05, n.d., Manuscripts Dept., Alderman Library, University of Va.
96. Wood, Big I, 46–47.
97. Supplement to the OR, V, pt. 1, 312–13. Letter, Edmund Berkeley to John W. Daniel, September 26, n.d.
98. The evidence tends to indicate that Armistead placed his hat on his sword during the last advance prior to volleying at the Federals before he stormed the wall. Kemper rode up to him as he crossed the Emmitsburg Road which is why Kemper's brigade temporarily stopped in front of Stannard's Vermonters. That would have placed Armistead's brigade in the hollow about 200 yards from Cowan, as Cowan stated. At 75 yards, Kemper rode back a second time and told him to come up because Kemper's brigade was getting used up. At 60 feet, he mixed with what was left of Garnett's brigade to volley, then charged.
   R. W. Martin, "Armistead at the Battle of Gettysburg," SHSP (XXXIX:186).
99. Ladd and Ladd, The Bachelder Papers, II, 1192. Letter, James L. Kemper. Ibid., III, 1415. Letter, Anthony W. McDermott, June 2, 1886.
100. John H. Smith, "Captain John Holmes Smith's Account," SHSP (XXXII:191). Report of Joseph Mayo, Jr., The Robert L. Brake Collection, The Gettysburg Campaign, USAMHI, Carlisle Barracks, Pa.

101. Joseph C. Mayo, "Pickett's Charge at Gettysburg," SHSP (XXXIV:333).

102. J. Risque Hutter, "Ninth Virginia, Kemper's Brigade," The Richmond Times, Sept. 10, 1905, John W. Daniel Papers, Box 28, Newspaper Clippings, Accession #158, Folder (1905 Aug. 20–Nov. 12), Manuscripts Dept., Alderman Library, University of Va.

103. Rody Landregan said that three Confederates broke into his crew and caused the casualties as stated here. Lt. G. W. Finley of the 56th Virginia wrote that his men broke over the wall at the same time as Archer's men and that Armistead's charge came afterward. Capt. J. B. Turney, 1st Tennessee, talks about the regiment crossing the wall there. Once ahead of the Virginians, then with Garnett's Virginians, and then when Armistead made his charge. Wiley Woods, 1st Tennessee, said that the 1st Tennessee went over the wall twice, once with Armistead, once with Turney. He apparently reversed the order of the attack. Nevertheless, enough evidence exists to show that Confederates broke the wall prior to Armistead's advance. This makes sense.

The guns were silent at the Angle on the north side. The 71st Pennsylvania had fled or surrendered. It makes sense.

Rody Landregan, "Battery A, 4th U.S.—Its Savage Work on Pickett's Column," The National Tribune, Sept. 2, 1909, 7. For the names of the two fatalities see Brown, Cushing of Gettysburg, 265–66. G. W. Finley, "Bloody Angle," Buffalo Evening News, May 29, 1894, 5. J. B. Turney, "The First Tennessee at Gettysburg," CV (VIII:536). Wiley Woods, "Gettysburg: The 1st Tennessee Flag at Gettysburg," Confederate Veteran Papers, Battles, 1861–1932, n.d., Box 1, Special Collections Dept., William R. Perkins Library, Duke University, Durham, N.C.

104. M. F. Newberry, "Cushing's Battery," The National Tribune, March 23, 1911, 3. Reed, et al., 220. Testimony Anthony McDermott, Co. I, 69th Pennsylvania.

105. Landregan's account in The National Tribune is somewhat suspect when it comes to the following paraphrase of his account of the fighting. Webb snatched him by the collar, stopping him cold. He needed more men for the guns, Landregan insisted. "No," Webb shouted, "you are wounded. Go behind the line." Landregan managed a salute. "General," he insisted, "I belong to that battery. I go back there." The general released his grip. Landregan turned toward the wall, saw the Rebs getting too close, and decided it was time to get some medical attention.

Too many infantrymen saw a justifiably frightened artilleryman struggle with the general to keep going to the rear to believe Landregan's quotes, in this instance, to be very reliable. Rody Landregan, "Battery A, 4th U.S.—Its Savage Work on Pickett's Column," The National Tribune, Sept. 2, 1909, 7.

106. Reed. et al., 63, 110. Testimony of William H. Porter, Co. E, Elwood N. Hamilton, Co. B, 72nd Pennsylvania.

107. While neither Buckley nor McDermott said they fired away all of their spare weapons at this time, it is implied because McDermott said that Armistead immediately charged after the 71st Pennsylvania broke. Garnett's brigade no longer existed as an intact unit because it had been shot up before Armistead arrived on the field.
Ladd and Ladd, The Bachelder Papers, III, 1403, 1410–11.

108. Letter, Webb to P. F. Rothermal, Jan., n.d. (Peter F. Rothermal Papers, Pa. Historical and Museum Commission, Harrisburg, Pa.), Box 4, Northern Commanders and Staff Officers, Brake Collection, USAMHI, Carlisle Barracks, Pa.

109. Ladd and Ladd, The Bachelder Papers, III, 1411–12, 1414, 1468–69. Letters, Anthony W. McDermott, June 2, 1886, and January 27, 1887. McDermott, 69th Pennsylvania, 31.

110. Turney confused Moore with another company of the 7th Tennessee. It is evident, however, that small groups of men from Fry's various regiments did cross the north wall of the Angle.
J. H. Moore, "Heroism in the Battle of Gettysburg," CV (IX:15–16). J. B. Turney, "The First Tennessee at Gettysburg," CV (VIII:536).

111. Reed, et al., 244. Testimony of SGM William Stockton, 71st Pennsylvania.

112. G. W. Finley, "Bloody Angle," Buffalo *Evening News*, May 29, 1894, 5.

113. J. B. Turney, "The First Tennessee at Gettysburg," CV (VIII:536).

114. Robert B. Damron, John W. Daniel Papers, Box 23, #158 5383 A–E, Folder Civil War Material: Gettysburg, 3 July 1863 (Pickett's Charge), 1903–05, n.d., Manuscripts Dept., Alderman Library, University of Va.

115. J. B. Turney, "The First Tennessee at Gettysburg," CV (VIII:536).

116. Robert B. Damron, John W. Daniel Papers, Box 23, #158 5383 A–E, Folder Civil War Material: Gettysburg, 3 July 1863 (Pickett's Charge), 1903–05, n.d., Manuscripts Dept., Alderman Library, University of Va.

117. Reed, et al., 274. Testimony of Charles H. Banes.

118. Ibid., 55–56, 75, 78, 79, 86. Testimony of Thomas Read, Co. F, and Charles B. Vessels, Co. H, Frederick Mannes, Co. B, 72nd Pennsylvania.

119. M. F. Newberry, "Cushing's Battery," *The National Tribune*, March 23, 1911, 3. Christopher Smith, Buffalo *Evening News*, May 29, 1894, 6.

120. G. W. Finley, "Bloody Angle," Buffalo *Evening News*, May 29, 1894, 5.

121. James W. Clay, "About the Death of General Garnett," CV (XIV:81).

122. Polak would have never asked such an obvious question had he seen Patton with his jaw shot away. He might not have seen a chest wound, however. Patton had to have been shot in the lung, then in the face.

      Charles T. Loehr, "The 'Old First' Virginia at Gettysburg, SHSP (XXXII:35). Harrison and Busey, *Nothing But Glory*, 207.

123. J. R. McPherson, "A Private's Account of Gettysburg," CV (VI:149).

124. Letter, H. C. Mitchie to Lieutenant Topscott, Feb. 21, 1904, John W. Daniel Papers, Manuscripts Dept., Alderman Library, University of Va.

125. Rollins, *"The Damned Red Flags of the Rebellion,"* 170.

126. Page, *14th Conn.*, 155.

127. Letter, A. S. Van de Graaf to his wife, July 8, 1863, Patricia Hanson Collection, GNBP.

128. Mrs. N. G. Robertson, "In regard to My Father's capture at Gettysburg, he has this to say in his memoirs," *Confederate Veteran* Papers, Reminiscences, n.d., Box 8, Special Collections Dept., William R. Perkins Library, Duke University, Durham, N.C.

129. F. S. Harris, "From Gettysburg," *Lebanon Democrat*, Aug. 10, 1899.

130. William F. Fulton, II, *Family Record and War Reminiscences*, s.n., n.d., 103. Confederate Muster Roll Collection, 5th Alabama Infantry Battalion, Box 52, Folder 1-1-1-4, Alabama State Archives, Montgomery, Ala.

131. Kimble said in a later writing that he ran from the Federal works to the slab fence which meant that he had gotten inside the Federal works.

      June Kimble, "W. H. McCulloch," Manuscript Dept., Eleanor S. Brockenbrough Library, Museum of the Confederacy, Richmond, Va.

132. June Kimble, "Capt. James W. Lockhardt," Manuscript Dept., Eleanor S. Brockenbrough Library, Museum of the Confederacy, Richmond, Va. Page, *14th Conn.*, 154, 155–56.

133. Scott, "Pickett's Charge," *Gettysburg Papers*, II, 909.

134. Thompson, "Scrap of Gettysburg," *Gettysburg Papers*, II, 963.

135. The regiment had 135 officers and men wounded and captured and wounded. According to Davis' testimony, none of the regiment got away from the board fence close to the stone wall. They were all captured there. The estimate of 150 men on the line includes all of the wounded and captured and the captured.

      S. A. Ashe, "North Carolinians at Gettysburg: A Critical Review of the Famous Confederate Charge on July 3, 1863," *The National Tribune*, Oct. 3, 1901, 3. Jordan, *N.C. Troops*, XI:244–363. Letter, Joseph J. Davis, Sept. 20, 1877, *The Raleigh Observer*, Nov. 30, 1877.

136. Lt. John H. Moore (Co. B, 7th Tennessee) and Maj. A. S. Van de Graaf of the 5th Alabama Battalion clearly state that there was a farm lane beyond the Emmitsburg Road. Seville, *First Regiment, Delaware Vols.*, 81–82. J. H. Moore, "Heth's Division at Gettysburg," *The Southern Bivouac* (III:392). Letter, A. S. Van de Graaf to his wife, July 8, 1863. Patricia Hanson Collection, GBNP.

137. Seville, *First Regiment, Delaware Vols.*, 81–82.

138. S. A. Ashe, "North Carolinians at Gettysburg: A Critical Review of the Famous Confederate Charge On July 3, 1863," *The National Tribune*, Oct. 3, 1901, 3.

139. Letter, B. F. Little, Sept. 20, 1877, in *The Raleigh Observer*, Nov. 30, 1877.

140. Letter, Albert S. Haynes, Oct. 8, 1877, as printed in *The Raleigh Observer*, Nov. 30, 1877.

141. R. M. Tuttle, "An Unparalleled Loss: A Whole North Carolina Company Destroyed at Gettysburg," *The National Tribune*, July 2, 1903, 6.

142. W. R. Bond, "Pickett or Pettigrew: It Was Pettigrew's North Carolinians Rather Than Pickett's Virginians Who Bore the Brunt of the Charge at Gettysburg," *The National Tribune*, Oct. 31, 1901, 2.

143. Seville, *First Regiment, Delaware Vols.*, 81–82.

144. R. M. Tuttle, "An Unparalleled Loss: A Whole North Carolina Company Destroyed at Gettysburg," *The National Tribune*, July 2, 1903, 6.

145. Letter, B. F. Little, Sept. 20, 1877, in *The Raleigh Observer*, Nov. 30, 1877.

146. Seville, *First Regiment, Delaware Vols.*, 81–82.

147. Ibid., 83.

148. Ladd and Ladd, *The Bachelder Papers*, III, 1398. Letter, John L. Brady, May 24, 1886.

149. Scott, "Pickett's Charge," *Gettysburg Papers*, II, 910.

150. Thompson, "Scrap of Gettysburg," *Gettysburg Papers*, II, 964. Page, *14th Conn.*, 151–52. The account from the 14th Connecticut confirms what Thompson observed.

151. Thompson, "Scrap of Gettysburg," *Gettysburg Papers*, II, 964. Page, *14th Conn.*, 151–52.

152. Ladd and Ladd, *The Bachelder Papers*, II, 967. Letter, Samuel Roberts, Aug. 18, 1883.

153. Rollins, *Pickett's Charge!*, 254–55.

154. Ladd and Ladd, *The Bachelder Papers*, II, 1199. Letter, Isaac R. Trimble, Feb. 8, 1886.

155. The article by S. A. Ashe misstated the location of the 33rd North Carolina. The 37th not the 33rd split to the right and the left. The 33rd was on the extreme left of the line. S. A. Ashe, "North Carolinians at Gettysburg: A Critical Review of the Famous Confederate Charge on July 3, 1863," *The National Tribune*, Sept. 26, 1901, 3. Ibid., Oct. 3, 1901, 3.

156. Ladd and Ladd, *The Bachelder Papers*, II, 1199. Letter, Isaac R. Trimble, Feb. 8, 1886.

157. According to Mr. Bacarella, the Garibaldi Guard lost 95 men to combat—30% of its strength. The regiment lost an additional 64 men—20%—to desertion, which tends to support Charles Richardson's assertion that the Guard did not perform very well upon the field at Gettysburg. Michael Bacarella, *Lincoln's Foreign Legion: The 39th New York Infantry, The Garibaldi Guard* (Shippensburg, Pa.: White Mane, 1996), 140, 210 and 219. Ladd and Ladd, *The Bachelder Papers*, I, 343. Letter, Charles A. Richardson to Bachelder, May 14, 1868. Raus, *The Union Army at Gettysburg*, 58.

158. The 28th North Carolina lost its colors to the 126th New York. It had to have been in the field east of the Emmitsburg Road.

159. Letter, from McLeod Turner, Oct. 10, 1877, in *The Raleigh Observer*, Nov. 30, 1877.

160. Letter, H. C. Moore, Nov. 6, 1877, *The Raleigh Observer*, Nov. 30, 1877. Petersburg, Va., *Enterprise*, March 3, 1894, George S. Bernard Diary-Scrapbook, 1861–1911, Special Collections Dept., William R. Perkins Library, Duke University, Durham, N.C.

161. Letter, from McLeod Turner, Oct. 10, 1877, in *The Raleigh Observer*, Nov. 30, 1877.

162. Letter, H. C. Moore, Nov. 6, 1877, *The Raleigh Observer*, Nov. 30, 1877.

163. Letter, from McLeod Turner, Oct. 10, 1877, in *The Raleigh Observer*, Nov. 30, 1877.

164. Both of those flags were captured at the wall or very close to it. The troops who captured the 38th North Carolina at the wall were from the 14th Connecticut. Adjutant Moore said the 38th was captured in front of an abandoned battery—Cushing's.
Letter, H. C. Moore, Nov. 6, 1877, *The Raleigh Observer*, Nov. 30, 1877.

165. *Supplement to the OR*, V, pt. 1, 336. Postwar account of John C. Timberlake.

166. Letter, Thomas L. Norwood, Oct. 6, 1877, as printed in *The Raleigh Observer*, Nov. 30, 1877.

167. Letter, from McLeod Turner, Oct. 10, 1877, in *The Raleigh Observer*, Nov. 30, 1877.

168. Ladd and Ladd, *The Bachelder Papers*, II, 964. Letter, Emerson L. Bicknell, Aug. 6, 1883.

169. Ibid., 1199. Letter, Isaac R. Trimble, Feb. 8, 1886.

170. Ibid., 1001, 1019. Letters, Samuel C. Armstrong, Feb. 6, 1884, and Feb. 13, 1884.

171. Letter, Joseph H. Saunders, Sept. 22, 1877, as printed in *The Raleigh Observer*, Nov. 30, 1877.

172. Ladd and Ladd, *The Bachelder Papers*, III, 1399. Letter, John L. Brady, May 24, 1886.

173. Ibid., II, 964. Letter, Emerson L. Bicknell, Aug. 6, 1883; I, 316. Letter, Charles A. Richardson, Aug. 18, 1867.

174. Letter, James Lane, Sept. 7, 1877, *The Raleigh Observer*, Nov. 30, 1877. Sorrel, *Recollections*, 164.

175. Letter, Joseph H. Saunders, Sept. 22, 1877, as printed in *The Raleigh Observer*, Nov. 30, 1877. Michael W. Taylor, "North Carolina in the Pickett-Pettigrew-Trimble Charge at Gettysburg," *Gettysburg Magazine*, Jan. 1, 1993, 76, fn. 14.

176. Letter, J. Jones, July 30, 1863, *The Raleigh Observer*, Nov. 30, 1877.

177. Ladd and Ladd, *The Bachelder Papers*, II, 964. Letter, Emerson L. Bicknell, Aug. 6, 1883; I, 316. Letter, Charles A. Richardson, Aug. 18, 1867.

178. Rollins, *Pickett's Charge!*, 255.

179. Thompson, "Scrap of Gettysburg," *Gettysburg Papers*, II, 964. Page, *14th Conn.*, 156.

180. Thompson, "Scrap of Gettysburg," *Gettysburg Papers*, II, 964. Page, *14th Conn.*, 156.

181. Ladd and Ladd, *The Bachelder Papers*, I, 316–17. Latter, Charles A. Richardson, Aug. 18, 1867. For the identification of the flag see Editors of Time-Life Books, *Echoes of Glory: Arms and Equipment of the Confederacy* (Alexandria: Time-Life Books), 252.

182. Rollins, *Pickett's Charge!*, 255.

183. I changed the verb tense in Marshall's second quote to make it correct with the way he should have said it at the time.
Robert A. Bright, "Pickett's Charge at Gettysburg," CV (38:265).

184. William Thomas Poague, *Gunner with Stonewall* (Wilmington: Broadfoot Publishing Co., 1989), 74–77.

185. Ladd and Ladd, *The Bachelder Papers*, II, 853–54. Letter, George Meade, May 6, 1882.

186. Sorrel, *Recollections*, 164.

187. Andrew Cowan, "Cowan's New York Battery: Its Old Captain Tells of Its Glorious Share in Repulsing Pickett's Charge," *The National Tribune*, Nov. 12, 1908, 7. James F. Crocker, "Gettysburg—Pickett's Charge," SHSP (XXXIII:132–33). James T. Carter, "Flag of the Fifty-Third Va. Regiment," CV (X:263).

188. James T. Carter, "Flag of the Fifty-Third Va. Regiment," CV (X:263).

189. Ladd and Ladd, *The Bachelder Papers*, III, 1411–12, 1414, 1468–69. Letters, Anthony W. McDermott, June 2, 1886, and Jan. 27, 1887. McDermott, *69th Pennsylvania*, 31. Lewis,

Recollections From 1860–1865, 84. J. Irving Sale, "Pickett's Charge," *The Philadelphia Press*, July 4, 1887, 1.

190. Letter, F. M. Bailey, undated, J. W. Daniel Collection, Manuscripts Dept., Alderman Library, University of Va.

191. James T. Carter, "Flag of the Fifty-Third Va. Regiment," CV (X:263).

192. J. Irving Sale, "Pickett's Charge," The Philadelphia Press, July 4, 1887, 1.

193. James T. Carter, "Flag of the Fifty-Third Va. Regiment," CV (X:263).

194. Easley erroneously said there were brass pieces at the wall. Cushing's guns were 3" ordnance rifles.
      D. B. Easley, "With Armistead When He Was Killed," CV (XX:379). *Supplement to the OR*, V, pt. 1, 335. Postwar account of John C. Timberlake.

195. Erasmus Williams, "A Private's Experience in Gettysburg," J. W. Daniel Papers, Manuscripts Dept., Alderman Library, University of Va.

196. *Supplement to the OR*, V, pt. 1, 336. Postwar account of John C. Timberlake.

197. Calvin P. Dearing, "Experiences of a Virginia Private," CV (XXI:592).

198. Letter, H. C. Mitchie to Lieutenant Topscott, February 21, 1904, John W. Daniel Papers, Manuscripts Dept., Alderman Library, University of Va.

199. Ladd and Ladd, *The Bachelder Papers*, III, 1411–12, 1414, 1468–69. Letters, Anthony W. McDermott, June 2, 1886 and January 27, 1887. McDermott, *69th Pennsylvania*, 31. James F. Crocker, "Gettysburg—Pickett's Charge," SHSP (XXXIII:132).

200. Erasmus Williams, "A Private's Experience in Gettysburg," J. W. Daniel Papers, Manuscripts Dept., Alderman Library, University of Va.

201. Ladd and Ladd, *The Bachelder Papers*, III, 1411–12, 1414, 1468–69. Letters, Anthony W. McDermott, June 2, 1886, and Jan. 27, 1887. McDermott, *69th Pennsylvania*, 31. James F. Crocker, "Gettysburg—Pickett's Charge," SHSP (XXXIII:132).

202. Reed, et al., 99. Testimony of Henry Russell, Co. A, 72nd Pennnsylvania.

203. Ladd and Ladd, *The Bachelder Papers*, III, 1629. Letter, Anthony W. McDermott, Sept. 17, 1889.

204. Ibid., 1412. Letter, Anthony W. McDermott, June 2, 1886. McDermott, *69th Pennsylvania*, 31–32.

205. Ladd and Ladd, Ibid., 1403. Letter, John Buckley, n.d.

206. Reed, et al., 81. Testimony of Robert T. Whittick, Co. E, 69th Pennsylvania.

207. Andrew Cowan, "Reminiscences of Gettysburg," *The National Tribune*, Oct. 28, 1915, 3.

208. Ladd and Ladd, *The Bachelder Papers*, I, 282–83, and 441. Letters, Andrew Cowan, Aug. 26, 1866, and Henry Hunt. Ibid., II, 1155. Letter, Andrew Cowan, Dec. 2, 1885.

209. Andrew Cowan, "Cowan's New York Battery: Its Old Captain Tells of Its Glorious Share in Repulsing Pickett's Charge," *The National Tribune*, Nov.12, 1908, 7.

210. *OR*, XXVII, pt. 1, 448. Report of Maj. S. W. Curtis, 7th Michigan.

211. Ladd and Ladd, *The Bachelder Papers*, I, 282–83, and 441. Letters, Andrew Cowan, Aug. 26, 1866, and Henry Hunt. Ibid., II, 1155. Letter, Andrew Cowan, Dec. 2, 1885. Andrew Cowan, "Reminiscences of Gettysburg," *The National Tribune*, Oct. 28, 1915, 3. H. T. Owen, "Pickett at Gettysburg," The Philadelphia *Times*, NPS clippings, vol. 6, 9.

212. Sturtevant, *13th Vermont*, 309.

213. Andrew Cowan, "Cowan's New York Battery: Its Old Captain Tells of Its Glorious Share in Repulsing Pickett's Charge," *The National Tribune*, Nov. 12, 1908, 7.

214. Gibbon, *Recollections*, 152–53. Ladd and Ladd, *The Bachelder Papers*, I, 263. Letter, Edward Moale, June 25, 1866. Raus, *The Union Army at Gettysburg*, Map II.

215. Letter, W. Raymond Lee to Alexander Webb, April 22 (no year), Alexander Stewart Webb Papers, Select List of Correspondence, Historical Manuscripts Div., Yale University Library, New Haven, Conn., in the Gettysburg Campaign, Robert L. Brake Collection,

USAMHI, Carlisle Barracks, Pa. Ladd and Ladd, *The Bachelder Papers*, I, 249, 252–53. Letters, George N. Macy, May 10, 1866, May 12, 1866.

216. This is the author's conjecture. Only one flag was captured by an officer on that end of the line. Lieutenant Hunt claimed the flag of the 18th Virginia. Private Deming was the only enlisted man in that area who claimed his flag was taken by a mounted officer, which he thought was a colonel. Every Confederate battle flag captured in the southern end of the field can be accounted for. It is only logical to assume that Hunt, who apparently broke with his small regiment, was the mounted officer who took the flag from Deming.

OR, XXVII, pt. 1, 441, and 448. Reports of Col. Norman J. Hall, and Maj. S. W. Curtis, 7th Michigan.

217. Ladd and Ladd, *The Bachelder Papers*, I, 393. Letter, A. C. Plaisted, June 11, 1870.

218. Gibbon never learned the identity of the regiment. The 143rd Pennsylvania occupied the short earthwork formerly used by the 13th Vermont.

Gibbon, *Recollections*, 152–53. Ladd and Ladd, *The Bachelder Papers*, I, 263. Letter, Edward Moale, June 25, 1866. Raus, *The Union Army at Gettysburg*, Map II.

219. M. F. Newberry, "Cushing's Battery," *The National Tribune*, March 23, 1911, 3.

220. Williams, in his recollections, erroneously referred to Martin as major. I have corrected the error.

Erasmus Williams, "A Private's Experience in Gettysburg," J. W. Daniel Papers, Manuscripts Dept., Alderman Library, University of Va.

221. Wiley Woods, "The 1st Tennessee Flag at Gettysburg," *Confederate Veteran* Papers, Battles, 1861–1932, n.d., Box 1, Special Collections Dept., William R. Perkins Library, Duke University, Durham, N.C.

222. D. B. Easley, "With Armistead When He Was Killed," CV (XX:379).

223. Turney said that he saw the general grasp his left arm as he dropped his sword, which would agree with McDermott's account. When hit, the left arm contracted across the stomach under the impact. Armistead dropped his sword and instinctively grabbed his left arm. Turney said that he caught and supported Armistead which could have happened so quickly in the confusion that other witnesses did not see it or remember it. Turney's recollection that Armistead's men carried him behind the wall is not substantiated, however. Therefore I have gone with the more traditional accounts of him being found by the gun. The doctor who worked on Armistead said that he was hit in the arm and the leg on opposite sides but did not remember which arm or leg it was, though he thought it was the left leg and the right arm. The descriptions of Armistead's fall in the Angle indicate the opposite to be true.

J. B. Turney, "The 1st Tennessee at Gettysburg," CV (VIII:536). Ladd and Ladd, *The Bachelder Papers*, III, 1413. Letter, Anthony W. McDermott, June 2, 1886. Milton Harding, "Where General Armistead Fell," CV (XIX:371).

224. June Kimble, "An Incident at Gettysburg," Manuscripts Dept., Eleanor S. Brockenbrough Library, Museum of the Confederacy, Richmond, Va.

225. G. W. Finley, "The Angle," Buffalo *Evening News*, May 29, 1894, 5.

226. *Supplement to the OR*, V, pt. 1, 313. Letter, Edmund Berkeley to John W. Daniel, Sept. 26, n.d.

227. Thompson, "Scrap of Gettysburg," *Gettysburg Papers*, II, 964. Page, *14th Conn.*, 153, 154, 155–56.

228. Milton Harding, "Where General Armistead Fell," CV (XIX:371).

229. D. B. Easley, "With Armistead When He Was Killed," CV (XX:379). Milton Harding, "Where General Armistead Fell," CV (XIX:371).

230. M. F. Newbury, "Cushing's Battery," *The National Tribune*, March 23, 1911, 3.

231. Reed, et al., 244. Testimony of SGM William Stockton, 71st Pennsylvania.

232. *Supplement to the OR*, V, pt. 1, 336. Postwar account of John C. Timberlake.

233. Ladd and Ladd, *The Bachelder Papers*, III, 1413. Letter, Anthony W. McDermott, June 2, 1886.
234. Letter, M. A. Cogbill to Charles Pickett, Sept. 28, 1894, Virginia Historical Society, Richmond, Va., VIAMSS2P5868b3.
235. Erasmus Williams, "A Private's Experience in Gettysburg," J. W. Daniel Papers, Manuscripts Dept., Alderman Library, University of Va. *Supplement to the OR*, V, pt. 1, 336. Postwar account of John C. Timberlake.
236. Rollins, *Pickett's Charge!*, 178. Account of D. B. Easley.
237. Robert A. Bright, "Pickett's Charge at Gettysburg," CV (XXXVIII:265–66).
238. J. B. Turney, "The 1st Tennessee at Gettysburg," CV (VIII:536).
239. June Kimble, "An Incident at Gettysburg," Manuscript Dept., Eleanor S. Brockenbrough Library, Museum of the Confederacy, Richmond, Va.
240. G. W. Finley, "The Angle," Buffalo *Evening News*, May 29, 1894, 5.
241. Charles T. Loehr, "The 'Old First' Virginia at Gettysburg, SHSP (XXXII:35–36).
242. Parmelee did not say exactly where they were when he was almost hit. He did note that they were crossing a run-down stone fence when it occurred. Hancock was riding to the left, apparently, to bolster the line.
    Letter Uriah N. Parmelee to his mother, July 13, 1863, and Uriah N. Parmelee to his father, July 5, 1863, S.S. and U.N. Parmelee, 1845–1863, Special Collections Library, Duke University, Durham, N.C.
243. *19th Mass.*, 242–43.
244. Ibid., 239–41.
245. Lochren, "1st Minn.," *Gettysburg Papers*, II, 613–14. Hazzard, *1st Minnesota*, 368, 370 and 378. St. Paul *Daily Press*, July 25, 1863, Box 10, Minn. to N.Y., Brake Collection, USAMHI, Carlisle Barracks, Pa.
246. R. M. Eastman, "Cemetery Hill, How the 1st Minn. Gathered in the Prisoners," *The National Tribune*, Nov. 16, 1905, 3. William Harmon, "Company C at Gettysburg," *The Minnesota Journal*, June 30, 1897, 7. Box, 10 Minn. to N.Y., Brake Collection, USAMHI, Carlisle Barracks. Pa.
247. Cook, "Personal Reminiscences," *Gettysburg Papers*, II, 929.
248. Ibid.
249. Benedict, *Army Life in Virginia*, 177–78.
250. Ladd and Ladd, *The Bachelder Papers*, III, 1413. Letter, Anthony W. McDermott, June 2, 1886. Letter, Alexander Webb to his father, July 17, 1863, The Robert L. Brake Collection, The Gettysburg Campaign, USAMHI, Carlisle Barracks, Pa.
251. Reed. et al., 34–37. Testimony of William H. Good, Pvt., Co. K, 72nd Pennsylvania.
252. Ibid., 63–64, 86–87, 99. Testimony of William H. Porter, Co. E, Frederick Mannes, Co. B, Henry Russell, Co. A, 72nd Pennsylvania.
253. Reed, et al., 137, 151. Testimony of James Wilson, Co. F, Samuel Roberts, Major, 72nd Pennsylvania.
254. Ladd and Ladd, *The Bachelder Papers*, III, 1609–10. Letter, Arthur F. Devereaux, July 22, 1889. Letter, Arthur Devereaux, May 1, 1875. Manuscript, NA. *19th Mass.*, 241.
255. Rollins, *Pickett's Charge!*, 178. Account of D. B. Easley.
256. Lewis, *Recollections of 1860–1865*, 86.
257. J. R. McPherson, "A Private's Account of Gettysburg" (VI:149).
258. Sherman's own account of how he took the flag is somewhat suspect. According to Bond, the Rebels were crossing the wall around him and Sherman took the flag. Sherman said he was barefoot and threadbare which does not correlate with other accounts which clearly state that his Co. C were the best dressed in the regiment because they were the provost guard.

Rollins, *"The Damned Red Flags of the Rebellion,"* 170–73. Rollins, *Pickett's Charge!,* 220. Account of Daniel Bond.

259. Reed, et al., 125, 127, 138. Testimony of Robert McBride, Co. F, James Wilson, Co. F, 72nd Pennsylvania.

260. There is some confusion in relating this account. Falls is cited in the *OR*s as being in Co. A and in the regimental history as being in Co. F. He apparently started out in Co. A and later transferred to Co. F.

19th Mass., 242, and 246. *OR*, XXVII, pt. 1, 444. Report of Col. Arthur Devereaux.

261. James T. Carter, "The Flag of the Fifty-Third Va. Regiment," CV (X:263). *19th Mass.,* 246.

262. *19th Mass.,* 246.

263. J. Irving Sale, "Pickett's Charge," The Philadelphia Press, July 4, 1887, 1.

264. *Supplement to the OR*, V, pt. 1, 336–37. Postwar account of John C. Timberlake.

265. G. W. Finley, "Bloody Angle," The Buffalo *Evening News*, May 29, 1894, 5.

266. *Supplement to the OR*, V, pt. 1, 337. Postwar account of John C. Timberlake.

267. Reed. et al., 36–37, 149. Testimony of William H. Good, Pvt., Co. K, Samuel Roberts, Major. 72nd Pennsylvania.

268. Ibid. 55–56, 99–100, 108. Testimony of Thomas Read, Co. F, Henry Russell, Co. A, Elwood N. Hamilton, Co. B, 72nd Pennsylvania.

269. J. B. Turney, "The 1st Tennessee at Gettysburg–The Retreat," CV (VIII:536).

270. Wiley Woods, "The First Tennessee Flag at Gettysburg," *Confederate Veteran* Papers, Battles, 1861–1932, n.d. Box 1, Special Collections Dept., William R. Perkins Library, Duke University, Durham, N.C.

271. J. H. Moore, "Heth's Division at Gettysburg," *The Southern Bivouac* (III:392).

272. June Kimble, "An Incident at Gettysburg," Manuscripts Dept., Eleanor S. Brockenbrough Library, Museum of the Confederacy, Richmond, Va. June Kimble, "Tennesseans at Gettysburg The Retreat," CV (XVIII:461).

273. Letter, A. S. Van de Graaf, Letter to his wife, July 8, 1863, Patricia Hanson Collection.

274. Joseph C. Mayo, "Pickett's Charge at Gettysburg," SHSP (XXXIV:334).

275. Smith did not see a lot of the fence because it was brush-covered. He talks about trees and brush obscuring his vision.

John H. Smith, "Captain John Holmes Smith's Account," SHSP (XXXII:192 and 194).

276. *Supplement to the OR*, V, pt. 1, 314. Letter, Edmund Berkeley to John W. Daniel, Sept. 26, n.d.

277. Ladd and Ladd, *The Bachelder Papers,* II, 1199. Letter, Isaac R. Trimble, Feb. 8, 1886.

278. J. H. Moore, "Heth's Division at Gettysburg," *The Southern Bivouac* (IIII:392). F. S. Harris, "From Gettysburg," *Lebanon Democrat*, Aug. 10, 1899.

279. Letter, from McLeod Turner, Oct. 10, 1877, in *The Raleigh Observer*, Nov. 30, 1877.

280. A. Wright, "The 2nd U.S. Sharpshooters: The Regiment That Took Part in Repelling Pickett's Charge," *The National Tribune*, Feb. 18, 1909, 7.

281. Letter, Thomas L. Norwood, Oct. 6, 1877, as printed in *The Raleigh Observer*, Nov. 30, 1877. Michael W. Taylor, "North Carolina in the Pickett-Pettigrew-Trimble Charge at Gettysburg," *Gettysburg Magazine*, Jan. 1, 1993, 92.

282. Letter, W. B. Shepard, Sept. 18, 1877, *The Raleigh Observer*, Nov. 30, 1877.

283. Letter, J. Jones, July 30, 1863, *The Raleigh Observer*, Nov. 30, 1877.

284. Ladd and Ladd, *The Bachelder Papers,* III, 1526. Letter, H. Judson, Oct. 17, 1887.

285. Ibid., II, 1133. Letter, Franklin Sawyer, Oct. 20, 1885. Thaddeus S. Potter, "On Skirmish: Gallant Behavior of the 8th Ohio at Gettysburg," *The National Tribune*, Jan. 24, 1895, 3.

286. *OR*, XXVII, pt. 1, 462. Report of Col. Franklin Sawyer, 8th Ohio.

287. Rollins, *Pickett's Charge!,* 240. Report of William S. Christian.

288. Egan did not identify what troops followed Hays. He merely said they were to the right front. They had to have been from the 111th New York.

   Letter, Egan to George Meade, Feb. 8, 1870. Peter F. Rothermal Collection, Pennsylvania Historical and Museum Commission, Harrisburg, Pa.

289. Rollins, *"The Damned Red Flags of the Rebellion,"* 193.

290. Letter, Egan to George Meade, Feb. 8, 1870. Peter F. Rothermal Papers, Pennsylvania Historical and Museum Commission, Harrisburg, Pa.

291. Scott, "Pickett's Charge," *Gettysburg Papers*, II, 910.

292. Letter, Egan to George Meade, Feb. 8, 1870. Peter F. Rothermal Papers, Pennsylvania Historical and Museum Commission, Harrisburg, Pa.

293. Ladd and Ladd, *The Bachelder Papers*, II, 854. Letter, George Meade, May 6, 1882.

Chapter 5

1. Ladd and Ladd, *The Bachelder Papers*, III, 1399. Letter, John L. Brady, May 24, 1886.

2. In a phone discussion with Howard M. Madaus I learned that Brady probably took the colors of the 5th Alabama Battalion. The colors showed evidence of being pulled from under a heavy weight and they were bloodstained.

   Ibid. Letter, John L. Brady, May 24, 1886. See Rollins, *"The Damned Red Flags of the Rebellion."*

3. Seville, *First Regiment, Delaware Vols.*, 83.

4. Letter, H. Moore, Nov. 6, 1877, *The Raleigh Observer*, Nov. 30, 1877. Page, *14th Conn.*, 156, 166.

5. Seville, *First Regiment, Delaware Vols.*, 83.

6. A. Wright, "The 2nd U.S. Sharpshooters: The Regiment That Took Part in Repelling Pickett's Charge," *The National Tribune*, Feb. 18, 1909, 7.

7. Page, *14th Conn.*, 165–66.

8. Mrs. N. G. Robertson, "In regard to My Father's capture at Gettysburg, he has this to say in his memoirs," *Confederate Veteran* Papers, Reminiscences, n.d., Box 8, Special Collections Dept., William R. Perkins Library, Duke University, Durham, N.C. Page, *14th Conn.*, 158.

9. Ladd and Ladd, *The Bachelder Papers*, II, 964. Letter, Emerson L. Bicknell, Aug. 6, 1883.

10. Seville, *First Regiment, Delaware Vols.*, 89.

11. The only Confederate major recorded as killed in action in Pettigrew's division was Richardson. According to Weymouth T. Jordan, Richardson was killed instantly by rifle fire while leading the left wing of Marshall's brigade.

   Thompson, "Scrap of Gettysburg," *Gettysburg Papers*, II, 966–67. Jordan, *North Carolina Troops*, XII, 415. F. Ray Sibley, Jr., *The Confederate Order of Battle: The Army of Northern Virginia*, I (Shippensburg, Pa.: White Mane, 1996), 52.

12. Letter, Thomas L. Norwood, Oct. 6, 1877, *The Raleigh Observer*, Nov. 30, 1877.

13. The lieutenant colonel had to have been George. The other lieutenant colonel which the regiment captured was Lt. Col. Marcus A. Parks (52nd North Carolina) who was wounded and probably did not come in under his own power.

   Page, *14th Conn.*, 156, 165. Sibley, *Confederate Order of Battle*, I. 52.

14. "Bloody Angle," The Buffalo *Evening News*, May 29, 1894, 6.

15. Ladd and Ladd, *The Bachelder Papers*, III, 1496. Letter, John C. Brown to Bachelder, July 1, 1887.

16. Reed, et al., 275. Testimony of Charles H. Banes.

17. I inserted the line where Bingham identified himself in quotes because it read in the letter as a quote. I did not capitalize the word "staff" which Bingham capitalized in his letter. Bingham did not say what ornaments on the uniform he recognized as those of a general

officer, but more than likely it was Armistead's braid on his sleeves. He was being taken off in a blanket. He would have likely held his wounded arm across his chest or stomach to try and alleviate some of the pressure on the wound. Hunched up in a blanket, it would have been very difficult to have seen his collar insignia.

Ladd and Ladd, *The Bachelder Papers*, I, 351–52. Letter, Henry H. Bingham, Jan. 5, 1869.

18. Ibid., 358. Letter, Daniel G. Brinton, March 22, 1869.

19. Ibid., 282–83. Letter, Andrew Cowan, Aug. 26, 1866, 282–83.

20. Andrew Cowan, "Cowan's New York Battery: Its Old Captain Tells of Its Glorious Share in Repulsing Pickett's Charge," *The National Tribune*, Nov. 12, 1908, 7.

21. Andrew Cowan, "When Cowan's Battery Withstood Pickett's Splendid Charge," *New York Herald*, July 2, 1911.

22. Cook, "Personal Reminiscences," *Gettysburg Papers*, II, 930.

23. Miller was the only staff officer other than Armistead who was wounded and captured in Pickett's division.

Cook, "Personal Reminiscences," *Gettysburg Papers*, II, 930–31. Harrison and Busey, *Nothing But Glory*, 256.

24. Ladd and Ladd, *The Bachelder Papers*, I, 393. Letter, A. C. Plaisted, June 11, 1870.

25. Johnston, *The Story of a Confederate Boy*, 215.

26. It is the author's supposition that McHugh and Carey took the two Virginia flags from the 19th Maine. The Mainers would have reached the Confederate lines ahead of the 82nd New York, which was deployed farther south in the Federal line. Again, every flag from Garnett's, Armistead's, and Kemper's brigade can be accounted for as captures by specific regiments. Three flags were reported stolen from three Federal enlisted men—one by an officer and two by enlisted men. The only flags it could have been were those of the 1st, 7th, and the 18th Virginia.

OR, XXVII, pt. 1, 422 and 426. Reports of Col. F. E. Heath, 19th Maine, and Capt. John Darrow, 82nd New York. Richard Rollins, *"The Damned Red Flags of the Rebellion"*, 158. This is a tremendous source for any Gettysburg student.

27. Reed, et al., 308. Testimony of James C. Lynch, Co. B, 106th Pennsylvania. Cook, "Personal Reminiscences," Gettysburg Papers, II, 930.

28. John H. Smith, "Captain John Holmes Smith's Account," SHSP (XXXII:193).

29. Joseph C. Mayo, "Pickett's Charge at Gettysburg," SHSP (XXXIV:333–35).

30. John H. Smith, "Captain John Holmes Smith's Account," SHSP (XXXII:193–94).

31. R. M. Eastman, "Cemetery Hill: How the 1st Minn. Gathered in the Prisoners," *The National Tribune*, Nov. 16, 1905, 3.

32. William Harmon, "Company C at Gettysburg," *The Minnesota Journal*, June 30, 1897, 7. Box, 10 Minn. to N.Y., Brake Collection, USAMHI, Carlisle Barracks. Pa.

33. R. M. Eastman, "Cemetery Hill: How the 1st Minn. Gathered in the Prisoners," *The National Tribune*, Nov. 16, 1905, 3. Benjamin T. Arrington, *The Medal of Honor at Gettysburg* (Gettysburg: Thomas Publications, 1996), 38.

34. Letter, from McLeod Turner, Oct. 10, 1877, in *The Raleigh Observer*, Nov. 30, 1877.

35. Letter, D. F. Kinney, Oct. 23, 1877, *The Raleigh Observer*, Nov. 30, 1877.

36. *Supplement to the OR*, V, pt. 1, 333. Report of Major Joseph R. Cabell.

37. Letter, from McLeod Turner, Oct. 10, 1877, in *The Raleigh Observer*, Nov. 30, 1877.

38. Frank E. Moran, "A Fire Zouave: Memoirs of a Member of the Excelsior Brigade," *The National Tribune*, Nov. 13, 1890, 3.

39. Rollins, *Pickett's Charge*, 164–65. Account of James B. Johnson.

40. There was no third flag captured by the 16th Vermont. Benedict clearly describes the colors of the 8th Virginia as those thrown down by the color bearer. It is apparent that two men went after the same flag and only one brought it off.

Rollins, *The Damned Red Flags of the Rebellion*, 178. Benedict, *Army Life in Virginia*, 179.

41. Cook, "Personal Reminiscences," *Gettysburg Papers*, II, 929–30.
42. J. Risque Hutter, "Ninth Virginia, Kemper's Brigade," The Richmond *Times*, Sept. 10, 1905. John W. Daniel Papers, Box, 28, Newspaper Clippings, Accession #158, Folder (1905 Aug. 20–Nov. 12), Manuscripts Dept., Alderman Library, University of Va.
43. F. S. Harris, "From Gettysburg," *Lebanon Democrat*, Aug. 10, 1899.
44. J. H. Moore, "Heth's Division at Gettysburg," *The Southern Bivouac* (III: 392–93).
45. F. S. Harris, "From Gettysburg," *Lebanon Democrat*, Aug. 10, 1899.
46. June Kimble, "Tennesseeans at Gettysburg," CV (XVIII:461).
47. J. H. Moore, "Heth's Division at Gettysburg," *The Southern Bivouac* (III:392–93). Poague, *Gunner with Stonewall*, 76.
48. Longstreet, *From Manassas to Appomattox*, 395.
49. *OR*, XXVII, pt. 2, 620. Report of Cadmus Wilcox.
50. Letter, Sept. 4, 1863, found in Diary, Raymond J. Reid, Raymond J. Reid Papers, St. Augustine Historical Society.
51. George Clark, "Wilcox's Alabama Brigade at Gettysburg," CV (XVII:230).
52. Gallagher, *Fighting for the Confederacy*, 264.
53. Andrew Cowan, "Cowan's New York Battery: Its Old Captain Tells of Its Glorious Share in Repulsing Pickett's Charge," *The National Tribune*, Nov. 12, 1908, 7.
54. *OR*, XXVII, pt. 2, 620. Report of Cadmus Wilcox.
55. Benedict, *Army Life in Virginia*, 182–84.
56. Ibid..
57. Ladd and Ladd, *The Bachelder Papers*, I, 351. Letter, Henry H. Bingham, Jan. 5, 1869.
58. *OR*, XXVII, pt. 2, 620. Report of Cadmus Wilcox.
59. "The Wentworth Diary," *The United Daughters of the Confederacy Magazine* (January 1990), 22.
60. Rollins, *Pickett's Charge*, 164–65. Account of James B. Johnson.
61. Benedict, *Army Life in Virginia*, 179. Ladd and Ladd, *The Bachelder Papers*, I, 56–57, 60–62, Diary, July 3, 1863, George J. Stannard, Letter, Wheelock Veazey (undated). OR, XXVII, pt. 2, 632. Report of Col. David Lang. Rollins, "*The Damned Red Flags of the Rebellion*," 178.
62. Rollins, *Pickett's Charge*, 164–65. Account of James B. Johnson.
63. Ibid.
64. It appears that the Kemper incident happened twice, perhaps an hour apart. Bright and Alexander are both very accurate sources. The incident did probably occur twice. It would be quite easy to see Lee, while trying to piece his divisions together, to have inquired about any wounded officer being drawn to the rear.
Gallagher, *Fighting for the Confederacy*, 265–66.
65. Longstreet, *From Manassas to Appomattox*, 395.
66. Benedict, *Army Life in Virginia*, 184. Hazzard, *1st Minnesota*, 365. Ladd and Ladd, *The Bachelder Papers*, III, 1363. Report of Lt. Col. Charles H. Morgan.
67. Ladd and Ladd, *The Bachelder Papers*, I, 231. Letter, William G. Mitchell, Jan. 10, 1866.
68. When Benedict first wrote of being sent to take care of brigade duties he did not mention the 14th Vermont. He did cite the regiment later on in relation to Stannard's wounding. Benedict, *Army Life in Virginia*, 185 and 188. Ladd and Ladd, *The Bachelder Papers*, I, 56. Diary, July 3, 1863, George J. Stannard.
69. Ladd and Ladd, *The Bachelder Papers*, II, 768. Letter, Homer R. Stoughton to Bachelder, Dec. 29, 1881.

70. Benedict, *Army Life in Virginia*, 180–81.

71. Ibid., 187–88, 189.

72. Ibid., 185.

73. Reed, et al., 87. Testimony of Frederick Mannes, Co. B, Longstreet, *From Manassas to Appomattox*, 395.

    72nd Pennsylvania.

74. Wiley Woods, "The 1st Tennessee Flag at Gettysburg," *Confederate Veteran* Papers, Battles, 1861–1932, n. d., Box 1, Special Collections Dept., William R. Perkins Library, Duke University, Durham, N.C.

75. Ladd and Ladd, *The Bachelder Papers*, II, 854–55. Letter, George Meade, May 6, 1882.

76. Haskell said that Meade and his son both cheered upon hearing that the battle had ended. No other reliable accounts, including that of Capt. George Meade, mention this event.

    Haskell, *Gettysburg*, 118–19.

77. Cook, "Personal Reminiscences," *Gettysburg Papers*, II, 930–31. Harrison and Busey, *Nothing But Glory*, 256.

78. Ladd and Ladd, *The Bachelder Papers*, I, 231, 321. Letters, William G. Mitchell, Jan. 10, 1866, and James Mead, Jan. 24, 1868.

79. Ibid., II, 855. Letter, George Meade, May 6, 1882.

80. Haskell, *Gettysburg*, 119.

81. Reed, et al., 187. Testimony of Colonel Arthur Devereaux, 19th Massachusetts.

82. Gregg S. Clemmer, *Valor in Gray*, 313. John Cheves Haskell, Memoirs, 1861–1865, Special Collections Library, William R. Perkins Library, Duke University, Durham, N.C., 34. *OR*, XXVII, pt. 2, 379 and 384. Reports of E. S. McCarthy and C. W. Motes.

83. Benedict, *Army Life in Virginia*, 179–80. Sturtevant, *13th Vermont*, 314.

84. Ibid.

85. Ladd and Ladd, *The Bachelder Papers*, II, 1151. Letter, Abner Doubleday, Nov. 25, 1885.

86. Sgt. Frederick Fuger and a few other men remained on active duty with Cushing's battery. The only surviving officer in the battery was Samuel Canby.

    Ladd and Ladd, *The Bachelder Papers*, II, 855–56. Letter, George Meade, May 6, 1882.

87. Ladd and Ladd, *The Bachelder Papers*, I, 445. Letter, Charles H. Tompkins, May 24, 1875.

88. *OR*, XXVII, pt. 1, 893. Report of Capt. Frederick M. Edgell.

89. Ladd and Ladd, *The Bachelder Papers*, III, 1628. Letter, Anthony W. McDermott, Sept. 17, 1889.

90. Reed, et al., 235. Testimony of Anthony McDermott, Co. I, 69th Pennsylvania. Richard Rollins, ed., *Returned Battle Flags* (Redondo Beach, Calif.: Rank and File Publications, 1995), 7. Ladd and Ladd, *The Bachelder Papers*, III, 1656. Letter, Anthony W. McDermott, Oct. 21, 1889.

91. D. S. Koons, "The 8th Ohio at Gettysburg: The Brigade Presented Arms to Them After Their Great Achievement," *The National Tribune*, Nov. 5, 1908, 7.

92. J. Risque Hutter, "Ninth Virginia, Kemper's Brigade," The Richmond *Times*, Sept. 10, 1905. John W. Daniel Papers, Box, 28, Newspaper Clippings, Accession #158, Folder (1905 Aug. 20–Nov. 12), Manuscripts Dept., Alderman Library, University of Va.

93. Harrison and Busey place the ambulance incident on Pitzer's Lane and seem to indicate that Lee encountered Kemper before he went to the aid station. The only logical place for an ambulance which would be on a lane in direct line of fire from Federal batteries was Spangler's lane. That would have placed the ambulance very close to Co. H, 14th Virginia's left flank, south of Spangler's Woods. It also makes sense that Kemper would not have assumed his wound was mortal until after surgeons had checked it at an aid station, Kemper was carried on a blanket to the field hospital. From there they would have transported him on a stretcher where he would have had an opportunity to meet Lee.

Harrison and Busey, *Nothing But Glory*, 121–22. Erasmus Williams, "A Private's Experience in Gettysburg," J. W. Daniels Papers, Manuscripts Dept., Alderman Library, University of Va.

94. According to Loehr, Lee said, "General, your men have done all that men could do; the fault is entirely my own." Bright's account is more detailed.

Loehr, *First Virginia Regiment*, 38. Charles T. Loehr, "The 'Old First' Virginia at Gettysburg (XXXII:37). Robert A. Bright, "Pickett's Charge at Gettysburg," CV (XXXVIII:266). Gallagher, *Fighting for the Confederacy*, 266.

95. Letter, Charles Pickett to the editor *Richmond Times*, Nov. 11, 1894, Virginia Historical Society, Richmond, Va. VIMSS2P5068B2.

96. William Youngblood, "Unwritten History of the Gettysburg Campaign," SHSP (XXXVIII:317).

97. Wood, *Big I*, 47.

Appendix A

1. Janet B. Hewett, et al. (ed.), *Supplement to the Official Records of the Union and Confederate Armies*, vol. 5, pt. 1 (Wilmington, N.C.: Broadfoot Publishing Co., 1995), 358–59.

2. Robert U. Johnson and Clarence C. Buel (ed.), *Battles and Leaders of the Civil War*, III (Secaucus, N.J.: Castle), 362.

3. "Letter from General E. P. Alexander to J. William Jones," SHSP (IV:103).

4. Edwin Porter Alexander, *Military Memoirs of a Confederate* (N.Y.: Da Capo Press, 1993), 418. (Reprint of 1907 edition.)

5. Gary Gallagher (ed.), *Fighting for the Confederacy: The Personal Recollections of General Edward Porter Alexander* (Chapel Hill: UNC Press, 1989), 248–49.

6. Robert Scott (ed.), *The Official Records of the War of the Rebellion*, XXVII, pt. 2, Washington, D.C.: U.S. Government Printing Office), 355.

7. David G. Martin, *Confederate Monuments at Gettysburg: The Gettysburg Battle Monuments*, I (Highstown, N.J.: Longstreet House, 1986). Pages will be cited as they come into use. Martin printed every Confederate marker upon the field and located them on a map insert. In addition, he corrected errors in the plaque texts.

8. For the individual battery citations see Martin, *Confederate Monuments*, I:65, 68, 71, 72, 73, 74, 75, 83, 84, 85, 86, 87, 90, 91, 92, 93, 97, 100, 111, 118, 124.

9. *OR*, XXVII, pt. 2, 355.

10. Ibid.

11. Martin, *Confederate Monuments*, I:81, 84, 85, 86, 87.

12. SHSP (XXIII:230).

13. Martin, *Confederate Monuments*, I: (Ward) 79; (Graham) 82; (Wyatt) 88–89; (Brooke) 94; (Grandy) 107–8, 200.

14. Gallagher said that the major commanded nine guns, all of which he assumed came from Garnett's Battalion.

Gallagher, *Fighting for the Confederacy*, 586, fn. 68.

15. Martin, *Confederate Monuments*, I: (McIntosh—16 guns), 177; (Lane—17 guns), 186; (Garnett—15 guns), 193; (Pegram—20 guns), 178; (Poague—16 guns), 199; (Cabell—16 guns), 145; (Dearing—18 guns), 151; (Eshleman—10 guns), 124; (Alexander—24 guns), 123; (Henry—19 guns), 134.

16. *OR*, XXVII, pt. 2, 603, 605–6.

17. Martin, *Confederate Monuments*, I, 104. See the commentary.

18. *OR*, XXVII, pt. 2, 675. Report of Maj. D. G. McIntosh. Martin, *Confederate Monuments*, I, 63. See commentary.

19. Martin, *Confederate Monuments*, I (Reese), 64; (W. Carter), 103; (Fry), 108; (Page), 107; (Battalion), 175. *OR*, XXVII, pt. 2, 603. Report of Lt. Col. Thomas H. Carter. Martin,

Confederate Monuments, I, 64. Lawrence R. Laboda, *From Selma to Appomattox* (Shippensburg, Pa.: White Mane, 1994), 147.

Neither of these sources show the exact position of each battery, except for Reese's map in Laboda's book. Using Reese as the battalion flank, and eliminating Page's battery which did not take part in the assault, leaves no other positions for the rest of the battalion than to the north.

20. R. Snowden Andrews, *Andrews' Mounted Artillery Drill* (Charleston: Evans and Cogswell, 1863), 68.

A section of artillery from hub to hub measured 18 yards. Fourteen yards frontage plus two yards for the width of the gun was allowed for each piece. The required battery front for four guns was, according to Andrews, 82 yards. The regulations in the U.S. manuals, which both sides used, was 64 yards (16 yards per piece).

21. Martin, *Confederate Monuments*, I, 108.

22. Martin, *Confederate Monuments*, I, 64. Lawrence R. Laboda, *From Selma to Appomattox* (Shippensburg, Pa.: White Mane, 1994), 147.

23. *OR*, XXVII, pt. 2, 604. Report of Capt. Willis J. Dance. Martin, *Confederate Monuments*, I, 109–10.

24. Martin, *Confederate Monuments*, I (Rice), 60–61; (Hurt), 62; (Johnson), 83–84; and (Wallace), 115.

25. *OR*, XXVII, pt. 2, 604. Report of Capt. Willis J. Dance. Martin, *Confederate Monuments*, I (Watson), 112–13; (Smith), 114; and (Griffin), 116.

26. Martin, *Confederate Monuments*, I: (Zimmerman), 88; (Johnston), 96; (Marye), 99; (Brander), 104; and (McGraw), 110.

27. Martin, *Confederate Monuments*, I: (Ross), 66; Wingfield, 67. Brunson's report—*OR*, XXVII, pt. 2, 677–79—has no position information for July 3.

28. *OR*, XXVII, pt. 2, 673. Report of Maj. William T. Poague. Martin, *Confederate Monuments*, I: (Ward), 79; (Graham), 82; (Wyatt), 88–89; and (Utterback), 93–94.

29. Martin W. Hazlewood, "Gettysburg Charge," SHSP (XXIII:231).

30. Stewart, *Pickett's Charge*, 162.

31. Harrison and Busey, *Nothing But Glory*, 22.

32. Gallagher, *Fighting for the Confederacy*, 253. William Miller Owen, *In Camp And Battle with the Washington Artillery of New Orleans* (Boston: Ticknor and Co., 1885), 248.

33. *OR*, XXVII, pt. 2, 434. Report of Maj. B. F. Eshleman.

34. *OR*, XXVII, pt. 2, 375 and 434. Reports of Col. Henry C. Cabell and Maj. Benjamin F. Eshleman, respectively. Martin, *Confederate Monuments*, I: (Fraser and Manly), 83.

Eshleman said that Cabell put five guns between Battle and Richardson. The evidence indicates that eight guns were between Eshleman's sections.

35. *OR*, XXVII, pt. 2, 379, 380, 382, 434. Reports of Capt. E. S. McCarthy, Capt. B. C. Manly, Lt. W. J. Furlong, and Maj. B. F. Eshleman, respectively. Martin, *Confederate Monuments*, I: (Fraser), 65; (Richardson), 73; (Battles), 74–75; (Manly), 83; (McCarthy), 111.

36. Martin, *Confederate Monuments*, I: (Jordan), 91–92; (Parker), 109. *Supplement to the OR*, V, pt. 1, 367. Report of Capt. William W. Parker.

Martin's reference to the Peach Orchard refers to its present location. The northern face of the orchard during the war ended about 200 feet south of Trostle's Lane. Parker said that his battery was the right of the battalion.

37. Martin, *Confederate Monuments*, I: (Blount), 92; (Macon), 111; (Caskie), 100, and (Stribling), 97.

38. *Supplement to the OR*, V, pt. 1, 341. Abstract of Capt. Robert M. Stribling's report.

39. Martin, *Confederate Monuments*, I: 90–91.

40. Gallagher, *Fighting for the Confederacy*, 258.
41. Coddington, *The Gettysburg Campaign*, 493, 787 (fn. 2).
42. *OR*, XXVII, pt. 2, 384. Report of Lt. C. W. Motes. Martin, *Confederate Monuments*, I, 68–69.
43. Martin, *Confederate Monuments*, I: 111–12. *OR*, XXVII, pt. 2, 379. Report of Capt. E. S. McCarthy.
44. Fairfax Downey, *The Guns at Gettysburg* (N.Y.: David McKay, 1958), 144. Douglas Southall Freeman, *Lee's Lieutenants: A Study in Command*, III (New York: Charles Scribner's Sons, 1944), 148.
45. Harrison and Busey, *Nothing But Glory*, 22, 32.
46. Glenn Tucker, *High Tide at Gettysburg* (Dayton: Morningside Bookshop, 1973), 359.
47. Stewart, *Pickett's Charge*, 127, 159.
48. Coddington, *The Gettysburg Campaign*, 493.
49. *Supplement to the OR*, V, pt. 1, 361.
50. Coddington, *The Gettysburg Campaign*, 502, and fn.. 2, 787–88.
51. Ibid., fn. 54, 792. *OR*, XXVII, pt. 1, 373, 428, 437. Haskell, 94. Richard Rollins (ed.), *Pickett's Charge! Eyewitness Accounts* (Redondo Beach, Calif.: Rank and File Publications, 1994), 170.
52. Stewart, *Pickett's Charge*, 159.
53. Gallagher, *Fighting for the Confederacy*, 246, 251.
54. John Gibbon, *The Artillerist's Manual* (New York: C. A. Alvord, 1863), 250. Board of Artillery Officers, *Instruction for the Field Artillery* (New York: Greenwood Press, 1968 reprint), 42.
55. Stewart, *Pickett's Charge*, 160.
56. *OR*, XXVII, pt. 1, 883–84. Report of Lt. Col. Freeman McGilvery.
57. Ibid., 885. Report of Capt. Charles A. Phillips.
58. Felix R. Galloway, "Gettysburg—The Battle and the Retreat," CV (XXI:388).
59. *B & L*, III, 372.
60. Haskell, 82–93. Gibbon, *Recollections*, 147–50.
61. N. F. Newberry, "Cushing's Battery," *The National Tribune*, March 23, 1911, 3. Kent M. Brown, *Cushing of Gettysburg, The Story of a Union Artillery Commander* (Lexington, Ky.: U. of Ky. Press, 1993), 266.

    Norton L. Newberry was wounded and missing in action on July 2. The *Tribune* article was written by Miles F. Newbury.
62. Frederick Fuger, "Cushing's Battery at Gettysburg," Journal of Military Service Institution of the U.S. (Nov.–Dec. 1907), 41:407.
63. *B & L*, III, 364.
64. *OR*, XXVII, pt. 2, 435. Report of Maj. B. F. Eshleman.
65. Ibid., 388–89. Report of Maj. James Dearing.
66. *OR*, XXVII, pt. 2, 381. Report of Capt. B. C. Manly.
67. *OR*, XXVII, pt. 2, 435. *Supplement to the OR*, V, pt. 1, 361. *OR*, XXVII, pt. 1, 898. Christopher Smith, "Bloody Angle," The Buffalo *Evening News*, May 29, 1894, 5. A. H. Belo, "The Battle of Gettysburg," CV (VIII:165–68).

Appendix B

1. Harrison and Busey, *Nothing But Glory*, 456.
2. Ibid., 461.
3. Ibid., 466.

4. Martin, *Confederate Monuments*, 189.
5. Ibid., 192. Jordan, *N.C. Troops*, V:6–105; VI:415–601; XII:415–521; XX:244–63.
6. Martin, *Confederate Monuments*, 191. Jordan, *N.C. Troops*, XIII:375, 386, 430–532. Stubbs, "They Suffered the Most."
7. Richard O'Sullivan, *55th Virginia Infantry*. (Lynchburg: H. E. Howard, 1989), 56. Rollins, *Pickett's Charge!* These returns are estimates at best for Brockenbrough.
8. Martin, *Confederate Monuments*, 195. Jordan, *N.C. Troops*, IV:405–514; V:305–424; VIII: 110–231; IX: 118–244; XI: 468–604.
9. Martin, *Confederate Monuments*, 197. Jordan, *N.C. Troops*, V:283–385; VI:10–117; VII:10–132; IX:253–353; X:8–104.
10. *OR*, XXVII, pt. 2, 620. Report of C. Wilcox. Martin, *Confederate Monuments*, 183.
11. *OR*, XXVII, pt. 2, 632. Report of D. Lang. Martin, *Confederate Monuments*, 181.

Bibliography

PRIMARY SOURCES

Adams, Silas. "The Nineteenth Maine at Gettysburg," *Papers Read Before the commandery of the State of Maine M.O.L.L.U.S.* Wilmington: Broadfoot Publishing, 1992.

Aldrich, Thomas M. *The History of Battery A: First Regiment Rhode Island Light Artillery in the War to Preserve the Union 1861–1865.* Providence: Snow and Farnham, Printers, 1904.

Alexander, Edward Porter. *Military Memoirs of a Confederate.* New York: Da Capo, 1993.

Andrews, Snowden. *Andrews' Mounted Artillery Drill.* Charleston: Evans and Cogswell, 1863.

Autobiography of Eppa Hunton. n.d.

Bandy, Ken, and Florence Freeland, ed. *The Gettysburg Papers*, II. Dayton: Morningside Bookshop, 1978.

Bartlett, Napier. *Military Record of Louisiana.* Baton Rouge: Louisiana State University Press, 1992.

Benedict, George Grenville. *Army Life in Virginia.* Burlington: Free Press Association, 1895.

Beyer, W. F., and O. F. Keydel, ed. *Deeds of Valor.* Woodbury, N.Y.: Longmeadow Press, 1992.

Brown, Maud Marrow. *The University Grays, Company A, Eleventh Mississippi Regiment, Army of Northern Virginia, 1861–1865.* Richmond: Garrett and Massie, Inc., 1940.

Clark, Walter, ed. *Historiea of the Several Regiments and Battalions From North Carolina in the Great War 1861–'65.* Wilmington: Broadfoot Publishing, 1991.

Crumb, Herb S., ed. *The Eleventh Corps Artillery at Gettysburg: The Papers of Major Thomas Ward Osborne*. Hamilton, N.Y.: Edmontson Publishing Co., Inc., 1991.

Dooley, John E. *John Dooley, Confederate Soldier*. Joseph T. Durkin, S.J., ed. Washington, D.C.: Georgetown University Press, 1945.

Editors of Time-Life Books. *Voices of the Civil War: Gettysburg*. Alexandria: Time Life, 1996.

Fulton, Jr., William F. *Family Record and Reminiscences*. s.n., n.d.

Gallagher, Gary W., ed. *Fighting for the Confederacy*. Chapel Hill: University of North Carolina Press, 1989.

Galwey, Thomas Francis. *The Valiant Hours*. W. S. Nye, ed. Harrisburg: Stackpole, 1951.

Gibbon, John. *Personal Recollections of the Civil War*. Dayton: Morningside Bookshop, 1978.

Haines, William P. *History of the Men of Co. F, With Description of the Marches and Battles of the 12th New Jersey Vols*. Mickelyon, N.J., 1897.

Hazzard, George H. *History of the First Regiment Minnesota Volunteer Infantry 1861–1864*. Stillwater, Minn.: Easton and Masterson, 1918.

Hewett, Janet B., et al. *Supplement to the Official Records of the Union and Confederate Armies*, V, part 1. Wilmington: Broadfoot Publishing, 1995.

History Committee. *History of the Nineteenth Regiment Massachusetts Volunteer Infantry 1861–1865*. Salem: Salem Press, 1906.

Johnson, Robert U., and Clarence C. Buel. *Battles and Leaders of the Civil War*, III. Secaucus, N.J.: Castle.

Johnston, David E. *The Story of a Confederate Boy in the Civil War*. Radford, Va.: Commonwealth Press, Inc., 1980.

Ladd, David L., and Audrey J. Ladd, ed. *The Bachelder Papers*. Dayton: Morningside Bookshop, 1995.

Lewis, John H. *Recollections From 1860–1865*. Dayton: Morningside Bookshop, 1983.

Longstreet, James. *From Manassas to Appomattox*. New York: Da Capo, 1992.

Mulholland, St. Clair A. *The Story of the 116th Regiment, Pennsylvania Infantry*. Gaithersburg: Olde Soldier Books, Inc.

New Jersey Battlefield Commission 1886–1892. *Final Report of the Gettysburg Battlefield Commission of New Jersey*. Trenton: John T. Murphy Publishing Co., 1891.

Owen, William Miller. *In Camp and Battle With the Washington Artillery of New Orleans.* Boston: Ticknor and Co., 1885.

Page, Charles D. *History of the Fourteenth Regiment Connecticut Volunteer Infantry.* Meriden, Conn.: Horton Printing Co., 1906.

Personal Narratives of Events in the War of the Rebellion Being Read Before the Rhode Island Soldiers and Sailors in the War to Preserve the Union. Wilmington: Broadfoot Publishing, 1993.

Poague, William Thomas. *Gunner With Stonewall,* Wilmington, N.C.: Broadfoot Publishing, 1989.

Poriss, Harder, and Ralph G. Poriss, ed. *While My Country Is in Danger: The Life and Letters of Lieutenant Colonel Richard S. Thompson, Twelfth New Jersey Volunteers.* Hamilton, N.Y.: Edmontson Publishing Co., 1994.

Priest, John M., ed. *John T. McMahon's Diary of the 136th New York 1861–1864.* Shippensburg, Pa.: White Mane, 1993.

Reed, John, et al., v. The Gettysburg Battle-Field Memorial Association, et al., *Supreme Court of Pennsylvania, Middle District, May Term, 1891, Nos. 20 and 30.*

Report of the Committee. *Five Points in the Record of North Carolina in the Great War of 1861–5.* Farmville, Va.: Farmville Printing, 1995.

Rhodes, John H. *The History of Battery B First Rhode Island Light Artillery in the War to Preserve the Union.* Providence: Snow and Farnham, 1894.

Rollins, Richard, ed. *Pickett's Charge: Eyewitness Accounts.* Redondo Beach, Calif.: Rank and File Publications, 1994.

Sawyer, Franklin. *A Military History of the 8th Ohio Vol. Inf'y.* Huntington, W.V.: Blue Acorn Press, 1994.

Scott, Robert Garth, ed. *Fallen Leaves: The Civil War Letters of Major Henry Livermore Abbott.* Kent, Ohio: Kent State University Press, 1991.

Scott, Robert N. comp. *The Official Records of the War of the Rebellion,* XXVII, parts 1 and 2. Washington, D.C.: U.S. Government Printing Office, 1887.

Seville, William P. *History of the First Regiment, Delaware Volunteers, from the Commencement of the "Three Months' Service" to the Final Muster Out at the Close of the Rebellion.* Highstown, N.J.: Longstreet House.

Sorrell, G. Moxley. *Recollections of a Confederate Staff Officer.* Wilmington: Broadfoot Publishing, 1995.

Sturtevant, Ralph Orson. *Pictorial History of the Thirteenth Regiment Vermont Volunteers, War of 1861–1865.* Burlington: Self-Appointed Committee of Three, 1911.

Underwood, Adin B. *Three Years' Service of the Thirty-Third Infantry Regiment, 1862–1865.* Huntington, Va.: Blue Acorn Press, 1993.

Ward, Joseph R. C. *History of the One Hundred and Sixth Regiment Pennsylvania Volunteers.* Philadelphia: McManus, Jr. and Co., 1906.

Washburn, George H. *A Complete Military History and Record of the 108th New York Volunteers From 1862 to 1894.* Rochester, 1894.

Willson, Arabella M. *Disaster, Struggle, Triumph, The Adventures of 1000 Boys in Blue from August, 1862, to June, 1865.* Albany: The Argus Co., 1870.

Wood, William N. *Reminiscences of Big I.* Wilmington: Broadfoot Publishing Co., 1987.

The National Tribune

Ashe, S. A. "North Carolinians at Gettysburg, A Critical Review of the Famous Confederate Charge on July 3, 1864," October 31, 1901, 2.

Blaisdell, O. P. "Gettysburg Memories of Several Comrades—Stannard's brigade—The Cavalry," July 17, 1904, 3.

Bond, W. R. "Pickett or Pettigrew: It Was Pettigrew's North Carolinians Rather Than Pickett's Virginians Who Bore the Brunt of the Charge at Gettysburg," October 31, 1901, 2.

Cowan, Andrew. "Cowan's New York Battery: Its Old Captain Tells of Its Glorious Share in Repulsing Pickett's Charge," November 12, 1908, 7.

Eastman, R. M. "Cemetery Hill: How the 1st Minnesota Gathered in the Prisoners," November 16, 1905, 3.

Fuger, Frederick. "Lieut. Cushing at Gettysburg: The Heroic Fight of His Battery Against Pickett's Charge," January 28, 1909, 7.

Hand, John W. "Gettysburg: A Graphic Account of the Battle by an Eleventh Corps Captain," July 24, 1890, 3.

Koons, D. S. "The 8th Ohio at Gettysburg: The Brigade Presented Arms to Them After Their Great Achievement," November 5, 1908, 7.

Landregan, Rody. "Battery A, 4th U.S.—Its Savage work on Pickett's Column," September 2, 1909, 7.

Moon, Thomas. "The Heroic Cushing: A Plain Old Veteran's Story of the fight at Gettysburg," December 3, 1908, 7.

Moran, Frank E. "A Fire Zouave: Memories of a Member of the Excelsior Brigade," November 13, 1890, 3.

Newberry, Norton L. "Cushing's Battery," March 23, 1911, 3.

Potter, Thaddeus S. "On Skirmish: Gallant Behavior of the 8th Ohio at Gettysburg," January 31, 1895, 3.

Thompson, Benjamin W. "Pickett Did Not Lead," January 25, 1915, 7.

Tuttle, R. M. "An Unparallelled Loss: A Whole North Carolina Company Destroyed at Gettysburg," July 2, 1903, 3.

Wright, A. "The 2nd U.S. Sharpshooters: The Regiment That Took Part in Repelling Pickett's Charge," February 18, 1909, 7.

Southern Historical Society Papers

Alexander, E. P. to J. William Jones, March 17, 1872, IV, 97.

Crocker, James F. "Gettysburg—Pickett's Charge," XXXIII, 132.

Fry, B. D. "Pettigrew's Charge at Gettysburg," VII, 92.

Hazlewood, Martin W. "Gettysburg charge. Paper as to Pickett's Men," XXIII, 231.

"Letter from General Trimble, October 15th, 1875," IX, 33.

Loehr, Charles T. "The Old first Virginia at Gettysburg," XXXII, 35.

Martin, R. W. "Armistead at the Battle of Gettysburg," XXXIX, 186.

Martin, Rawley. "Rawley Martin's Account," XXXII, 184.

Mayo, Joseph C. "Pickett's Charge at Gettysburg," XXXIV, 328.

Report of Col. H. C. Cabell, X, 166.

Smith, John H. "Captain John Holmes Smith's Account," XXXII, 189.

Youngblood, William. "Unwritten History of the Gettysburg Campaign," XXXVIII, 317.

Confederate Veteran

Berkeley, Edmund. "Rode With Pickett," XXXVIII, 175.

Bright, Robert A. "Pickett's Charge at Gettysburg," XXXVIII, 264.

Carter, James T. "Flag of the Fifty-Third Virginia Regiment," X, 263.

Clark, George. "Wilcox's Alabama Brigade at Gettysburg," XVII, 230.

Clay, James W. "About the Death of General Garnett," XIV, 81.

Dearing, Calvin P. "Experiences of a Virginia Private," XXI, 592.

Easley, D. B. "With Armistead When He Was Killed," XX, 379.

Farrington, LeRoy. "Testimony About Battle of Gettysburg," XVIII, 524.

Galloway, Felix Richard. "The Battle and the Retreat," XXI, 388.

Harding, Milton. "Where General Armistead Fell," XIX, 371.

Kimble, June. "Tennesseeans at Gettysburg—The Retreat," XVIII, 460.

McCulloch, Robert. "About the Charge of Pickett's Division," XXI, 474.

McPherson, J. R. "A Private's Account of Gettysburg," VI, 149.

Moore, J. H. "Heroism in the Battle of Gettysburg," IX, 15.

Turney, J. B. "The First Tennessee at Gettysburg," VIII, 536.

Miscellaneous Newspaper and Magazine Articles

Philadelphia Weekly Times

Sale, J. Irving. "Pickett's Charge," July 4, 1887.

Smith, R. Penn. "The Part Taken by the Philadelphia Brigade in the Battle," May 28, 1887.

Civil War Times Illustrated

Thompson, Benjamin W. "Personal Narrative of Experiences in the Civil War, 1861–1865," October 1973, 20.

Journal of Military Service Institute of the United States

Fuger, Frederick. "Cushing's Battery at Gettysburg," vol. 41:404.

Buffalo Evening News

Smith, Christopher, and G. W. Finley, "Bloody Angle, The Story of Cemetery Ridge from the Blue and Gray," May 29, 1894, 5.

Military Historical Society Papers

Hunt, Henry J. "Artillery," XIII, 94.

The Southern Bivouac

Moore, J. H. "Heth's Division at Gettysburg," III, 389.

New York Herald

Cowan, Andrew. "When Cowan's Battery Withstood Pickett's Splendid Charge," July 2, 1911.

The Minnesota Journal

Harmon, William. "Company C at Gettysburg," June 30, 1897, 7.

Toledo Blade

Ewing, William A. Letter to mother, July 4, 1863. Printed, July 11, 1863, 2.

Marietta Sunday Observer

Huntington, James F. "Notes of Service With a Light Artillery at Chancellorsville and Gettysburg," August 11, 1918.

Portage County Newspaper

Letter, August 5, 1863.

Lebanon Democrat

Harris, F. S. "From Gettysburg," August 10, 1899.

The Raleigh Observer, November 30, 1877.

Publications of the Mississippi Historical Society
  McFarland, Baxter. "The Eleventh Mississippi Regiment at Gettysburg,"
  II, 551.

The Vertical Files. Gettysburg National Battlefield Park.
  Letter, A. S. Van de Graaf to his wife, July 8, 1863.
  Letter, James L. Kemper to W. H. Swallow, February 2, 1896.
  Owen, H. T. "Pickett at Gettysburg," *The Philadelphia Weekly Times.*

Manuscripts
Saint Augustine Historical Society, Saint Augustine, Fla.
  Letter to Hall, September 4, 1863, Raymond J. Reid Papers.

Yale University Library, New Haven, Connecticut.
  Cowan, Andrew. Letter to Alexander Webb, November 6, 1885, Alexander
  Stewart Webb Papers, Select List of Correspondence.
  Raymond, W. Letter to Alexander Webb, April 22, n.d., Alexander Stewart
  Webb Papers, Select List of Correspondence.

George Staley Collection
  McCrae, Tully. "Reminiscences About Gettysburg," March 30, 1904.

Pennsylvania Historical and Museum Collection, Harrisburg, Pa.
  Egan, John. Letter to George Meade, February 8, 1870, Peter F.
  Rothermal Papers.
  Webb, Alexander. Letter to P. F. Rothermal, n.d., Peter F. Rothermal
  Papers.

Eleanor S. Brockenbrough Library, Museum of the Confederacy, Richmond,
Va.
  Kimble, June, "W. H. McCulloch."
  Kimble, June, "Capt. James W. Lockhardt."
  Kimble, June, "An Incident at Gettysburg."

**United States Army Military History Institute, Carlisle Barracks,
Pennsylvania**
Belknap, Charles Wesley. 125th New York, Diary, 14 September 1862–21
  October 1863, Civil War Miscellaneous Collection, Bee–Ber.
Burns, William J. Diary, July 3, 1863, Co. G, 71st Pennsylvania, "Civil
  War Diary, September 27, 1861–December 31, 1863," Save the Flag
  Collection.

Cowan, Andrew J. "Undated Remarks by Andrew J. Cowan," The Gettysburg Campaign, The Robert L. Brake Collection.

Mayo, Joseph, Jr. Report, The Gettysburg Campaign, The Robert L. Brake Collection.

Metcalf, George P. "Recollections of Boyhood Days," Harrisburg Civil War Round Table Collection.

St. Paul Daily Press, July 25, 1863, Box 10, Minn. to N.Y., The Gettysburg Campaign, The Robert L. Brake Collection.

Symington, William Stuart. Letter to Charles Pickett, October 17, 1892, The Gettysburg Campaign, The Robert L. Brake Collection.

Symington, William Stuart. Letter to James Longstreet, October 26, 1892, The Gettysburg Campaign, The Robert L. Brake Collection.

Webb, Alexander. Letter to his father, July 17, 1863, The Gettysburg Campaign, The Robert L. Brake Collection.

Special Collections Department, William R. Perkins Library, Duke University, Durham, N.C.

Bentley, W. W. Letter to W. Fry, July 9, 1863, George E. Pickett Papers.

Haskell, John Cheves. "Memoirs," 1861–1865.

Hunton, Eppa. Letter to John W. Daniel, July 15, 1904, George W. Jones Papers, 1832–1865.

Parmelee, Uriah. Letter to his father, July 5, 1863, S. S. and U. N. Parmelee, 1845–1863.

Parmelee, Uriah N. Letter to his mother, July 13, 1863, S. S. and U. N. Parmelee, 1845–1863.

Petersburg, Virginia, *Enterprise.* March 3, 1894, George S. Bernard Diary-Scrapbook 1861–1911.

Robertson, Mrs. N. G. "In Regard to My Father's Capture at Gettysburg, He Has This to Say in His Memoirs," *Confederate Veteran* Papers, Reminiscences, n.d., Box 8.

Woods, Wiley. "The First Tennessee Flag at Gettysburg," *Confederate Veteran* Papers, Battles, 1861–1932, n.d., box 1.

Virginia Historical Society, Richmond, Virginia

Bright, Robert A. Letter to Charles Pickett, October 15, 1892. ViH Mss 255868b1.

Cogbill, M. A. Letter to Charles Pickett, September 28, 1894. ViH Mss 2P586b3.

Friend, Thomas R. Letters to Major Charles Pickett, December 10, 1894. ViH Mss 2P5868b3.

Pickett, Charles. Letter to the Editor, *Richmond Times*, November 11, 1894. ViH Mss 2P5068b2.

Stubbs, Stephen H. "They Suffered the Most," unpublished manuscript.

Alabama State Archives, Montgomery, Alabama

Confederate Muster Roll Collection, 5th Alabama Infantry Battalion, Box 52, Folder 1-1-1-4.

Manuscripts Department, University of Va., Charlottesville, Va.

John W. Daniel Papers.

SECONDARY WORKS

Arrington, Benjamin T. *The Medal of Honor at Gettysburg*. Gettysburg: Thomas Publications, 1996.

Bacarella, Michael. *Lincoln's Foreign Legion: The 39th New York Infantry, The Garibaldi Guards*. Shippensburg, Pa.: White Mane, 1996.

Bessette, S. "Memorial Day 1989," *Cannon Fodder, Battery B Newsletter*, July–August 1989, II, #2.

Brown, Kent Masterson. *Cushing of Gettysburg, The Story of a Union Artillery Commander*. Lexington: University of Kentucky Press, 1993.

Christ, Elwood W. *"Over a Wide Hot...Crimson Plain," The Struggle for the Bliss Farm at Gettysburg*. Baltimore: Butternut and Blue, 1994.

Clemmer, Gregg, S. *Valor in Gray, The Recipients of the Confederate Medal of Honor*. Staunton, Va.: Hearthside Publishing, 1996.

Coddington, Edwin B. *The Gettysburg Campaign, A Study in Command*. New York: Charles Scribner's Sons, 1984.

Editors of Time-Life Books. *Echoes of Glory: Arms and Equipment of the Confederacy*. Alexandria: Time-Life Books.

Harrison, Kathy Georg, and John W. Busey. *Nothing But Glory, Pickett's Division at Gettysburg*. Gettysburg: Thomas Publications, 1993.

Heitmann, Francis B. *Historical Register and Dictionary of the United States Army*, I. Washington, D.C.: U.S. Government Printing Office, 1903.

Martin, David G. *Confederate Monuments at Gettysburg*, I. Highstown, N.J.: Longstreet House, 1986.

Jordan, Weymouth T., Jr. *North Carolina Troops 1861–1865, A Roster*. Raleigh: Division of Archives and History.

Raus, Edmund J. *A Generation on the March. The Union Army at Gettysburg*. Lynchburg: H. E. Howard, Inc., 1987.

Rollins, Richard. *"The Damned Red Flags of the Rebellion."* Redondo Beach, Calif.: Rank and File Publications, 1997.

Rollins, Richard. "Black Confederates at Gettysburg," *Black Southerners in Gray, Essays on Afro-Americans in Confederate Armies*, Journal of Confederate History, Series XI.

Sibley, F. Ray, Jr. *The Confederate Order of Battle: The Army of Northern Virginia*. Shippensburg, Pa.: White Mane, 1996.

Stewart, George R. *Pickett's Charge*. Boston: Houghton Mifflin, 1987.

Index

264

Mitchell, William G. (Maj., A.D.C. to W. S. Hancock), 80, 170, 174, 175, 176
Mitchell, William L. (Pvt., Co. D, 1st Virginia), 99
Moale, Edward (Lt., A.D.C. to J. Gibbon), 121, 142, 144
Mockbee, Robert (Sgt., Co. B, 14th Tennessee), 106
Moody, George V. (Capt., Louisiana Artillery), 97
Moore, Henry C. (3rd Lt., Adj., 38th North Carolina), 134
Moore, John H. (2nd Lt., Co. B, 7th Tennessee), 22, 29, 87, 106, 107, 112, 153, 156, 168, 169
Moore, John V. (2nd Lt., Co. A, 11th Mississippi), 107
Moore, Samuel A. (Capt., Co. F, 14th Connecticut), 35, 42, 160
Moran, Frank E. (2nd Lt., Co. H, 73rd New York), 9, 166
Morgan, Charles H. (Lt. Col., I.G, C.O.S., II Corps), 55
Motes, Columbus W. (Lt., Georgia Artillery), 97, 121, 175
Mulally, Peter (Cpl., 1st New York Independent Battery), 95
Mullen, Michael (Lt., Co. G, 69th Pennsylvania), 140
Munson, William D. (Lt. Col., 13th Vermont), 176
Murden, Joshua (Color Sgt., 3rd Virginia), 84
Murphy, James (Acting Sgt., Btty. A, 4th U.S. Artillery), 115
Murphy, Thomas (Sgt., Co. G, 72nd Pennsylvania), 150, 152
Murray, Elisha (1st Sgt., Co. F, 7th Virginia), 70
Murray, Henry W. (Pvt., Co. H, 69th Pennsylvania), 140

N

Newbury, Miles F. (Pvt., Btty. A, 4th U.S. Artillery), 116, 129, 146, 197
Newton, John (Maj. Gen., U.S.A.), 38, 45, 48, 93, 176
Nichols, William T. (Col., 14th Vermont), 117
Niemeyer, John C. (1st Lt., Co. A, 9th Virginia), 139
Niles, Robert A. (Stable Sgt., Btty. B, 1st Rhode Island Artillery), 67–68
Norcom, Joseph (Capt., Louisiana Artillery), 2
Norton, George F. (Capt., Co. D, 1st Virginia), 119

Norton, George W. (2nd Lt., Btty. H, 1st Ohio Artillery), 38, 58, 93
Norwood, Thomas L. (1st Lt., Co. A, 37th North Carolina), 135, 157, 161

O

O'Brien, Billy (Pvt., Co. C, 11th Mississippi), 122
O'Brien, Henry D. (Color Bearer, 1st Minnesota), 149
O'Donnell, Frank (Cpl., Co. D, 72nd Pennsylvania), 128
O'Kane, Dennis (Col., 69th Pennsylvania), 106, 140
Ogden, Dewees (Pvt., McCarthy's Battery), 9
Osborn, Thomas (Maj., XI Artillery), 4, 36, 51, 58, 59, 64, 78, 79, 93
Ostrander, Dwight H. (1st Lt., Co. A., 108th New York), 17, 20
Owen, Henry T. (Capt., Co. C, 18th Virginia), 117

P

Parker, William W. (Capt., Virginia Artillery), 1, 8, 11, 12, 33, 106, 189
Parks, Marcus A. (Lt. Col., 52nd North Carolina), 131
Parmelee, Uriah (Cpl., Co. I, 6th New York Cavalry), 56, 148, 170
Parsons, Augustus (Lt., Co. A, New Jersey Battery), 93
Parsons, Theron (2nd Lt., Co. D, 108th New York), 62, 66
Patton, Waller Tazwell (Col., 7th Virginia), 31, 69, 70, 74, 129
Patton, William (Pvt., Btty. A, 4th U.S. Artillery), 127
Peel, William H. (Lt., Co. C, 11th Mississippi), 71, 87, 97, 98, 122, 132, 136
Pendleton, William N. (Brig. Gen., C.S.A.), 24, 25, 181, 182, 183
Perrin, William (Lt., Btty. B, 1st Rhode Island Artillery), 68
Pettigrew, J. Johnston (Brig. Gen., C.S.A.), 13, 29, 86, 89, 92, 97, 98, 102, 106, 107, 112, 130–32, 157, 168, 192
Phillips, Charles A. (Capt., Btty. E, 5th Massachusetts Light Artillery), 10, 114, 115
Pickett, Charles (Maj., A.D.C. to G. E. Pickett), 77, 102, 180
Pickett, George E. (Maj. Gen., C.S.A.), 7, 13, 14, 25, 30, 46, 47, 48, 77, 78, 82, 83, 84, 89, 98, 102, 103, 105, 113, 115, 137, 138, 147, 173, 179, 180